Kubernetes Recipes

A Practical Guide for Container Orchestration and Deployment

Grzegorz Stencel
Luca Berton

Apress®

Kubernetes Recipes: A Practical Guide for Container Orchestration and Deployment

Grzegorz Stencel
Bournemouth, UK

Luca Berton
BOURNEMOUTH, UK

ISBN-13 (pbk): 979-8-8688-1324-5
ISBN-13 (electronic): 979-8-8688-1325-2
https://doi.org/10.1007/979-8-8688-1325-2

Managing Director, Apress Media LLC: Welmoed Spahr
Acquisitions Editors: James Robinson-Prior, Divya Modi
Development Editor: James Markham
Coordinating Editor: Gryffin Winkler

Cover Image by Kerstin Riemer from Pixabay (pixabay.com)

Distributed to the book trade worldwide by Springer Science+Business Media New York, 233 Spring Street, 6th Floor, New York, NY 10013. Phone 1-800-SPRINGER, fax (201) 348-4505, e-mail orders-ny@springer-sbm.com, or visit www.springeronline.com. Apress Media, LLC is a California LLC and the sole member (owner) is Springer Science + Business Media Finance Inc (SSBM Finance Inc). SSBM Finance Inc is a **Delaware** corporation.

For information on translations, please e-mail booktranslations@springernature.com; for reprint, paperback, or audio rights, please e-mail bookpermissions@springernature.com.

Apress titles may be purchased in bulk for academic, corporate, or promotional use. eBook versions and licenses are also available for most titles. For more information, reference our Print and eBook Bulk Sales web page at http://www.apress.com/bulk-sales.

Any source code or other supplementary material referenced by the author in this book can be found here: https://www.apress.com/gp/services/source-code.

If disposing of this product, please recycle the paper

Writing this book has been a journey of growth, one that required me to step out of my comfort zone and set aside my ego. I owe a debt of gratitude to my good friend and coauthor, Luca, for inspiring me to embark on this book and my family—my beloved wife, Malgorzata; my greatest treasure, my son Xavier; and of course my mum, Ewa—for their unwavering support. Their love and understanding have allowed me to dedicate more time to this project.

Throughout my career, I have learned and known how important it is to appreciate others and say a simple (or big) "thank you" to peers who helped. This also shows that the part of this book I wrote is not my own experience but the cumulative experience of brilliant people I had the honor to work with. So firstly, for infecting me with knowledge sharing, to Paul TID. Secondly but not less importantly, to the people who brought me into the advanced enterprise Kubernetes world, the real "Kubernetes experts," my mentor John F. and all the magnificent people he introduced me to—his little army of best k8s engineers I was honored to work with, Sven, Neil, Eric, and Alen. And finally, for the most significant architectural inspiration, to my other mentor Bryn who can "destroy" you constructively but when he "destroys" you, you enjoy it because you take lessons from it that you won't learn anywhere else. Also a big thanks to Allan for his immense support and coaching. Chris for teaching how to appreciate others and be a good leader—"a happy developer is a performing developer." And, lastly, Aleksander (Olek) for motivating me to always improve and to pursue success.
—Greg

For my son, Filippo, the joy of my life.
—Luca

Table of Contents

About the Authors

Grzegorz Stencel is a versatile technologist and staff engineer at JPMorgan Chase and a holder of two patents. Greg designs and develops new systems, products, and features while providing technical guidance and mentorship. His experience spans prestigious organizations like Ericsson, ING, and Oxford University Press, with expertise in networks, cyber security, and programming. An electronics enthusiast, Greg creates PCB designs for home automation and alarms and explores robotics integrated with AI using Jetson Nano. With 17 years of experience as a Linux admin, Greg also holds a Certified Kubernetes Application Developer (CKAD) certificate. He has built a Kubernetes cluster from laptop motherboards, contributing to the cloud community through teaching and leadership.

Luca Berton is an IT infrastructure expert. He spent two years at JPMorgan Chase & Co. and three years with Red Hat. Luca is the author of *Ansible for VMware by Examples* and *Ansible for Kubernetes by Example* and the creator of the Ansible Pilot project. With over 18 years of experience in the IT industry, Luca specializes in infrastructure hardening and automation. An open source enthusiast, he actively supports the community by sharing his knowledge at public events.

About the Technical Reviewer

Nikhil Kumar is a seasoned software engineer at HPE, specializing in Kubernetes, AI, DevOps, and MLOps. With a versatile skill set spanning development, architecture, and consultancy, Nikhil has made impactful contributions across diverse domains for numerous clients and organizations. His expertise includes designing scalable Kubernetes architectures, implementing AI-driven DevOps pipelines, and advancing MLOps practices to streamline machine learning workflows. Nikhil is a recognized authority in the field, holding prestigious certifications such as Red Hat Certified Engineer (EX294) and Red Hat Certified OpenShift Administrator (EX280). As a passionate advocate for knowledge sharing, he actively contributes to the software engineering community through technical blogs, YouTube tutorials, and by serving as a technical reviewer for books on Kubernetes, DevOps, Cloud, and MLOps.

Acknowledgments

Writing a book is never a solitary endeavor, and *Kubernetes Recipes* is no exception. This book is the result of years of experience, collaboration, and support from many individuals and communities. We would like to express our heartfelt gratitude to those who have contributed to making this book possible.

First and foremost, we extend our deepest thanks to our families and loved ones for their patience, encouragement, and unwavering support throughout this journey. Your understanding during the late nights, endless research, and countless hours spent writing has been invaluable.

We would like to acknowledge our mentors, colleagues, and friends in the Kubernetes, cloud-native, and DevOps communities, whose expertise and insights have helped shape our knowledge and perspectives. The open source community has been a constant source of inspiration, and we are grateful to all the contributors, maintainers, and developers who continue to push Kubernetes forward.

A special thanks to the Kubernetes and CNCF (Cloud Native Computing Foundation) communities, whose contributions have made Kubernetes the powerful, flexible platform it is today. Without the collective efforts of developers, engineers, and advocates worldwide, Kubernetes would not be where it is today.

We would also like to thank our editors and publishing team at Apress for their guidance, feedback, and patience throughout the writing process. Your insights have helped us refine our ideas and structure this book so that it is accessible and practical for readers.

To our readers, thank you for picking up this book. We hope that *Kubernetes Recipes* serves as a valuable resource in your journey. Whether you are just beginning or an experienced professional looking for quick solutions, we appreciate your trust in us as your guide.

Finally, we extend our gratitude to our professional networks, including colleagues at JPMorgan Chase, Dell Technologies, Red Hat, and the various organizations we've worked with over the years. Your discussions, challenges, and real-world scenarios have provided invaluable insights that helped shape the content of this book.

It has been a privilege to write this book, and we hope it provides practical, real-world solutions to Kubernetes practitioners worldwide.

—Grzegorz Stencel and Luca Berton

Introduction

Kubernetes has become the de facto standard for container orchestration, providing a powerful, scalable, and resilient platform for deploying and managing containerized applications. As cloud-native technologies continue to evolve, mastering Kubernetes is essential for developers, system administrators, DevOps professionals, and anyone involved in modern application deployment.

Kubernetes Recipes is designed as a hands-on, problem-solving guide that provides immediate, actionable solutions to common and advanced challenges in Kubernetes environments. Whether you're setting up Kubernetes for the first time, managing complex workloads, or optimizing performance and security, this book offers a structured, easy-to-follow approach with real-world examples and best practices.

Who This Book Is For

This book is designed for developers, system administrators, DevOps engineers, and IT professionals who want to enhance their Kubernetes skills. Readers should have a basic understanding of Linux and container concepts, but no extensive prior knowledge of Kubernetes is necessary. The book caters to both beginners looking for foundational knowledge and experienced users seeking advanced techniques.

It is also beneficial for

- Technical managers overseeing Kubernetes implementations
- Students and researchers exploring cloud-native technologies
- Technology enthusiasts eager for hands-on Kubernetes experience

How This Book Is Structured

The book is organized as a collection of recipes, allowing readers to quickly find solutions to specific problems. It starts with the fundamentals and gradually explores advanced Kubernetes topics, making it a great reference for both on-the-job troubleshooting and structured learning.

Overview of Chapters

1. **Getting Started**: A primer on Kubernetes, installation methods, and core concepts
2. **Configuring Stateless Applications**: Deploying lightweight applications and managing resources efficiently
3. **Configuring Stateful Applications**: Managing databases and persistent workloads in Kubernetes
4. **Kubernetes on Cloud Providers**: Running Kubernetes clusters on Amazon Web Services, Azure, Google Cloud, and other platforms

5. **Developer Experience in Kubernetes**: Tools and best practices for developers working with Kubernetes
6. **Scaling and Resiliency**: Strategies for autoscaling, load balancing, and ensuring high availability (HA)
7. **Storage in Kubernetes**: Managing storage options, persistent volumes (PVs), and dynamic provisioning
8. **Networking in Kubernetes**: Load balancing, service discovery, network policies, and advanced networking concepts
9. **Performance Observability in Kubernetes**: Monitoring, logging, and tracing applications effectively
10. **Control Plane Administration and Package Management**: Managing Kubernetes infrastructure and using Helm
11. **Security in Kubernetes**: Securing workloads, role-based access control (RBAC), network policies, and best practices
12. **Emerging and Advanced Kubernetes Concepts**: Exploring service meshes, AI/ML workloads, and Kubernetes extensions
13. **Best Practices in Kubernetes**: Industry best practices for deployment, scaling, and security
14. **Additional Kubernetes Resources**: Community involvement, CNCF ecosystem, and further learning resources

Why This Book?

Unlike theoretical guides, this book is based on practical knowledge from seasoned Kubernetes professionals. It is designed for quick reference and provides step-by-step solutions to common challenges. Each recipe is structured with clear explanations, example commands, YAML configurations, and troubleshooting tips, helping readers apply solutions immediately in their Kubernetes environments.

By the end of this book, you will

- Gain hands-on experience with Kubernetes, from basic operations to advanced workflows.
- Develop scalable and resilient applications on Kubernetes clusters.
- Understand security best practices and monitoring techniques.
- Leverage cloud-native technologies to streamline containerized application deployments.

Whether you are deploying your first Kubernetes cluster or optimizing an enterprise-scale system, *Kubernetes Recipes* will serve as your go-to guide for leveraging Kubernetes with real-world solutions.

CHAPTER 1

Getting Started

Introduction

Kubernetes is an open source container orchestration platform that automates the deployment, scaling, and management of containerized applications. It provides a platform for automating application container deployment, scaling, and operations across clusters of hosts. With Kubernetes, you can easily deploy, scale, and manage containerized applications, ensuring they run efficiently and reliably. Everybody is talking about Kubernetes and cloud-native applications. Articles and documentation for Kubernetes are abundant, and so is the customization we can do. Kubernetes is a complex technology, and finding the information we need to perform our task might be daunting. Open source software is distributed online rather than in shiny box sets. This chapter guides us through the first steps in the orchestration technology because the customization options are literally infinite.

G. Stencel and L. Berton, *Kubernetes Recipes*,
https://doi.org/10.1007/979-8-8688-1325-2_1

1.1 Installing the kubectl Tool

Problem

We're ready to dive into the world of Kubernetes and manage our containerized applications efficiently, but we need to install the `kubectl` tool first.

Solution

Step 1: Check for Existing Installation

Before installing, check if kubectl is already installed on our system. Open our terminal and type the following command:

```
kubectl version --client
```

If kubectl is installed, we will see version information. If not, move on to the next step.

Step 2: Choose the Installation Method

2.1 Homebrew (MacOS)

If we are using MacOS and have Homebrew installed, we can install kubectl with a single command:

```
brew install kubectl
```

The result is displayed in Figure 1-1.

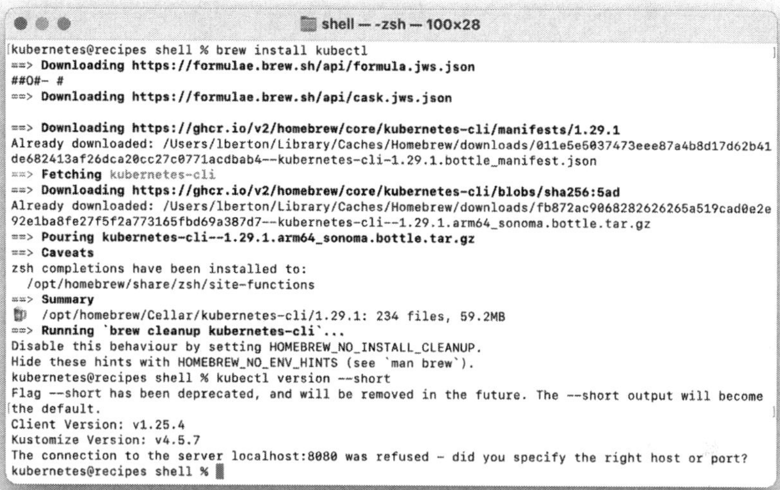

```
kubernetes@recipes shell % brew install kubectl
==> Downloading https://formulae.brew.sh/api/formula.jws.json
##O#- #
==> Downloading https://formulae.brew.sh/api/cask.jws.json

==> Downloading https://ghcr.io/v2/homebrew/core/kubernetes-cli/manifests/1.29.1
Already downloaded: /Users/lberton/Library/Caches/Homebrew/downloads/011e5e5037473eee87a4b8d17d62b41
de682413af26dca20cc27c0771acdbab4--kubernetes-cli-1.29.1.bottle_manifest.json
==> Fetching kubernetes-cli
==> Downloading https://ghcr.io/v2/homebrew/core/kubernetes-cli/blobs/sha256:5ad
Already downloaded: /Users/lberton/Library/Caches/Homebrew/downloads/fb872ac9068282626265a519cad0e2e
92e1ba8fe27f5f2a773165fbd69a387d7--kubernetes-cli--1.29.1.arm64_sonoma.bottle.tar.gz
==> Pouring kubernetes-cli--1.29.1.arm64_sonoma.bottle.tar.gz
==> Caveats
zsh completions have been installed to:
  /opt/homebrew/share/zsh/site-functions
==> Summary
🍺  /opt/homebrew/Cellar/kubernetes-cli/1.29.1: 234 files, 59.2MB
==> Running `brew cleanup kubernetes-cli`...
Disable this behaviour by setting HOMEBREW_NO_INSTALL_CLEANUP.
Hide these hints with HOMEBREW_NO_ENV_HINTS (see `man brew`).
kubernetes@recipes shell % kubectl version --short
Flag --short has been deprecated, and will be removed in the future. The --short output will become
the default.
Client Version: v1.25.4
Kustomize Version: v4.5.7
The connection to the server localhost:8080 was refused - did you specify the right host or port?
kubernetes@recipes shell %
```

Figure 1-1. *kubectl on MacOS*

2.2 Chocolatey (Windows)

For Windows users with Chocolatey, execute the following command:

```
choco install kubernetes-cli
```

2.3 Linux (Package Managers)

On Linux, the package manager varies by distribution:

For Debian/Ubuntu:

```
sudo apt-get update && sudo apt-get install -y kubectl
```

For Red Hat-based systems:

```
sudo yum install -y kubectl
```

For other Linux distributions, refer to the official documentation.

Install kubectl.

Step 3: Verify the Installation

After installation, verify that kubectl is correctly set up by checking its version:

```
kubectl version
```

This should display the installed version of kubectl. The "`--short`" and "`--client`" arguments might be needed in the version before 1.29.

Step 4: Configure kubectl

We need to configure `kubectl` with the appropriate context to interact with a Kubernetes cluster. If we are using a local cluster like Minikube, we can set it as the default context:

```
kubectl config use-context minikube
```

To connect to a remote cluster, we will need the cluster's `kubeconfig` file.

In Google Kubernetes Engine (GKE), we can install kubectl using the `glcoud` command:

```
gcloud components install kubectl
```

The latest versions of `minikube` can invoke `kubectl` as a subcommand that matches the cluster version:

```
minikube kubectl
```

Discussion

Installing `kubectl` is a fundamental step in working with Kubernetes. The choice of installation method depends on our operating system and package manager preferences. Once installed, we can use kubectl to interact with Kubernetes clusters, deploy applications, and manage resources.

See Also

– Command line tool (kubectl) `https://kubernetes.io/docs/reference/kubectl`

1.2 Installing Lightweight Kubernetes

Problem

We need a lightweight and efficient Kubernetes cluster for our project, one that is easy to install and manage, especially in resource-constrained environments. How can we quickly set up a streamlined Kubernetes cluster that conserves resources and is suitable for various use cases, from development to production?

Solution

k3s is a lightweight Kubernetes distribution designed for scenarios where a minimalistic and efficient Kubernetes cluster is required. It's an ideal choice for resource-constrained environments, IoT devices, edge computing, or situations where simplicity and ease of use are paramount. Follow these steps to set up a lightweight Kubernetes cluster with k3s:

- **Step 1**: Installation

  Connect the target machine using the SSH where we want to install k3s. We can install k3s on various Linux distributions, including Ubuntu, CentOS, and Raspberry Pi OS.

  Run the following command to download and install k3s:

  ```
  curl -sfL https://get.k3s.io | sh -
  ```

This command will install both the k3s server and k3s agent on the target machine, creating a single-node Kubernetes cluster.

- **Step 2**: Verification

  To verify that our k3s cluster is up and running, run the following command on the target machine:

  ```
  k3s kubectl get nodes
  ```

  This should display the node where k3s is installed, indicating that our cluster is active, as shown in Figure 1-2.

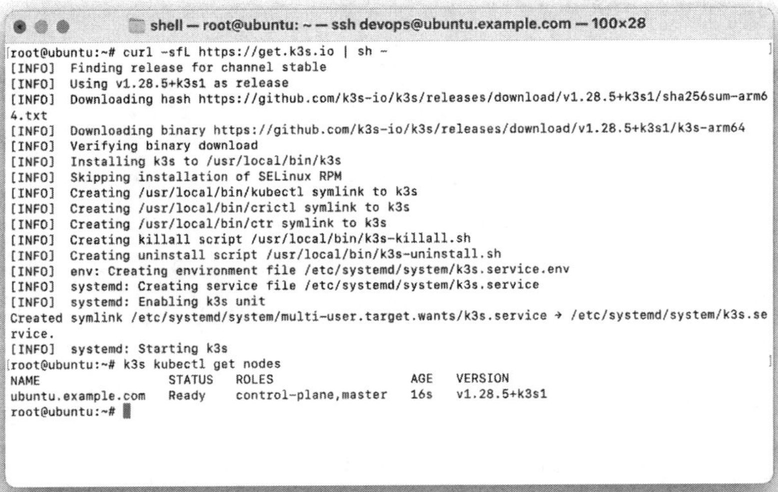

```
shell — root@ubuntu: ~ — ssh devops@ubuntu.example.com — 100×28
root@ubuntu:~# curl -sfL https://get.k3s.io | sh -
[INFO]  Finding release for channel stable
[INFO]  Using v1.28.5+k3s1 as release
[INFO]  Downloading hash https://github.com/k3s-io/k3s/releases/download/v1.28.5+k3s1/sha256sum-arm6
4.txt
[INFO]  Downloading binary https://github.com/k3s-io/k3s/releases/download/v1.28.5+k3s1/k3s-arm64
[INFO]  Verifying binary download
[INFO]  Installing k3s to /usr/local/bin/k3s
[INFO]  Skipping installation of SELinux RPM
[INFO]  Creating /usr/local/bin/kubectl symlink to k3s
[INFO]  Creating /usr/local/bin/crictl symlink to k3s
[INFO]  Creating /usr/local/bin/ctr symlink to k3s
[INFO]  Creating killall script /usr/local/bin/k3s-killall.sh
[INFO]  Creating uninstall script /usr/local/bin/k3s-uninstall.sh
[INFO]  env: Creating environment file /etc/systemd/system/k3s.service.env
[INFO]  systemd: Creating service file /etc/systemd/system/k3s.service
[INFO]  systemd: Enabling k3s unit
Created symlink /etc/systemd/system/multi-user.target.wants/k3s.service → /etc/systemd/system/k3s.se
rvice.
[INFO]  systemd: Starting k3s
root@ubuntu:~# k3s kubectl get nodes
NAME                 STATUS   ROLES                  AGE   VERSION
ubuntu.example.com   Ready    control-plane,master   16s   v1.28.5+k3s1
root@ubuntu:~#
```

Figure 1-2. *k3s on Ubuntu*

- **Step 3**: Interact with k3s

  Now that our lightweight Kubernetes cluster is operational, we can interact with it using `kubectl` as we would with any other Kubernetes cluster. For example, we can deploy applications, create pods and services, and manage our cluster resources.

Discussion

k3s is an excellent choice for scenarios where a lightweight, efficient, and easy-to-manage Kubernetes cluster is required. It is particularly well-suited for resource-constrained environments, edge computing, and IoT deployments. Despite its reduced footprint, it maintains compatibility with standard Kubernetes features and APIs, making it versatile for various use cases.

However, it's essential to understand that k3s is designed for single-node or small-scale cluster deployments. If our project requires a more extensive cluster with high availability and advanced features, we may need to consider other Kubernetes distributions like Kubernetes itself or solutions such as Rancher.

See Also

- k3s Official Documentation `https://k3s.io`

1.3 Dashboard

Problem

You would like to set up and access the Kubernetes Dashboard to monitor and manage your Kubernetes cluster.

Solution

Follow these steps to download, configure, and access the Kubernetes Dashboard:

1. Download the latest version of the dashboard:

```
wget https://raw.githubusercontent.com/
kubernetes/dashboard/v2.7.0/aio/deploy/
recommended.yaml
```

2. Apply the YAML configuration:

```
kubectl apply -f recommend.yaml
```

3. Create and apply the YAML files for the “admin-user” in the dashboard namespace in order to access the dashboard:

   - dashboard-adminuser.yaml

```
apiVersion: v1
kind: ServiceAccount
metadata:
      name: admin-user
      namespace: kubernetes-dashboard
```

   - clusterrolebind.yaml

```
apiVersion: rbac.authorization.k8s.io/v1
kind: ClusterRoleBinding
metadata:
     name: admin-user
```

```
roleRef:
    apiGroup: rbac.authorization.k8s.io
    kind: ClusterRole
    name: cluster-admin
subjects:
- kind: ServiceAccount
  name: admin-user
  namespace: kubernetes-dashboard
```

```
# kubectl apply -f dashboard-adminuser.yaml
# kubectl apply -f clusterrolebind.yaml
```

4. Generate the token for the "`admin-user`":

   ```
   kubectl -n kubernetes-dashboard create token
   admin-user
   ```

   This command copies the authentication token for the dashboard to our clipboard.

5. Access the Kubernetes Dashboard.

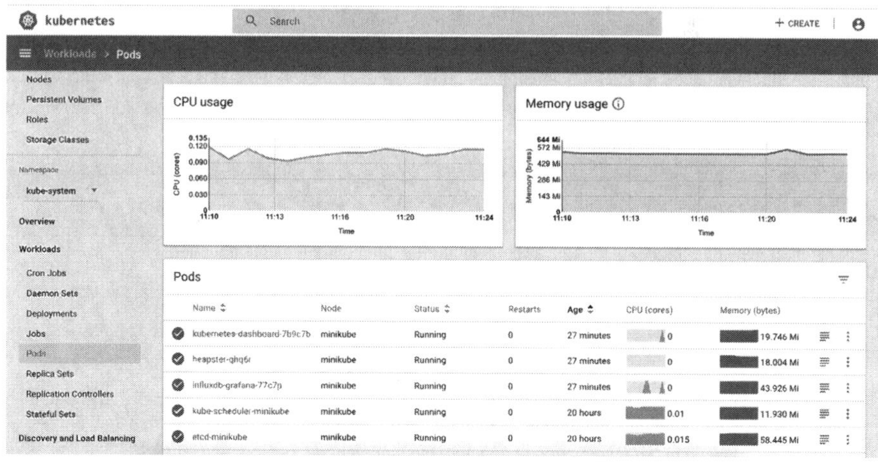

***Figure 1-3.** Kubernetes Dashboard*

Open our browser and navigate to `https://<server-ip>:6443`, where `<server-ip>` is the machine's IP add where Kubernetes is installed. Paste the token to access the dashboard.

Discussion

The Kubernetes Dashboard provides a user-friendly interface for managing and monitoring your Kubernetes cluster. This includes viewing workloads, managing cluster resources, and troubleshooting common issues.

Ensure that the dashboard is accessible only within your network or through secure means such as a VPN. Use role-based access control (RBAC) to limit dashboard access to authorized users only. If you encounter issues accessing the dashboard, verify that the Kubernetes API server is accessible at the specified IP and port. Ensure that the `ServiceAccount` and `ClusterRoleBinding` are correctly applied and that the token has not expired.

See Also

- Kubernetes Dashboard GitHub Repository
- Kubernetes Documentation on Dashboard

1.4 Set Up a Local Kubernetes with Minikube

Problem

We want to develop and test our Kubernetes applications on our local machine without the need for a full-scale cluster. Setting up a local Kubernetes environment is essential for development and debugging but can be challenging if we are new to Kubernetes. How can we quickly and easily set up a local Kubernetes cluster for our development needs?

Solution

Minikube is a fantastic tool that allows us to run a single-node Kubernetes cluster on our local machine. It's a perfect solution for developers who want to experiment with Kubernetes or test their applications in a local environment before deploying them to a production cluster. Follow these steps to set up a local Kubernetes cluster using Minikube:

- **Step 1**: Install Minikube

  First, make sure we have Minikube installed on our machine. We can download and install Minikube by following the instructions on the official Minikube website (`https://minikube.sigs.k8s.io/docs/start`) using the package manager of the major operating systems.

- **Step 2**: Start Minikube

  Open our terminal and run the following command to start Minikube:

  ```
  minikube start
  ```

  Minikube will create a virtual machine and configure a Kubernetes cluster inside it.

- **Step 3**: Verify Our Cluster

  To verify that our Minikube cluster is up and running, use the following command:

  ```
  minikube status
  ```

  This command should display that our cluster is running and the kubectl context is set to use the Minikube cluster, as shown in Figure 1-4.

Figure 1-4. *Minikube on MacOS*

- **Step 4**: Interact with Minikube

  Now that our local Kubernetes cluster is running, we can use `kubectl` to interact with it like a remote cluster. For example, we can deploy applications, create pods, and manage cluster resources.

Minikube comes out of the box with many add-ons. We can list all the available add-ons using the command

```
$ minikube addons list
```

The command produces a list of the available and enabled add-ons, like Figure 1-5.

```
lberton — -zsh — 91×46
lberton@Lucas-MacBook-Pro ~ % minikube addons list
|-----------------------------|----------|--------------|--------------------------------|
|         ADDON NAME          | PROFILE  |    STATUS    |           MAINTAINER           |
|-----------------------------|----------|--------------|--------------------------------|
| ambassador                  | minikube | disabled     | 3rd party (Ambassador)         |
| auto-pause                  | minikube | disabled     | minikube                       |
| cloud-spanner               | minikube | disabled     | Google                         |
| csi-hostpath-driver         | minikube | disabled     | Kubernetes                     |
| dashboard                   | minikube | enabled ✅   | Kubernetes                     |
| default-storageclass        | minikube | enabled ✅   | Kubernetes                     |
| efk                         | minikube | disabled     | 3rd party (Elastic)            |
| freshpod                    | minikube | disabled     | Google                         |
| gcp-auth                    | minikube | disabled     | Google                         |
| gvisor                      | minikube | disabled     | minikube                       |
| headlamp                    | minikube | disabled     | 3rd party (kinvolk.io)         |
| helm-tiller                 | minikube | disabled     | 3rd party (Helm)               |
| inaccel                     | minikube | disabled     | 3rd party (InAccel             |
|                             |          |              | [info@inaccel.com])            |
| ingress                     | minikube | disabled     | Kubernetes                     |
| ingress-dns                 | minikube | disabled     | minikube                       |
| inspektor-gadget            | minikube | disabled     | 3rd party                      |
|                             |          |              | (inspektor-gadget.io)          |
| istio                       | minikube | disabled     | 3rd party (Istio)              |
| istio-provisioner           | minikube | disabled     | 3rd party (Istio)              |
| kong                        | minikube | disabled     | 3rd party (Kong HQ)            |
| kubeflow                    | minikube | disabled     | 3rd party                      |
| kubevirt                    | minikube | disabled     | 3rd party (KubeVirt)           |
| logviewer                   | minikube | disabled     | 3rd party (unknown)            |
| metallb                     | minikube | disabled     | 3rd party (MetalLB)            |
| metrics-server              | minikube | disabled     | Kubernetes                     |
| nvidia-device-plugin        | minikube | disabled     | 3rd party (NVIDIA)             |
| nvidia-driver-installer     | minikube | disabled     | 3rd party (Nvidia)             |
| nvidia-gpu-device-plugin    | minikube | disabled     | 3rd party (Nvidia)             |
| olm                         | minikube | disabled     | 3rd party (Operator Framework) |
| pod-security-policy         | minikube | disabled     | 3rd party (unknown)            |
| portainer                   | minikube | disabled     | 3rd party (Portainer.io)       |
| registry                    | minikube | disabled     | minikube                       |
| registry-aliases            | minikube | disabled     | 3rd party (unknown)            |
| registry-creds              | minikube | disabled     | 3rd party (UPMC Enterprises)   |
| storage-provisioner         | minikube | enabled ✅   | minikube                       |
| storage-provisioner-gluster | minikube | disabled     | 3rd party (Gluster)            |
| storage-provisioner-rancher | minikube | disabled     | 3rd party (Rancher)            |
| volumesnapshots             | minikube | disabled     | Kubernetes                     |
| yakd                        | minikube | disabled     | 3rd party (marcnuri.com)       |
|-----------------------------|----------|--------------|--------------------------------|
lberton@Lucas-MacBook-Pro ~ %
```

Figure 1-5. *Minikube add-ons list*

For example, we can enable the dashboard and enable the connection from other hosts using the following commands:

```
$ minikube addons enable dashboard
$ minikube addons enable ingress
```

We can access the `minikube` dashboard using the following command:

```
minikube dashboard
```

This opens a web-based Kubernetes Dashboard in our default web browser.

We can deploy a sample application:

```
kubectl create deployment hello-minikube --image=k8s.gcr.io/
echoserver:1.4
```

Discussion

Minikube is an excellent tool for setting up a local Kubernetes environment for development and testing purposes. It allows us to avoid the complexity of managing a full-scale cluster while providing an authentic Kubernetes experience. With Minikube, we can develop, debug, and experiment with our Kubernetes applications locally before deploying them to a production cluster. Remember that Minikube is a single-node cluster, which means it's unsuitable for testing scenarios requiring multiple nodes or high availability. Consider other Kubernetes solutions like `kind` (Kubernetes in Docker) or using cloud-based Kubernetes services.

1.5 Running Local Kubernetes Clusters in Docker Containers

Problem

We want to set up a local Kubernetes cluster for development or testing purposes, and we prefer to use Docker containers for a lightweight and isolated environment.

Solution

Running a local Kubernetes cluster in Docker containers is a popular choice for developers who want a quick and isolated Kubernetes environment. Follow these steps to create our Kubernetes cluster using Docker containers:

- **Step 1**: Install Docker

  Ensure Docker is installed on our machine. We can download Docker from the official website: Docker Downloads (`https://www.docker.com/get-started`).

- **Step 2**: Download Kubernetes in Docker (KinD)

  KinD is a tool for running local Kubernetes clusters using Docker container "nodes." Install KinD using a package manager or download the binary from the official releases page: KinD Releases (`https://github.com/kubernetes-sigs/kind/releases`).

- 2.1 Homebrew (MacOS)

  ```
  brew install kind
  ```

- 2.2 Chocolatey (Windows)

  ```
  choco install kind
  ```

- 2.3 Manual Installation (Linux/MacOS/Windows)

  Download the KinD binary and follow the installation instructions for our operating system.

- **Step 3**: Create a Kubernetes Cluster

  Run the following command to create a local Kubernetes cluster using KinD:

  ```
  kind create cluster
  ```

  This command sets up a cluster with a default name (kind), and we are ready to go.

- **Step 4**: If kubectl is not in your PATH, you can create a symlink to it. Open your terminal and execute the following command:

  ```
  sudo ln -s $(which kubectl) /usr/local/bin/kubectl
  ```

- **Step 5**: Verify the Cluster

  Check that the cluster is running:

  ```
  kubectl cluster-info
  ```

  This command should display information about the Kubernetes cluster.

- **Step 6**: Interact with the Cluster

  Now that our Kubernetes cluster is up and running, use `kubectl` to interact with it. For example, deploy a sample application:

  ```
  kubectl create deployment hello-kind --image=k8s
  .gcr.io/echoserver:1.4
  ```

Discussion

Running local Kubernetes clusters in Docker containers using KinD provides an isolated environment for development and testing. It enables us to experiment with Kubernetes features without needing a dedicated cluster. Remember that this setup is suitable for local development and learning purposes.

See Also

- KinD Documentation `https://kind.sigs.k8s.io/docs/`
- Kubernetes—Using KinD for local clusters `https://kubernetes.io/docs/setup/learning-environment/kind/`

1.6 Set Up a Cluster Using Kubeadm

Problem

Setting up a Kubernetes cluster manually can be a daunting task, often prone to errors and inconsistencies. Without a reliable and streamlined approach, beginners may find it challenging to initiate a cluster and get their applications up and running.

Solution

Install Docker: Ensure Docker is installed on all machines. Use our package manager to install Docker.

```
apt-get update
apt-get install docker.io
```

Disable Swap: Disable swap to meet Kubernetes requirements.

```
swapoff -a
```

Install Kubeadm, Kubelet, and Kubectl:

```
apt-get update && sudo apt-get install -y kubelet
kubeadm kubectl
```

Initialize the Master Node: On the designated master node, initialize the cluster using Kubeadm.

```
kubeadm init
```

Set Up Kubeconfig: Copy the `kubeconfig` file to the user's home directory.

```
mkdir -p $HOME/.kube
cp -i /etc/kubernetes/admin.conf $HOME/.kube/config
chown $(id -u):$(id -g) $HOME/.kube/config
```

Join Worker Nodes: On each worker node, run the join option provided by the `kubeadm` command.

```
kubeadm join <MASTER_IP>:<MASTER_PORT> --token <TOKEN>
--discovery-token-ca-cert-hash <HASH>
```

Verify Cluster Status: Check the status to ensure the cluster is up and running.

```
kubectl get nodes
```

Discussion

Setting up a Kubernetes cluster using Kubeadm provides a straightforward and standardized approach. It automates many of the complex tasks, allowing users to focus on deploying and managing applications rather than dealing with the intricacies of cluster initialization. This recipe serves as a fundamental step in our Kubernetes journey, enabling us to build a solid foundation for scalable and resilient containerized applications.

See Also

- Kubeadm Official Documentation `https://kubernetes.io/docs/setup/production-environment/tools/kubeadm`

1.7 Set Up a Cluster Using Kubernetes Operations

Problem

Manually setting up a Kubernetes cluster can be a time-consuming and error-prone process. The need for a streamlined, automated solution becomes evident as organizations embrace Kubernetes for container orchestration.

Solution

Install kOps: Install kOps on our local machine. For example, on Linux:

```
wget https://github.com/kubernetes/kops/releases/
download/$(curl -s https://api.github.com/repos/kubernetes/
kops/releases/latest | grep tag_name | cut -d '"' -f 4)/kops-
linux-amd64 -O /usr/local/bin/kops
chmod +x /usr/local/bin/kops
```

Create a Cluster Configuration: Generate a cluster configuration using kOps. This includes specifying the cluster name, region, and other essential parameters.

```
kops create cluster --name=<cluster-name> --state=s3://<s3-
bucket-name> --zones=<availability-zones> --node-count=
<num-nodes> --node-size=<node-instance-type>
```

Edit Cluster Configuration (Optional): If needed, we can edit the cluster configuration to customize aspects like network settings, instance types, or Kubernetes version.

```
kops edit cluster --name <cluster-name>
```

Create and Update the Cluster: Once the configuration is finalized, create the cluster and update the DNS.

```
kops update cluster --name <cluster-name> --yes
```

Validate the Cluster: Ensure the cluster is in a valid state and ready for use.

```
kops validate cluster --name <cluster-name>
```

Discussion

kOps simplifies the deployment and management of production-ready Kubernetes clusters. It automates the tedious tasks involved in cluster creation, making it a valuable tool for both beginners and experienced users. The ability to version-control cluster configurations further enhances collaboration and repeatability.

By leveraging kOps, users can easily scale their clusters, apply updates, and manage infrastructure changes without delving into the complexities of manual setup. The tool aligns with the infrastructure-as-code (IaC) philosophy, promoting consistency and reducing the risk of configuration drift.

See Also

– kOps Official Documentation `https://kops.sigs.k8s.io/`

1.8 Running on Raspberry Pis Using MicroK8s

Problem

Running Kubernetes clusters on small-scale or edge devices like Raspberry Pi presents unique challenges. Traditional Kubernetes setups are often too resource-intensive for the limited hardware of Raspberry Pis or any alternative single-board computers. This can lead to performance issues, difficulty in managing cluster operations, and complexities in implementing high availability and resilience.

Solution

MicroK8s offers an efficient solution for running Kubernetes on Raspberry Pis. It is a lightweight, self-contained Kubernetes distribution designed for small-scale and IoT devices. MicroK8s requires minimal resources, making it ideal for Raspberry Pis. It simplifies the deployment and management of Kubernetes clusters on these devices while offering all essential features. Here are the steps to install and run MicroK8s on Raspberry Pi:

1. **Prepare the Raspberry Pi**: Ensure the Raspberry Pi is set up with the latest OS and has network connectivity.
2. **Install MicroK8s**: Use the command sudo snap install microk8s --classic.

3. **Configure MicroK8s**: Run "`microk8s status --wait-ready`" to check the status and enable necessary add-ons like DNS, dashboard, etc., using "`microk8s enable <addon-name>`".

4. **Deploy Applications**: Use "`microk8s kubectl`" to deploy and manage our applications.

Discussion

MicroK8s offers several advantages for those looking to deploy Kubernetes on Raspberry Pi devices. Firstly, it excels in resource efficiency, consuming fewer CPU and memory resources, making it an excellent fit for Raspberry Pi's limited hardware capabilities. Its user-friendly nature simplifies the deployment and management of Kubernetes, making it accessible to users with limited Kubernetes experience. Scalability is another key benefit, allowing for the straightforward addition of more Raspberry Pi nodes to the cluster. Moreover, MicroK8s enjoys the support of strong communities from both Raspberry Pi and Kubernetes, providing users with valuable resources and assistance. However, it's essential to consider the hardware limitations of Raspberry Pi, as high-demand applications may still be constrained by the device's physical constraints in terms of CPU, memory, and storage. Setting up networking for a Raspberry Pi cluster can be complex, especially for beginners, so it's crucial to plan and execute networking configurations carefully. Lastly, maintaining security is paramount, as IoT devices like Raspberry Pi can be vulnerable to attacks, requiring diligent security practices to safeguard the cluster.

See Also

- MicroK8s website `https://microk8s.io`

1.9 Building a Hybrid Architecture Cluster

Problem

In today's diverse computing environment, organizations often need to integrate different types of computing architectures, such as ARM, x86, and RISC-V, into a single cohesive system. This hybrid architecture approach poses significant challenges in terms of compatibility, management, and resource optimization. Ensuring seamless communication and efficient workload distribution across different architectures can be complex and resource-intensive.

Solution

Building a hybrid architecture cluster involves integrating different computing architectures under a unified management system. This can be achieved by using containerization technologies like Docker and orchestration tools like Kubernetes. These technologies abstract the underlying hardware differences and provide a common platform for deploying and managing applications.

Here are the steps to build a hybrid architecture cluster:

- **Assess Requirements**: Understand the specific needs and constraints of each architecture in the cluster.
- **Set Up Hardware**: Prepare servers with different architectures (e.g., ARM-based and x86-based) and ensure they are networked together.
- **Install Containerization Software**: Install Docker on all nodes to containerize applications.
- **Set Up Kubernetes**: Install and configure Kubernetes to orchestrate containers across different architectures. Ensure that Kubernetes is set up to handle multi-architecture images.

- **Deploy Applications**: Create Docker images for our applications that are compatible with multiple architectures and deploy them using Kubernetes.

Discussion

A hybrid architecture cluster offers a plethora of advantages for organizations seeking versatility and resource optimization in their IT infrastructure. One notable advantage is its flexibility, as it accommodates a wide array of applications and services, taking advantage of the specific strengths each architecture brings to the table. Resource optimization is another key benefit, as it intelligently balances workloads across different architecture types to achieve optimal performance. Scalability is also a strong suit, as new nodes, regardless of their architecture, can seamlessly integrate into the cluster. Nevertheless, there are important considerations to bear in mind. Managing a hybrid cluster can be more intricate than overseeing a single-architecture cluster due to the need to harmonize diverse components. Ensuring software and applications are compatible across various architectures can be challenging. Additionally, the potential for increased costs, encompassing hardware investments, software licensing, and ongoing maintenance, must be carefully evaluated before committing to a hybrid cluster approach.

See Also

- Arm workloads on GKE `https://cloud.google.com/kubernetes-engine/docs/concepts/arm-on-gke`

1.10 Cluster Access Kubeconfig Files

Problem

Effectively managing multiple Kubernetes clusters requires organizing access to them without frequently switching `kubeconfig` files or editing the configuration manually.

Solution

Use the following `kubectl` command-line tool to manage and combine multiple `kubeconfig` files into one organized file configuration:

1. **Locate Existing Kubeconfig Files**: Identify the `kubeconfig` files for your clusters. Typically, these are found in `~/.kube/config` or provided during cluster creation.

   ```
   ls ~/.kube
   ```

2. **Set the KUBECONFIG Environment Variable**: Temporarily set the `KUBECONFIG` variable to include all your configuration files.

   ```
   export KUBECONFIG=~/.kube/config:/path/to/
   another/config:/path/to/third/config
   ```

3. **Merge Configurations**: Merge all the specified `kubeconfig` files into one, making it easier to manage clusters.

   ```
   kubectl config view --flatten > ~/.kube/
   merged-config
   ```

4. **Back Up and Replace the Original Config**: Back up your original kubeconfig and replace it with the merged one.

```
cp ~/.kube/config ~/.kube/config.bak
mv ~/.kube/merged-config ~/.kube/config
```

5. **Verify Contexts**: List all contexts to ensure access to all clusters.

```
kubectl config get-contexts
```

6. **Switch Between Contexts**: Use the following command to switch contexts when interacting with different clusters:

```
kubectl config use-context <context-name>
```

7. **Set a Default Context (Optional)**: Define a default context for convenience.

```
kubectl config set-context --current
--namespace=default
```

Discussion

Effectively managing multiple Kubernetes clusters requires a centralized and streamlined approach to organizing kubeconfig files, particularly in large-scale environments that span various cloud providers, regions, or settings like development, staging, and production. Consolidating kubeconfig files into a single, merged configuration ensures ease of access and reduces the cognitive load associated with managing separate configurations. It also minimizes errors, such as applying operations to the wrong cluster or namespace, by making context switching explicit. Security is crucial; `kubeconfig` files should utilize RBAC with minimal privileges, scoped credentials, and regular audits to prevent unauthorized access. For teams operating CI/CD pipelines, dynamically generating `kubeconfig` files with ephemeral access and the least privilege ensures secure deployments. Tools like `kubectx`, `kubens`, or comprehensive platforms like Rancher can further simplify multi-cluster management. Defaulting namespaces, audit logging, and proper tool integration reduce misconfigurations and enhance operational efficiency. Organizations should also prepare for scale by future-proofing `kubeconfig` management through automation and adopting centralized fleet management tools for comprehensive oversight, ensuring smooth operations as their Kubernetes footprint expands and grows.

See Also

- kubectl config `https://kubernetes.io/docs/reference/kubectl/generated/kubectl_config/`

1.11 Implementing Kubernetes HA

Problem

In a Kubernetes environment, ensuring high availability (HA) is crucial for maintaining the reliability and stability of applications. A single point of failure in a Kubernetes cluster can lead to significant downtime and disrupt services. This challenge involves ensuring that the Kubernetes control plane and worker nodes are resilient to failures and can handle loads efficiently without any service disruption.

Solution

Implementing Kubernetes HA involves setting up a cluster with multiple master nodes and worker nodes distributed across different failure domains (e.g., different physical servers, racks, or data centers). This setup ensures that the failure of one component does not affect the overall availability of the system.

Here are the steps to implement Kubernetes HA:

- **Set Up Multiple Master Nodes**: Deploy at least three master nodes to ensure the Kubernetes control plane remains available even if one node fails.
- **Use a Load Balancer**: Implement a load balancer in front of the master nodes to distribute traffic and provide a single point of contact for the Kubernetes API server.
- **Distributed Storage for ETCD**: Use a distributed storage solution for the ETCD cluster, which is the Kubernetes backing store, to ensure data is replicated across master nodes.
- **High Availability for Worker Nodes**: Distribute worker nodes across different physical or virtual machines to prevent a single point of failure.
- **Implement Pod Disruption Budgets (PDBs)**: Use Pod Disruption Budgets to ensure that a minimum number of replicas for critical applications are always running.

Discussion

High-availability (HA) Kubernetes clusters offer several advantages for organizations seeking robust and uninterrupted operations. First and foremost, they provide unparalleled reliability by minimizing the risk of system downtime, thereby ensuring the continuous functioning of critical applications. Scalability is another key benefit, as HA Kubernetes clusters make it easier to expand applications and resources while maintaining system availability. Load balancing capabilities efficiently distribute traffic and workloads across multiple nodes, enhancing overall performance. However, it's important to consider the associated complexities, as setting up and managing an HA Kubernetes cluster can be more intricate than a standard single-master setup. Furthermore, HA configurations demand additional hardware and network resources, potentially driving up costs. Regular monitoring and maintenance are essential to keep all components running smoothly and maintain the cluster's high availability. In addition to providing unparalleled reliability and scalability, high-availability (HA) Kubernetes clusters offer automatic failover capabilities, ensuring quick recovery from master node failures. These clusters also prioritize data replication to maintain data consistency and availability, which is particularly crucial for stateful applications. While HA configurations can incur higher hardware and networking costs, they play a vital role in disaster recovery strategies and bolster security through enhanced communication and access control mechanisms.

See Also

- etcd Clustering Guide `https://etcd.io/docs/latest/op-guide/clustering`

Summary

This chapter serves as an introductory guide to the essential tools and strategies for setting up and managing Kubernetes environments. It covers the installation of crucial components like `kubectl`, `k3s`, and `minikube`, providing step-by-step instructions tailored to various operating systems and preferences. The chapter highlights the versatility of Kubernetes in different contexts, from lightweight, resource-constrained setups with k3s to local development environments using Minikube and Docker-based Kubernetes clusters with KinD. It also touches on advanced setups like HA clusters and hybrid architecture clusters, addressing diverse needs and scenarios. Overall, this chapter equips readers with the foundational knowledge and practical skills necessary to navigate the complexities of Kubernetes and leverage its capabilities effectively in various operational environments.

CHAPTER 2

Configuring Stateless Applications

This chapter focuses on the configuration of stateless applications in Kubernetes, covering various aspects such as namespace creation, pod deployment, environment variable configuration, multi-container pod setups, resource limits, JSON patch operations, secret management, and the utilization of enterprise and Linux-based images.

2.1 List All the Namespaces

Kubernetes namespaces provide a mechanism for isolating resources within a single cluster. It does not apply to cluster-wide objects like storage, nodes, or persistent volumes.

Let's see our namespaces first. For the sake of productivity, we should assign an alias to our `kubectl`, like alias `kc=kubectl`. Still, for presentation details, we will use `kubectl` throughout the book so all commands are executable in case we don't have an alias set.

Problem

In a Kubernetes environment, we need to list all the namespaces to manage and monitor the isolated groups of resources effectively. This is crucial in a multi-tenant environment with resources divided among

G. Stencel and L. Berton, *Kubernetes Recipes*,
https://doi.org/10.1007/979-8-8688-1325-2_2

teams or projects. Our challenge is to retrieve a list of all namespaces efficiently, understanding their role in resource isolation and how they apply to namespaced objects.

Solution

```
$ kubectl get namespace
```

We can also use aliases:

```
$ kubectl get ns
```

The output of the command looks like the following:

```
NAME              STATUS   AGE
default           Active   26m
kube-node-lease   Active   26m
kube-public       Active   26m
kube-system       Active   26m
```

Discussion

Remember that Kubernetes comes with four default namespaces: `default`, `kube-node-lease`, `kube-public`, and `kube-system`. While creating namespaces, we must avoid being reserved by Kubernetes names, starting with "`kube-`".

2.2 Create a Namespace

Problem

We manage a Kubernetes cluster and must isolate resources for different teams or projects. This is crucial in a multi-tenant environment, where efficient resource management and security are paramount. Our challenge is to create and manage namespaces effectively, ensuring resources like deployments, pods, services, etc. are uniquely identified within each namespace.

Solution

First of all, let's create the `test1` namespace:

```
$ kubectl create ns test1
namespace/test1 created
```

To confirm that the namespace is there, let's list all the namespaces:

```
$ kubectl get ns
NAME              STATUS   AGE
default           Active   31m
kube-node-lease   Active   31m
kube-public       Active   31m
kube-system       Active   31m
test1             Active   4s
```

Let's create another namespace and switch the context to the first one:

```
$ kubectl create ns test2
namespace/test2 created
```

Problem

Create a namespace definition in the YAML file named `test3-ns.yaml` without applying it to the cluster.

Solution

```
$ kubectl create ns test3 -o yaml --dry-run=client >
test3-ns.yaml
apiVersion: v1
kind: Namespace
metadata:
  creationTimestamp: null
  name: test3
spec: {}
status: {}
```

Discussion

If we don't provide the `--dry-run=client` option, it doesn't matter if it's piped to the file or not. It will be applied to the cluster.

Problem

Create a namespace from `stdin` (standard input) definition.

Solution

```
$ kubectl apply -f - <<EOF
apiVersion: v1
kind: Namespace
```

```
metadata:
  creationTimestamp: null
  name: test3
spec: {}
status: {}
EOF
```

2.3 Create a Pod in a Namespace

Problem

We are tasked with creating a pod running Nginx in one namespace (namespace `test1`) and then verifying if this pod is visible or accessible from another namespace (namespace `test2`). This experiment will help us understand the isolation level provided by Kubernetes namespaces and how resources interact across these boundaries.

Solution

First of all, let's switch to namespace `test1`:

```
$ kubectl config set-context --current --namespace=test1
Context "minikube" modified.
$ kubectl run nginx --image=nginx
pod/nginx created
$ kubectl get pods
NAME    READY   STATUS    RESTARTS   AGE
nginx   1/1     Running   0          108s
$kubectl config set-context --current --namespace=test2
Context "minikube" modified.
$ kubectl get pods
```

```
No resources found in test2 namespace.
```

We can see our pod from "namespace 1" is nicely isolated from other namespaces.

2.4 Create a Pod with Environment Variables as Configuration

Problem

In a production environment, applications often need to adapt to different settings based on the environment in which they are deployed. This includes variations in database connections, API endpoints, and other configuration parameters that change between development, testing, and production environments. Hardcoding these configurations in the application code or Docker images can lead to security risks and a lack of flexibility. Kubernetes offers a solution to this by allowing environment variables to be set directly in the pod specifications.

The challenge here is to create a Kubernetes pod that can dynamically adapt its behavior based on environment-specific configurations without the need to rebuild or redeploy the application. This setup should facilitate easy updates to the configuration, promote consistency across different environments, and ensure secure handling of sensitive information.

Let's assign `SERVICE_PORT` variable with value 8000 on `nginx` image.

Solution

Let's have the pod YAML definition:

```
apiVersion: v1
kind: Pod
metadata:
```

```
  name: dependent-envars-demo
spec:
  containers:
    - name: dependent-envars-demo
      image: nginx
      env:
        - name: SERVICE_PORT
          value: "8000"
```

A similar would apply to mysql image

```
apiVersion: apps/v1
kind: Deployment
metadata:
  name: mysql-deployment
spec:
  replicas: 1
  selector:
    matchLabels:
      app: mysql
  template:
    metadata:
      labels:
        app: mysql
    spec:
      containers:
      - name: mysql
        image: mysql:5.7  # Use the desired MySQL version
        env:
        - name: MYSQL_ROOT_PASSWORD
          value: "myrootpw"
        - name: MYSQL_DATABASE
          value: "mydb"
```

```
        - name: MYSQL_USER
          value: "myuser"
        - name: MYSQL_PASSWORD
          value: "mypw"
        - name: MYSQL_HOST
          value: "myhost"
        ports:
        - containerPort: 3306
```

The MySQL Docker image would check first if the env vars set are in place and will override them with the user-defined values in the YAML file above. It is strongly discouraged to set passwords inside the YAML. The above example should be treated as an antipattern.

2.5 Create a Multi-container Pod

Remember that this might be misleading, but the containers are not the smallest deployable units; the pods are in Kubernetes. A pod is a group of containers.

Problem

In modern microservices architectures, it's common to have a situation where multiple interdependent containers must run together in a single pod in Kubernetes. This might be due to shared resources, such as storage volumes or networking, or because these containers represent tightly coupled components of a larger application (such as a main application and its caching service). The challenge lies in effectively managing these containers within a single pod, ensuring they can communicate, share resources efficiently, and maintain high availability and resilience.

The complexities include setting up inter-container communication, resource allocation, lifecycle management, and handling dependencies and ordering. Additionally, strategies must be implemented for logging, monitoring, and updating these multi-container pods without disrupting the service.

Solution

Let's have the pod YAML definition:

```
apiVersion: v1
kind: Pod
metadata:
  name: multi-container-pod
  labels:
    purpose: multi-containers
spec:
  containers:
  - name: web-app
    image: my-web-app:latest
    ports:
    - containerPort: 80
    volumeMounts:
    - name: shared-logs
      mountPath: /var/log

  - name: log-sidecar
    image: my-logging-sidecar:latest
    volumeMounts:
    - name: shared-logs
      mountPath: /var/log

  volumes:
```

```
  - name: shared-logs
    emptyDir: {}
```

```
$ kubectl apply -f multicontainer.yaml
pod/multi-container-pod created
```

Let us verify it if is running:

```
$ kubectl get pods
NAME                   READY   STATUS    RESTARTS     AGE
multi-container-pod    2/2     Running   1 (3s ago)   8s
```

We can see it says 2/2, which means there are two containers running within our pod.

Let's get into the first one to see how resource share works between containers.

To get inside the first container in our `multi-container-pod`, we need to add the `-c` flag specifying our container name, in this case `web-app`:

```
kubectl exec -it multi-container-pod /bin/bash
```

Explanation:

```
-i, --stdin=false:
```

Pass stdin to the container.

```
 -t, --tty=false:
```

Stdin is a TTY.

We can also execute any process running in the container. Actually, this is how containers are designed. We just execute our application process, which will run in a container:

```
$ kubectl exec -it multi-container-pod -c web-app -- /bin/bash
root@multi-container-pod:/#
ls -la /var/log/shared-logs/
```

```
total 8
drwxrwxrwx 2 root root 4096 Dec 10 23:31 .
drwxr-xr-x 1 root root 4096 Dec 10 23:13 ..
echo "container-web-app-was-here" > /var/log/shared-logs/
message1
$ cat /var/log/shared-logs/message1
container-web-app-was-here
CTRL+D
```

If we don't know the YAML location and any container name, we can just describe the pod to see all the containers, or we can just run `kubectl`:

```
kubectl get pods POD_NAME_HERE -o jsonpath='{.spec.
containers[*].name}'
```

2.6 Create a Pod with Resource Limits

Problem

In Kubernetes, a common challenge is ensuring that pods use resources efficiently without overwhelming the cluster. Without proper resource limits, a pod could consume more CPU or memory than it should, potentially affecting other pods and leading to resource starvation. The goal is to define resource limits for a pod to optimize resource usage and maintain the stability of the system.

Create a Kubernetes pod with specific CPU and memory limits to ensure efficient resource usage and prevent the pod from consuming excessive resources.

Solution

```yaml
apiVersion: v1
kind: Pod
metadata:
  name: example-pod
  labels:
    purpose: demonstrate-resource-limits
spec:
  containers:
  - name: example-container
    image: nginx
    resources:
      requests:
        memory: "64Mi"
        cpu: "250m"
      limits:
        memory: "128Mi"
        cpu: "500m"
  - name: log-aggregator
    image: log-aggregator:v1
    resources:
      requests:
        memory: "64Mi"
        cpu: "250m"
      limits:
        memory: "128Mi"
        cpu: "500m"
```

Discussion

We have to learn Kubernetes resource limits and requests defining CPU and memory limits for a Kubernetes pod and the memory resource units Below cheat sheet can help us understanding it.

Limits and requests for memory are measured in bytes. We can express memory using one of these quantity suffixes: E, P, T, G, M, k. We can also use the power-of-two equivalents: Ei, Pi, Ti, Gi, Mi, and Ki.

The below suffixes are based on the power of two, which aligns with the way computer memory is structured.

The base unit of memory is B (bytes), for example, 500 B (500 bytes).

Table 2-1. *The power of two*

Unit	Name	1 unit	Power of 2	Bytes equivalent
Ki	Kibibytes	1 Ki	2^10	1,024 bytes
Mi	Mebibytes	1 Mi	2^20	1,048,576 bytes
Gi	Gibibytes	1 Gi	2^30	1,073,741,824 bytes
Ti	Tebibytes	1 Ti	2^40	1,099,511,627,776 bytes
Pi	Pebibytes	1 Pi	2^50	1,125,899,906,842,624 bytes
Ei	Exbibytes	1 Ei	2^60	1,152,921,504,606,846,976 bytes

In Kubernetes, we can also specify memory limits and requests using units that are not based on powers of two, though it's less common:

Bytes (B): The base unit, as in the power-of-two units.

Example: 500 B (500 bytes)

Kilobytes (KB): 1 KB = 10^3 = 1,000 bytes.

Example: 100 KB (100 × 1,000 bytes = 100,000 bytes)

Megabytes (MB): 1 MB = 10^6 = 1,000,000 bytes.

Example: 50 MB (50 × 1,000,000 bytes = 50,000,000 bytes)

Gigabytes (GB): 1 GB = 10^9 = 1,000,000,000 bytes.

Example: 2 GB (2 × 1,000,000,000 bytes = 2,000,000,000 bytes)

Terabytes (TB): 1 TB = 10^12 = 1,000,000,000,000 bytes.

Example: 1 TB (1 × 1,000,000,000,000 bytes = 1,000,000,000,000 bytes)

Petabytes (PB): 1 PB = 10^15 = 1,000,000,000,000,000 bytes.

Example: 500 PB (500 × 1,000,000,000,000,000 bytes = 500,000,000,000,000,000 bytes)

Exabytes (EB): 1 EB = 10^18 = 1,000,000,000,000,000,000 bytes.

Example: 1 EB (1 × 1,000,000,000,000,000,000 bytes = 1,000,000,000,000,000,000 bytes)

For the CPU resource limit cheat sheet, CPU resources are measured in units of Kubernetes CPU, which are equivalent to CPU cores. We can specify CPU limits and requests using whole numbers or fractional values. Here are the units and examples:

- CPU resources can be specified in terms of whole CPU cores, for example, 1 equals 1 CPU core.
- **Millicores (m)**: This is a more granular unit where 1,000 m (millicores) equals 1 full CPU core. This allows for more precise allocation.

Table 2-2. *Correspondence between CPU cores and millicore units*

CPU core count	YAML core unit	YAML in millicore unit
2 CPU cores	cpu: "2"	cpu: "2000m"
1 CPU core	cpu: "1"	cpu: "1000m"
0.5, half a CPU core	cpu: "0.5"	cpu: "500m"
0.25, quarter of a CPU core	cpu: "0.25"	cpu: "250m"
0.1, one-tenth of a CPU core	cpu: "0.1"	cpu: "100m"

2.7 Apply a JSON Patch Operation

Problem

In Kubernetes, we can update resources such as pods, deployments, and services using a patch operation. This allows us to change specific parts of the resource without replacing the entire configuration. There are different patch strategies, with JSON patch being one of them.

Solution

Create a JSON patch file.

JSON patch files are written in JSON format and describe a series of operations to be performed on the resource. Below is an example to update the number of replicas in a deployment:

op: The operation to perform (add, remove, replace)

path: The JSON pointer indicating the field to update

value: The new value to set (only for add and replace)

```
[
  {
    "op": "replace",
    "path": "/spec/replicas",
    "value": 5
  }
]
```

Apply the JSON patch using kubectl:

```
kubectl patch deployment <deployment-name> --type=
'json' --patch-file=patch.json
```

2.8 Create Secrets

Kubernetes secrets are used to store and manage sensitive information, such as passwords, OAuth tokens, and SSH keys. They are particularly important in Kubernetes environments to maintain security and prevent sensitive data from being exposed in container logs or configurations.

Problem

Let's assume we have an application running in Kubernetes that requires access to a database. The database credentials (username and password) are sensitive information that should be kept secret.

Solution

Creating a Secret

We can create a Kubernetes secret to store the database credentials.

Let's get the base64 encoded values of our username and password first.

In Linux let's run

```
$ echo "myuser" | base64
bXl1c2VyCg==
$ echo "mypassword" | base64
 bXlwYXNzd29yZAo=
```

Here's a simple example in YAML format `secret.yaml`:

```
apiVersion: v1
kind: Secret
metadata:
  name: db-secret
type: Opaque
```

```
data:
  username: bXl1c2VyCg==
  password: bXlwYXNzd29yZAo=
```

To apply it to our current namespace, we would run

```
kubectl apply -f secret.yaml.
```

Using Secrets in a Pod

Once the secret is created, we can reference it in our pod definition:

```
apiVersion: v1
kind: Pod
metadata:
  name: myapp-pod
spec:
  containers:
  - name: myapp-container
    image: myapp:1.0
    env:
      - name: DB_USERNAME
        valueFrom:
          secretKeyRef:
            name: db-secret
            key: username
      - name: DB_PASSWORD
        valueFrom:
          secretKeyRef:
            name: db-secret
            key: password
```

This configuration will set the environment variables **DB_USERNAME** and **DB_PASSWORD** in our container using the values from the secret db-secret.

Discussion

We should always ensure only necessary pods have access to the secrets—don't make them widely available. If we create a secret YAML file, it should never be committed to the version control. Secrets should be stored in vaults like HashiCorp Vault, Infisical, Mozilla SOPS, etc.

2.9 Use Enterprise and Linux-Based Images for Our Pod

Problem

The world of containerized applications is evolving rapidly, and enterprises are facing the challenge of maintaining robust, secure, and scalable systems while leveraging the flexibility and efficiency of Kubernetes. One crucial aspect of this challenge is the effective utilization of enterprise and Linux-based container images within Kubernetes environments. Despite Kubernetes' popularity and powerful capabilities, many organizations still struggle with this aspect.

Solution

Here are examples of enterprise-grade container images that are widely used in Kubernetes environments due to their reliability, security, and enterprise support:

Red Hat Universal Base Images (UBI)

Image Name: registry.access.redhat.com/ubi8/ubi

Description: UBI images are lightweight, secure, and certified for enterprise use, built on Red Hat Enterprise Linux (RHEL). They are free to use and provide compatibility with RHEL environments.
Usage: Ideal for applications requiring RHEL-based environments.
Image: registry.access.redhat.com/ubi8/ubi:8.6
SUSE Linux Enterprise Server (SLES) Containers
Image Name: registry.suse.com/sles15
Description: These images are optimized for SUSE Linux Enterprise environments, providing enterprise-grade security and stability.
Usage: Suitable for workloads already integrated with SUSE ecosystems.
Image: registry.suse.com/sles15:latest
Canonical Ubuntu Pro Images
Image Name: docker.io/ubuntu:pro
Description: Ubuntu Pro images come with expanded security coverage and are optimized for enterprises needing a secure, stable Linux base.
Usage: Versatile for general-purpose workloads, especially cloud-native applications.
Image: docker.io/ubuntu:22.04-pro
Oracle Linux Images
Image Name: container-registry.oracle.com/os/oraclelinux
Description: Free, optimized, and secure Linux container images based on Oracle Linux. They are tailored for Oracle Cloud and on-prem environments.
Usage: Best for Oracle Cloud Infrastructure (OCI) or database-heavy applications.
Image: container-registry.oracle.com/os/oraclelinux:8-slim
Amazon Linux
Image Name: amazonlinux
Description: A secure, lightweight image provided by AWS, designed for AWS services and environments.

Usage: Preferred for workloads running in AWS environments.

Image: amazonlinux:2

Alpine Linux with Enterprise Enhancements

Image Name: alpine:enterprise

Description: While Alpine Linux is lightweight by default, enterprise-focused variants often include enhanced security features and support.

Usage: Ideal for minimal, performance-focused applications.

Image: alpine:3.18-enterprise

VMware Photon OS

Image Name: vmware/photon

Description: A lightweight Linux container image optimized for VMware environments and Kubernetes clusters.

Usage: Best for applications running on VMware Tanzu or ESXi.

Image: vmware/photon:4.0

Microsoft CBL-Mariner

Image Name: mcr.microsoft.com/cbl-mariner

Description: A container image optimized for Microsoft Azure and Kubernetes workloads. Designed for security and minimalism.

Usage: Recommended for Azure-based applications.

Image: mcr.microsoft.com/cbl-mariner:2.0

Debian Enterprise Variants

Image Name: debian:enterprise

Description: Enterprise-supported variants of Debian tailored for robust, secure deployments.

Usage: Reliable for general-purpose workloads in secure environments.

Image: debian:11-enterprise

IBM Cloud Pak Base Images

Image Name: icr.io/ibm/base

Description: Optimized for IBM Cloud environments and enterprise applications using IBM's Cloud Pak solutions.

Usage: Best for applications hosted on IBM Cloud or using IBM middleware.

Image: icr.io/ibm/base:latest

These images are commonly used in enterprise environments where stability, security, and support are critical. Each vendor provides extended documentation and tools to integrate these images seamlessly with Kubernetes workloads.

Discussion

Here are best practices for using images:

Minimalist Base Images: Images like Alpine Linux are popular because of their minimal size, which reduces the attack surface. Fewer components mean fewer vulnerabilities.

Official and Verified Images: Use images from official repositories or verified publishers. For instance, Docker Hub and other container registries often have official images for popular software, which are maintained and regularly updated for security.

Regularly Updated and Patched: Security vulnerabilities are constantly being discovered and fixed. Images that are regularly updated and patched are essential. This includes not just the base operating system but also all the software and dependencies within the image.

Built for Specific Purposes: Images that are tailored for specific applications tend to be more secure than general-purpose ones, as they can be stripped of unnecessary packages and services.

Scanned for Vulnerabilities: Utilizing images that are scanned for vulnerabilities with tools like Clair, Trivy, or Docker's own scanning features helps in identifying and mitigating security issues.

Non-root User Configuration: Images configured to run processes as non-root users are generally considered more secure, as this reduces the potential damage from a container breakout.

Hardened Images: Some images are specifically hardened for security. For instance, the Center for Internet Security (CIS) provides benchmarks and hardened images for various operating systems.

Enterprise-Grade Images: Images provided by enterprise vendors (like Red Hat Enterprise Linux (RHEL) UBI, SUSE Linux Enterprise, or Ubuntu Pro) often come with additional security features and support.

Signed Images: Using image signing (like Docker Content Trust) ensures that the images are not tampered with and are from a trusted source.

Compliance with Security Standards: Images that comply with security standards and best practices (like those adhering to NIST guidelines, CIS benchmarks, or ISO standards) are generally more secure.

Distroless Images: Google's "distroless" images provide just the runtime dependencies (no shell or package manager), minimizing the potential for security exploits.

Immutable Images: Images designed to be immutable, where the file system is read-only, can significantly improve security by preventing changes at runtime.

Summary

This chapter covers the configuration of stateless applications in Kubernetes, focusing on namespace creation, pod deployment, environment variable setup, and multi-container pods. It starts by explaining how namespaces enable resource isolation within a cluster, allowing teams to manage resources effectively. Commands like "kubectl get namespace" help list all namespaces, including the defaults: "default," "kube-node-lease," "kube-public," and "kube-system." Creating namespaces is demonstrated with both commands and YAML definitions, highlighting their role in secure resource management. The chapter then addresses pod operations, showing how pods in separate namespaces remain isolated. An example with Nginx illustrates this point. It also discusses environment variables that allow applications to dynamically adjust to their environments without code changes. A configuration example for MySQL demonstrates the flexibility and security of this approach while emphasizing the importance of avoiding sensitive data in configuration files. Multi-container pods are presented as a solution for tightly coupled services that share resources. Effective management strategies, including inter-container communication and shared volumes, are outlined, alongside the necessity of defining resource limits to ensure efficient CPU and memory usage. The chapter wraps up with advanced topics such as using JSON patches for updates and managing sensitive information with Kubernetes secrets, which allow secure storage of credentials. Lastly, it highlights the significance of using minimal, secure, and regularly updated images to enhance Kubernetes deployment security and efficiency.

CHAPTER 3

Configuring Stateful Applications

Stateful applications require data persistence. A typical example is the deployment and management of containerized databases, a cornerstone for any robust cloud-native architecture. Usually, these use cases are more complex than stateless applications and require the simultaneous application of multiple YAML files, streamlining the configuration process in Kubernetes environments. Delving deeper, the chapter explores the cloud-native Software Development Lifecycle (SDLC), offering insights into the best practices and methodologies that underpin successful cloud-native deployments. Complex applications mark an increase in the realm of polyglot, multi-language cloud application development, highlighting the versatility and adaptability required in today's diverse technological landscape.

3.1 Containerized Databases

In the realm of software development and database management, the shift toward containerization represents a significant advancement. This section delves into the challenges posed by traditional database management systems and offers containerized databases as a solution, explaining their benefits and discussing potential concerns. Additionally, it provides further resources for readers interested in exploring this topic in depth.

G. Stencel and L. Berton, *Kubernetes Recipes*,
https://doi.org/10.1007/979-8-8688-1325-2_3

Problem

Traditional database management systems often grapple with issues such as

- **Scalability Limitations**: Scaling a traditional database can be a complex and resource-intensive process.
- **Inconsistent Environments**: Differences in development, testing, and production environments can lead to unexpected errors.
- **Resource Inefficiency**: These databases often underutilize the underlying hardware, leading to inefficiencies.
- **Deployment Complexity**: Deploying and managing databases across various platforms can be cumbersome and time-consuming.

Solution

The following YAML configuration deploys PostgreSQL in Kubernetes. This configuration includes a deployment and a service. The deployment manages the PostgreSQL container, while the service exposes PostgreSQL to other parts of the cluster or outside. Remember that we should adjust the values like passwords, storage sizes, and other configurations to suit our specific needs and environment. Also, it's crucial to handle secrets like passwords more securely in a production environment, possibly using Kubernetes secrets or another secure method:

```
apiVersion: v1
kind: Service
metadata:
  name: postgres-service
```

```
spec:
  selector:
    app: postgres
  ports:
    - protocol: TCP
      port: 5432
      targetPort: 5432
  type: ClusterIP

---
apiVersion: apps/v1
kind: Deployment
metadata:
  name: postgres-deployment
spec:
  replicas: 1
  selector:
    matchLabels:
      app: postgres
  template:
    metadata:
      labels:
        app: postgres
    spec:
      containers:
        - name: postgres
          image: postgres:latest
          env:
            - name: POSTGRES_DB
              value: mydatabase
            - name: POSTGRES_USER
              value: myuser
```

```
          - name: POSTGRES_PASSWORD
            value: mypassword
        ports:
          - containerPort: 5432
        volumeMounts:
          - mountPath: /var/lib/postgresql/data
            name: postgres-storage
    volumes:
      - name: postgres-storage
        persistentVolumeClaim:
          claimName: postgres-pvc
```

Discussion

In this solution

- A service named postgres-service is defined to expose PostgreSQL.
- A deployment named postgres-deployment is created for PostgreSQL.
- Environment variables (POSTGRES_DB, POSTGRES_USER, POSTGRES_PASSWORD) are set for the initial database setup.
- Port 5432 is exposed as it's the default for PostgreSQL.
- A volume (postgres-storage) is attached for persistent data storage. We need to create a PersistentVolumeClaim (PVC) named postgres-pvc in our cluster for this to work.

3.2 Understanding Data Persistency on Kubernetes

Problem

Deploying a stateful application, like a MySQL database, on Kubernetes can be challenging, especially when it comes to ensuring data persistence.

Solution

The solution involves using a PersistentVolumeClaim (PVC) object. Here's a step-by-step guide:

Create a PVC Request:

Prepare a YAML manifest (`data.yaml`) to request storage, for example, 1 GB.

Example of `data.yaml`:

```
apiVersion: v1
kind: PersistentVolumeClaim
metadata:
  name: data
spec:
  accessModes:
    - ReadWriteOnce
  resources:
    requests:
      storage: 1Gi
```

Apply this manifest using the Kubernetes command line:

```
$ kubectl apply -f data.yaml
```

Verify the Creation of the PVC and PV:

Check the status of the PVC and corresponding persistent volume (PV) using

```
$ kubectl get pvc
$ kubectl get pv
```

Utilize the Claim in Our Pod:

In our pod's YAML, under the volumes section, reference the PVC.

Mount this volume inside the container, for example, for MySQL, at `/var/lib/mysql`.

Example snippet for the pod manifest:

```
apiVersion: v1
kind: Pod
metadata:
  name: db
spec:
  containers:
  - image: mysql:8.3.0
    name: db
    volumeMounts:
    - mountPath: /var/lib/mysql
      name: data
    env:
      - name: MYSQL_ROOT_PASSWORD
        value: root
  volumes:
  - name: data
    persistentVolumeClaim:
      claimName: data
```

Discussion

In Kubernetes, the default storage class automatically creates a matching PV when a PVC is requested. This dynamic provisioning is crucial for data persistence in stateful applications. The storage class in Minikube typically uses a hostPath provisioner, which means the data is stored on the Minikube VM itself. This setup allows for data persistency, ensuring that if the pod restarts or is deleted, the data remains intact.

See Also

- **Kubernetes Persistent Volume Claim Documentation** (`https://kubernetes.io/docs/concepts/storage/persistent-volumes/`): For more details on how a PVC works and how to configure it for different needs
- **Kubernetes Storage Class Documentation** (`https://kubernetes.io/docs/concepts/storage/storage-classes/`): To understand storage classes and how they provide abstraction over physical storage

3.3 Database Migrations to Kubernetes Environments

Problem

Transitioning an existing database to Kubernetes is another challenge. Many teams containerize and integrate traditional migration tools. As applications evolve, so do their database schemas.

Solution

The Atlas Kubernetes Operator:

- **Declarative Schema Management**: Allows defining the desired database schema in a declarative manner, aligning with GitOps principles.
- **Continuous Reconciliation**: Utilizes a reconciliation loop to manage the database schema, effectively handling changes and failures.
- **Rich Semantic Management**: Provides a more transparent and manageable approach using CRDs (custom resource definitions) and Kubernetes tooling.
- **Automated Backup and Restore**: The Atlas Kubernetes Operator provides capabilities for automated backup and restore of the database, ensuring data durability and enabling recovery in case of data loss or corruption.
- **Scaling and High Availability**: The operator supports scaling the database horizontally or vertically to meet changing demands as well as provides high availability features to minimize downtime and ensure reliability.

Discussion

Traditional migration tools, which typically follow an imperative approach, are not aligned with the GitOps principles, specifically regarding declarative configuration and continuous reconciliation. From ORM and language-specific tools like Alembic for Python to versatile tools like Flyway and Liquibase, developers have plenty of options. Let's see the pros and cons of the most widely used techniques:

Running Migrations In-App

The simplest method triggers migrations within the Kubernetes environment during the application's startup. It doesn't fully leverage Kubernetes' capabilities and presents security risks, leaving migration tools and sensitive database credentials within the runtime environment vulnerable to exploitation. Furthermore, when deploying multiple application replicas, the in-app migration approach forces sequential loading, posing risks of simultaneous database modifications and significantly slowing down the deployment process.

Pros: Simple to implement

Cons: Does not fully leverage Kubernetes' capabilities; presents security risks by exposing migration tools and sensitive database credentials within the runtime environment; forces sequential loading when deploying multiple application replicas, posing risks of simultaneous database modifications and significantly slowing down the deployment process

Migrations as Init Containers

A better approach involves using Kubernetes' init containers to run migrations before the main application starts. While this method removes the migration tools from the runtime environment, it still faces synchronization challenges and doesn't adequately address failure scenarios, where failed migrations could result in numerous pods stuck in a crash loop, potentially causing downtime.

Pros: Removes migration tools from the runtime environment

Cons: Faces synchronization challenges; does not adequately address failure scenarios, where failed migrations could result in numerous pods stuck in a crash loop, potentially causing downtime

Kubernetes Jobs for Migrations

Another method employs Kubernetes jobs, which executes migrations as a separate step before application rollout. This approach, often implemented using tools like Helm pre-upgrade hooks or Argo CD pre-sync hooks, ensures migrations run once and in isolation from the runtime environment. However, this method still needs to fully embrace GitOps principles.

Pros: Executes migrations as a separate step before application rollout

Cons: Needs to fully embrace GitOps principles; often requires additional tools like Helm pre-upgrade hooks or Argo CD pre-sync hooks

The Operator Pattern

Embracing GitOps principles in database migrations using Git as the central hub for code and infrastructure management emphasizes automated, auditable deployments. The Atlas Kubernetes Operator exemplifies this approach. It allows for defining and applying a desired database schema through Kubernetes, supporting both a declarative workflow and a versioned approach. The operator continuously reconciles the desired and actual database states, offering a more robust and semantically rich solution than traditional jobs. This process is shown in Figure 3-1.

Pros: Embraces GitOps principles by using Git as the central hub for code and infrastructure management; allows for defining and applying a desired database schema through Kubernetes, supporting both a declarative workflow and a versioned approach; continuously reconciles the desired and actual database states, offering a more robust and semantically rich solution than traditional jobs

Cons: Requires familiarity with Kubernetes operators and potentially more complex setup compared with traditional migration approaches

Suppose we would like to add the "`bio`" column in the "`users`" table, we need the following `schema.yaml` manifest:

```
apiVersion: db.atlasgo.io/v1alpha1
kind: AtlasSchema
metadata:
  name: atlasschema-mysql
spec:
  urlFrom:
    secretKeyRef:
      key: url
      name: mysql-credentials
```

```
schema:
  sql: |
    create table users (
      id int not null auto_increment,
      name varchar(255) not null,
      email varchar(255) unique not null,
      bio varchar(255) not null,
      primary key (id)
    );
```

We can apply this schema using the Atlas Operator by typing the command

```
kubectl apply -f schema.yaml
```

Behind the scenes, the Atlas Operator is applying the schema as shown in Figure 3-1.

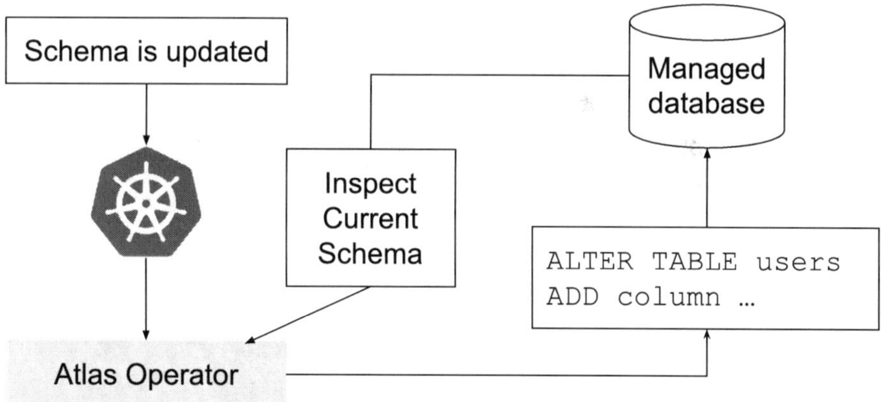

Figure 3-1. *Declarative schema migrations*

See Also

- The Atlas Kubernetes Operator `https://atlasgo.io/integrations/kubernetes/operator`

3.4 Apply Multiple YAML Files at Once on Kubernetes

Problem

Kubernetes administrators and developers often face the challenge of managing multiple YAML files for configuring various Kubernetes resources such as pods, services, and deployments. Applying these files individually can be time-consuming and error-prone, especially in large-scale deployments or complex applications.

Solution

To efficiently manage and apply multiple YAML files in Kubernetes, we can use the `kubectl apply` command with a directory or multiple files as arguments. This method allows us to apply all YAML configurations contained within a directory or specified in multiple files in a single command, streamlining the deployment process.

Steps:

1. **Organize YAML Files**: Place all our YAML files in a specific directory. Ensure that each file is correctly formatted and contains the necessary Kubernetes resource configuration.
2. **Use `kubectl apply` with a Directory**: To apply all YAML files in a directory, use the following command:

   ```
   kubectl apply -f <directory_path>/
   ```

3. This command applies all YAML files in the specified directory.

4. **Use `kubectl apply` with Multiple Files**: If we want to apply selected YAML files, list them in the command:

```
kubectl apply -f <file1.yaml> -f <file2.yaml> -f
<file3.yaml>
```

5. This applies only to the specified files.

6. **Verify Deployment**: After applying the files, use `kubectl get` commands to verify that the resources are correctly deployed and running as expected.

Discussion

This solution is particularly useful in scenarios where configurations are modularized into different files for better organization. For instance, we might have separate YAML files for each deployment, service, and config map. Applying them all at once ensures consistency and efficiency in our deployment process.

However, be cautious about file dependencies. If certain resources depend on others (e.g., a service depending on a deployment), ensure the dependent resources are defined first or manage the order of file application accordingly.

It's also important to note that `kubectl apply` intelligently manages changes. If a resource defined in a YAML file already exists, `kubectl apply` will update it if there are changes rather than creating a new instance. This idempotent behavior is crucial for continuous deployment (CD) pipelines and automated workflows.

3.5 Cloud-Native Software Development Lifecycle (SDLC)

Problem

Traditional Software Development Lifecycle (SDLC) models often struggle to keep pace with the dynamic and distributed nature of cloud-native environments. Cloud-native development requires an approach that accommodates rapid iteration, continuous delivery, and scalable architectures, such as microservices and serverless computing.

Solution

Adopting a cloud-native SDLC involves integrating principles like DevOps, continuous integration and continuous deployment (CI/CD), and microservices architecture. This approach emphasizes automation, collaboration, and flexibility, ensuring that software development aligns with the dynamic nature of cloud-native technologies.

Steps:

1. **Plan and Design**: Begin with a clear understanding of the cloud-native architecture, focusing on scalability, resilience, and independence. Design microservices and select appropriate cloud-native technologies.

2. **Develop**: Write code in small, manageable chunks. Implement CI/CD pipelines to automate the building, testing, and deployment processes. Utilize containerization (e.g., Docker) and orchestration tools like Kubernetes for managing and deploying services.

3. **Testing**: Adopt a rigorous testing strategy that includes unit, integration, and end-to-end testing. Leverage cloud-native features like service meshes for traffic control and fault injection during testing.

4. **Deployment**: Automate deployment using Kubernetes. Employ blue-green or canary deployment strategies to minimize downtime and reduce risks associated with deploying new versions.

5. **Monitoring and Maintenance**: Utilize cloud-native monitoring tools to track the performance and health of applications. Implement logging and monitoring at every layer of our application to quickly identify and address issues.

6. **Feedback and Iteration**: Collect feedback continuously through monitoring tools and user feedback channels. Iterate rapidly based on this feedback, ensuring constant improvement and adaptation.

7. **Security**: Implement robust security measures throughout the SDLC, including secure coding practices, vulnerability scanning of dependencies, and regular security audits.

Discussion

In a cloud-native SDLC, the focus is on small, frequent updates and resilience. Microservices allow teams to update parts of a system independently, reducing the risk of system-wide failures. The emphasis on DevOps culture fosters collaboration between development and operations teams, ensuring that the operational environment's realities are considered early in the development process.

Moreover, the cloud-native approach often involves leveraging managed services and serverless computing, reducing infrastructure management overhead and allowing teams to focus more on core business logic.

3.6 Polyglot, Multi-language, Cloud Application Development

Problem

As businesses expand and diversify, the need for building complex and scalable applications across various cloud platforms and regions becomes more apparent. These applications often require a mix of programming languages to leverage the strengths of different ecosystems and libraries. However, managing a polyglot, multi-language, cloud application development environment can be challenging. Developers need guidance on designing, developing, and maintaining such applications efficiently.

Solution

Polyglot programming involves multiple programming languages for cloud application development. Using multiple programming languages, we will explore best practices, tools, and techniques to create resilient, efficient, and maintainable cloud-native applications, whether dealing with microservices, serverless architectures, or complex distributed systems.

Discussion

1. **Choose the Right Mix of Languages**

   Selecting the appropriate programming languages for our project can significantly impact its success. Consider the strengths and weaknesses of different languages and libraries in our project's context. Aim for a balance between productivity, performance, and developer expertise. This section will delve into the factors to consider when choosing languages, and it will provide examples of successful language combinations for various use cases.

2. **Design Microservices Effectively**

   Developing microservices in a polyglot environment can lead to integration and compatibility issues. Adopt a clear design strategy that includes API contracts, versioning, and standardized communication protocols such as REST or gRPC. We will explore design patterns and tools for building polyglot microservices, ensuring they work seamlessly together.

3. **Managing Dependencies and Libraries**

   Coordinating dependencies across different languages and versions can be complex. Use package managers, dependency management tools, and containerization techniques like Docker to isolate dependencies for each language. We'll provide practical examples of managing dependencies effectively and avoiding version conflicts.

4. **Monitoring and Debugging**

   Diagnosing issues and debugging in a polyglot environment can be time-consuming. Implement robust monitoring and tracing solutions and leverage cross-language debugging tools where available. This section will explore monitoring tools like Prometheus and tracing frameworks like Jaeger, along with debugging techniques to streamline the process.

5. **Continuous Integration and Deployment (CI/CD)**

   Automating CI/CD pipelines for multiple languages can be challenging. Adopt CI/CD best practices, containerization, and infrastructure as code (IaC) to automate deployment and testing for polyglot applications. We'll provide examples of CI/CD configurations and deployment strategies to ensure efficient delivery of our multi-language applications.

6. **Error Handling and Resilience**

   Ensuring error handling and resilience across languages is crucial for maintaining application stability. Implement standardized error handling strategies, circuit breakers, and retry mechanisms. This section will discuss techniques to make our application resilient in a polyglot environment, reducing downtime and improving user experience.

Chapter Summary

We learned how to configure stateful applications, from the initial deployment to managing them in Kubernetes. Common use cases include containerized databases that require persistent data storage. The advantages of using containerized stateful applications over traditional systems involve addressing challenges like scalability, deployment complexity, and resource inefficiencies. It includes practical YAML code for configuring a PostgreSQL database deployment with PersistentVolumeClaims (PVCs) to ensure data persistence. It also highlights the importance of securely handling sensitive data, aligning configurations with application needs, and leveraging Kubernetes tools like `kubectl` to streamline the deployment and management of stateful applications to facilitate the deployment and administration of stateful applications.

CHAPTER 4

Kubernetes on Cloud Providers

In this chapter, we learn how to set up and manage Kubernetes clusters across various major public cloud providers. As organizations scale, the demand for resources that can seamlessly scale and provide global availability becomes critical. Kubernetes offers a robust solution for orchestrating containerized applications across a cluster of machines, and doing so on a cloud platform combines Kubernetes' capabilities with the cloud's elasticity and depth of services. The Cloud Native Computing Foundation (CNCF) has set standards through the Certified Kubernetes Conformance Program to ensure that implementations of Kubernetes across different cloud providers maintain consistent API compatibility and feature sets. This certification guarantees that applications developed for one certified Kubernetes environment are portable to another, preventing vendor lock-in and fostering a vibrant ecosystem of cloud-native tools.

4.1 Google Kubernetes Engine (GKE)

Problem

Creating a Kubernetes cluster and deploying applications (workloads) can be complex, involving the management of computing, storage, networking, and other resources. Google Kubernetes Engine (GKE) Autopilot mode

G. Stencel and L. Berton, *Kubernetes Recipes*,
https://doi.org/10.1007/979-8-8688-1325-2_4

offers a managed environment where Google handles the cluster configuration and scaling. Terraform is the alternative if our organization prefers infrastructure as code (IaC).

Solution

GKE Autopilot mode targets developers and teams seeking a simplified, managed Kubernetes experience, enabling them to focus on application deployment without operational complexities. Terraform, on the other hand, caters to DevOps engineers and infrastructure architects who need robust, code-driven automation and control over Kubernetes and associated resources.

Autopilot Mode

We can create a Kubernetes cluster using this step-by-step guide in GKE Autopilot mode and deploying a "`hello world`" application. This method ensures Google manages most of the operational complexities, allowing us to focus on application development:

1. **Enable the Kubernetes Engine API**
    - Visit the Kubernetes Engine page in the Google Cloud Console.
    - Create or select a project.
    - Enable the API and wait for the process to complete.
2. **Create a Cluster in GKE Autopilot Mode**
    - Navigate to the GKE Clusters page in the Google Cloud Console and click Create.

- Set up a cluster:
    - **Name**: Enter hello-world-cluster.
    - Keep default values for other settings.
- Create the cluster and monitor the deployment status until verified.

3. **Deploy a Sample App**

- Navigate to the GKE Workloads page and click Deploy.
- Configure the container:
    - **Image Path**: `us-docker.pkg.dev/google-samples/containers/gke/hello-app`
- Set a deployment name: hello-world-app.
- Link to a cluster: choose hello-world-cluster.
- Expose our app:
    - Select Expose deployment as a new service.
    - Set Port to 80 and Target Port to 8080.
- Deploy and wait for the IP address to be assigned.

4. **Access Our App**

- Navigate to the Deployment Details for hello-world-app.
- Open the public IP address in a browser to view the "Hello, world!" message.

Terraform

1. **Environment Setup**

    - Enable APIs and set permissions.
    - Enable the Kubernetes Engine API in our Google Cloud project.
    - Ensure billing is enabled.
    - Assign necessary roles: `roles/container.admin`, `roles/compute.networkAdmin`, `roles/iam.serviceAccountUser`.

    Prepare our local environment using Google Cloud Shell, which has Terraform and other necessary tools installed. Set the default project:

    ```
    gcloud config set project PROJECT_ID
    ```

    Clone the Terraform configuration sample repository:

    ```
    git clone https://github.com/terraform-google-modules/terraform-docs-samples.git --single-branch
    cd terraform-docs-samples/gke/quickstart/autopilot
    ```

2. **Review and Initialize Terraform Configuration**

    Review Terraform files:

    - Inspect the “`cluster.tf`” to understand the VPC and GKE Autopilot cluster configurations.
    - View the “`app.tf`” to review the application deployment and service exposure settings.

Initialize Terraform by executing the "`terraform init`" command to prepare our directory for other commands.

3. **Apply Terraform Configuration**

   Create an infrastructure by executing the "`terraform plan`" to see the execution plan and apply the configuration:

   ```
   terraform apply
   ```

   Confirm the setup by typing `yes` when prompted.

4. **Verify and Access the Deployment**

   Check workloads:

   - Navigate to the "Workloads" page in the GKE console to see our deployed application.
   - Ensure the deployment is correctly configured and running.

   Access the application:

   - Go to the "Services & Ingress" page to find the LoadBalancer created for our app.
   - Use the provided IP address to access our web browser's "Hello World" application.

Discussion

Selecting between GKE Autopilot mode and Terraform depends on your operational needs and expertise. Autopilot mode simplifies Kubernetes management by handling scaling, security, and resource optimization, making it ideal for developers who prefer to focus on application development, though it limits customizations and may not be cost-effective for predictable workloads. On the other hand, Terraform is geared toward DevOps professionals seeking automation, consistency, and reproducibility in managing GKE clusters. It enables infrastructure as code, integrates with CI/CD pipelines, and supports version control, though debugging resource dependencies can be complex. Each option excels in different scenarios, catering to diverse team requirements.

Autopilot Mode

- **Managed Infrastructure**: Google handles scaling, security, and configuration, optimizing resource usage based on actual app needs.
- **Simplified Operations**: Reduces the need for in-depth Kubernetes infrastructure knowledge.
- **Cost**: While Autopilot provides a simplified operational model, it might be more cost-effective for predictable workloads to use GKE Standard mode, where we manage the node infrastructure.
- **Customizations**: Autopilot limits certain customizations due to its managed nature, which might not be suitable for all types of workloads.
- **Security**: Google ensures security best practices in Autopilot mode, including regular security patches and updates, reducing the burden on users to manage security aspects.

Terraform with GKE

- **Consistency and Reproducibility**: Terraform allows us to create reproducible infrastructure configurations, which is crucial for production environments and CI/CD pipelines.
- **Automation**: Automate the creation and management of GKE clusters and their associated resources, which reduces manual overhead and potential human errors.
- **Version Control**: Manage our infrastructure definitions in version control systems alongside our application code, improving collaboration and change management.
- **Debugging**: Troubleshooting Terraform can be complex, especially when managing resource dependencies.
- **State Management**: Terraform uses state files to keep track of the current state of the infrastructure. Understanding and managing the state file is important for ensuring consistency and avoiding conflicts in a collaborative environment.

See Also

- Google GKE Documentation `https://cloud.google.com/kubernetes-engine/docs/concepts/kubernetes-engine-overview`

4.2 Azure Kubernetes Service (AKS)

Problem

Setting up a Kubernetes cluster and deploying applications can be complex, especially when managing configurations manually. Azure Kubernetes Service (AKS) simplifies this process. We can efficiently deploy and manage clusters using Azure Command-Line Interface (CLI), particularly for a microservices architecture involving multiple containers, or use Terraform as IaC.

Solution

Azure CLI

We can deploy an AKS cluster using Azure CLI and a sample multi-container application. This setup will leverage AKS's managed services to efficiently handle complex configurations and scaling:

1. **Prerequisites**

   - **Azure Subscription**: Ensure we have an Azure subscription or create a new account.
   - **Azure CLI Installation**: Install Azure CLI locally or use Azure Cloud Shell for command execution.
   - **Configure Azure CLI**: Log in using "`az login`" and set the appropriate subscription using "`az account set`".

2. **Define Environment Variables**

   Set up the necessary variables to streamline the creation commands:

```
export MY_RESOURCE_GROUP_NAME="myAKSResourceGro
up$RANDOM"
export REGION="westeurope"
export MY_AKS_CLUSTER_NAME="myAKSCluster$RANDOM"
export MY_DNS_LABEL="mydnslabel$RANDOM"
```

3. **Create a Resource Group**

   Resource groups hold related resources for an Azure solution. Create one for our AKS cluster:

```
az group create --name $MY_RESOURCE_GROUP_NAME
--location $REGION
```

4. **Create an AKS Cluster**

   Deploy an AKS cluster with a system-assigned managed identity and generate SSH keys automatically:

```
az aks create --resource-group $MY_RESOURCE_GROUP_NAME
--name $MY_AKS_CLUSTER_NAME --enable-managed-identity
--node-count 1 --generate-ssh-keys
```

5. **Configure `kubectl`**

   Install kubectl locally using "`az aks install-cli`", and set it up to connect to our newly created AKS cluster:

```
az aks get-credentials --resource-group $MY_RESOURCE_
GROUP_NAME --name $MY_AKS_CLUSTER_NAME
```

6. **Deploy the Application**

   Create a manifest file "`quickstart.yaml`" that includes the deployment and service definitions for our microservices and execute

   ```
   kubectl apply -f quickstart.yaml
   ```

7. **Verify the Deployment**

   Ensure that our services are running correctly:

   ```
   kubectl get services
   ```

   This will display the external IP addresses for accessing the services.

Terraform

We can set up AKS using Terraform in a repeatable manner:

1. **Set Up Your Environment**

   - **Azure Account**: Ensure you have an Azure subscription or create a new account.
   - **Install Terraform**: Download and install Terraform on our local machine or use it directly in Azure Cloud Shell.
   - **Install Azure CLI**: Necessary for Terraform to interact with Azure.
   - **Log Into Azure**: Authenticate using Azure CLI with az login.
   - **Create a Service Principal**: Terraform will use this for Azure resource management.

2. **Write Terraform Configuration**

   - Create Terraform files using the "azurerm" provider to define the Terraform required for Azure:

```
provider "azurerm" {
  features {}
}
```

   - Define resources like the Azure resource group and AKS cluster:

```
resource "azurerm_resource_group" "aks" {
  name     = "myResourceGroup"
  location = "East US"
}
resource "azurerm_kubernetes_cluster" "aks" {
  name                = "myAKSCluster"
  location            = azurerm_resource_group.aks.
                        location
  resource_group_name = azurerm_resource_group.
                        aks.name
  dns_prefix          = "myakscluster"
  default_node_pool {
    name       = "default"
    node_count = 1
    vm_size    = "Standard_DS2_v2"
  }
  identity {
    type = "SystemAssigned"
  }

}
```

3. **Initialize and Apply Terraform**

   - **Initialize Terraform**: Run "`terraform init`" to initialize the directory and pull the required providers.
   - **Plan Deployment**: Execute "`terraform plan`" to see the execution plan and make adjustments if necessary.
   - **Apply Configuration**: Use "`terraform apply`" to create the resources. Confirm the deployment to proceed.

4. **Verify Deployment**

   - **Set Kubeconfig**: Use "`az aks get-credentials --resource-group myResourceGroup --name myAKSCluster`" to configure `kubectl` to use your new AKS cluster.
   - **Check Nodes**: Run "`kubectl get nodes`" to verify that the cluster nodes are correctly configured and running.

Discussion

Creating a Kubernetes cluster on AKS simplifies Kubernetes deployment and management by offering a managed service that handles much of the complexity of infrastructure management. This approach allows developers and operations teams to focus on deploying and scaling their applications without worrying about the underlying infrastructure. It's important to carefully plan our cluster's configuration, such as the node size and count, as these settings can impact the cost and performance of our applications. Additionally, consider leveraging Azure's native integrations and services, such as Azure Monitor and Azure Policy, to enhance the observability and security of our cluster and workloads.

Azure CLI

- **Simplified Management**: AKS abstracts and automates complex management tasks, making it easier to deploy, manage, and scale applications.
- **Scalability**: Easily scale our applications with AKS's automatic scaling features.
- **Cost-Effective**: Only pay for the resources we use and manage costs effectively through Azure's management tools.
- **Network Configuration**: Carefully plan our network configuration, especially for production environments, to ensure security and performance.
- **Monitoring and Logging**: Integrate Azure monitoring and logging tools to keep track of our application's performance and health.

Terraform

- **Automation**: Automates the deployment of AKS clusters, reducing the potential for human error and speeding up the process.
- **Reproducibility**: Ensures reproducible environments are crucial for testing and production parity.

- **Scalability**: Simplifies scaling operations, both up and down, as your application requirements change.
- **Complexity**: The initial setup of Terraform and understanding its configuration can be complex for new users.
- **State Management**: Terraform state files must be managed and backed up, as they hold the state of your managed resources.

See Also

- **AKS Documentation**: Provides comprehensive guides and tutorials on deploying, managing, and scaling applications with Azure Kubernetes Service (`https://learn.microsoft.com/en-us/azure/aks/`)

4.3 Amazon Elastic Kubernetes Service (EKS)

Problem

Setting up and managing a Kubernetes cluster can be a complex task involving configuring various components such as nodes, pods, and services. Amazon Elastic Kubernetes Service (EKS) simplifies this process by providing a managed Kubernetes service. This allows users to focus on deploying and managing their applications rather than the underlying infrastructure. However, the initial setup of an EKS cluster, including configuring the necessary tools and access permissions, can still pose challenges for new users.

Discussion

Follow these steps to create a Kubernetes cluster on Amazon EKS. This guide assumes we have the AWS CLI installed and configured on our system:

1. **Install AWS CLI and `eksctl`**: Ensure we have the latest version of AWS CLI and `eksctl` installed. `eksctl` is a simple CLI tool for creating clusters on EKS. It simplifies many of the complexities around node and cluster management. We can install the software using our favorite package manager for our operating system or directly via the AWS website. In this way, we guarantee to retrieve the latest version of the software:

   ```
   curl "https://awscli.amazonaws.com/awscli-exe-
   linux-x86_64.zip" -o "awscliv2.zip"
   unzip awscliv2.zip
   sudo ./aws/install
   curl --silent --location "https://github.com/
   weaveworks/eksctl/releases/latest/download/
   eksctl_$(uname -s)_amd64.tar.gz" | tar xz -C /tmp
   sudo mv /tmp/eksctl /usr/local/bin
   ```

2. **Create an EKS Cluster**: Use `eksctl` to create our cluster. This step will create a cluster named `MyCluster`, with a specified node count and region. Adjust the parameters as needed:

   ```
   eksctl create cluster --name MyCluster --region us-
   west-2 --nodegroup-name standard-workers --node-type
   t3.medium  --nodes 3
   ```

The `eksctl` command automatically configures `kubectl` for us. Verify the configuration by listing the nodes:

```
kubectl get nodes
```

See Also

- **AWS CLI Documentation**: For more detailed information on configuring and using AWS CLI
- **EKS User Guide**: Provides an in-depth guide to using Amazon EKS, including advanced configuration, security, and networking features
- **Kubernetes Official Documentation**: For a broader understanding of Kubernetes concepts and how to deploy and manage applications on a Kubernetes cluster
- **eksctl Documentation**: For more advanced `eksctl` usage and scenarios, including cluster upgrades, scaling, and integration with other AWS services

4.4 DigitalOcean

Problem

Deploying Kubernetes clusters typically involves managing the control plane and containerized infrastructure, which can be complex and time-consuming. DigitalOcean Kubernetes (DOKS) simplifies this by providing a managed service that integrates natively with DigitalOcean load balancers, volumes, and allows for high-availability configurations. However, users may need guidance on utilizing DOKS efficiently through different interfaces like the API, CLI, and the Control Panel.

Solution

This guide outlines three methods to create Kubernetes clusters on DigitalOcean: using the DigitalOcean Command-Line Interface (CLI), the DigitalOcean API, and the DigitalOcean Control Panel. This will enable us to choose the approach that best fits our needs, whether we are scripting our setup for automation or using the graphical interface for manual setup.

Create a Cluster Using the DigitalOcean CLI

1. **Install the CLI**: Download and install the DigitalOcean CLI (`doctl`).

2. **Authenticate**: Authenticate our CLI with our DigitalOcean account using

   ```
   doctl auth init
   ```

3. **Create the Cluster**: Specify the region, node size, and Kubernetes version. Retrieve the options using

   ```
   doctl kubernetes options versions
   ```

4. Create the cluster by running

   ```
   doctl kubernetes cluster create <cluster-name> --region
   nyc1 --version <version> --count 3 --size s-1vcpu-2gb
   ```

Create a Cluster Using the DigitalOcean API

1. **Generate an API Token**: Create a token from the DigitalOcean dashboard with the necessary permissions.

2. **Set Up an API Request**: Use the following curl command template to create a cluster:

```
curl -X POST -H "Content-Type: application/json" -H
"Authorization: Bearer $TOKEN" -d '{
    "name": "example-cluster",
    "region": "nyc3",
    "version": "1.20.7-do.0",
    "node_pools": [{
        "size": "s-1vcpu-2gb",
        "count": 3,
        "name": "worker-pool"
    }]
}' "https://api.digitalocean.com/v2/kubernetes/
clusters"
```

Create a Cluster Using the Control Panel

1. **Open the Create Menu**: Log into the DigitalOcean Control Panel. Click "Create" and select "Kubernetes."

2. **Configure the Cluster**:

    - **Kubernetes Version**: Select the latest stable release.

    - **Data Center Region**: Choose a region (e.g., NYC1).

    - **VPC Network**: Opt for the default or a specific VPC network.

    - **Node Pools**: Add a node pool with the desired capacity and machine type.

    - **Additional Options**: If required, enable the HA control plane for increased uptime.

3. **Finalize and Create**:
    - **Name Our Cluster**: Optionally customize the name.
    - **Review and Create**: Check the cost and hit the "Create Cluster" button.

Discussion

Choose the right method:

- **CLI**: Best for users who need quick, scriptable access without manual interaction.
- **API**: Suitable for integrations into custom applications or automated infrastructure setups.
- **Control Panel**: This is the most user-friendly, graphical method, suitable for users who prefer a visual setup process.

The HA control plane is a critical feature for production environments where downtime directly impacts business continuity. It provides redundancy and resilience, ensuring that the Kubernetes control plane remains available even if some components fail.

See Also

DigitalOcean How to Create Kubernetes Clusters `https://docs.digitalocean.com/products/kubernetes/how-to/create-clusters/`

4.5 OVH

Problem

Setting up a Kubernetes cluster often involves dealing with the complexities of cluster management and network configuration and ensuring high availability. OVH Kubernetes Service (OVH KS) offers a managed Kubernetes environment to alleviate these challenges, but initial setup and configuration might be unclear for those new to OVH Cloud or Kubernetes.

Solution

To create a Kubernetes cluster on OVH Cloud, we will typically follow these steps, assuming we have access to OVH Cloud and are familiar with its user interface:

1. **Access the OVH Cloud Panel**: Log into our OVH Cloud Panel to manage our resources.
2. Create a Kubernetes cluster.
3. Navigate to the "Public Cloud" section, and then select "Kubernetes" from the sidebar.
4. Click the "Create a Kubernetes Cluster" button and follow the on-screen instructions.
5. Select the desired region for our cluster.

6. Choose the Kubernetes version we wish to deploy. OVH Cloud supports multiple versions, allowing us to use the latest features or stick with more stable, established releases.

7. Configure our node pools, including the size and number of instances to fit our workload needs.

8. **Configure Access**:

   a. Once our cluster is created, we need to set up kubectl to interact with it. OVH Cloud provides a `kubeconfig` file that we can download directly from the cloud panel.

   b. Use the `kubeconfig` file with `kubectl` to set up access to our cluster: `kubectl --kubeconfig=/path/to/our/kubeconfig.yaml get nodes`

9. **Deploy Applications**: With our cluster up and running, we can deploy our applications using kubectl or other CI/CD tools that integrate with Kubernetes.

Discussion

OVH's managed Kubernetes service handles the underlying server infrastructure, including setup, scaling, and maintenance, allowing us to focus on deploying and managing our applications. Considerations when using OVH Kubernetes Service include planning for scalability, resource management, and cost. It's essential to size our cluster according to our application's needs and budget while leaving room for growth as our application scales.

4.6 Hetzner

Problem

Deploying a Kubernetes cluster using Hetzner Cloud, these tasks can be streamlined using a tool like Claudie, which effectively manages multi-cloud and hybrid-cloud Kubernetes clusters.

Solution

1. **Install Claudie—Create a Management Cluster**: Install Claudie on an existing Kubernetes cluster, such as one created by KinD:

   ```
   kind create cluster --name claudie-mgmt
   kubectl cluster-info --context kind-claudie-mgmt
   ```

   Install Dependencies: Install cert-manager, required by Claudie:

   ```
   kubectl apply -f https://github.com/cert-manager/cert-
   manager/releases/download/v1.12.0/cert-manager.yaml
   ```

   Deploy Claudie:

   ```
   kubectl apply -f https://github.com/berops/claudie/
   releases/latest/download/claudie.yaml
   ```

2. **Create a Hetzner API Key—Generate an API Token**: Create a new API token from the Hetzner Cloud Console with read and write permissions. Create a Kubernetes secret:

   ```
   kubectl create secret generic hetzner-secret --from-
   literal=credentials='OUR_API_TOKEN'
   ```

3. **Create a Claudie Manifest File—Define Cluster Configuration**:

```
apiVersion: claudie.io/v1beta1
kind: InputManifest
metadata:
  name: kubernetes-hetzner
spec:
  providers:
    - name: hetzner-secret
      providerType: hetzner
      secretRef:
        name: hetzner-secret
        namespace: default
  nodePools:
    dynamic:
      - name: control-hetzner-1
        providerSpec:
          name: hetzner-secret
          region: fsn1
          zone: fsn1-dc14
          count: 1
          serverType: cpx21
          image: ubuntu-22.04
      - name: compute-hetzner-1
        providerSpec:
          name: hetzner-secret
          region: fsn1
          zone: fsn1-dc14
          count: 3
          serverType: cpx21
          image: ubuntu-22.04
          storageDiskSize: 50
```

```
kubernetes:
  clusters:
    - name: hetzner-cluster
      version: v1.27.0
      network: 192.168.2.0/24
      pools:
        control:
          - control-hetzner-1
        compute:
          - compute-hetzner-1
```

4. **Deploy the Cluster—Apply the Manifest**:

   ```
   kubectl apply -f inputmanifest.yml
   ```

   Monitor Deployment:

   ```
   kubectl get inputmanifest kubernetes-hetzner
   ```

5. **Access the Cluster**

   Retrieve Kubeconfig:

   ```
   kubectl get secrets -n claudie hetzner-cluster-mgcdv9x-
   kubeconfig -o jsonpath='{.data.kubeconfig}' | base64 -d
   > ~/.kube/hetzner
   export KUBECONFIG=~/.kube/hetzner
   ```

   Confirm Cluster Status:

```
kubectl get nodes
NAME                          STATUS   ROLES    AGE   VERSION
compute-hetzner-1-cyxbuh6-1   Ready    <none>   19m   v1.27.0
compute-hetzner-1-cyxbuh6-2   Ready    <none>   19m   v1.27.0
compute-hetzner-1-cyxbuh6-3   Ready    <none>   19m   v1.27.0
control-hetzner-1-ivfw0xn-1   Ready    <none>   20m   v1.27.0
```

Discussion

Using Claudie significantly simplifies the deployment of Kubernetes clusters on Hetzner Cloud by abstracting complex configurations into a declarative manifest file. This approach not only ensures consistency across deployments but also integrates seamlessly with Hetzner's infrastructure, providing a robust solution for managing multi-cloud and hybrid-cloud environments. Alternatively, we can use the "`hetzner-ocp4`" project to set up an OpenShift cluster.

See Also

- Kubernetes on Hetzner with Claudie! `https://community.hetzner.com/tutorials/kubernetes-with-claudie`
- `hetzner-ocp4` project `https://github.com/RedHat-EMEA-SSA-Team/hetzner-ocp4`

4.7 Kubespray

Problem

Deploying Kubernetes across various infrastructures such as AWS, GCE, Azure, OpenStack, vSphere, Equinix Metal, Oracle Cloud Infrastructure, or even on bare-metal and air-gapped environments can be complex and error-prone. The process often varies significantly depending on the underlying infrastructure, leading to inconsistencies and potential failures. Kubespray, powered by Ansible, offers a robust solution to standardize and automate the deployment of production-ready Kubernetes clusters, aiming to reduce complexity and ensure repeatability.

Solution

1. **Preparation**

   - Install dependencies by ensuring all prerequisite software and tools, including Python and Ansible, are installed on the controller machine.
   - Setup Inventory by preparing the inventory of hosts that form our Kubernetes cluster. This includes defining your master and worker nodes in Ansible's inventory file:

   ```
   git clone https://github.com/kubernetes-sigs/kubespray
   cp -r inventory/sample inventory/mycluster
   declare -a IPS=(10.10.1.3 10.10.1.4 10.10.1.5)
   CONFIG_FILE=inventory/mycluster/hosts.yml python3
   contrib/inventory_builder/inventory.py ${IPS[@]}
   ```

2. **Configuration**

   Customize Configuration: Edit inventory/mycluster/group_vars/all/all.yml and inventory/mycluster/group_vars/k8s-cluster/k8s-cluster.yml to set up network configurations, cluster names, and API settings and customize Kubernetes components like the network plugin (Calico, Flannel, Canal).

3. **Deployment**

   Run Kubespray Playbook: Execute the Ansible playbook to deploy Kubernetes. This will set up Kubernetes and the necessary components on all the specified hosts:

   ```
   ansible-playbook -i inventory/mycluster/hosts.yml
   cluster.yml -b -v --private-key=~/.ssh/private_key
   ```

4. **Verification**

   Check cluster health, verifying that the cluster is up and running correctly. Check the status of nodes and pods to ensure all components are functioning as expected:

   ```
   kubectl get nodes
   kubectl get pods --all-namespaces
   ```

Discussion

- **Versatility and Extensibility**: Kubespray provides the flexibility to deploy Kubernetes on almost any platform, making it ideal for hybrid and multi-cloud environments.
- **Configuration Management**: Leveraging Ansible for configuration management simplifies the process of maintaining and updating the cluster settings.
- **Scalability**: Easily scale your cluster by modifying the inventory file and rerunning the playbook.
- **Security**: Kubespray includes roles for setting up highly secure clusters, which by default apply best practices for network policies and other security settings.
- **Complexity in Setup**: While Kubespray abstracts much of the complexity in setting up Kubernetes, the initial configuration and tuning of parameters can be daunting for new users.

- **Dependency on Ansible**: Operational proficiency in Ansible is required to effectively use Kubespray, which might be a barrier for teams unfamiliar with configuration management tools.
- **High Availability**: Kubespray supports high availability configurations, allowing you to deploy Kubernetes clusters that ensure uninterrupted service in production environments. By configuring multiple master nodes and using redundancy mechanisms, Kubespray enhances the reliability and resilience of your Kubernetes clusters, minimizing the impact of potential failures and ensuring continuous availability of your applications.

4.8 Certified Kubernetes Software Conformance by CNCF (Sonobuoy)

Problem

The Certified Kubernetes Software Conformance program, overseen by the Cloud Native Computing Foundation (CNCF), ensures that every vendor's version of Kubernetes supports the required APIs and offers a consistent experience. The goal is to maintain interoperability and consistency across different Kubernetes solutions, making it safer and easier for users to adopt Kubernetes in their projects without being locked into a specific vendor. This certification helps verify that Kubernetes products and services meet a set of standards established by the CNCF.

Organizations using Kubernetes face the challenge of ensuring their deployment is compatible with the wide array of Kubernetes services and tools available. With the proliferation of Kubernetes offerings from different vendors, there's a risk of fragmentation, where some services might not work consistently across different environments or could lead to vendor lock-in.

Solution

The solution provided by CNCF through the Certified Kubernetes Conformance Program involves a suite of tests that any vendor can run against their Kubernetes distribution or platform to certify that it conforms to CNCF standards. CNCF recommends Sonobuoy as the tool to run these conformance tests. It is an open source diagnostic tool that performs compliance and diagnostic tests against a Kubernetes cluster. Sonobuoy runs the Kubernetes conformance tests to ensure a cluster is properly configured and compliant with the official Kubernetes specifications.

Discussion

Adopting certified Kubernetes solutions brings numerous benefits, including

- **Interoperability**: Ensures applications and services can run across different Kubernetes environments without modification.
- **Vendor Neutrality**: Prevents vendor lock-in by providing a consistent and standardized platform across different providers.
- **Community Confidence**: By ensuring a baseline quality and feature set, Kubernetes builds trust among developers and organizations in using it for their critical applications.

- **Ecosystem Growth**: This policy encourages the development of Kubernetes-native applications and services that can run anywhere, fostering a rich ecosystem of tools and services.

The certification process, while beneficial, requires vendors to regularly update their Kubernetes offerings and rerun the conformance tests for each release to remain certified. This ongoing commitment helps ensure the quality and consistency of the Kubernetes ecosystem as it evolves.

Chapter Summary

We examined the setup and management of Kubernetes clusters on leading public cloud platforms, utilizing their scalability and worldwide reach. Important subjects covered included Google Kubernetes Engine (GKE), Azure Kubernetes Service (AKS), and Amazon Elastic Kubernetes Service (EKS), all of which provide managed environments that simplify the deployment and operations of Kubernetes. Tools like Terraform and cloud-specific CLIs are used to automate infrastructure and ensure reproducibility. This chapter also addressed the significance of Certified Kubernetes Software Conformance by CNCF in promoting interoperability across environments, preventing vendor lock-in, and supporting a strong cloud-native ecosystem. The best practices ensure efficient cluster and application deployment, balancing operational requirements and flexibility.

CHAPTER 5

Developer Experience in Kubernetes

This chapter aims to enhance the developer experience in Kubernetes by exploring tools and practices that streamline development workflows. The focus is on creating an efficient and developer-friendly environment, covering topics such as setting up Lens integrated development environment (IDE), leveraging dev spaces, using kubens/kubectx for namespace management, and incorporating Gitpods into the development process.

There are plenty of IDEs. One of the free and the best is Visual Studio (VS) Code, which has Kubernetes extensions that are installable.

5.1 Command-Line Tools

Problem

Managing Kubernetes clusters is undeniably complex and time-consuming, particularly when dealing with repetitive tasks such as deployments, scaling, and maintenance. It is imperative to ensure consistency, reliability, and efficiency in these operations for maintaining a robust Kubernetes environment. Manual handling of these tasks can result in errors, inefficiencies, and challenges in managing large-scale

G. Stencel and L. Berton, *Kubernetes Recipes*,
https://doi.org/10.1007/979-8-8688-1325-2_5

environments. Furthermore, iterative and interactive command-line operations are absolutely essential for immediate feedback, facilitating rapid troubleshooting and adjustments.

Solution

kubectl

Let's start with the main tool for CLI in Kubernetes, which is kubectl.

kubectl is the primary command-line tool for interacting with Kubernetes clusters. It can be used to create, scale, edit, view, and list all k8s resources. Create custom aliases for frequently used kubectl commands to speed up your workflow.

Normally you need to write kubectl commands for all actions to get resources/put resources into an API server. To avoid typing kubectl before every action, you can make an alias if using Linux and put it to your ~/.bashrc or ~/.zshrc. Add the below line to the end of the file:

```
alias k=kubectl
```

You can use kubectl autocompletion if you are a Linux user. Again, you can add autocomplete to your zshrc or bashrc.

Full instructions for all operating systems can be found under `https://kubernetes.io/docs/reference/kubectl/generated/kubectl_completion/`.

oh-my-zsh

If you are a Linux user, you might use zsh and oh-my-zsh—these have nice autocompletion and selection of Kubernetes resources, which eliminates the need to list resources first, as double tab shows us all available resources.

If you are a zsh user, you can install the oh-my-zsh kubectl plugin by simply adding kubectl to the zshrc file:

```
plugins=(git history kubectl)
```

Starting a new zsh process or sourcing a new zshrc will enable a new plugin, so now whenever you write kubectl and double tab, it will display all the options even more. If you try listing resources, kubectl will send request to the master API and will return the results. See examples in Figure 5-1.

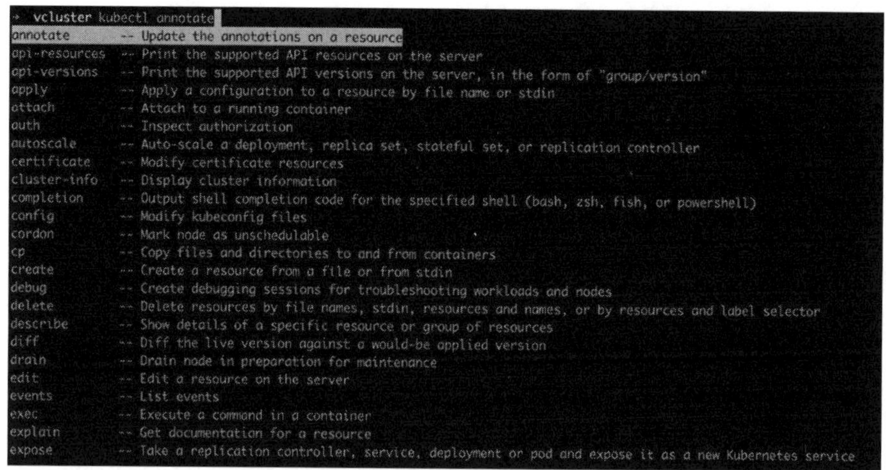

***Figure 5-1.** Kubectl annotate options with autocomplete in place*

Also, if we want to “get pod”, we would normally list it with kubectl get pods and then kubectl would describe the pod with the pod name displayed from the first command output. With the autocomplete plugin, we can just do kubectl describe pods and double tab. This way, we will get a list from the API server with all available pods.

```
→ vcluster kubectl get pods my-
→ vcluster kubectl describe pods my-
my-daemonset-g9bx9              my-deployment-544587cc57-rklqz  my-statefulset-0            my-statefulset-2
my-deployment-544587cc57-6cx4f  my-deployment-544587cc57-tpwlf  my-statefulset-1
```

Figure 5-2. *Kubectl autocompletion listing pods*

krew

A plugin manager for kubectl that makes it easy to discover and install plugins.

Install krew for kubectl from `https://krew.sigs.k8s.io/`.

To check if it was installed, run kubectl krew.

Now we can automatically add plugins to kubectl with the usage of krew:

```
kubectl krew install ctx
```

CTX is for easy context switching.

kubectl ctx yourc_ontext_name

kubectl krew install ns

vcluster kubectl ns kube-public

Context "kind-kind" modified.

Active namespace is "`kube-public`".

helm

Helm is a package manager for Kubernetes, which simplifies the deployment and management of applications.

Helm Charts: Use pre-configured templates (charts) to deploy applications.

Automation with Helm: Automate deployments and updates of applications using Helm charts:

```
helm install my-release my-chart
helm upgrade my-release my-chart
```

kustomize

Kustomize allows you to customize Kubernetes configurations without templating.

Overlays: Use overlays to manage different environments (e.g., dev, prod):

```
kustomize build overlays/prod | kubectl apply -f -
```

5.2 Lens as k8s IDE

Problem

Investigate a dedicated Kubernetes IDE for faster visual debugging and inspecting your Kubernetes cluster resources.

Solution

There is another great tool on the market called Lens, an IDE specifically designed for Kubernetes. It is widely used by developers and DevOps teams to manage and troubleshoot Kubernetes clusters. Key features and benefits of using Lens as a Kubernetes IDE are shown in Figure 5-3.

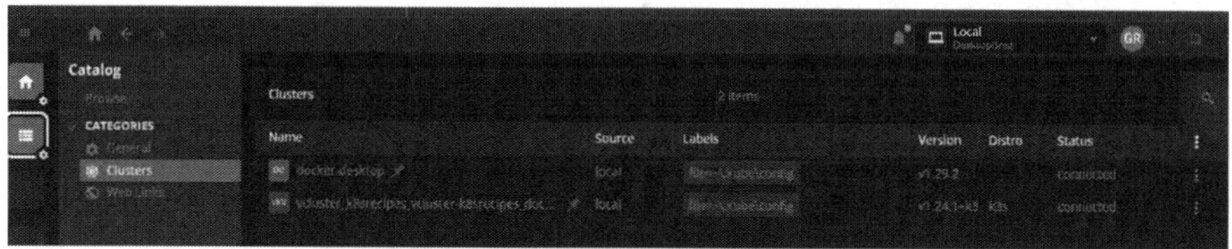

Figure 5-3. *Lens cluster dashboard*

The Lens overview shows us the real-time state of our resources.

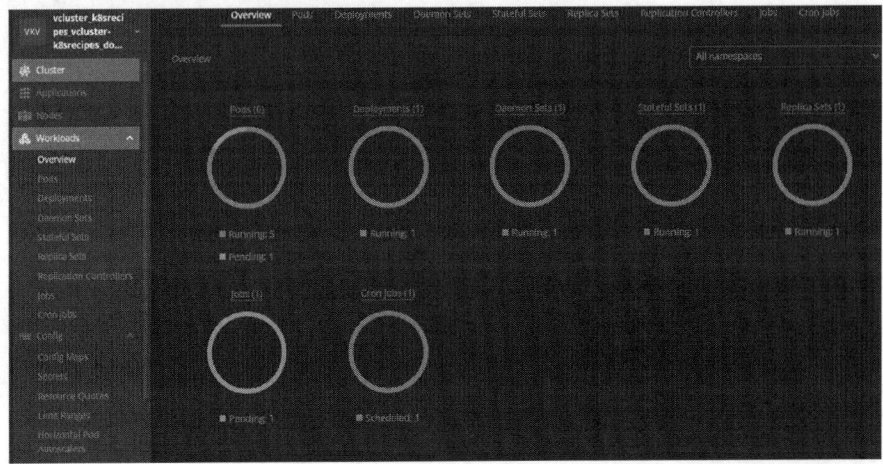

Figure 5-4. *Lens workload dashboard*

Lens enables nice visual metrics for resources like jobs.

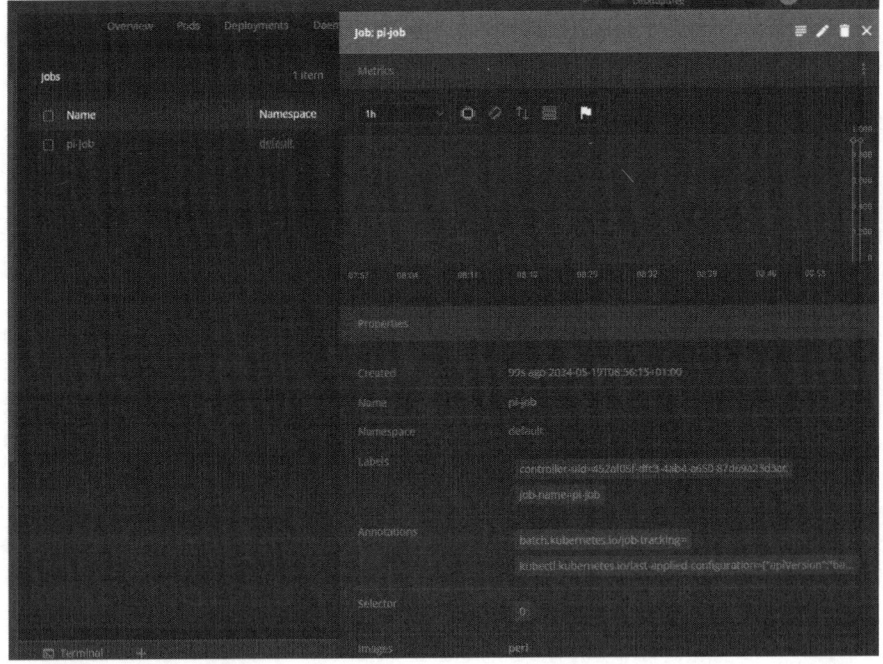

Figure 5-5. *Lens job modification*

We can browse through all cluster resources and even modify them as shown in Figure 5-6.

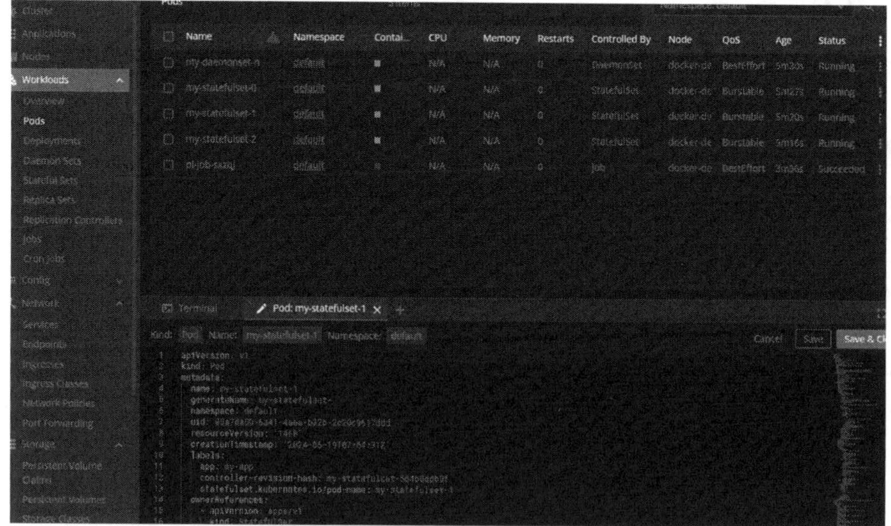

Figure 5-6. *Lens workloads listing and editing*

Bear in mind, modifying resources by hand will write the desired state to the etcd. This is an antipattern as you don't keep a version of your state anywhere if you manually modify resources—this is also like using the kubectl edit option.

You can add your cluster by specifying the kubeconfig location in Cluster Management View ➤ Add Cluster and then selecting the location of your kubeconfig.

5.3 DevSpace

Problem

Being an admin of Kubernetes clusters, ensuring efficient development workflows can hinder productivity and requires extensive Kubernetes expertise. There is a need for a tool that can simplify these processes, making them accessible and manageable for all team members, regardless of their Kubernetes proficiency. To simplify and streamline the development and deployment processes for Kubernetes clusters, we can utilize DevSpace, a next-generation tool designed for fast cloud-native software development. DevSpace aims to make it easier for teams to standardize and automate their workflows, thus reducing the need for extensive Kubernetes knowledge among all team members.

Solution

Implement DevSpace to leverage its features for declarative workflows, team collaboration, hot reloading, automation, and broad compatibility. This will streamline the development and deployment processes, reduce the learning curve for Kubernetes, and enhance overall productivity and consistency within the development team.

Here are expected outcomes:

- Simplified Kubernetes management with reduced complexity for developers
- Standardized and automated workflows, improving efficiency and consistency
- Enhanced collaboration within development teams, minimizing the need for deep Kubernetes knowledge
- Faster development cycles with immediate code changes and automated deployment processes

By integrating DevSpace into the development pipeline, teams can focus more on coding and less on managing Kubernetes intricacies, leading to more rapid and reliable software delivery.

DevSpace is a client-only, open source developer tool for Kubernetes that lets you develop and deploy cloud-native software faster:

- Build, test, and debug applications directly inside Kubernetes.
- Develop with hot reloading: updating your running containers without rebuilding images or restarting containers.
- Unify deployment workflows within your team and across dev, staging, and production.
- Automate repetitive tasks for image building and deployment.

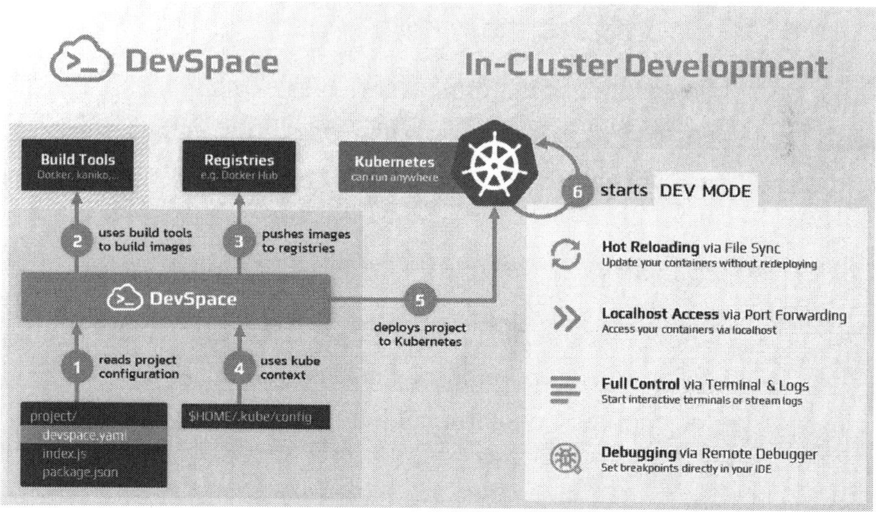

Figure 5-7. *DevSpace workflow*

The above workflow describes functionality DevSpace offers, which are

1. **Declarative Workflows**
    a. Centralize all workflows in a single devspace.yaml configuration file.
    b. Codify and version workflows alongside the codebase, enabling easy retrieval and deployment of any project version.
    c. Facilitate sharing of workflows among team members, promoting consistency and efficiency.
2. **Team Collaboration**
    a. Allow DevOps and Kubernetes experts to configure DevSpace and share configurations via Git.
    b. Enable other developers to deploy projects with a single command (devspace deploy), minimizing the need for Kubernetes expertise.
    c. Use dynamic configuration variables to maintain a base configuration while allowing individual customization (e.g., different sub-domains for testing).
3. **Hot Reloading**
    a. Support high-performance, bidirectional file synchronization for immediate code change detection and synchronization between local development environments and Kubernetes containers.
    b. Provide capabilities to stream logs, connect debuggers, and open container terminals directly from the IDE.

4. **Automation**

    a. Automate image building, tagging, and application deployment with a single command, including dependency management.

    b. Automatically handle port forwarding and log streaming, eliminating the need for manual execution of repetitive commands.

5. **Compatibility**

    a. Ensure compatibility with a wide range of Kubernetes distributions, including local clusters (Minikube, k3s, MikroK8s, KinD), managed clusters (GKE, EKS, AKS, DOKS), and self-managed clusters (e.g., created with Rancher).

To install DevSpace, head to devspace.sh and follow your installation instruction accordingly to your operating system (`https://www.devspace.sh/docs/getting-started/introduction`).

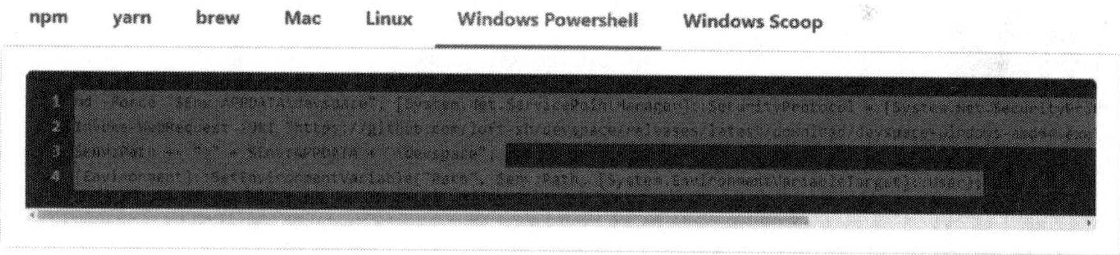

Figure 5-8. *DevSpace installation options*

It's best to investigate DevSpace UI.

→ vcluster devspace ui
[info] Using namespace 'kube-public'
[info] Using kube context 'kind-kind'
[info] Start listening on http://localhost:8090

Figure 5-9. *DevSpace up and running*

We will start the web server, and DevSpace UI will be available on the 8090 port on our localhost, where we can browse all local or remote Kubernetes clusters that we have access to via .kube/config.

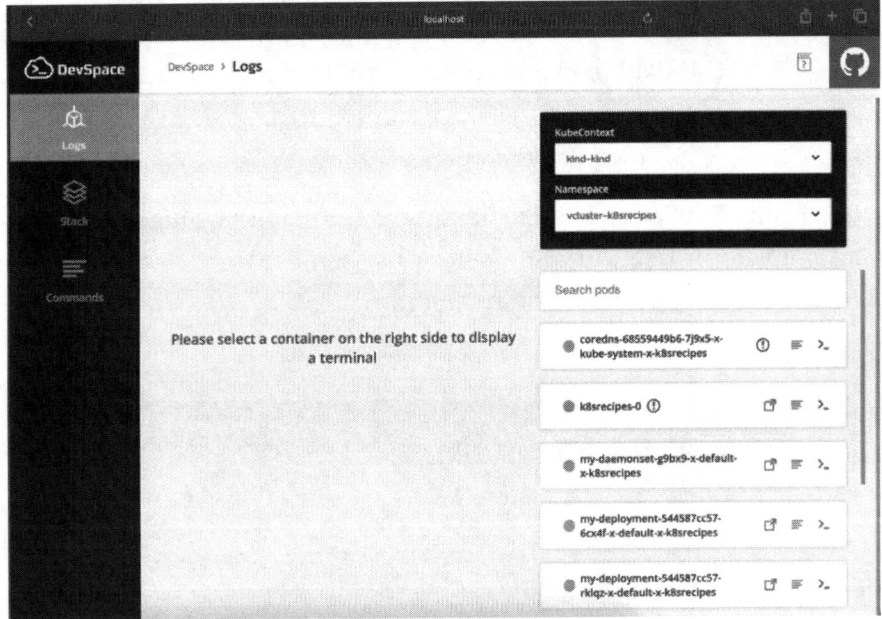

Figure 5-10. *DevSpace log functionality*

By clicking a pod on the right, we open more productive way of browsing pod logs to inspect what went wrong if we have problems launching it.

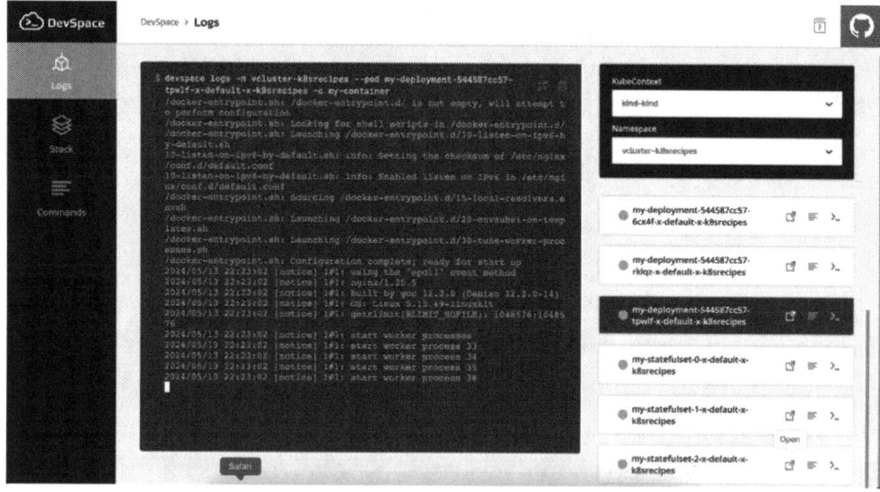

***Figure 5-11.** DevSpace terminal functionality*

We can also open a terminal and exec into a container and get their YAMLs.

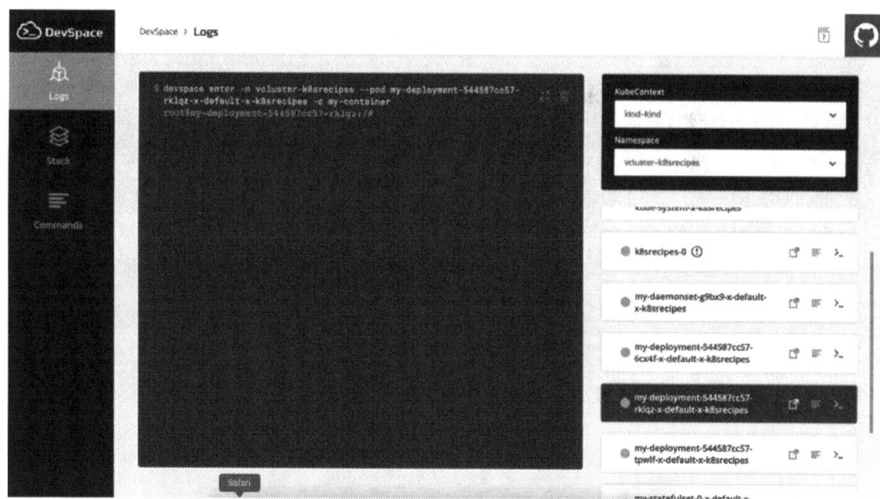

***Figure 5-12.** DevSpace workloads view*

5.4 VS Code as k8s IDE

Problem

Managing a Kubernetes cluster involves dealing with complex configurations and resources using command-line tools like kubectl. Although effective, the command-line interface can be challenging for users who prefer a graphical interface or need more integrated tooling for efficient management. The goal is to develop an integrated development environment (IDE) setup using Visual Studio Code (VS Code) that enhances the user experience and productivity in managing Kubernetes clusters. This IDE setup should leverage VS Code's extensibility and existing Kubernetes-related extensions to provide a robust, user-friendly environment for Kubernetes cluster management.

Solution

Install VS Code: If you haven't already, download and install Visual Studio Code from its official website.

Install Kubernetes Extensions: VS Code has several extensions that enhance Kubernetes' functionality. The most essential ones are

- **Kubernetes Extension by Microsoft**: This extension provides support for Kubernetes in various ways, such as viewing your clusters in an explorer, and it adds IntelliSense for Kubernetes resources, which helps write the YAML files.

  Open Visual Studio Code.

  Go to the extensions view by clicking the extensions icon in the Activity Bar on the side of the window or by pressing Ctrl+Shift+X.

Search for "Kubernetes" in the search box.

Install the "Kubernetes" extension by Microsoft.

Alternatively, you can install it from the VS Code Marketplace.

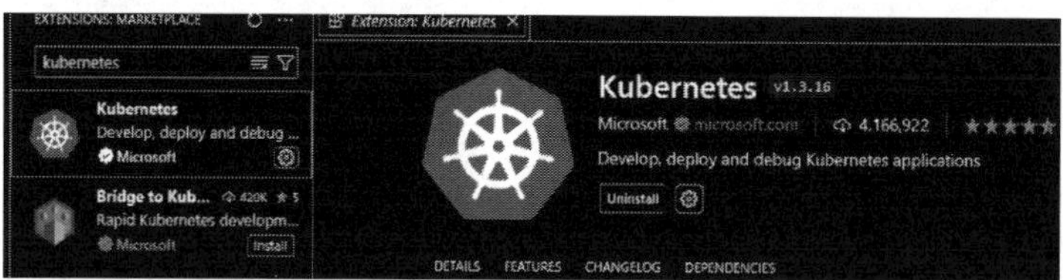

***Figure 5-13.** VS Code Kubernetes plugin*

- **YAML by Red Hat**: Since Kubernetes configurations often involve a lot of YAML, this extension provides YAML validation, autocompletion, and formatting.

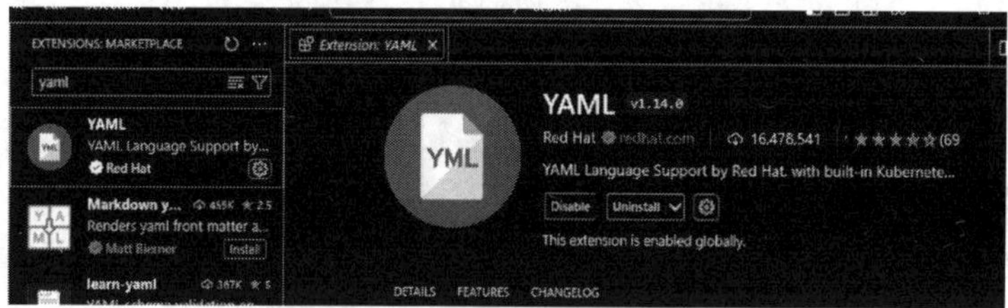

***Figure 5-14.** VS Code YAML plugin*

If you are on Windows, you will be prompted if you want to use the native containers provisioner Windows Subsystem for Linux (WSL).

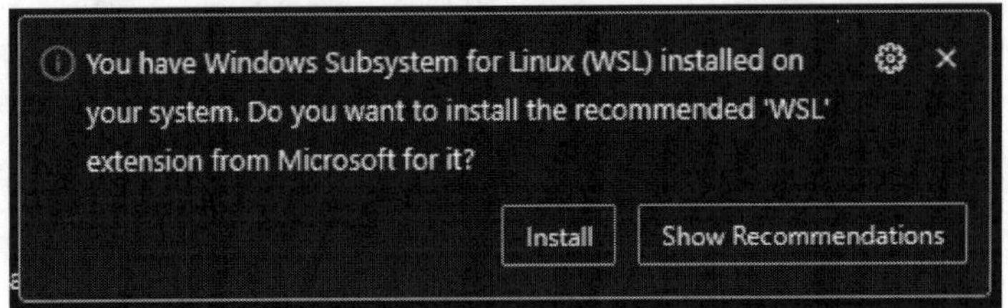

Figure 5-15. *WSL extension*

Use the Kubernetes extension.

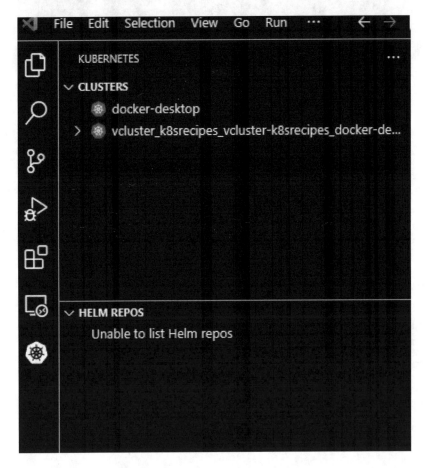

Figure 5-16. *VS Code Kubernetes extension view*

Cluster Explorer: Once installed and configured, the Kubernetes extension allows you to interact with your Kubernetes cluster directly from VS Code. You can explore nodes, pods, and deployments in the VS Code sidebar.

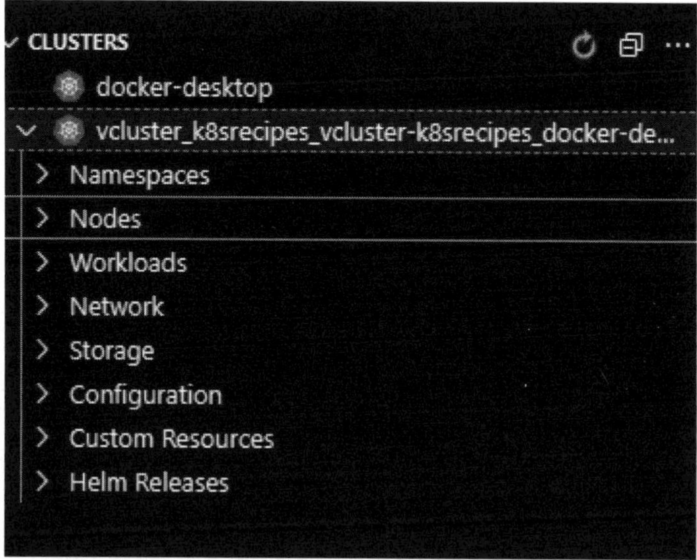

***Figure 5-17.** VS Code Kubernetes extension listing cluster resources*

Terminal Access: You can open an integrated terminal in VS Code to run kubectl commands directly, making it convenient to manage your cluster without switching between tools.

We can apply a default pod resource from the terminal with kubectl.

```
PS C:\Users\gsten\OneDrive\Dokumenty\book> kubectl apply -f .\pod.yaml
pod/my-pod created
```

***Figure 5-18.** VS Code terminal usage*

```
PS C:\Users\gsten\OneDrive\Dokumenty\book> kubectl apply -f .\pod.yaml
pod/my-pod created
PS C:\Users\gsten\OneDrive\Dokumenty\book> kubectl get pods
NAME     READY   STATUS    RESTARTS   AGE
my-pod   1/1     Running   0          3m34s
PS C:\Users\gsten\OneDrive\Dokumenty\book> 
```

Figure 5-19. *VS Code terminal applying kubectl*

Resource Management: You can create, edit, and delete Kubernetes resources directly from the IDE. The extension also allows you to apply configurations directly to your cluster.

Figure 5-20. *VS Code Kubernetes YAML editing inline*

Summary

This chapter focuses on improving the developer experience in Kubernetes by introducing tools and practices that streamline workflows and enhance productivity. It highlights using command-line tools like kubectl, with features like aliases, autocompletion, and plugins through krew to simplify tasks like context and namespace switching. Helm and Kustomize are also emphasized for managing deployments and customizing configurations effectively.

Lens IDE is presented as a dedicated Kubernetes tool for visual management, offering real-time resource insights, visual debugging, and streamlined configuration modification. DevSpace is introduced as a solution for simplifying Kubernetes workflows, enabling declarative configurations, team collaboration, and automation and reducing the need for extensive Kubernetes expertise.

VS Code, with its extensibility and Kubernetes-related extensions, is highlighted as an integrated development environment for efficient cluster management, offering features like a cluster explorer, terminal integration, and YAML editing. Together, these tools enhance productivity, reduce complexity, and provide a cohesive development environment for Kubernetes.

CHAPTER 6

Scaling and Resiliency

This chapter aims to build confidence by offering strategies for managing resources, scaling deployments, and implementing resilience mechanisms in a Kubernetes environment. It discusses setting resource limits and requests, utilizing deployment strategies, exploring customization for efficient configuration management, and implementing various forms of autoscaling. Furthermore, it delves into securing the control plane, managing container image registries, and strategies for updating applications, all of which contribute to the resilience of your applications.

6.1 Create Resource Limits and Requests in Pods and Containers

Problem

In a Kubernetes environment, managing resource allocation for pods and containers is crucial for scalability and application resiliency. Resource limits and requests help avoid contention, inefficient utilization, and potential downtime. Define resource limits and requests to ensure the Kubernetes scheduler assigns enough resources and prevents pods from consuming more than their allocated share, protecting cluster stability.

G. Stencel and L. Berton, *Kubernetes Recipes*,
https://doi.org/10.1007/979-8-8688-1325-2_6

Solution

Defining and managing resource requests and limits is crucial for improving application scalability and resilience when working with a Kubernetes cluster. This ensures that your applications have the necessary resources to operate efficiently while preventing any single pod from using up all the cluster resources, thus maintaining overall system stability and performance.

To implement resource limits and requests in Kubernetes, it's important to understand their differences and assess your application's needs:

1. **Identify Resource Requirements**: Analyze your application's resource requirements to determine suitable CPU and memory requests and limits.

2. **Define Resource Requests and Limits in Pod Specifications**:

    – Resource requests specify the minimum CPU and memory required for a container.

    – Resource limits define the maximum CPU and memory a container can use.

3. **Update Deployment YAML Files**: Incorporate the resource requests and limits into the deployment YAML files of your pods and containers.

4. **Apply and Test the Configuration**: Deploy the updated YAML files to your Kubernetes cluster and monitor the resource usage to ensure the configurations are practical.

limitsexample.yaml

```yaml
apiVersion: v1
kind: Pod
metadata:
  name: example-pod
spec:
  containers:
  - name: example-container
    image: nginx:latest
    resources:
      requests:
        memory: "64Mi"
        cpu: "250m"
      limits:
        memory: "128Mi"
        cpu: "500m"
```

After creating the above YAML file, we can apply it using the following command:

```
kubectl apply -f limitsexample.yaml
```

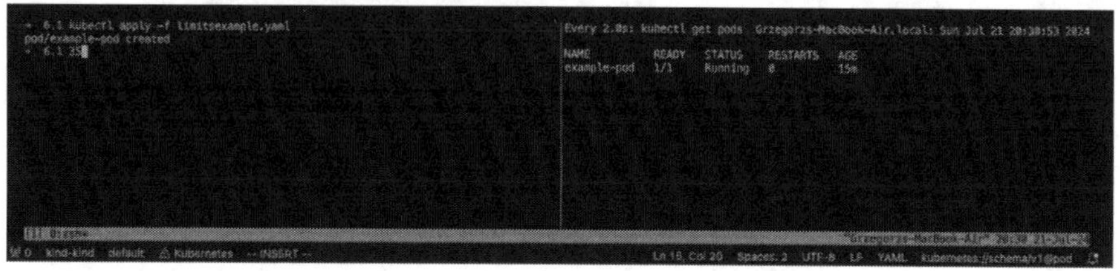

***Figure 6-1.** Applying limitsexample.yaml while monitoring it on the right*

Explanation

memory: "64Mi" and cpu: "250m" under requests specify that the container requires 64 MiB of memory and 250 milliCPU to be scheduled.

memory: "128Mi" and cpu: "500m" under limits ensure that the container cannot use more than 128 MiB of memory and 500 milliCPU.

Monitoring and Adjusting

After deploying the pod, monitor its resource usage using Kubernetes tools like kubectl top or the metrics server. Based on the observed usage, you may need to adjust the resource requests and limits to optimize performance and resource utilization:

```
kubectl top pod example-pod
```

```
→ 6.1 kubectl apply -f limitsexample.yaml
pod/example-pod created
→ 6.1 kubectl top pod example-pod
error: Metrics API not available
→ 6.1 kubectl top pod example-pod
error: Metrics API not available
→ 6.1
```

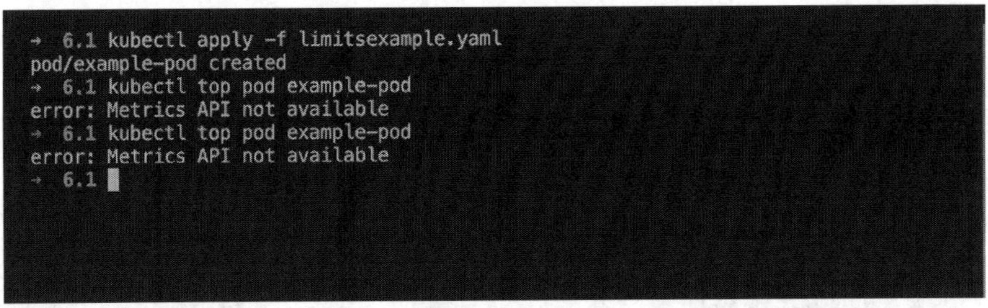

Figure 6-2. *Unexpected error from a non-existing metrics server*

If we have a fresh Kubernetes installation (e.g., KinD, Minikube, k3s, etc.) and encounter an error when running "kubectl top", it means we need the metrics server installed. You can install the metrics server using the official Kubernetes metrics server manifests:

```
kubectl apply -f https://github.com/kubernetes-sigs/metrics-server/releases/latest/download/components.yaml
```

After applying, we need to verify the installation:

```
kubectl get deployment metrics-server -n kube-system
```

Ensure the metrics server deployment is running and all its pods are up with a one-liner like the one below (which gets the name of the pod and then runs the logs command on it):

```
kubectl logs -n kube-system $(kubectl get pods -n kube-system
-l k8s-app=metrics-server -o name)
```

If you can see an error

```
"Metrics server error Warning Unhealthy 25s (x21 over 3m25s)
kubelet Readiness probe failed: HTTP probe failed with
statuscode: 500"
```

that also means you are getting an SSL certification issue because the metrics server requires secure communication with the kubelet. Still, you might need to configure it to skip Transport Layer Security (TLS) verification or use internal IPs (not advised for production environments). Still, for our learning, we are allowed with this approach, so what we need to do next is to edit metrics server deployment by adding arguments to handle insecure TLS and using internal IPs:

```
kubectl edit deployment metrics-server -n kube-system
```

And locate the path below in the deployment:

```
spec:
  containers:
  - name: metrics-server
    args:
```

Make sure these arguments are under metrics-server:

```
- --kubelet-insecure-tls
- --kubelet-preferred-address-types=InternalIP
```

So it should look similar to

```
spec:
  containers:
  - name: metrics-server
    args:
      - --kubelet-insecure-tls
      - --kubelet-preferred-address-types=InternalIP
```

When we save, Kubernetes will redeploy the new pod and kill the old one.

We just need to check when it's available.

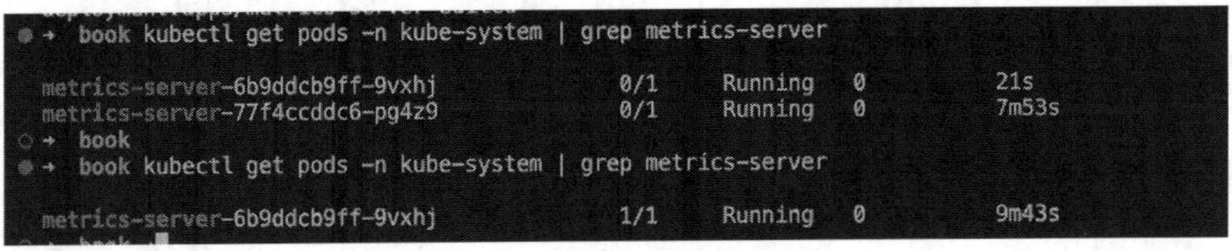

```
→ book kubectl get pods -n kube-system | grep metrics-server

metrics-server-6b9ddcb9ff-9vxhj          0/1     Running   0          21s
metrics-server-77f4ccddc6-pg4z9          0/1     Running   0          7m53s
→ book
→ book kubectl get pods -n kube-system | grep metrics-server

metrics-server-6b9ddcb9ff-9vxhj          1/1     Running   0          9m43s
```

***Figure 6-3.** Monitoring presence of the metrics server*

Now, we can run the top command.

```
→ book kubectl top pod example-pod
NAME          CPU(cores)   MEMORY(bytes)
example-pod   0m           4Mi
```

***Figure 6-4.** Checking the Kubernetes pod with the top command*

6.2 Deployment, ReplicaSet, Replication Controller, or Job

Problem

Maintaining high availability and resilience is critical in a cloud-native application. The application must scale dynamically based on the load, ensure zero downtime during updates, and recover quickly from failures.

A company has deployed a microservices-based application on a Kubernetes cluster. This application is designed to handle varying loads, particularly during peak times (e.g., sales events or new feature releases). However, the current setup does not handle scaling efficiently and faces downtime issues during updates. Additionally, the application fails to recover promptly from pod failures, impacting the user experience.

Dynamic Scaling: The application cannot automatically scale based on load, leading to performance degradation during high-traffic periods.

Zero-Downtime Updates: The deployment process occasionally causes downtime, affecting the application's availability.

Pod Resilience: Failed pods are not replaced promptly, which decreases the service's overall reliability.

Solution

Implement autoscaling to adjust the number of running pods based on the current load.

Ensure zero downtime during application updates by configuring rolling updates.

Improve the resiliency by configuring pod health checks and auto-replacement of failed pods.

Dynamic Scaling with Horizontal Pod Autoscaling (HPA):

Configure HPA: Use Kubernetes Horizontal Pod Autoscaling to adjust the number of pods based on CPU utilization or other custom metrics. To discover more about HPA, head to section "Application Horizontal Pod Autoscaling."

Zero-Downtime Updates with Rolling Updates:

Configure Deployment for Rolling Updates: Ensure the deployment strategy is set to rolling updates to avoid downtime during updates.

#6.2/rolling.yaml

```
apiVersion: apps/v1
kind: Deployment
metadata:
  name: my-app-deployment
spec:
  replicas: 3
  strategy:
    type: RollingUpdate
    rollingUpdate:
      maxUnavailable: 1
      maxSurge: 1
  selector:
    matchLabels:
      app: my-app
```

```
  template:
    metadata:
      labels:
        app: my-app
    spec:
      containers:
      - name: my-app-container
        image: nginx:latest
        ports:
        - containerPort: 80
```

We will apply the above with kubectl apply -f rolling.yaml.

To check if our deployment is running, we will run

```
kubectl get pods -l app=my-app
```

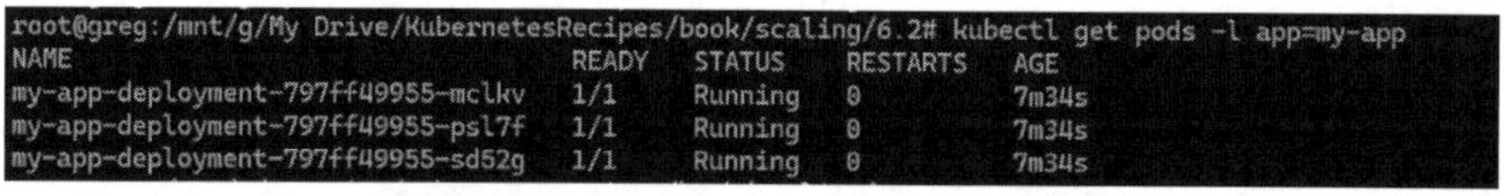

```
root@greg:/mnt/g/My Drive/KubernetesRecipes/book/scaling/6.2# kubectl get pods -l app=my-app
NAME                                 READY   STATUS    RESTARTS   AGE
my-app-deployment-797ff49955-mclkv   1/1     Running   0          7m34s
my-app-deployment-797ff49955-psl7f   1/1     Running   0          7m34s
my-app-deployment-797ff49955-sd52g   1/1     Running   0          7m34s
```

***Figure 6-5.** Getting pods by label*

Our app was nicely scaled to three running pods.

To test the rolling update, you need to update the deployment. For example, update the container image to a different version of Nginx (e.g., nginx:1.21.0).

We can do it with the set image command or with the edit command:

```
kubectl set image deployment/my-app-deployment my-app-
container=nginx:1.21.0
```

or

```
kubectl edit deployment my-app-deployment
```

And let's change the image from the latest to 1.21.0:

```
image: nginx:1.21.0
```

If we save the deployment, it will automatically pick up changes and will apply them to the cluster.

Pods with the old version will be gradually terminated. Pods with the new version will be created and running before the old ones are fully terminated.

```
root@greg:/mnt/g/My Drive/KubernetesRecipes/book/scaling# kubectl  get pods -w
NAME                               READY   STATUS    RESTARTS   AGE
my-app-deployment-7459d78798-728tm   1/1     Running   0          30s
my-app-deployment-7459d78798-dkv6x   1/1     Running   0          30s
my-app-deployment-7459d78798-hkmmk   1/1     Running   0          24s
my-app-deployment-7bc87574d7-bjsp4   0/1     Pending   0          0s
my-app-deployment-7bc87574d7-bjsp4   0/1     Pending   0          0s
my-app-deployment-7459d78798-hkmmk   1/1     Terminating   0          91s
my-app-deployment-7bc87574d7-bjsp4   0/1     ContainerCreating   0          0s
my-app-deployment-7bc87574d7-b8x5h   0/1     Pending             0          0s
my-app-deployment-7bc87574d7-b8x5h   0/1     Pending             0          0s
my-app-deployment-7bc87574d7-b8x5h   0/1     ContainerCreating   0          0s
my-app-deployment-7459d78798-hkmmk   0/1     Completed           0          92s
my-app-deployment-7459d78798-hkmmk   0/1     Completed           0          93s
my-app-deployment-7459d78798-hkmmk   0/1     Completed           0          93s
my-app-deployment-7bc87574d7-bjsp4   1/1     Running             0          6s
my-app-deployment-7459d78798-dkv6x   1/1     Terminating         0          103s
my-app-deployment-7bc87574d7-q6g7h   0/1     Pending             0          0s
my-app-deployment-7bc87574d7-q6g7h   0/1     Pending             0          0s
my-app-deployment-7bc87574d7-q6g7h   0/1     ContainerCreating   0          0s
my-app-deployment-7459d78798-dkv6x   0/1     Completed           0          103s
my-app-deployment-7bc87574d7-b8x5h   1/1     Running             0          7s
my-app-deployment-7459d78798-dkv6x   0/1     Completed           0          104s
my-app-deployment-7459d78798-dkv6x   0/1     Completed           0          104s
my-app-deployment-7459d78798-728tm   1/1     Terminating         0          104s
my-app-deployment-7459d78798-728tm   0/1     Completed           0          104s
my-app-deployment-7bc87574d7-q6g7h   1/1     Running             0          2s
my-app-deployment-7459d78798-728tm   0/1     Completed           0          105s
my-app-deployment-7459d78798-728tm   0/1     Completed           0          105s
```

Figure 6-6. *Getting pods with -w (watch, live-refresh) flag*

Let's check rollout:

```
kubectl rollout status deployment/my-app-deployment
```

```
root@greg:/mnt/g/My Drive/KubernetesRecipes/book/scaling# kubectl rollout st
atus deployment/my-app-deployment
deployment "my-app-deployment" successfully rolled out
root@greg:/mnt/g/My Drive/KubernetesRecipes/book/scaling# kubectl port-forwa
rd deployment/my-app-deployment 8080:80
Forwarding from 127.0.0.1:8080 -> 80
Forwarding from [::1]:8080 -> 80
Handling connection for 8080
Handling connection for 8080
```

Figure 6-7. *Checking rollout status of the deployment*

If we additionally want to check the web server status, we can

```
kubectl port-forward deployment/my-app-deployment 8080:80
```

and access the browser from your machine (you need to run kubectl on the same machine).

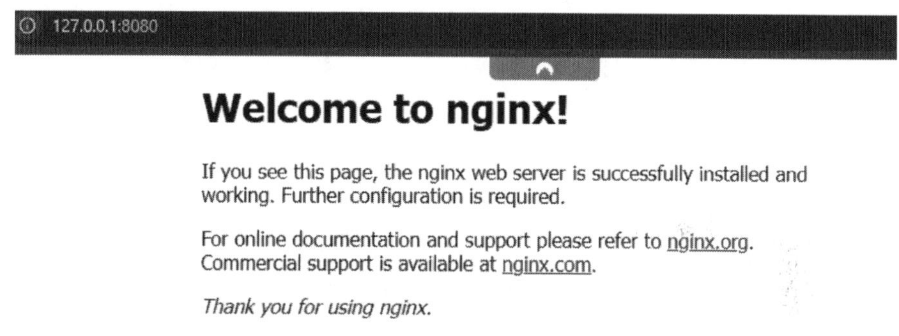

Figure 6-8. *Nginx default welcome page*

Improving Pod Resiliency:

Health Checks: Define liveness and readiness probes to detect and replace unhealthy pods.

```
apiVersion: apps/v1
kind: Deployment
metadata:
  name: my-app-deployment
spec:
  replicas: 3
  selector:
    matchLabels:
      app: my-app
  template:
    metadata:
      labels:
        app: my-app
    spec:
      containers:
      - name: my-app-container
        image: nginx:latest
        ports:
        - containerPort: 80
        livenessProbe:
          httpGet:
            path: /
            port: 80
          initialDelaySeconds: 3
          periodSeconds: 3
        readinessProbe:
          httpGet:
```

```
        path: /
        port: 80
      initialDelaySeconds: 3
      periodSeconds: 3
```

Let's apply the above:

```
kubectl apply -f healthchecks.yaml
```

```
root@greg:/mnt/g/My Drive/KubernetesRecipes/book/scaling/6.2# kc get pods -w
 READY   STATUS    RESTARTS   AGE
my-app-deployment-6fcbd7cf87-dgtpz   1/1     Running   0          9s
my-app-deployment-6fcbd7cf87-kf5wx   1/1     Running   0          9s
my-app-deployment-6fcbd7cf87-v5kph   1/1     Running   0          9s
```

***Figure 6-9.** Getting status of live pods*

To check how health checks are working, we are going to simulate health check failure.

Let's exec into one of the pods:

```
kubectl exec -it my-app-deployment-6fcbd7cf87-dgtpz -- /bin/sh\
and stop nginx
nginx -s stop
```

We can see that the health check failed and a new pod was instantiated.

```
root@greg:/mnt/g/My Drive/KubernetesRecipes/book/scaling/6.2# kc get pods -w
 READY   STATUS    RESTARTS   AGE
my-app-deployment-6fcbd7cf87-dgtpz   1/1     Running   0          9s
my-app-deployment-6fcbd7cf87-kf5wx   1/1     Running   0          9s
my-app-deployment-6fcbd7cf87-v5kph   1/1     Running   0          9s
^[my-app-deployment-6fcbd7cf87-dgtpz   0/1     Completed   0          3m49s
my-app-deployment-6fcbd7cf87-dgtpz   0/1     Running     1 (2s ago)   3m50s
my-app-deployment-6fcbd7cf87-dgtpz   1/1     Running     1 (6s ago)   3m54s
```

***Figure 6-10.** New pod instantiation after health check failure*

Let's break the health check by removing the file from the path.

```
root@greg:/mnt/g/My Drive/KubernetesRecipes/book/scaling/6.2# kubectl exec -it my-app-deployment-6fcbd7cf87-dgtp
z -- /bin/sh
# rm /usr/share/nginx/html/index.html
# command terminated with exit code 137
root@greg:/mnt/g/My Drive/KubernetesRecipes/book/scaling/6.2#
```

Figure 6-11. *Forcing health check failure for debug purposes*

We can see, the second pod that we were exec into was killed.

```
NAME                                 READY   STATUS    RESTARTS        AGE
my-app-deployment-6fcbd7cf87-dgtpz   0/1     Running   1 (3m43s ago)   7m31s
my-app-deployment-6fcbd7cf87-kf5wx   1/1     Running   0               7m31s
my-app-deployment-6fcbd7cf87-v5kph   1/1     Running   0               7m31s
my-app-deployment-6fcbd7cf87-dgtpz   0/1     Running   2 (1s ago)      7m32s
my-app-deployment-6fcbd7cf87-dgtpz   1/1     Running   2 (5s ago)      7m36s
```

Figure 6-12. *The pod's status*

Using Jobs for Batch Processing and Resilience:

Implement Jobs: Use Kubernetes jobs for batch processing tasks and ensure they are retried in case of failure.

```
apiVersion: batch/v1
kind: Job
metadata:
  name: my-batch-job
spec:
  template:
    metadata:
      labels:
        job-name: my-batch-job
    spec:
      containers:
      - name: my-job-container
        image: busybox
        command: ["echo", "Hello, World!"]
      restartPolicy: OnFailure
  backoffLimit: 4
```

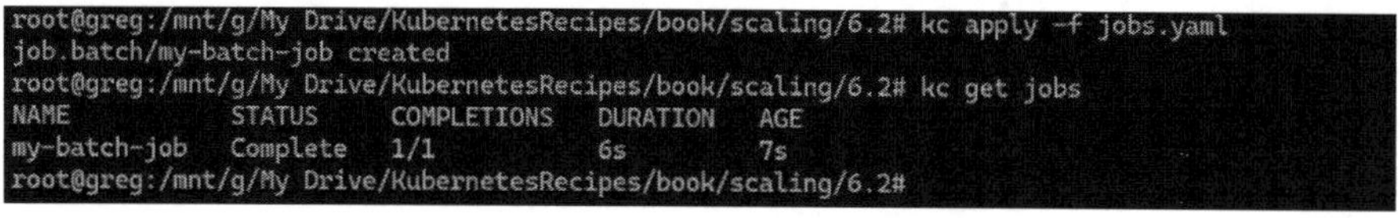

```
root@greg:/mnt/g/My Drive/KubernetesRecipes/book/scaling/6.2# kc apply -f jobs.yaml
job.batch/my-batch-job created
root@greg:/mnt/g/My Drive/KubernetesRecipes/book/scaling/6.2# kc get jobs
NAME           STATUS     COMPLETIONS   DURATION   AGE
my-batch-job   Complete   1/1           6s         7s
root@greg:/mnt/g/My Drive/KubernetesRecipes/book/scaling/6.2#
```

Figure 6-13. *Applying above file (jobs.yaml)*

By implementing HPA, configuring rolling updates, defining health checks, and using Kubernetes jobs for batch processing, the application can achieve better scaling, zero downtime during updates, and improved resiliency. These steps will ensure the application is robust, highly available, and capable of handling varying loads efficiently.

6.3 Kustomize: Do More with Less

Problem

Organizations that adopt Kubernetes for container orchestration often face challenges in scaling applications efficiently and ensuring their resiliency. As the number of microservices grows, managing configurations across multiple environments becomes increasingly complex. Traditional handling of configuration files can lead to redundancy, increased errors, and difficulties maintaining consistency across different application lifecycle stages.

Kustomize, a configuration management tool native to Kubernetes, promises to alleviate these challenges. However, many organizations may feel uncertain about fully harnessing its capabilities due to a lack of understanding of its features and best practices. The key challenges it can help address include the following:

- Managing multiple configurations for different environments (development, testing, production) is a common and significant challenge. It often leads to duplicated efforts and increases the potential for errors, underscoring the need for a more efficient solution like Kustomize.

- Maintaining configuration consistency while ensuring efficient resource utilization becomes difficult as applications scale.
- Ensuring applications remain resilient during scaling and configuration changes is not just a challenge; it's critical. This is especially true in dynamic environments, where adapting quickly is paramount. Kustomize can play a significant role in this aspect.

Solution

Organizations can adopt a systematic approach to leveraging Kustomize to address these challenges. This involves utilizing its robust features to simplify configuration management, boost scalability, and enhance application resilience. Here's a suggested solution.

Leveraging Kustomize for Enhanced Scaling and Resiliency

Leveraging Kustomize for enhanced scaling and resiliency in Kubernetes involves utilizing Kustomize's configuration management capabilities to create reusable, composable, and environment-specific Kubernetes manifests.

1. **Basic Kustomize Structure**

   First, let's set up a basic Kustomize structure:

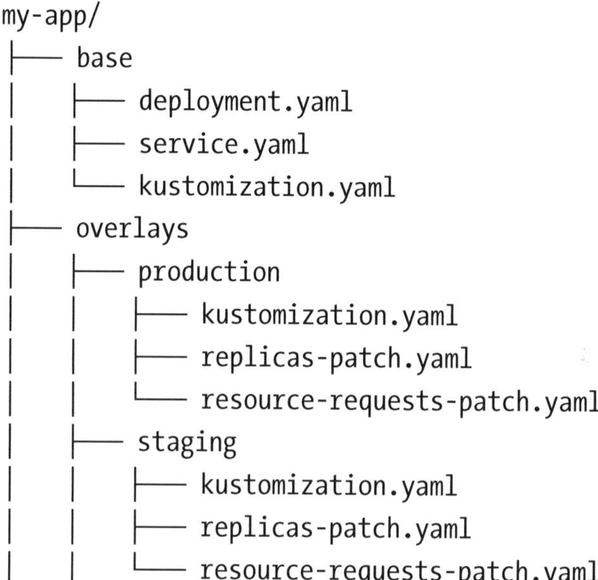

2. **Base Deployment**

   The base directory contains the standard configuration:

   # base/deployment.yaml

```
apiVersion: apps/v1
kind: Deployment
metadata:
  name: nginx-deployment
  labels:
    app: nginx
spec:
  replicas: 1
  selector:
```

```
    matchLabels:
      app: nginx
  template:
    metadata:
      labels:
        app: nginx
    spec:
      containers:
      - name: nginx
        image: nginx:1.21.1
        ports:
        - containerPort: 80
```

base/service.yaml

```
apiVersion: v1
kind: Service
metadata:
  name: nginx-service
spec:
  selector:
    app: nginx
  ports:
    - protocol: TCP
      port: 80
      targetPort: 80
```

base/kustomization.yaml

```
resources:
  - deployment.yaml
  - service.yaml
```

3. **Overlays for Production**

   The overlays/production directory contains environment-specific customizations:

   # overlays/production/replicas-patch.yaml

```
apiVersion: apps/v1
kind: Deployment
metadata:
  name: nginx-deployment
spec:
  replicas: 5
```

   # overlays/production/resource-requests-patch.yaml

```
apiVersion: apps/v1
kind: Deployment
metadata:
  name: nginx-deployment
spec:
  template:
    spec:
      containers:
      - name: nginx
        resources:
          requests:
            memory: "64Mi"
            cpu: "250m"
          limits:
            memory: "128Mi"
            cpu: "500m"
```

overlays/production/kustomization.yaml

```
resources:
  - ../../base
patchesStrategicMerge:
  - replicas-patch.yaml
  - resource-requests-patch.yaml
```

4. **Overlays for Staging**

   Similarly, the overlays/staging directory contains customizations for the staging environment:

   # overlays/staging/replicas-patch.yaml

```
apiVersion: apps/v1
kind: Deployment
metadata:
  name: nginx-deployment
spec:
  replicas: 2
```

   # overlays/staging/resource-requests-patch.yaml

```
apiVersion: apps/v1
kind: Deployment
metadata:
  name: nginx-deployment
spec:
  template:
    spec:
      containers:
      - name: nginx
        resources:
          requests:
```

```
          memory: "32Mi"
          cpu: "125m"
        limits:
          memory: "64Mi"
          cpu: "250m"
```

overlays/staging/kustomization.yaml

```
resources:
  - ../../base

patchesStrategicMerge:
  - replicas-patch.yaml
  - resource-requests-patch.yaml
```

5. **Applying Configurations**

   To validate Kubernetes files without applying them, we can run

   ```
   kubectl apply --dry-run=client
   ```

   To apply the configurations for a specific environment, you navigate to the appropriate overlay directory and apply the Kustomize configuration.

   For production:

   ```
   kustomize build overlays/production | kubectl
   apply -f -
   ```

   For staging:

   ```
   kustomize build overlays/staging | kubectl
   apply -f -
   ```

```
root@greg:/mnt/g/My Drive/KubernetesRecipes/book/scaling/6.3/my-app# kustomize build overlays/staging | kubectl apply -f -
# Warning: 'patchesStrategicMerge' is deprecated. Please use 'patches' instead. Run 'kustomize edit fix' to update your Kustomizat
ion automatically.
service/nginx-service created
deployment.apps/nginx-deployment created
root@greg:/mnt/g/My Drive/KubernetesRecipes/book/scaling/6.3/my-app# kc get pods
kc: command not found
root@greg:/mnt/g/My Drive/KubernetesRecipes/book/scaling/6.3/my-app# kubectl get pods
NAME                               READY   STATUS    RESTARTS   AGE
nginx-deployment-599658bd-m264s    1/1     Running   0          7s
nginx-deployment-599658bd-rr4mz    1/1     Running   0          7s
root@greg:/mnt/g/My Drive/KubernetesRecipes/book/scaling/6.3/my-app#
                                   Ln 7, Col 1  Spaces: 2  UTF-8  CRLF  YAML  kustomization.yaml
```

Figure 6-14. *Applying Kustomize for staging YAMLs*

We can see we have a staging version running with two replica sets specified in the staging.

If our pipeline runs production overlay, we can see five replica sets.

```
root@greg:/mnt/g/My Drive/KubernetesRecipes/book/scaling/6.3/my-app# kustomize build overlays/production | kubectl apply -f -
# Warning: 'patchesStrategicMerge' is deprecated. Please use 'patches' instead. Run 'kustomize edit fix' to update your Kustomizat
ion automatically.
service/nginx-service unchanged
deployment.apps/nginx-deployment configured
root@greg:/mnt/g/My Drive/KubernetesRecipes/book/scaling/6.3/my-app# kc get pods
kc: command not found
root@greg:/mnt/g/My Drive/KubernetesRecipes/book/scaling/6.3/my-app# kubectl get pods
NAME                                READY   STATUS    RESTARTS   AGE
nginx-deployment-cb446ffcd-28662    1/1     Running   0          8s
nginx-deployment-cb446ffcd-f48vn    1/1     Running   0          8s
nginx-deployment-cb446ffcd-gcm9v    1/1     Running   0          7s
nginx-deployment-cb446ffcd-sxm5d    1/1     Running   0          7s
nginx-deployment-cb446ffcd-xqljk    1/1     Running   0          8s
root@greg:/mnt/g/My Drive/KubernetesRecipes/book/scaling/6.3/my-app#
```

Figure 6-15. *Checking staging status*

6. **Enhanced Resiliency with Health Checks**

   Add liveness and readiness probes to the deployment for enhanced resiliency:
   # base/deployment.yaml (updated)

```
apiVersion: apps/v1
kind: Deployment
metadata:
  name: nginx-deployment
  labels:
    app: nginx
```

```
spec:
  replicas: 1
  selector:
    matchLabels:
      app: nginx
  template:
    metadata:
      labels:
        app: nginx
    spec:
      containers:
      - name: nginx
        image: nginx:1.21.1
        ports:
        - containerPort: 80
        livenessProbe:
          httpGet:
            path: /
            port: 80
          initialDelaySeconds: 10
          periodSeconds: 10
        readinessProbe:
          httpGet:
            path: /
            port: 80
          initialDelaySeconds: 5
          periodSeconds: 5
```

Liveness Probe:

The livenessProbe checks if the application is running properly. If the liveness probe fails, Kubernetes will restart the container.

httpGet specifies that the liveness probe should send an HTTP GET request to the root path (/) on port 80.

initialDelaySeconds: The number of seconds after the container has started before the probe is initiated.

periodSeconds: How often (in seconds) is the probe performed?

Readiness Probe:

The readinessProbe checks if the application is ready to accept traffic. If the readiness probe fails, Kubernetes will stop sending traffic to the container until it passes.

httpGet: Like the liveness probe, it sends an HTTP GET request to the root path (/) on port 80.

initialDelaySeconds: The number of seconds after the container has started before the probe is initiated.

periodSeconds: How often (in seconds) is the probe performed?

These probes ensure that Kubernetes can automatically detect and respond to problems with your application, helping maintain the availability and reliability of your services.

Using Kustomize in this manner, you can efficiently manage different environments, ensure scalability by adjusting replicas and resources, and enhance resiliency with proper health checks. This approach simplifies managing complex configurations and makes your Kubernetes deployments more robust and adaptable to various environments.

Hierarchical Configuration Management

Utilize Kustomize's base and overlay features to manage configurations hierarchically. Define a common base configuration for all environments and create environment-specific overlays to customize settings without duplicating the base configuration.

Example: Define a base configuration for a microservice with common settings. Create overlays for development, staging, and production environments, each adjusting only the necessary parameters.

Environment-Specific Customizations

Use Kustomize transformers and patches to apply environment-specific changes dynamically. This allows for a clean separation of common and environment-specific configurations.

Example: Use transformers to modify resource limits or replica counts based on the environment, ensuring efficient resource use and better scalability.

Version Control and Consistency

Store Kustomize configurations in version control systems (e.g., Git) to maintain a history of changes and ensure consistency across deployments. Implement GitOps practices to automate the deployment process, reducing the risk of human error.

Example: Use Git repositories to manage Kustomize configurations and employ continuous integration/continuous deployment (CI/CD) pipelines to automate deployments based on changes in the repository.

Store all base and overlay configurations in a Git repository.

Here's an example repository structure:

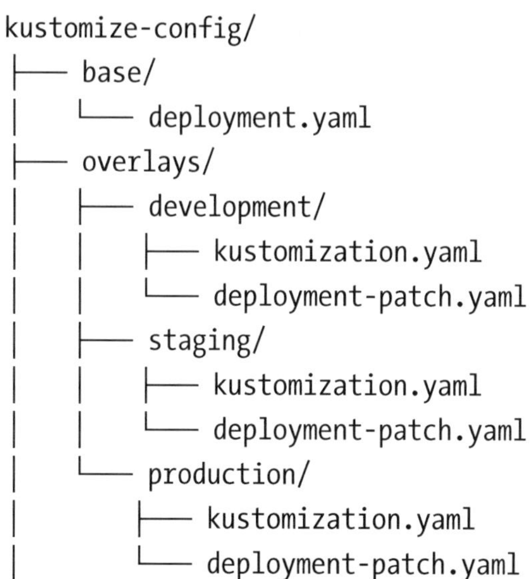

```
kustomize-config/
├── base/
│   └── deployment.yaml
├── overlays/
│   ├── development/
│   │   ├── kustomization.yaml
│   │   └── deployment-patch.yaml
│   ├── staging/
│   │   ├── kustomization.yaml
│   │   └── deployment-patch.yaml
│   └── production/
│       ├── kustomization.yaml
│       └── deployment-patch.yaml
│
```

Implement CI/CD pipeline (e.g., using GitHub Actions, GitLab CI, or Jenkins) to automate deployments.

Resiliency Enhancements

Implement health checks, liveness probes, and readiness probes within Kustomize configurations to ensure that applications remain resilient and recover quickly from failures.

Example: Configure liveness and readiness probes in the base configuration to monitor application health, ensuring that the service is only considered available when it is ready to handle traffic. Let's add "liveness and readiness" probes (base/deployment.yaml):

```
apiVersion: apps/v1
kind: Deployment
metadata:
  name: my-app
spec:
  replicas: 2
  selector:
    matchLabels:
      app: my-app
  template:
    metadata:
      labels:
        app: my-app
    spec:
      containers:
      - name: my-app
        image: my-app:1.0
        ports:
        - containerPort: 80
        livenessProbe:
```

```
    httpGet:
      path: /healthz
      port: 80
    initialDelaySeconds: 30
    periodSeconds: 10
  readinessProbe:
    httpGet:
      path: /readyz
      port: 80
    initialDelaySeconds: 5
    periodSeconds: 10
```

Automation and Validation

Utilize Kustomize plugins and external tools to automate configuration validation and testing before applying them to clusters. This reduces the likelihood of configuration errors impacting live environments.

Example: Integrate Kustomize with tools like kubeval or kube-score kubeconform to validate Kubernetes manifests and ensure they adhere to best practices and standards:

```
kustomize build overlays/production | kubeconform
```

```
oot@greg:/mnt/g/My Drive/KubernetesRecipes/book/scaling/6.3/my-app# kustomize build overlays/production | kubeconform
 Warning: 'patchesStrategicMerge' is deprecated. Please use 'patches' instead. Run 'kustomize edit fix' to update your Kustomizat
on automatically.
tdin - Deployment nginx-deployment is invalid: problem validating schema. Check JSON formatting: jsonschema: '/spec' does not val
date with https://raw.githubusercontent.com/yannh/kubernetes-json-schema/master/master-standalone/deployment-apps-v1.json#/proper
ies/spec/required: missing properties: 'selector'
oot@greg:/mnt/g/My Drive/KubernetesRecipes/book/scaling/6.3/my-app# kustomize build overlays/production | kubeconform
 Warning: 'patchesStrategicMerge' is deprecated. Please use 'patches' instead. Run 'kustomize edit fix' to update your Kustomizat
on automatically.
oot@greg:/mnt/g/My Drive/KubernetesRecipes/book/scaling/6.3/my-app#
```

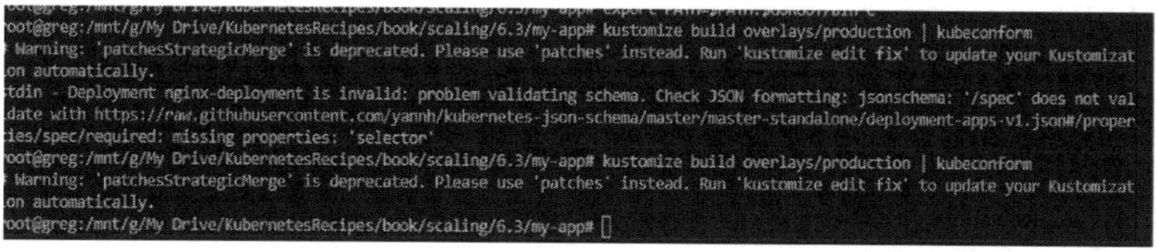

Figure 6-16. *Applying production YAMLs with later verification with plugin kubeconform*

Integrate Kubeval/Kubeconform for validation (CI/CD pipeline example).

These examples demonstrate practical uses of Kustomize for managing configurations, customizing environments, maintaining version control, improving resiliency, and automating validation. These aspects effectively address the challenges of scaling and resiliency in Kubernetes environments.

6.4 Cluster Autoscaler (Google, Azure, AWS, DigitalOcean, OVH Cloud)

Problem

As organizations increasingly adopt containerized applications, managing the infrastructure to support dynamic workloads becomes a critical challenge. Kubernetes, a popular container orchestration platform, provides robust solutions for deploying, managing, and scaling containerized applications. However, ensuring that a Kubernetes cluster can efficiently scale and remain resilient under varying load conditions requires effectively utilizing cluster autoscaler mechanisms.

Different cloud providers, such as Google Cloud Platform (GCP), Microsoft Azure, Amazon Web Services (AWS), DigitalOcean, and OVH Cloud, offer their implementations of cluster autoscalers. These autoscalers dynamically adjust the number of nodes in a Kubernetes cluster based on the demands of the workloads. Despite their availability, many organizations need help configuring and optimizing these autoscalers to achieve optimal performance, cost efficiency, and resiliency.

Challenges:

Dynamic Workloads: Handling unpredictable and fluctuating workloads without over-provisioning or under-provisioning resources

Cost Management: Balancing the need for high availability and performance with the cost of running additional resources

Cross-Provider Differences: Configuring and managing autoscalers across cloud platforms with varying features and limitations

Resiliency: Ensuring the cluster remains resilient during scaling events, preventing downtime and maintaining service quality

Resource Limits: Dealing with cloud provider-specific resource limits and quotas that can impact scaling capabilities

Solution

Solution: Implementing and Optimizing Cluster Autoscaler for Kubernetes

To address these challenges, organizations need a well-defined strategy for implementing and optimizing cluster autoscalers across different cloud platforms. Here are the key steps and best practices to achieve this:

- **Cluster Autoscaler Configuration**:

  Google Cloud Platform (GCP): Use the Google Kubernetes Engine (GKE) autoscaler. Configure node pools with autoscaling enabled, set minimum and maximum node limits, and choose the appropriate machine types based on workload requirements.

Azure: Utilize the Azure Kubernetes Service (AKS) autoscaler. Set up node pools, configure scaling parameters, and monitor scaling activities through Azure Monitor.

AWS: Implement the AWS Elastic Kubernetes Service (EKS) autoscaler. Use autoscaling groups, configure scaling policies, and leverage AWS CloudWatch for monitoring.

DigitalOcean: Use the DigitalOcean Kubernetes autoscaler. Define node pool scaling settings, set appropriate limits, and monitor cluster health through DigitalOcean's monitoring tools.

OVH Cloud: Implement the OVH Cloud Kubernetes autoscaler. Configure node pool settings, set scaling parameters, and monitor them through OVH Cloud's management interface.

- **Monitoring and Metrics**:

Integrate monitoring tools like Prometheus and Grafana to gather real-time metrics on cluster performance and scaling activities.

Set up alerts for critical events like node failures, scaling errors, and resource saturation.

- **Cost Optimization**:

Use cloud provider–specific cost management tools to track spending and identify opportunities for cost savings.

Implement policies to prevent over-provisioning, such as setting reasonable scaling limits and leveraging spot instances where applicable.

- **Resiliency Strategies**:

Design stateless and horizontally scalable applications, reducing node failures' impact during scaling events.

Implement automated backups and disaster recovery plans to ensure data integrity and availability.

- **Cross-Provider Management**:

Use multi-cloud management tools like Rancher or Anthos to manage clusters across different providers from a single interface.

Standardize configuration and management practices to reduce complexity and improve operational efficiency.

Implementing these strategies, organizations can effectively utilize cluster autoscale to handle dynamic workloads, optimize costs, and maintain high resiliency in their Kubernetes environments. This approach ensures the infrastructure adapts to changing demands while providing a seamless and reliable user experience.

6.5 Kubernetes Event-Driven Autoscaling (KEDA)

Problem

High availability, responsiveness, and resource efficiency are essential in modern cloud-native applications. Traditional autoscaling based on CPU and memory usage may need to be revised for event-driven workloads that experience bursty and unpredictable traffic patterns.

Scenario:

A company runs a real-time analytics platform on a Kubernetes cluster. The platform processes events from various sources, such as user interactions, IoT devices, and third-party integrations. During peak periods, the volume of events can surge dramatically, leading to performance bottlenecks and delayed processing. Based on CPU utilization, the current scaling mechanism needs to be improved for these event-driven workloads. Additionally, the platform must ensure quick failure recovery to maintain high availability.

Challenges:

Event-Driven Scaling: The current CPU-based scaling does not effectively respond to fluctuating event-driven traffic, causing performance issues during peak loads.

Resource Efficiency: Inefficient resource usage during low-traffic periods leads to unnecessary costs.

Resiliency: The system must ensure quick failure recovery to maintain uninterrupted service.

Solution

Implement event-driven autoscaling to dynamically adjust the number of running pods based on the volume of events.

Ensure efficient resource utilization by scaling down during periods of low traffic.

Improve resiliency by configuring KEDA to handle pod failures and ensure quick recovery.

Install KEDA (Kubernetes Event-Driven Autoscaling):

```
kubectl apply -f https://github.com/kedacore/keda/releases/
download/v2.5.0/keda-2.5.0.yaml
```

Configure an Event Source for Scaling:

Define an event source (e.g., a message queue like Kafka, RabbitMQ, or Azure Event Hubs) that KEDA will monitor for scaling.

Create a ScaledObject:

Implementation: Define a ScaledObject to scale the deployment based on the number of events in the message queue.

```
apiVersion: keda.sh/v1alpha1
kind: ScaledObject
metadata:
  name: my-scaledobject
spec:
  scaleTargetRef:
    apiVersion: apps/v1
    kind: Deployment
    name: my-app-deployment
  minReplicaCount: 1
  maxReplicaCount: 10
  triggers:
  - type: kafka
    metadata:
      bootstrapServers: my-kafka-broker:9092
      topic: my-topic
      consumerGroup: my-group
      lagThreshold: "100"
```

Deploy the Application:

Implementation: Define the deployment for the application that KEDA will scale.

```
apiVersion: apps/v1
kind: Deployment
metadata:
  name: my-app-deployment
```

```
spec:
  replicas: 1
  selector:
    matchLabels:
      app: my-app
  template:
    metadata:
      labels:
        app: my-app
    spec:
      containers:
      - name: my-app-container
        image: my-app:latest
        ports:
        - containerPort: 80
```

Define Health Checks for Resiliency:

Implementation: Configure liveness and readiness probes to ensure the application pods are healthy and replaced if they fail.

```
apiVersion: apps/v1
kind: Deployment
metadata:
  name: my-app-deployment
spec:
  replicas: 1
  template:
    metadata:
      labels:
        app: my-app
```

```
    spec:
      containers:
      - name: my-app-container
        image: my-app:latest
        ports:
        - containerPort: 80
        livenessProbe:
          httpGet:
            path: /healthz
            port: 80
          initialDelaySeconds: 3
          periodSeconds: 3
        readinessProbe:
          httpGet:
            path: /ready
            port: 80
          initialDelaySeconds: 3
          periodSeconds: 3
```

By implementing KEDA, the application can dynamically scale based on the volume of events, ensuring efficient resource utilization and improved performance during peak loads. Configuring health checks will enhance the system's resiliency, providing quick recovery from pod failures. This solution addresses the challenges of scaling and resiliency in an event-driven architecture, maintaining the high availability and responsiveness of the real-time analytics platform.

6.6 Application Horizontal Pod Autoscaling

Problem

In modern cloud-native environments, applications must handle varying loads efficiently while maintaining high availability and performance. Kubernetes provides a mechanism called Horizontal Pod Autoscaling (HPA) to address these needs. HPA automatically adjusts the number of pod replicas in a Kubernetes deployment based on observed CPU utilization or other select metrics. However, implementing and optimizing HPA poses several challenges, including configuring appropriate scaling metrics, ensuring cost-effectiveness, and maintaining application resiliency during scaling events.

Challenges:

Metric Selection: Choosing the right metrics (CPU, memory, custom metrics) to trigger scaling actions.

Threshold Configuration: Setting appropriate threshold values for scaling up and down to avoid thrashing and ensure stability.

Resource Allocation: Balancing resource allocation to avoid over-provisioning or under-provisioning, impacting cost and performance.

Scaling Latency: Minimize the latency in scaling actions to ensure a timely response to changes in load.

Resiliency: Ensuring the application remains resilient and available during scaling operations, including handling pod restarts and network disruptions.

Solution

Implementing and Optimizing Kubernetes Horizontal Pod Autoscaling

To effectively utilize HPA for enhancing application scalability and resiliency, the following steps and best practices should be adopted:

Metric Selection and Monitoring:

CPU/Memory Utilization: Start with CPU and memory metrics, commonly used and supported by default in Kubernetes. These metrics are good indicators of pod resource demands.

Custom Metrics: Use custom metrics to gain more granular control over scaling decisions. Tools like Prometheus and custom metrics adapters can help expose application-specific metrics (e.g., request count and latency).

Metrics Server: Ensure the Kubernetes metrics server is properly installed and configured to collect and expose the required metrics.

Configuring HPA:

Define HPA Resources: Create HorizontalPodAutoscaler resources in Kubernetes, specifying the target deployment, metric types, and scaling thresholds.

Threshold Values: Set appropriate threshold values for scaling up and down. Avoid setting thresholds too low to prevent thrashing (frequent scaling actions) or too high to ensure timely scaling.

Min/Max Replicas: Define minimum and maximum replica counts to control the scaling range and avoid excessive resource consumption.

Advanced HPA Configurations:

Multiple Metrics: Configure HPA to use various metrics for a more balanced and accurate scaling strategy. This can include combining CPU usage with custom application metrics.

Rate Limiting: Implement rate limiting on scaling actions to prevent rapid scaling changes that could destabilize the application.

Testing and Optimization:

Load Testing: Conduct load testing to simulate different load scenarios and observe how HPA responds. Tools like Apache JMeter or K6 can be used for load testing.

Tuning Parameters: Monitor application performance and adjust HPA parameters based on observed behaviors and metrics.

Debugging: Use Kubernetes events and logs to debug and understand the behavior of HPA during scaling events.

Ensuring Resiliency:

Graceful Shutdown: Implement graceful shutdown mechanisms in applications to handle pod terminations smoothly and ensure no in-flight requests are lost.

Pod Disruption Budgets: Define PodDisruptionBudget (PDB) to limit the number of pods that can be taken down simultaneously during scaling events, maintaining application availability.

Health Checks: Ensure robust readiness and liveness probes are in place to detect and mitigate issues promptly during scaling.

Cost Management:

Resource Requests and Limits: Properly configure resource requests and limits for each pod to optimize resource utilization and control costs.

Monitoring Costs: Use cost management tools and dashboards to monitor the cost implications of scaling actions and adjust policies accordingly.

6.7 Application Vertical Pod Autoscaling

Problem

In dynamic cloud-native environments, ensuring optimal resource allocation for applications is critical for maintaining performance and efficiency. Kubernetes Vertical Pod Autoscaling (VPA) automatically adjusts the resource requests and limits (CPU and memory) of containers running in pods. This helps to optimize resource utilization, improve performance, and reduce costs. However, implementing and optimizing VPA presents several challenges, including configuring appropriate resource limits, managing scaling latency, and ensuring application resiliency during scaling adjustments.

Challenges:

Resource Allocation: Determining the appropriate CPU and memory requests and limits to prevent under-provisioning (causing performance issues) or over-provisioning (leading to resource wastage)

Scaling Impact: Minimizing the impact on running applications during scaling adjustments, especially since VPA can restart pods to apply new resource configurations

Latency in Scaling: Ensuring timely adjustments to resource allocation to respond to workload changes without significant delays

Cost Management: Balancing the need for sufficient resources with cost efficiency to avoid unnecessary spending

Application Resiliency: Maintaining application availability and performance during and after VPA adjustments, including handling pod restarts and disruptions

Solution

Implementing and Optimizing Kubernetes Vertical Pod Autoscaling

To effectively utilize VPA for enhancing application performance and resiliency, the following steps and best practices should be adopted:

VPA Configuration:

Install VPA: Deploy the Vertical Pod Autoscaler components in the Kubernetes cluster, ensuring the VPA Admission Controller, Recommender, and Updater are properly configured.

Define VPA Resources: Create VerticalPodAutoscaler custom resources (CRs) specifying the target deployment, resource policy, and update mode (e.g., "Auto," "Off," or "Initial").

Resource Policy and Limits:

Resource Policy: Define resource policies to control how VPA makes recommendations and updates resource requests and limits. This includes specifying minimum and maximum allowed resource values.

Update Mode: Choose the appropriate update mode for the VPA:

"Auto": VPA automatically updates resource requests and limits, potentially restarting pods.

"Initial": VPA sets resource requests and limits only at pod creation time, not affecting running pods.

"Off": VPA makes recommendations but does not apply changes automatically.

Monitoring and Metrics:

Collect Metrics: Use monitoring tools like Prometheus to collect CPU and memory usage metrics. These metrics inform VPA recommendations.

Analyze Usage Patterns: Regularly analyze resource usage patterns to understand the application's resource needs and adjust VPA configurations accordingly.

Testing and Optimization:

Load Testing: Conduct load testing to observe how VPA recommendations impact application performance and resource usage. Tools like Apache JMeter or K6 can simulate different load scenarios.

Tuning Parameters: Continuously monitor VPA recommendations and application performance and tune VPA parameters based on observed behaviors and metrics.

Dry-Run Mode: Use the dry-run mode to observe VPA recommendations without applying them, allowing for safe testing and analysis.

Ensuring Resiliency:

Graceful Shutdown: Implement graceful shutdown mechanisms in applications to handle pod restarts smoothly and ensure no in-flight requests are lost.

Pod Disruption Budgets: Define a PodDisruptionBudget (PDB) to limit the number of pods that can be disrupted simultaneously during scaling events while maintaining application availability.

Health Checks: Ensure robust readiness and liveness probes are in place to detect and mitigate issues promptly during scaling.

Cost Management:

Resource Requests and Limits: Configure each pod's initial resource requests and limits based on historical usage and VPA recommendations to optimize resource utilization and control costs.

Monitoring Costs: Use cost management tools and dashboards to monitor the cost implications of VPA adjustments and adjust policies accordingly.

Organizations can implement and optimize Vertical Pod Autoscaling in Kubernetes by following these best practices to enhance application performance and resiliency. This ensures that the applications can dynamically adapt to changing resource demands while maintaining efficiency and cost-effectiveness.

6.8 High-Performance Kubernetes Cluster Autoscaler with Karpenter

Problem

As organizations strive to meet dynamic and unpredictable workloads in their Kubernetes environments, efficient autoscaling becomes critical. Traditional cluster autoscalers often need more latency, flexibility, and resource optimization support. Karpenter, an open source high-performance Kubernetes cluster autoscaler, aims to address these limitations by providing faster and more efficient scaling, better resource utilization, and enhanced integration with cloud providers. However, implementing and optimizing Karpenter poses challenges, including configuring it for optimal performance, managing cost-effectiveness, and ensuring the resiliency of applications during scaling events.

Challenges:

Latency in Scaling: Minimizing the time taken to scale up or down in response to workload changes, ensuring timely resource availability

Resource Optimization: Efficiently utilizing resources to prevent over-provisioning or under-provisioning, impacting performance and cost

Configuration Complexity: Configuring Karpenter to integrate seamlessly with existing Kubernetes clusters and cloud provider APIs

Cost Management: Balancing the need for high availability and performance with the cost of additional resources

Resiliency: Ensuring the cluster and applications remain resilient during scaling events, avoiding downtime and performance degradation

Solution

Implementing and Optimizing Karpenter for High-Performance Kubernetes Cluster Autoscaling

Karpenter automatically launches the right compute resources to handle your cluster's applications. It is designed to let you take full advantage of the cloud with fast and straightforward computing provisioning for Kubernetes clusters.

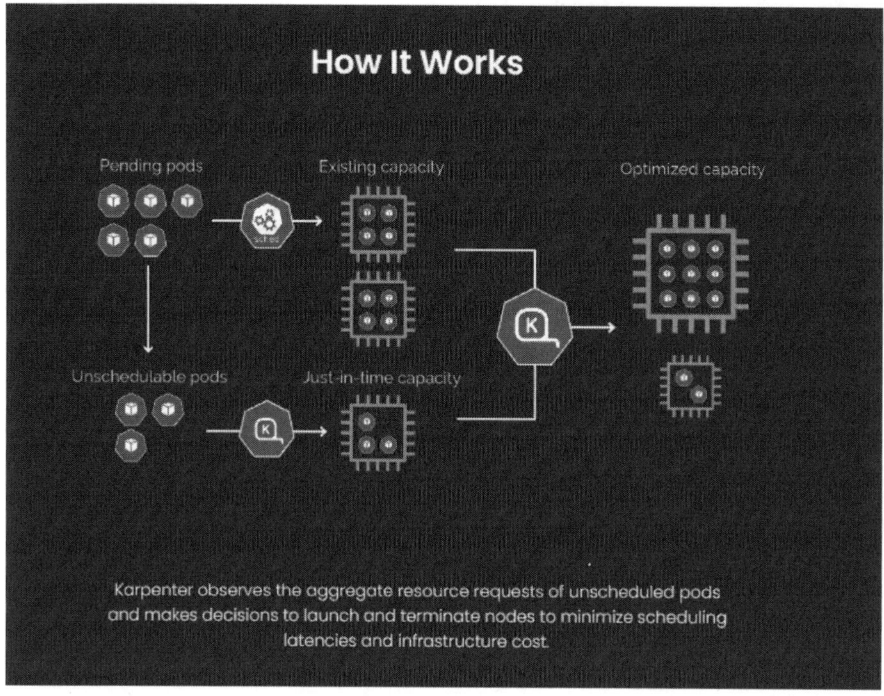

Figure 6-17. *Karpenter logical decision flow*

`src:karpenter.sh`

To leverage Karpenter for high-performance autoscaling, the following steps and best practices should be adopted:

Karpenter Installation and Configuration:

Install Karpenter: Deploy Karpenter in the Kubernetes cluster, ensuring all necessary components are correctly installed and configured.

Cloud Provider Integration: Configure Karpenter to integrate with your cloud provider (e.g., AWS, GCP). This includes setting up necessary permissions, credentials, and API access.

Defining Scaling Policies:

Provisioner Configuration: Define Karpenter Provisioners that specify scaling policies, including instance types, zones, and resource limits. Provisioners help manage how and when Karpenter scales nodes.

Scheduling Constraints: Use scheduling constraints to ensure that the right types of nodes are provisioned based on the workload requirements (e.g., GPU instances for machine learning workloads).

Resource Optimization:

Efficient Node Utilization: Configure Karpenter to optimize node utilization by efficiently packing pods on fewer nodes, reducing the number of nodes needed.

Instance Flexibility: Enable Karpenter to dynamically use various instance types and sizes to match workloads, improving cost efficiency and performance.

Monitoring and Metrics:

Collect Metrics: Use monitoring tools like Prometheus and Grafana to gather real-time metrics on cluster performance, resource usage, and scaling activities.

Analyze Performance: Continuously analyze performance metrics to fine-tune Karpenter configurations and ensure optimal resource utilization.

Testing and Optimization:

Load Testing: Conduct load testing to simulate different scenarios and observe how Karpenter responds. This helps you understand the scaling behavior and make necessary adjustments.

Tuning Parameters: Adjust Karpenter parameters based on testing results and ongoing monitoring to achieve the desired balance between performance, cost, and resiliency.

Ensuring Resiliency:

Graceful Shutdown: Implement graceful shutdown mechanisms in applications to handle node terminations smoothly and ensure no in-flight requests are lost.

Pod Disruption Budgets: Define PodDisruptionBudget (PDB) to control the number of pods that can be disrupted simultaneously during scaling events, maintaining application availability.

Health Checks: Ensure robust readiness and liveness probes are in place to detect and mitigate issues promptly during scaling.

Cost Management:

Spot Instances: Leverage spot instances where appropriate to reduce costs. Karpenter can automatically replace interrupted spot instances with on-demand instances to maintain availability.

Cost Monitoring: Cloud provider cost management tools monitor spending and identify opportunities for cost savings. Based on cost insights, Karpenter configurations are adjusted to optimize resource allocation.

Following these best practices, organizations can implement and optimize Karpenter for high-performance autoscaling in their Kubernetes environments. This ensures the cluster can dynamically adapt to changing workloads while maintaining performance, cost efficiency, and application resiliency.

6.9 Ensuring Application Resiliency and Efficiency in Constrained Environments with Kubernetes PodTopologySpread

Problem

In Kubernetes environments, maintaining high availability and resiliency of applications often requires distributing workloads across different nodes and zones. This is particularly crucial in constrained environments where resources are limited and the risk of resource contention and single points of failure is higher. Kubernetes PodTopologySpread (PTS) allows administrators to define rules that spread pods across various topology domains, such as nodes, zones, or regions, to ensure balanced resource utilization and fault tolerance. However, implementing and optimizing PodTopologySpread in constrained environments poses challenges, including setting appropriate spread constraints, managing resource limitations, and maintaining application performance and resiliency.

Challenges:

Resource Limitations: Managing limited resources effectively to avoid overloading specific nodes or zones while ensuring application performance.

Setting Spread Constraints: Defining appropriate spread constraints to balance pods across different topology domains without causing resource fragmentation.

Single Points of Failure: Preventing single points of failure by ensuring that pods are adequately distributed to handle node or zone failures.

Performance Management: Ensuring performance is not compromised due to pod spreading, especially in latency-sensitive applications.

Complex Configuration: Configuring PodTopologySpread policies that align with the specific needs of constrained environments, ensuring compatibility with existing deployments.

Solution

Implementing and Optimizing PodTopologySpread for Constrained Environments

To leverage PodTopologySpread for enhancing application resiliency and efficiency in constrained environments, the following steps and best practices should be adopted:

Understanding PodTopologySpread:

PodTopologySpread Constraints: These constraints control how pods are distributed across topology domains, such as nodes or zones. Constraints can be based on labels, max skew, and topology keys.

Configuring PodTopologySpread:

Define Topology Keys: Identify the topology domains (e.g., node, zone, region) relevant to your deployment. Use topology keys like kubernetes.io/hostname for nodes and topology.kubernetes.io/zone for zones.

Set Max Skew: Determine the maximum allowable difference in the number of pods between topology domains. This helps prevent uneven distribution and resource contention.

Label Nodes and Pods: Ensure nodes and pods are appropriately labeled to enable effective topology spreading based on defined constraints.

Creating PodTopologySpread Constraints:

```
apiVersion: v1
kind: Pod
metadata:
  name: example-pod
spec:
  topologySpreadConstraints:
  - maxSkew: 1
```

```
topologyKey: "kubernetes.io/hostname"
whenUnsatisfiable: DoNotSchedule
labelSelector:
  matchLabels:
    app: example
```

maxSkew: Set to 1 to ensure that the number of pods per node does not differ by more than one.

topologyKey: Set to kubernetes.io/hostname to spread pods across different nodes.

whenUnsatisfiable: Set it to DoNotSchedule to prevent pods from being scheduled if the constraints cannot be satisfied.

Monitoring and Metrics:

Collect Metrics: Use monitoring tools like Prometheus and Grafana to gather metrics on pod distribution, node utilization, and application performance.

Analyze Spread: Continuously analyze the distribution of pods across topology domains to ensure that the constraints are being met effectively.

Testing and Optimization:

Simulate Failures: Conduct failure simulations to test your application's resiliency when nodes or zones fail. This helps validate the effectiveness of PodTopologySpread constraints.

Adjust Constraints: Based on monitoring and testing results, adjust PodTopologySpread constraints to optimize resource utilization and application resiliency.

Ensuring Performance:

Resource Requests and Limits: Properly configure resource requests and limits for pods to ensure they receive adequate resources without overloading nodes.

Health Checks: Implement robust readiness and liveness probes to detect and mitigate issues promptly, ensuring pods remain healthy and available.

Managing Resource Constraints:

Efficient Utilization: Ensure that resource requests and limits are set appropriately to maximize resource utilization while preventing contention.

Node Affinity and Anti-affinity: Use node affinity and anti-affinity rules in conjunction with PodTopologySpread to further control pod placement and avoid overloading specific nodes.

By following these best practices, organizations can implement and optimize PodTopologySpread in constrained environments, enhancing application resiliency and efficiency. This ensures that applications are distributed across topology domains in a balanced manner, preventing resource contention and improving fault tolerance.

6.10 Securing the Control Plane with Additional Resources

Problem

Organizations face significant challenges in securing the control plane of their infrastructure, particularly in cloud environments, container orchestration platforms (e.g., Kubernetes), or network systems. The control plane is critical for managing configurations, communications, and resource provisioning. If compromised, it can lead to severe consequences, including data breaches, service disruptions, and unauthorized access to critical systems. Common issues include weak access control, poor encryption practices, insufficient network segmentation, lack of logging and monitoring, and vulnerabilities in APIs and software components. Additionally, inadequate resource management and a lack of disaster recovery plans can expose the control plane to performance bottlenecks and potential attacks.

Solution

To address these security challenges, organizations can implement a multilayered approach to fortifying the control plane by utilizing the following key measures:

Identity and Access Management (IAM): Implement role-based access control (RBAC) and multi-factor authentication (MFA) to ensure only authorized users have access while enforcing least privilege principles.

Network Security: Isolate the control plane through network segmentation, enforce ingress and egress policies, and use VPNs and firewalls to prevent unauthorized access.

Encryption: Ensure all data in transit and at rest is encrypted with strong encryption protocols, including using TLS for communication.

Audit Logging and Monitoring: Enable comprehensive and centralized monitoring to detect suspicious activities and respond to security incidents.

Secure API Management: Secure the control plane's APIs by leveraging an API gateway with robust authentication protocols and limiting public API exposure.

Resource Quotas and Rate Limiting: Implement rate limiting and set appropriate resource quotas for the control plane to protect against resource exhaustion and denial-of-service (DoS) attacks.

Patching and Updates: Regularly update and patch the control plane software and components to mitigate known vulnerabilities.

High Availability and Disaster Recovery: Implement redundancy across multiple availability zones and maintain regular backups of control plane data to ensure resilience and disaster recovery.

Security Posture Management: Apply configuration hardening and compliance scanning to align with industry security standards and best practices.

Secret Management: Use centralized secret management tools with strict access controls to securely handle sensitive information such as API keys and passwords.

By implementing these security measures, organizations can significantly reduce the risk of control plane compromises, ensuring a strong and resilient infrastructure capable of withstanding internal and external threats.

6.11 Container Image Registries (AWS ECR, DockerHub, GCR, Quay.io, Harbor, JFrog)

Problem

Container image registries are critical for storing and distributing container images in a cloud-native environment. Popular registries include AWS Elastic Container Registry (ECR), DockerHub, Google Container Registry (GCR), Quay.io, Harbor, and JFrog Artifactory. These registries are crucial in the CI/CD pipeline, enabling seamless containerized application deployment. However, managing and securing container image registries poses several challenges, including access control, vulnerability scanning, image tagging, and compliance with security policies.

Challenges:

Access Control: Ensuring that only authorized users and systems can push, pull, and manage container images

Vulnerability Management: Identifying and mitigating vulnerabilities in container images

Image Tagging and Versioning: Managing image tags and versions effectively to ensure consistency and traceability

Compliance and Security: Ensuring compliance with security policies and industry standards

Performance and Availability: Maintaining the registry's high availability and performance to support continuous integration and deployment

Solution

Implementing and Optimizing Container Image Registries

To effectively manage and secure container image registries, the following steps and best practices should be adopted.

AWS ECR

Figure 6-18. AWS ECR logo

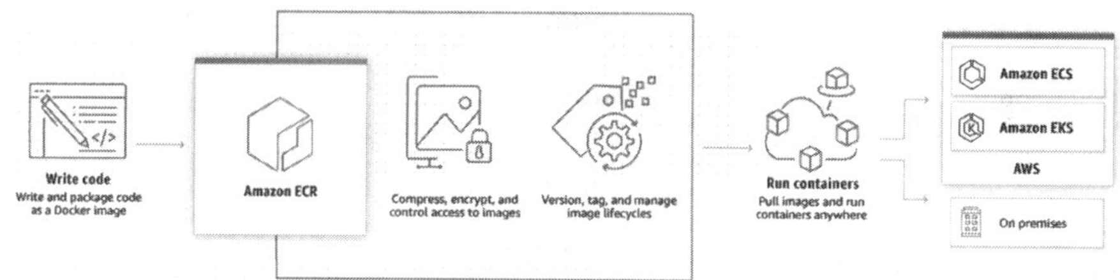

Figure 6-19. AWS ECR workflow

Access Control	Best Practices
Use AWS Identity and Access Management (IAM) policies to control access to ECR repositories.	Use lifecycle policies to manage image cleanup and retention.
Enable multi-factor authentication (MFA) for added security.	Enable encryption at rest and in transit for added security.

DockerHub

Figure 6-20. DockerHub logo

Access Control	Best Practices
Use DockerHub teams and organizations to manage access control.	Use private repositories for sensitive or proprietary images.
Enable two-factor authentication (2FA) for all user accounts.	Take advantage of DockerHub's automated build and scan features.

GCR

Figure 6-21. GCR logo

Access Control	Best Practices
Use Google Cloud IAM to manage access control for GCR.	Leverage Google Cloud's security features, such as VPC Service Controls and Private Google Access.

(*continued*)

Access Control	Best Practices
Implement least privilege access by assigning appropriate roles to users and service accounts.	Use GCR's native vulnerability scanning features.

Quay.io

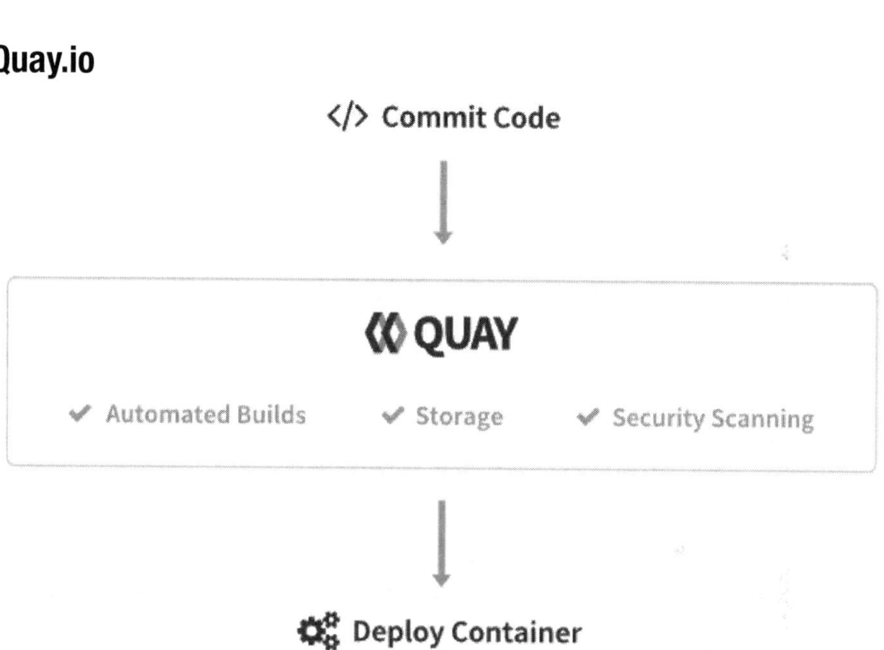

Figure 6-22. Quay workflow

Access Control	Best Practices
Use Quay.io teams and organizations to manage access control.	Use Quay.io's integrated security scanning to obtain a vulnerability report, and leverage its automated tag expiration features.
Enable SSO (Single Sign-On) and 2FA for enhanced security.	Use Quay.io's repository mirroring to enhance redundancy.

Harbor

Figure 6-23. Harbor logo

Access Control	Best Practices
Use Harbor's built-in role-based access control (RBAC) to manage access.	Use Harbor's built-in security features, including content trust and Notary for image signing.
Integrate with LDAP/AD for centralized user management.	Use Harbor's replication capabilities to synchronize images across multiple registries.

JFrog Artifactory

Figure 6-24. JFrog logo

Access Control	Best Practices
Use JFrog's RBAC to manage permissions.	Utilize Artifactory's advanced features like Xray for deep security and compliance scanning.
Integrate with SSO and LDAP for centralized access management.	Implement repository sharding and replication for high availability and disaster recovery.

Vulnerability Management

Automated Scanning: Enable automated vulnerability scanning for images stored in the registry. Use tools like Clair, Trivy, or Aqua Security to scan images.

Regular Updates: Update images regularly to include the latest security patches and fixes. Set up notifications and alerts for detected vulnerabilities to ensure timely remediation.

Image Tagging and Versioning

Follow a consistent tagging convention (e.g., semantic versioning) to manage image versions.

Immutable Tags: Avoid overwriting tags to ensure traceability and consistency.

Retention Policies: Implement retention policies to clean up old and unused images, freeing up storage space.

Compliance and Security

Policy Enforcement:

Use tools like Open Policy Agent (OPA) or Kyverno to enforce image security policies.

Audit Logs:

Enable and regularly review audit logs for registry operations to detect and investigate suspicious activities.

Compliance Checks:

Regularly run compliance checks to ensure adherence to industry standards and organizational policies.

Performance and Availability

Deploy the registry in a highly available configuration using multiple replicas and load balancers.

Caching and Mirroring: Use caching and mirroring to improve performance and reduce latency for frequently accessed images.

Implement monitoring and alerting to track registry performance and availability using tools like Prometheus and Grafana.

By following these best practices, organizations can effectively manage and secure their container image registries, ensuring that containerized applications are deployed safely, efficiently, and in compliance with security policies. This approach enhances the containerized environment's overall security posture and operational efficiency.

Integrating Vulnerability Scanning into CI/CD: A DevSecOps Perspective

By incorporating automated vulnerability scanning into your CI/CD pipelines, you enhance security and streamline remediation efforts, embodying the core DevSecOps principle of integrating security throughout the software delivery lifecycle.

> **Early and Frequent Scanning**: You can catch vulnerabilities as early as possible by embedding security checks in every stage of your CI/CD pipeline. Each code commit and container image build can trigger automated scanning, reducing the risk of shipping insecure artifacts.
>
> **Pipeline Gating**: Configure your pipeline to "fail fast" if scans detect severe vulnerabilities. This helps ensure that builds do not proceed to later stages (e.g., staging or production) unless critical issues are remediated.

Tooling and Automation:

CI/CD Platforms: Jenkins, GitLab CI, GitHub Actions, and others commonly provide plugins or integrations for popular vulnerability scanning tools.

Scanning Tools: Clair, Trivy, or Aqua Security can be run within pipeline stages to analyze dependencies, images, and code for known vulnerabilities.

DevSecOps Culture: By making security a shared responsibility among developers, operations, and security teams, you foster transparency and collaboration. Vulnerability reports become part of standard feedback mechanisms, helping teams fix issues quickly and continuously improve overall security posture.

Continuous Feedback Loop: The results of scans and compliance checks should feed back into your development cycle. This loop helps developers understand the root causes of vulnerabilities and apply secure coding practices in the future.

6.12 Update Your App: Deployment Strategy Types

Problem

Regularly updating applications in a dynamic cloud-native environment is crucial for deploying new features, security patches, and bug fixes. Kubernetes offers a range of deployment strategies to manage application updates, each tailored to specific scenarios and requirements. These strategies include Recreate deployment, rolling deployment, ramped slow rollout, best-effort controlled rollout, blue/green deployment, canary deployment, shadow deployment, A/B testing, rollback deployments, and DaemonSets. However, the challenge lies in selecting and implementing the right deployment strategy to ensure minimal downtime, maintain application performance, and avoid disruptions.

Challenges involve minimizing application downtime during updates to ensure uninterrupted availability and safeguarding against any decline in application performance. Properly configuring deployment strategies to align with specific application and operational requirements may take time and effort. Effectively managing the risks associated with deploying new versions, including potential bugs and incompatibilities, is essential. Furthermore, implementing robust rollback mechanisms to swiftly revert to a stable state in case of deployment issues is paramount.

Solution

To successfully oversee application updates in Kubernetes, it is essential to adopt the following steps and best practices for various deployment strategies.

Recreate Deployment

Suitable for applications where downtime is acceptable and there is no need for seamless updates.

Deploying the "Recreate" strategy in Kubernetes involves shutting down the existing pods before creating new ones. This strategy ensures no overlap between old and new versions, which can be helpful when the latest version is not backward compatible or when you want to ensure that no two versions run simultaneously.

First, ensure you have a deployment YAML file. This file defines your Kubernetes deployment. Here's an example of a deployment YAML with the Recreate strategy:

recreate_deployment.yaml

```
apiVersion: apps/v1
kind: Deployment
metadata:
  name: nginx-app
spec:
  replicas: 3
  strategy:
    type: Recreate
  selector:
    matchLabels:
      app: nginx-app
  template:
    metadata:
      labels:
        app: nginx-app
    spec:
      containers:
      - name: nginx-container
        image: nginx:1.26.1
        ports:
        - containerPort: 80
```

Let's prepare some terminals.

To check the deployment status, we can type

```
kubectl get deployments
kubectl get pods
kubectl rollout status deployment/nginx-app
```

or we can use it with tmux to have more commands running and observe the live status change of pods:

```
tmux
tmux split -h && tmux spit -v
```

Then, in each tmux window, we can run commands for apply in another one command for watch and status rollout like on the image attached:

```
kubectl get pods -l 'app=nginx-app' -w
```

Let's apply the YAML with the following:

```
kubectl apply -f recreate_deployment.yaml
```

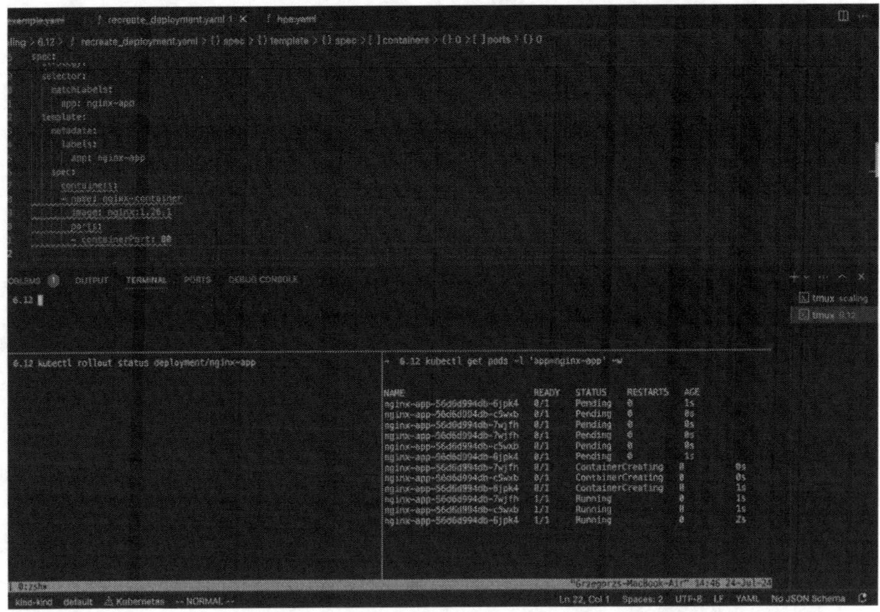

Figure 6-25. *Checking status of live pods while applying rollout*

Now, let's edit the image to recreate the strategy in action.

Let's change the image to nginx:1.27.0 so the deployment image should look like

```
- name: nginx-container
  image: nginx:1.27.0
```

And let's observe the rollout run:

```
kubectl rollout status deployment/nginx-app
```

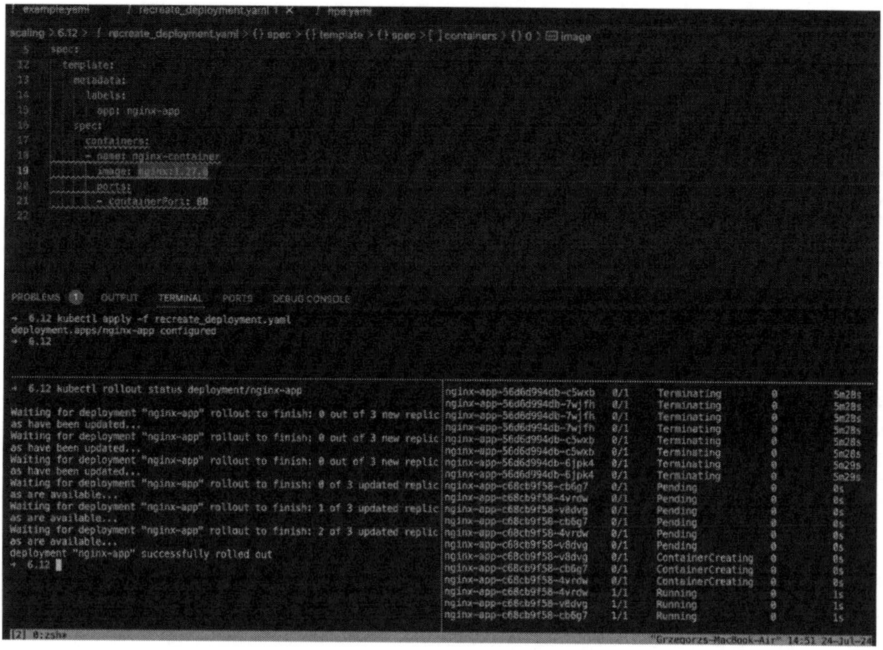

***Figure 6-26.** Rollout status visible with termination of old pods and creation of new ones*

Rolling Update Deployment

It is ideal for minimizing downtime and maintaining application availability during updates.

Let's start with our rollingupdatedeployment.yaml:

```
apiVersion: apps/v1
kind: Deployment
metadata:
  name: nginx-ru-app
  labels:
    app: nginx-ru-app
spec:
  replicas: 3
  strategy:
    type: RollingUpdate
    rollingUpdate:
      maxUnavailable: 1
      maxSurge: 1
  selector:
    matchLabels:
      app: nginx-ru-app
  template:
    metadata:
      labels:
        app: nginx-ru-app
    spec:
      containers:
      - name: my-app-container
        image: nginx:1.26.1
        ports:
        - containerPort: 80
```

In the example above

> **maxUnavailable**: 1 means one pod can be unavailable during the update process.
>
> **maxSurge**: 1 means that, at most, one additional pod (above the desired number of replicas) can be created during the update process.

Let's set watch with

```
kubectl get pods -l 'app=nginx-ru-app' -w
```

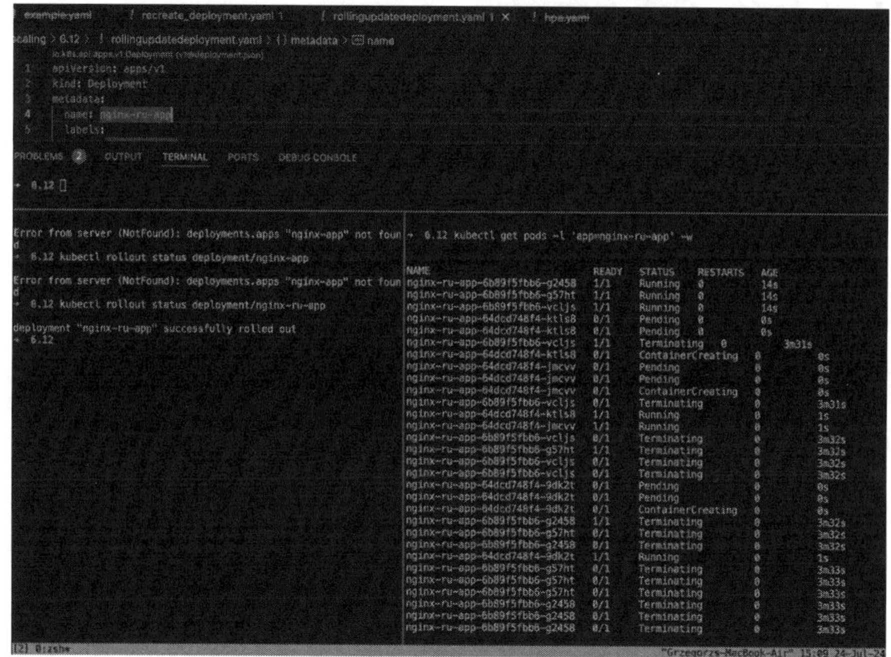

Figure 6-27. *Rollout changes with live watch*

In our live pod watch, we can see Kubernetes gradually replacing old pods with new pods, ensuring that a specified number of pods are always running.

Let's verify the update with

```
kubectl get pods -l app=nginx-ru-app -o jsonpath="{.items[*].
spec.containers[*].image}"
```

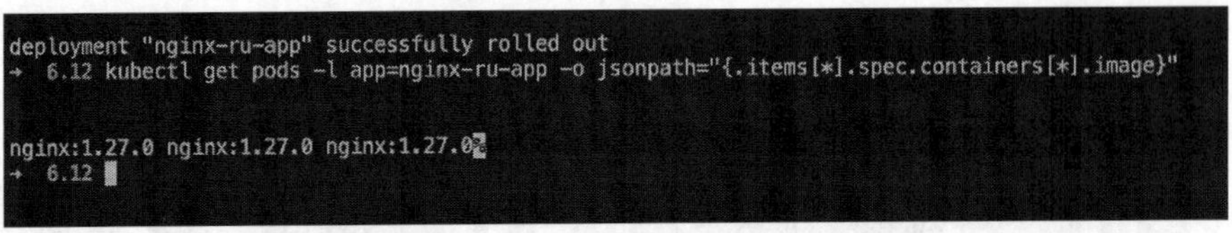

***Figure 6-28.** Checking Nginx pod image version*

We can see the pods were successfully upgraded with a new image.

In case something goes wrong or a new image is faulty, we can always do a rollback operation with

```
kubectl rollout undo deployment/ngingx-ru-app
```

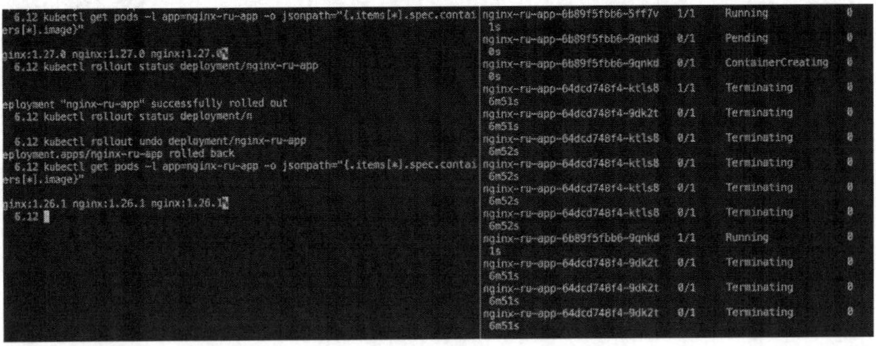

***Figure 6-29.** Undoing deployment rollout*

Blue–Green Deployment

Blue-green deployment is a technique that reduces downtime and risk by running two identical production environments, referred to as blue and green. At any time, only one of these environments is live, with the live environment serving all production traffic. The other environment is updated to the new application version and rigorously tested. Once the latest version is verified, traffic is switched from the live environment to the updated environment, ensuring a high-quality update.

Let's start with the blue deployment:

blue_deployment.yaml

```
apiVersion: apps/v1
kind: Deployment
metadata:
  name: nginx-blue
spec:
  replicas: 3
  selector:
    matchLabels:
      app: nginx
      version: blue
  template:
    metadata:
      labels:
        app: nginx
        version: blue
    spec:
      containers:
      - name: nginx
        image: nginx:1.26.1
        ports:
```

```
        - containerPort: 80
---
apiVersion: v1
kind: Service
metadata:
  name: nginx-service
spec:
  selector:
    app: nginx
    version: blue
  ports:
  - protocol: TCP
    port: 80
    targetPort: 80
```

Apply the above YAML with kubectl apply -f blue_deployment.yaml.

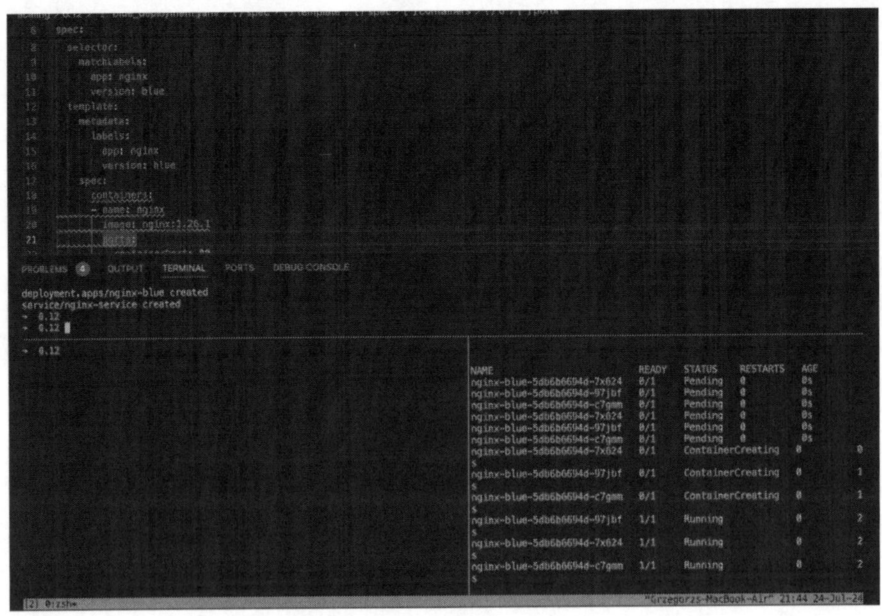

Figure 6-30. *Applying blue deployment*

Let's test the above pod image running and the Nginx response:

```
kubectl get svc nginx-service
```

Best-Effort Controlled Rollout:

Use Case: Ensures a controlled rollout with fallback mechanisms.

Implementation: Integrate with custom controllers or tools like Argo Rollouts to manage the rollout process.

Canary Deployment:

Use Case: Ideal for testing new versions with a subset of users before a full rollout.

Implementation: Gradually shift traffic to the new version and monitor.

```
apiVersion: apps/v1
kind: Deployment
metadata:
  name: my-app-canary
spec:
  replicas: 1
  ...
```

Shadow Deployment:

Use Case: Testing new versions with live traffic without impacting users.

Implementation: Route a copy of the live traffic to the new version for testing.

```
apiVersion: apps/v1
kind: Deployment
```

```
metadata:
  name: my-app-shadow
spec:
  replicas: 1
  ...
```

A/B Testing:

Use Case: Compare different versions of an application to determine the one that performs better.

Implementation: Route a percentage of users to different versions using ingress controllers or service meshes.

```
apiVersion: networking.k8s.io/v1
kind: Ingress
metadata:
  name: my-app-ab
spec:
  rules:
    - host: myapp.example.com
      http:
        paths:
          - path: /a
            backend:
              service:
                name: my-app-v1
                port:
                  number: 80
          - path: /b
            backend:
              service:
```

```
          name: my-app-v2
          port:
            number: 80
```

To test with curl, we need Kubernetes DNS; our host is unaware of that to curl from the pod. Knowing k8s infrastructure, we will deploy our test pod to curl afterward. We will use curl image curlimages/curl.

Rollback Deployments:

> **Use Case**: Quickly revert to a previous stable version in case of issues.
>
> **Implementation**: Use Kubernetes' rollback feature to revert to an earlier replica set.

```
kubectl rollout undo deployment/my-app
```

DaemonSets:

> **Use Case**: Ensuring that specific updates are applied to all nodes, particularly for system-level applications.
>
> **Implementation**: Deploy updates to all or a subset of nodes in the cluster.

```
apiVersion: apps/v1
kind: DaemonSet
metadata:
  name: my-daemon-app
spec:
  ...
```

Best Practices for Deployment Strategies

Monitoring and Metrics:

Use tools like Prometheus and Grafana to monitor deployment health, performance, and success rates.

Implement alerts to detect issues quickly during rollouts.

Testing and Validation:

Use CI/CD pipelines to automate testing and validation before production deployment.

Implement integration and end-to-end tests to ensure new versions work as expected.

Rollback Mechanisms:

Always have a rollback plan in place and test it regularly.

Use Kubernetes' built-in rollback features to quickly revert to previous stable states.

Traffic Management:

Use ingress controllers, service meshes, or load balancers to manage traffic during canary, blue/green, and A/B testing deployments.

Documentation and Training:

Document deployment strategies and processes to ensure team alignment and understanding.

Provide training to teams on using different deployment strategies and handling rollback scenarios.

By following these best practices, organizations can implement and optimize various deployment strategies in Kubernetes, ensuring smooth application updates with minimal downtime and disruptions. This approach enhances the applications' reliability, performance, and user experience.

6.13 vCluster: Instantly Spin Up Hundreds of Kubernetes Virtual Clusters in Seconds

In this Kubernetes chapter, one common challenge is managing multi-tenancy in large-scale Kubernetes environments. Multi-tenancy occurs when multiple users or teams share the same Kubernetes cluster but need isolation, performance guarantees, and application scaling flexibility. Achieving this in a traditional Kubernetes setup can be challenging due to the complexities of isolating resources, managing namespace conflicts, and maintaining security.

Problem

As organizations scale their Kubernetes usage, managing multiple teams and applications within a single cluster becomes more difficult. Key challenges include

Resource Contention: Multiple teams sharing the same cluster may compete for resources, leading to performance degradation or "noisy neighbor" problems.

Isolation: Traditional namespaces within Kubernetes do not provide complete isolation. A misconfigured or rogue application could affect others in the same cluster.

Cluster Management Overhead: Running multiple physical clusters for each team or environment (e.g., dev, staging, prod) increases operational overhead, including costs, maintenance, and monitoring complexity.

Customization: Each team may require specific Kubernetes configurations, policies, or versions, which can be difficult to achieve without running separate clusters.

Scaling: With growing workloads, managing horizontal scaling across multiple teams without impacting each other's operations becomes a bottleneck.

Solution

vCluster (Virtual Cluster) is an innovative solution to address these issues by allowing you to create lightweight virtual Kubernetes clusters within a single physical Kubernetes cluster. This enhances scaling and resiliency while addressing multi-tenancy challenges effectively.

Key benefits of vCluster in scaling and resiliency include

Full Isolation: Each virtual cluster runs in its own namespace within the physical cluster but behaves as a fully isolated Kubernetes environment. This provides complete isolation of resources, security policies, and configurations per team or environment.

Improved Resource Utilization: Instead of deploying multiple physical clusters, vClusters allow multiple isolated virtual clusters to run on the same physical infrastructure. This optimizes resource utilization and reduces operational costs while maintaining scalability.

Simplified Multi-tenancy: vClusters provide an easy way to manage multiple tenants (teams or environments) in a Kubernetes environment. Each tenant gets its own virtual cluster, avoiding conflicts in namespace, RBAC policies, or resource quotas.

	Namespace Per Tenant	vCluster Per Tenant	Cluster Per Tenant
Isolation	very weak	strong	very strong
Access for Tenants	very restricted	vCluster admin	cluster admin
Cost	very cheap	cheap	expensive
Resource Sharing	easy	easy	very hard
Overhead	very low	very low	very high

***Figure 6-31.** vCluster features comparison*

Version and Configuration Flexibility: Teams can run different Kubernetes versions or configurations within their own virtual clusters without affecting others. This is especially useful in scenarios where one team needs to upgrade to a newer Kubernetes version, while another team continues using an older one.

Resiliency and Fault Isolation: Since each virtual cluster is independent, issues like resource exhaustion, application crashes, or misconfigurations in one virtual cluster do not affect the other virtual clusters. This provides better fault tolerance and operational resiliency in large-scale environments.

Scalability: With vCluster, scaling becomes more granular and efficient. Each virtual cluster can be scaled independently based on workload requirements, allowing fine-tuned scaling policies without affecting the physical cluster's performance.

Consider a large organization with multiple development teams working on different microservices. Each team needs isolated Kubernetes environments for development, testing, and production, and each might require different Kubernetes versions or configurations. Using vClusters, the organization can deploy a single physical Kubernetes cluster while giving each team its own virtual cluster. Teams can operate independently, with the flexibility to scale and configure their virtual clusters without impacting the others, and the organization avoids the overhead of managing multiple physical clusters.

vCluster provides a scalable, resilient solution to the challenges of managing large, multi-tenant Kubernetes environments. By offering isolation, better resource utilization, and operational simplicity, it enhances both scaling and resiliency in Kubernetes-based infrastructure.

How vCluster Works

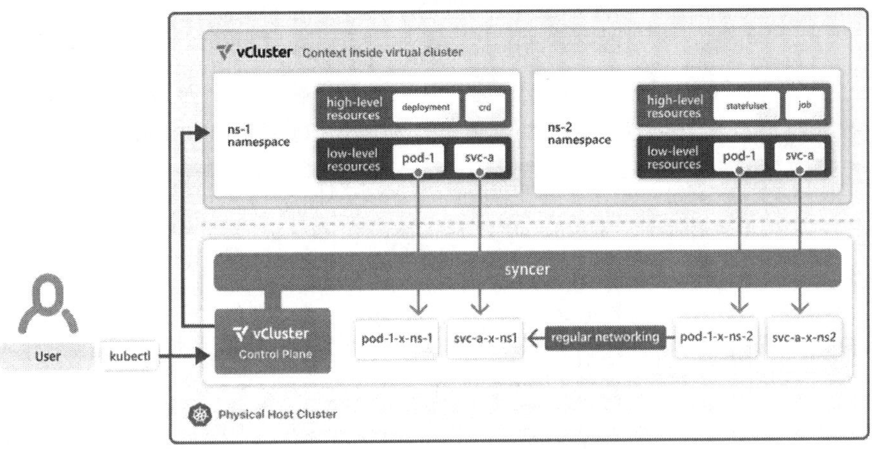

***Figure 6-32.** vCluster business logic*

We will install vCluster first.

Depending on your host system/Kubernetes distribution, please follow instructions on the vCluster page:

https://vcluster.com/docs/vcluster?x0=4#deploy-vcluster

We will use the Linux version, which we run on wsl2:

```
curl -L -o vcluster "https://github.com/loft-sh/vcluster/
releases/latest/download/vcluster-linux-amd64" && sudo install
-c -m 0755 vcluster /usr/local/bin && rm -f vcluster
```

Figure 6-33. *vCluster CLI execution*

Let's create the first vCluster within namespace team-x:

```
vcluster create my-vcluster --namespace team-x
```

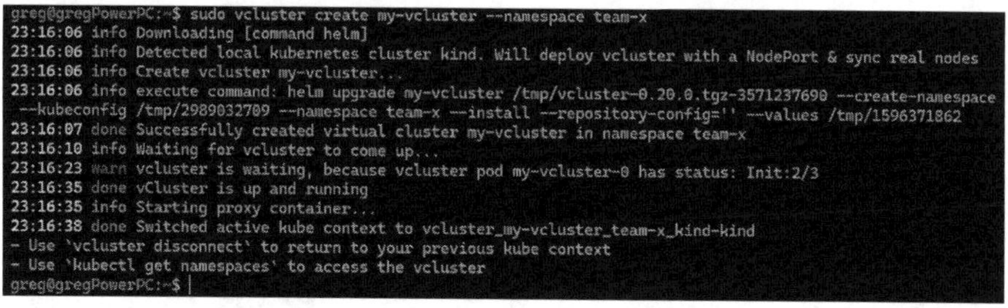

Figure 6-34. *Creating vCluster*

The example in Figure 6-35 is output from the vCluster.

```
greg@gregPowerPC:~$ sudo kubectl create namespace demo-nginx
namespace/demo-nginx created
greg@gregPowerPC:~$ sudo kubectl create deployment ngnix-deployment -n demo-nginx --image=nginx -r 2
deployment.apps/ngnix-deployment created
greg@gregPowerPC:~$ kc get pods
No resources found in default namespace.
greg@gregPowerPC:~$ kc get pods -n demo-nginx
NAME                                READY   STATUS    RESTARTS   AGE
ngnix-deployment-5bbc8d4644-7tzfj   1/1     Running   0          12s
ngnix-deployment-5bbc8d4644-g8lbj   1/1     Running   0          12s
greg@gregPowerPC:~$ |
```

***Figure 6-35.** Creating namespace demo-nginx, applying pods in it, and listing pods*

Now working on one cluster, we are not interfering with the other vCluster.

Now let's create a second cluster within ns team-z.

```
greg@gregPowerPC:~$ sudo vcluster create my-vcluster --namespace team-z

? You are creating a vcluster inside another vcluster, is this desired? No, switch back to context kind-kind
23:20:09 info Creating namespace team-z
23:20:09 info Detected local kubernetes cluster kind. Will deploy vcluster with a NodePort & sync real nodes
23:20:09 info Create vcluster my-vcluster...
23:20:09 info execute command: helm upgrade my-vcluster /tmp/vcluster-0.20.0.tgz-3978399705 --create-namespace
 --kubeconfig /tmp/128066143 --namespace team-z --install --repository-config='' --values /tmp/2535998901
23:20:09 done Successfully created virtual cluster my-vcluster in namespace team-z
23:20:12 info Waiting for vcluster to come up...
23:20:31 done vCluster is up and running
23:20:31 info Starting proxy container...
23:20:31 done Switched active kube context to vcluster_my-vcluster_team-z_kind-kind
- Use `vcluster disconnect` to return to your previous kube context
- Use `kubectl get namespaces` to access the vcluster
greg@gregPowerPC:~$ |
```

***Figure 6-36.** Creating a second virtual cluster*

We can see our second cluster environment is completely isolated from any workload or even CRDs or controllers we created any in the first cluster.

```
greg@gregPowerPC:~$ kc get pods -n demo-nginx
No resources found in demo-nginx namespace.
greg@gregPowerPC:~$ |
```

***Figure 6-37.** Getting pods from the new cluster*

Let's prove it. We couldn't isolate CRDs with namespaces as they are installed cluster-wide—this is super useful for our use case with vCluster. Below we create two vClusters within our master cluster, which runs on KinD.

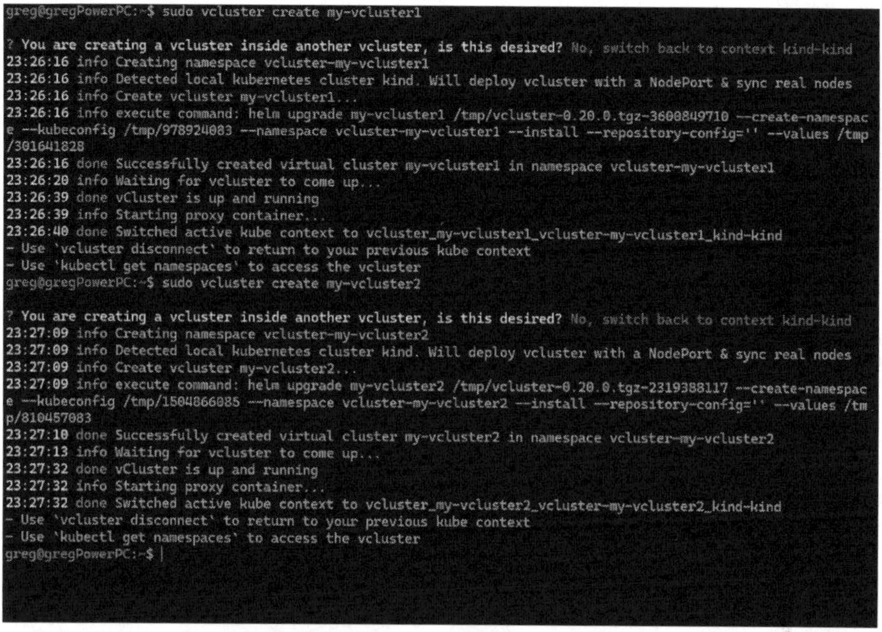

```
greg@gregPowerPC:~$ sudo vcluster create my-vcluster1

? You are creating a vcluster inside another vcluster, is this desired? No, switch back to context kind-kind
23:26:16 info Creating namespace vcluster-my-vcluster1
23:26:16 info Detected local kubernetes cluster kind. Will deploy vcluster with a NodePort & sync real nodes
23:26:16 info Create vcluster my-vcluster1...
23:26:16 info execute command: helm upgrade my-vcluster1 /tmp/vcluster-0.20.0.tgz-3600849710 --create-namespac
e --kubeconfig /tmp/978924083 --namespace vcluster-my-vcluster1 --install --repository-config='' --values /tmp
/301641828
23:26:16 done Successfully created virtual cluster my-vcluster1 in namespace vcluster-my-vcluster1
23:26:20 info Waiting for vcluster to come up...
23:26:39 done vCluster is up and running
23:26:39 info Starting proxy container...
23:26:40 done Switched active kube context to vcluster_my-vcluster1_vcluster-my-vcluster1_kind-kind
- Use `vcluster disconnect` to return to your previous kube context
- Use `kubectl get namespaces` to access the vcluster
greg@gregPowerPC:~$ sudo vcluster create my-vcluster2

? You are creating a vcluster inside another vcluster, is this desired? No, switch back to context kind-kind
23:27:09 info Creating namespace vcluster-my-vcluster2
23:27:09 info Detected local kubernetes cluster kind. Will deploy vcluster with a NodePort & sync real nodes
23:27:09 info Create vcluster my-vcluster2...
23:27:09 info execute command: helm upgrade my-vcluster2 /tmp/vcluster-0.20.0.tgz-2319388117 --create-namespac
e --kubeconfig /tmp/1504866085 --namespace vcluster-my-vcluster2 --install --repository-config='' --values /tm
p/810457083
23:27:10 done Successfully created virtual cluster my-vcluster2 in namespace vcluster-my-vcluster2
23:27:13 info Waiting for vcluster to come up...
23:27:32 done vCluster is up and running
23:27:32 info Starting proxy container...
23:27:32 done Switched active kube context to vcluster_my-vcluster2_vcluster-my-vcluster2_kind-kind
- Use `vcluster disconnect` to return to your previous kube context
- Use `kubectl get namespaces` to access the vcluster
greg@gregPowerPC:~$ |
```

Figure 6-38. *Listing cluster resources like CRDs*

Let's consider below CRD:

```
apiVersion: apiextensions.k8s.io/v1
kind: CustomResourceDefinition
metadata:
  name: myresources.example.com
spec:
  group: example.com
```

```
  versions:
  - name: v1
    served: true
    storage: true
    schema:
      openAPIV3Schema:
        type: object
        properties:
          spec:
            type: object
            properties:
              name:
                type: string
              size:
                type: integer
  scope: Namespaced
  names:
    plural: myresources
    singular: myresource
    kind: MyResource
    shortNames:
    - mr
```

Let's apply CRD in the first cluster:

```
sudo kubectl apply -f crd.yaml
```

```
greg@gregPowerPC:~$ sudo kubectl apply -f crd.yaml
customresourcedefinition.apiextensions.k8s.io/myresources.example.com created
greg@gregPowerPC:~$ sudo kubectl get crd
NAME                      CREATED AT
myresources.example.com   2024-09-20T22:31:01Z
greg@gregPowerPC:~$ |
```

Figure 6-39. *Applying CRD in one of the clusters*

Now we will switch to the second cluster to prove CRD is not visible there, which would not be possible using a native "physical" Kubernetes cluster.

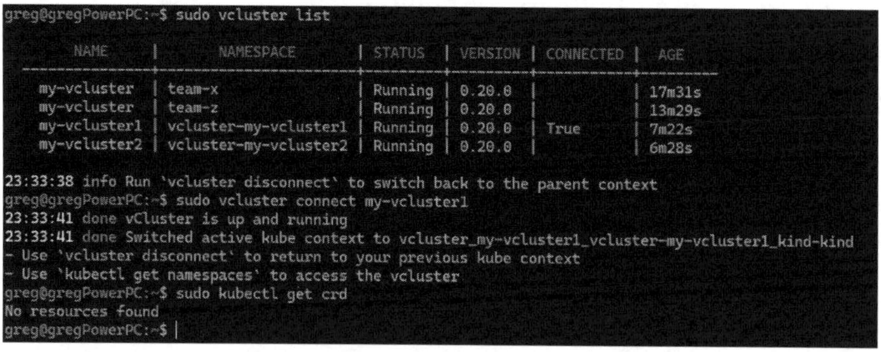

```
greg@gregPowerPC:~$ sudo vcluster list

      NAME      |       NAMESPACE        | STATUS  | VERSION | CONNECTED |  AGE
  --------------+------------------------+---------+---------+-----------+---------
   my-vcluster  | team-x                 | Running | 0.20.0  |           | 17m31s
   my-vcluster  | team-z                 | Running | 0.20.0  |           | 13m29s
   my-vcluster1 | vcluster-my-vcluster1  | Running | 0.20.0  | True      | 7m22s
   my-vcluster2 | vcluster-my-vcluster2  | Running | 0.20.0  |           | 6m28s

23:33:38 info Run `vcluster disconnect` to switch back to the parent context
greg@gregPowerPC:~$ sudo vcluster connect my-vcluster1
23:33:41 done vCluster is up and running
23:33:41 done Switched active kube context to vcluster_my-vcluster1_vcluster-my-vcluster1_kind-kind
- Use `vcluster disconnect` to return to your previous kube context
- Use `kubectl get namespaces` to access the vcluster
greg@gregPowerPC:~$ sudo kubectl get crd
No resources found
greg@gregPowerPC:~$ |
```

***Figure 6-40.** Checking if CRD applied in the first cluster wasn't created in the second cluster*

In the output we can see there are no CRDs installed in our second cluster or within our master cluster.

```
greg@gregPowerPC:~$ sudo kubectl cluster-info --context kind-kind
Kubernetes control plane is running at https://127.0.0.1:40243
CoreDNS is running at https://127.0.0.1:40243/api/v1/namespaces/kube-system/services/kube-dns:dns/proxy

To further debug and diagnose cluster problems, use 'kubectl cluster-info dump'.
greg@gregPowerPC:~$ sudo kubectl get crd
No resources found
greg@gregPowerPC:~$ |
```

***Figure 6-41.** Checking CRDs in the master cluster*

Scaling and Resiliency Chapter Summary

This chapter provides strategies to enhance scalability and resilience in Kubernetes environments. Key topics include setting resource limits and requests for efficient resource allocation, implementing deployment strategies like rolling updates and blue-green deployments, and leveraging autoscaling mechanisms such as HPA, VPA, and KEDA. Advanced configuration management with Kustomize and PodTopologySpread ensures efficient scaling and fault tolerance. The chapter also explores securing the control plane, optimizing container image registries, and deployment strategies for zero-downtime updates. Tools like Karpenter and vCluster are introduced for high-performance scaling and multi-tenancy management, addressing complex workloads while maintaining resiliency and operational efficiency.

CHAPTER 7

Storage in Kubernetes

As applications evolve, the demands for data storage for persistent and non-persistent data grow increasingly complex. In the dynamic environment of Kubernetes, managing persistent storage presents unique challenges, such as ensuring data consistency, handling the lifecycle of storage resources, and optimizing performance. Kubernetes offers robust solutions to these problems through its storage management features, including persistent volumes (PVs), Persistent Volume Claims (PVCs), and storage classes.

This chapter guides us into the intricacies of managing storage in Kubernetes, providing practical steps and insights for effectively leveraging these storage mechanisms. Whether we are dealing with stateful applications that require data persistence or seeking to automate storage provisioning for scalable applications, this chapter offers the guidance we need.

7.1 Storage for Containerized Workloads

Effectively managing storage for containerized workloads is crucial for ensuring data persistence, consistency, and optimal performance in dynamic and scalable environments like Kubernetes.

G. Stencel and L. Berton, *Kubernetes Recipes*,
https://doi.org/10.1007/979-8-8688-1325-2_7

Problem

Containerized applications often require persistent storage to retain data beyond the lifespan of individual containers. This persistent storage need presents challenges in dynamic and scalable environments like Kubernetes. Specifically, managing the lifecycle of storage resources, ensuring data consistency, and optimizing performance are common problems.

Solution

Kubernetes manages storage via persistent volumes (PVs), Persistent Volume Claims (PVCs), and storage classes. Here's how we can manage storage for containerized workloads:

1. **Define a Persistent Volume (PV)**: Create a YAML file to define a persistent volume, for example:

```
apiVersion: v1
kind: PersistentVolume
metadata:
  name: pv-example
spec:
  capacity:
    storage: 10Gi
  accessModes:
    - ReadWriteOnce
  persistentVolumeReclaimPolicy: Retain
  storageClassName: standard
  hostPath:
    path: "/mnt/data"
```

2. **Define a Persistent Volume Claim (PVC)**: Create a YAML file to define a Persistent Volume Claim, for example:

```
apiVersion: v1
kind: PersistentVolumeClaim
metadata:
  name: pvc-example
spec:
  accessModes:
    - ReadWriteOnce
  resources:
    requests:
      storage: 10Gi
  storageClassName: standard
```

3. **Deploy an Application Using the PVC**: Modify our application deployment YAML file to use the PVC, for example:

```
apiVersion: apps/v1
kind: Deployment
metadata:
  name: nginx-deployment
spec:
  replicas: 1
  selector:
    matchLabels:
      app: nginx
  template:
    metadata:
      labels:
        app: nginx
```

```
spec:
  containers:
  - name: nginx
    image: nginx:latest
    volumeMounts:
    - mountPath: "/usr/share/nginx/html"
      name: storage
  volumes:
  - name: storage
    persistentVolumeClaim:
      claimName: pvc-example
```

4. **Apply the Configurations**: Apply the PV, PVC, and application deployment configurations using `kubectl`:

```
kubectl apply -f pv.yaml
kubectl apply -f pvc.yaml
kubectl apply -f deployment.yaml
```

Discussion

Managing storage in Kubernetes involves understanding and correctly implementing persistent volumes, Persistent Volume Claims, and storage classes. PVs are storage resources in the cluster, while PVCs are requests for those resources. Storage classes provide a way to define different types of storage (e.g., fast SSDs, slow HDDs) and their provisioning parameters.

Persistent Volumes (PV)

PVs are resources in the cluster that provide durable storage. They have a lifecycle independent of any individual pod that uses the PV. They are defined by a YAML file and include details such as storage capacity and access modes (e.g., `ReadWriteOnce`, `ReadOnlyMany`, `ReadWriteMany`).

Persistent Volume Claims (PVC)

PVCs are requests for storage by a user. They are similar to a pod in that they consume resources in the cluster. PVCs can request specific sizes and access modes, and Kubernetes will bind the PVC to an available PV that meets the requirements.

Storage Classes

Storage classes allow administrators to define different types of storage offered in a cluster. Each storage class might map to a different quality-of-service level, such as IOPS performance or backup policies.

7.2 Defining StorageClass

Problem

Manually provisioning persistent volumes (PVs) can be time-consuming and error-prone, especially in dynamic environments where storage needs frequently change. This approach lacks flexibility and can lead to inefficiencies in resource utilization.

Solution

Use a **StorageClass** to enable dynamic provisioning of PVs. A **StorageClass** defines the parameters and provisioner for storage backends, allowing Kubernetes to automatically create PVs on demand based on PVC requests.

Here's an example **StorageClass** definition:

```
apiVersion: storage.k8s.io/v1
kind: StorageClass
metadata:
  name: fast-storage
```

```
provisioner: kubernetes.io/aws-ebs
provisioner
parameters:
  type: gp2
reclaimPolicy: Retain
volumeBindingMode: Immediate
```

This configuration sets up a **storage class** named `fast-storage`, which uses AWS EBS as the storage backend and gp2 as the storage type. Adjust the provisioner and parameters based on your environment (e.g., GCP PD, Azure Disk, or Network File System (NFS)).

Discussion

- **Dynamic Provisioning**: A StorageClass eliminates the need for predefined PVs by dynamically creating them when PVCs request storage. This significantly reduces administrative overhead and supports scalability.
- **Reclaim Policy**: The `reclaimPolicy` determines what happens to the PV when the PVC is deleted. Common options are `Retain`, `Delete`, and `Recycle`. Choose the policy based on your retention requirements.
- **Volume Binding Mode**: Modes like `Immediate` or `WaitForFirstConsumer` control when and where the volume is provisioned. Use `WaitForFirstConsumer` in environments where the volume must be provisioned close to the requesting workload (e.g., for zone-aware provisioning).
- **Flexibility**: Different StorageClasses can be defined to meet varying workload requirements, such as performance or cost considerations.

7.3 Static Provisioning

Problem

Deploying a stateful application, like a MySQL database, on Kubernetes can be challenging, especially when it comes to ensuring data persistence.

Solution

The solution involves using a PersistentVolumeClaim (PVC) object. Here's a step-by-step guide:

Create a PVC Request:

Prepare a YAML manifest (`data.yaml`) to request storage, for example, 1 GB.

Here's an example of `data.yaml`:

```
apiVersion: v1
kind: PersistentVolumeClaim
metadata:
  name: data
spec:
  accessModes:
    - ReadWriteOnce
  resources:
    requests:
      storage: 1Gi
```

Apply this manifest using the Kubernetes command line:

```
$ kubectl apply -f data.yaml
```

Verify Creation of PVC and PV:

Check the status of PVC and corresponding persistent volume (PV) using

```
$ kubectl get pvc
$ kubectl get pv
```

These commands display the details of the PV, including its status, access modes, and reclaim policy. The default value for the reclaim policy for a PersistentVolume is "Delete," which means the PV and its data are deleted when the PVC is deleted. To ensure data persists beyond the lifecycle of the PVC, set the persistentVolumeReclaimPolicy to the "Retain" value in the PV manifest. More insights are available using the "`describe`" parameter:

```
kubectl describe PersistentVolume data
```

We should see the **STATUS** of our PV change to **Bound**, which indicates a successful claim.

Utilize the Claim in Our Pod:

In our pod's YAML, under the volumes section, reference the PVC.

Mount this volume inside the container, for example, for MySQL, at `/var/lib/mysql`.

Here's an example snippet for a pod manifest:

```
apiVersion: v1
kind: Pod
metadata:
  name: db
spec:
  containers:
  - image: mysql:8.3.0
    name: db
    volumeMounts:
```

```
    - mountPath: /var/lib/mysql
      name: data
    env:
      - name: MYSQL_ROOT_PASSWORD
        value: root
  volumes:
  - name: data
    persistentVolumeClaim:
      claimName: data
```

Discussion

In Kubernetes, the default storage class automatically creates a matching PV when a PVC is requested. This dynamic provisioning is crucial for data persistence in stateful applications. The storage class in Minikube typically uses a `hostPath` provisioner, which means the data is stored on the Minikube virtual machine itself. This setup allows for data persistency, ensuring that if the pod restarts or is deleted, the data remains intact.

See Also

- **Kubernetes Persistent Volume Claim Documentation** (`https://kubernetes.io/docs/concepts/storage/persistent-volumes/`): For more details on how PVC works and how to configure it for different needs
- **Kubernetes Storage Class Documentation** (`https://kubernetes.io/docs/concepts/storage/storage-classes/`): To understand storage classes and how they provide abstraction over physical storage

7.4 Local Persistent Volumes

Problem

Interact with a local persistent volume as a local disk directly attached to a single Kubernetes node. This is necessary for scenarios where high-performance, low-latency storage is required and using remote storage solutions would introduce unacceptable overhead.

Solution

Step 1: Create the StorageClass

Define a StorageClass that uses the `kubernetes.io/no-provisioner` provisioner, which indicates that the volume will not be dynamically provisioned and must be manually created.

```
kind: StorageClass
apiVersion: storage.k8s.io/v1
metadata:
  name: sc-local
provisioner: kubernetes.io/no-provisioner
volumeBindingMode: WaitForFirstConsumer
```

Step 2: Create a Local PersistentVolume

Create a PersistentVolume that references a local path on the node. Ensure that the node affinity is set so that the volume is only used by pods on the specified node.

```
apiVersion: v1
kind: PersistentVolume
metadata:
  name: pv-local
spec:
```

```
  capacity:
    storage: 10Gi
  accessModes:
    - ReadWriteOnce
  persistentVolumeReclaimPolicy: Retain
  storageClassName: sc-local
  local:
    path: /data/volume1
  nodeAffinity:
    required:
      nodeSelectorTerms:
        - matchExpressions:
            - key: kubernetes.io/hostname
              operator: In
              values:
                - worker-01
```

Step 3: Create a PersistentVolumeClaim

Create a PersistentVolumeClaim to request the local storage defined in the PersistentVolume.

```
kind: PersistentVolumeClaim
apiVersion: v1
metadata:
  name: pvc-local
spec:
  accessModes:
    - ReadWriteOnce
  storageClassName: sc-local
  resources:
    requests:
      storage: 10Gi
```

Step 4: Deploy the Configurations

Apply the configurations using `kubectl`:

```
kubectl apply -f storageclass.yaml
kubectl apply -f persistentvolume.yaml
kubectl apply -f persistentvolumeclaim.yaml
```

Discussion

Local persistent volumes (PVs) are useful for workloads that require high-performance and low-latency access to storage. These volumes are physically attached to the Kubernetes nodes, and as such, they are limited by the node's lifecycle. If the node goes down, the data on the local PV may become unavailable.

The key components in this setup are

- **StorageClass**: Defines the class of storage and specifies that no dynamic provisioning should occur (`kubernetes.io/no-provisioner`). The `WaitForFirstConsumer` volume binding mode ensures that the PersistentVolumeClaim is only bound to a PersistentVolume when a pod that uses the PVC is scheduled, which helps in ensuring that the pod and volume are co-located on the same node.

- **PersistentVolume**: Represents a piece of storage in the cluster that has been manually created and made available to the cluster. It includes node affinity settings to restrict the use of the volume to a specific node.

- **PersistentVolumeClaim**: A user's request for storage that consumes the resources offered by a PersistentVolume.

Here's an example output after creating the PV and PVC:

```
kubectl get pv
NAME        CAPACITY   ACCESS MODES   RECLAIM POLICY
   STATUS       CLAIM   STORAGECLASS   AGE
pv-local    10Gi        RWO             Retain
   Available            sc-local        43s

kubectl get pvc
$ kubectl get pvc
NAME        STATUS    VOLUME      CAPACITY    ACCESS MODES
   STORAGECLASS    AGE
pvc-local    Bound     local-pv    10Gi         RWO
   sc-local        2m
```

The "Pending" status indicates that the `PersistentVolume` is available but has not yet been bound to a `PersistentVolumeClaim`, which will happen when a pod requests storage. The "Pending" status of a PVC typically indicates that Kubernetes cannot find a matching PV to bind to the PVC. Ensuring that the StorageClass is correctly configured and that there are matching PVs available are critical steps in resolving this issue. Checking events and logs provides additional insight into any underlying problems. The desired status for a PVC is "Bound," which indicates that the PVC has been successfully matched to a PersistentVolume (PV) and is ready for use by a pod.

7.5 Dynamic Provisioning Volumes

Problem

In a Kubernetes environment, applications often need persistent storage that survives pod restarts and failures. Manually provisioning storage volumes and binding them to specific pods is time-consuming and not scalable. There is a need for a system that can dynamically provision storage volumes based on the demands of the pods, ensuring data persistence while maintaining the flexibility and scalability that containerized applications require.

Solution

The solution involves creating a `StorageClass` resource that uses the NFS Container Storage Interface (CSI) driver for dynamic volume provisioning. When a pod requests persistent storage through a PVC, Kubernetes uses the specified `StorageClass` to automatically create the necessary storage on the NFS server and bind it to the pod. This approach streamlines storage management and integrates seamlessly with Kubernetes deployments.

Here's how to implement it:

1. Install the NFS CSI driver to enable Kubernetes to manage NFS-based persistent storage.

   ```
   kubectl apply -k "github.com/kubernetes-csi/csi-driver-nfs/deploy/kubernetes/overlays/stable?ref=master"
   ```

2. **Define the NFS StorageClass**

   Create a `storageclass.yaml` file to define a `StorageClass` that uses the NFS CSI provisioner. This StorageClass points to our NFS server and specifies the NFS version, among other mount options.

   ```
   apiVersion: storage.k8s.io/v1
   kind: StorageClass
   metadata:
     name: nfs-csi
   ```

```
provisioner: nfs.csi.k8s.io
parameters:
  server: nfs-server
  share: /export/volumes/pod
reclaimPolicy: Delete
volumeBindingMode: Immediate
mountOptions:
  - nfsvers=4.1
```

3. **Deploy a PersistentVolumeClaim**

   Create a `nfs-csi.nginx.yaml` file that includes a PVC definition. This PVC uses the previously defined `StorageClass` to request a 10 Gi volume.

```
apiVersion: v1
kind: PersistentVolumeClaim
metadata:
  name: pvc-nfs-csi
spec:
  accessModes:
    - ReadWriteOnce
  storageClassName: nfs-csi
  resources:
    requests:
      storage: 10Gi
```

4. **Deploy an Application Using the PVC**

   The same `nfs-csi.nginx.yaml` file should also define a deployment that mounts the dynamically provisioned volume into a Nginx container. This demonstrates how an application can use the NFS-backed persistent storage.

```
apiVersion: apps/v1
kind: Deployment
metadata:
  name: nginx-nfs-csi-deployment
spec:
  replicas: 1
  selector:
    matchLabels:
      app: nginx
  template:
    metadata:
      labels:
        app: nginx
    spec:
      volumes:
      - name: webcontent
        persistentVolumeClaim:
          claimName: pvc-nfs-csi
      containers:
      - name: nginx
        image: nginx
        ports:
        - containerPort: 80
        volumeMounts:
        - name: webcontent
          mountPath: "/usr/share/nginx/html/web-app"
```

Additionally, a service is defined as exposing the Nginx deployment.

5. **Apply the Configuration**

   Apply the configurations using the following:

   ```
   kubectl apply -f storageclass.yaml
   kubectl apply -f nfs-csi.nginx.yaml
   ```

Discussion

Kubernetes supports dynamic volume configuration, allowing us to create storage volumes on demand when needed. Therefore, administrators do not have to manually create new storage volumes and then create a `PersistentVolume` object for use in the cluster. When the user requests a specific type of storage, the entire process runs automatically.

This setup automates the provisioning of NFS-backed volumes for Kubernetes pods. When the pod that uses the PVC is deleted, the dynamic volume is also automatically deleted due to the `reclaimPolicy: Delete`. This behavior ensures efficient use of resources and simplifies cleanup. However, we can change the `reclaimPolicy` to Retain if we need to retain the data.

It's important to have our NFS server configured and accessible from within our Kubernetes cluster. Ensure proper network configurations and permissions are in place for seamless operation.

See Also

- **Kubernetes Documentation on Persistent Volumes**: For a deeper understanding of PVs, PVCs, and dynamic provisioning
- **NFS CSI Driver GitHub Repository**: To explore the driver's capabilities, configuration options, and updates
- **Ansible for Kubernetes**: Automate the deployment and management of our Kubernetes clusters and NFS configurations

7.6 NFS Volume

Problem

We need to deploy a Nginx application in Kubernetes with persistent storage provided by a NFS (Network File System) using the Container Storage Interface (CSI). This setup ensures that our Nginx deployment can store and retrieve data persistently across pod restarts and rescheduling.

Solution

Define the Kubernetes resources in a YAML file (`nfs-csi.nginx.yaml`), which include

- PersistentVolumeClaim (PVC) using the NFS CSI StorageClass
- Nginx deployment that mounts the volume from the PVC
- Service to expose the Nginx application

```
apiVersion: v1
kind: PersistentVolumeClaim
metadata:
  name: pvc-nfs-csi
spec:
  accessModes:
    - ReadWriteMany
  storageClassName: nfs-csi
  resources:
    requests:
      storage: 1Gi
---
```

```
apiVersion: apps/v1
kind: Deployment
metadata:
  name: nginx-nfs-csi-deployment
spec:
  replicas: 1
  selector:
    matchLabels:
      app: nginx-nfs-csi
  template:
    metadata:
      labels:
        app: nginx-nfs-csi
    spec:
      containers:
        - name: nginx
          image: nginx:latest
          volumeMounts:
            - mountPath: "/usr/share/nginx/html"
              name: nfs-csi-volume
      volumes:
        - name: nfs-csi-volume
          persistentVolumeClaim:
            claimName: pvc-nfs-csi
---
apiVersion: v1
kind: Service
metadata:
  name: nginx-nfs-csi-service
spec:
  selector:
```

```
    app: nginx-nfs-csi
  ports:
    - protocol: TCP
      port: 80
      targetPort: 80
```

Apply the YAML file:

```
kubectl apply -f nfs-csi.nginx.yaml
```

Here's an expected output:

```
persistentvolumeclaim/pvc-nfs-csi created
deployment.apps/nginx-nfs-csi-deployment created
service/nginx-nfs-csi-service created
```

Inspect the PersistentVolume (PV) and PersistentVolumeClaim (PVC)

Verify the PVC and its binding to the PV:

```
kubectl get PersistentVolume
kubectl get PersistentVolumeClaim
```

Check the Bound status to ensure the PVC is properly bound to the PV.

Retrieve the Service IP

Get the external IP address to access the Nginx service:

```
SERVICEIP=$(kubectl get service | grep nginx-nfs-csi-service |
awk '{ print $3 }')
echo $SERVICEIP
```

Check the status of the Nginx pod to ensure it is running:

```
kubectl get pods
```

Copy the Web Page into the PVC Volume

List the volumes and get the PVC directory name:

```
ls /export/volumes/pod/
```

This will return the directory name prefixed by `pvc`. Note this name for the following command to copy our web page (e.g., `demo.html`) into the PVC directory:

```
sudo cp -v /export/volumes/pod/demo.html /export/volumes/
pod/<<pvc_directory_name>>/
```

Verify the HTML File Contents in the Pod

Enter the Nginx pod and list the HTML directory:

```
kubectl exec -it <<pod_name>> -- /bin/bash
ls /usr/share/nginx/html/web-app
cat /usr/share/nginx/html/web-app/demo.html
exit
```

Access the Rendered Web Page

Use a browser to access the web page:

```
http://$SERVICEIP/web-app/demo.html
```

Discussion

Using NFS CSI for storage in a Kubernetes deployment allows for persistent storage that can be shared across multiple pods. This is particularly useful for applications that require shared access to the same storage volume. NFS CSI provides a flexible and scalable solution for such needs.

7.7 Azure Dynamic Provisioning

Problem

We need to set up and use Azure Kubernetes Service (AKS) to manage persistent storage using StorageClasses and dynamic provisioning. This involves creating, describing, and utilizing storage resources with the storage account type for the managed disk, which can be set only during the creation of the scale set, with various options like Standard HDD (Standard_LRS), Standard SSD (StandardSSD_LRS), Premium SSD (Premium_LRS), Ultra disk (UltraSSD_LRS for data disks only), and zone-redundant storage options (Premium_ZRS and StandardSSD_ZRS).

Solution

Step 1: Define the Custom StorageClass

1. Create a YAML file for the custom StorageClass:
   Create a file named `CustomStorageClass.yaml` with the following content:

```
apiVersion: storage.k8s.io/v1
kind: StorageClass
metadata:
  name: managed-standard-ssd
parameters:
  cachingmode: ReadOnly
  kind: Managed
  storageaccounttype: StandardSSD_LRS
provisioner: kubernetes.io/azure-disk
```

2. Apply the custom StorageClass configuration:

```
kubectl apply -f CustomStorageClass.yaml
```

Step 2: Verify the Custom StorageClass

1. List the current StorageClasses:

```
kubectl get storageclass
```

2. Describe the custom StorageClass:

```
kubectl describe storageclass managed-standard-ssd
```

Step 3: Use the Custom StorageClass

1. Create a PersistentVolumeClaim and deployment using the custom StorageClass:

   Create a file named `AzureDiskCustomStorageClass.yaml` with the following content:

```
apiVersion: v1
kind: PersistentVolumeClaim
metadata:
  name: pvc-azure-standard-ssd
spec:
  accessModes:
  - ReadWriteOnce
  storageClassName: managed-standard-ssd
  resources:
    requests:
      storage: 10Gi
---
apiVersion: apps/v1
kind: Deployment
metadata:
  name: nginx-azdisk-deployment-standard-ssd
spec:
  replicas: 1
```

```
  selector:
    matchLabels:
      app: nginx
  template:
    metadata:
      labels:
        app: nginx
    spec:
      volumes:
      - name: webcontent
        persistentVolumeClaim:
          claimName: pvc-azure-standard-ssd
      containers:
      - name: nginx
        image: nginx
        ports:
        - containerPort: 80
        volumeMounts:
        - name: webcontent

          mountPath: "/usr/share/nginx/html/web-app"
```

2. Apply the deployment configuration:

```
kubectl apply -f AzureDiskCustomStorageClass.yaml
```

Step 4: Verify Resources

1. Check the PersistentVolumeClaim:

```
kubectl get persistentvolumeclaim
```

2. Check the PersistentVolume:

```
kubectl get persistentvolume
```

3. Verify the pod creation:

```
kubectl get pods
```

Discussion

StorageClasses provide a way for administrators to describe the different types of storage available in the cluster. Each StorageClass can specify a different provisioner that knows how to create volumes of that type. Defining custom StorageClasses allows us to tailor the storage behavior to the specific needs of our applications, such as setting specific parameters for performance or redundancy. Dynamic provisioning allows Kubernetes to automatically provision storage resources when a PersistentVolumeClaim (PVC) is created. This removes the need for a cluster administrator to create storage resources manually. The same process applies to Amazon Web Services and Google Cloud Platform.

7.8 Amazon EFS

Problem

We need to dynamically provision storage for our Kubernetes applications using Amazon Elastic File System (EFS). Dynamic provisioning simplifies the process by automatically creating access points and PersistentVolumes (PVs) as needed. This approach avoids the manual intervention required for static provisioning.

Solution

To dynamically provision storage with Amazon EFS in Kubernetes, follow these steps:

1. Set up the Amazon EFS CSI driver to allow Kubernetes to handle EFS-based persistent storage. Verify that the appropriate security groups and network configurations are in place.

   ```
   kubectl apply -k "github.com/kubernetes-sigs/aws-
   efs-csi-driver/deploy/kubernetes/overlays/stable/
   ecr/?ref=release-2.x"
   ```

2. **Create an Amazon EFS File System:** Go to the Amazon EFS console and create a new file system (`myEFS2`).

3. Ensure you set up the necessary security groups and network configurations, including VPC and subnets, to allow access to the EFS file system from your Kubernetes cluster.

   ```
   aws ec2 create-security-group \
       --group-name EFSAccessSecurityGroup \
       --description "Security group for EFS access from
         Kubernetes cluster" \
       --vpc-id <your-vpc-id>

   aws ec2 authorize-security-group-ingress \
       --group-id <security-group-id> \
       --protocol tcp \
       --port 2049 \
       --cidr <kubernetes-cluster-cidr>
   ```

Replace `<your-vpc-id>` with your VPC ID, `<security-group-id>` with the ID from the first command, and `<kubernetes-cluster-cidr>` with your cluster's CIDR block.

```
aws efs create-mount-target \
    --file-system-id <efs-id> \
    --subnet-id <subnet-id> \
    --security-groups <security-group-id>
```

Replace `<efs-id>` with your EFS file system ID, `<subnet-id>` with the appropriate subnet ID in your VPC, and `<security-group-id>` with the ID of the security group created earlier.

4. **Create a StorageClass for EFS:** Define a `sc.yaml` StorageClass that references the EFS file system.

```
kind: StorageClass
apiVersion: storage.k8s.io/v1
metadata:
  name: efs-sc
provisioner: efs.csi.aws.com
parameters:
  provisioningMode: efs-ap
  fileSystemId: fs-029bb6e31bea97453
  directoryPerms: "700"
```

5. **Deploy the StorageClass:** Apply the StorageClass configuration to our cluster.

```
$ kubectl apply -f sc.yaml
```

Create a PersistentVolumeClaim (PVC) and a Pod: Define a `pvc_pod.yaml` PVC and a pod that will use the dynamically provisioned EFS storage.

```
apiVersion: v1
kind: PersistentVolumeClaim
metadata:
  name: efs-claim-1
spec:
  accessModes:
    - ReadWriteMany
  storageClassName: efs-sc
  resources:
    requests:
      storage: 5Gi
---
apiVersion: v1
kind: Pod
metadata:
  name: efs-app-1
spec:
  containers:
    - name: app
      image: centos
      command: ["/bin/sh"]
      args: ["-c", "while true; do echo $(date -u) >>
      /data/out; sleep 5; done"]
      volumeMounts:
        - name: persistent-storage
          mountPath: /data
```

```
volumes:
  - name: persistent-storage
    persistentVolumeClaim:
      claimName: efs-claim-1
```

6. **Deploy the PVC and Pod**: Apply the PVC and pod configuration to our cluster.

```
$ kubectl apply -f pvc_pod.yaml
```

7. **Verify the Deployment:** Check the status of the PVC, PV, and pod.

```
$ kubectl get pvc
$ kubectl get pv | grep efs-sc
$ kubectl get pods
```

8. **Monitor the Pod's Output:** Use `kubectl exec` to monitor the output generated by the pod, ensuring it is writing to the EFS volume.

```
$ kubectl exec -ti efs-app-1 -- tail -f /data/out
```

Discussion

Dynamic provisioning using the Amazon EFS CSI driver allows Kubernetes to handle the creation and management of storage resources. By specifying `provisioningMode: efs-ap`, the driver creates a unique access point for each PersistentVolumeClaim, ensuring multiple applications can share the same EFS file system while maintaining isolation through different POSIX UID/GID configurations. This method streamlines the deployment process by automating the setup of storage, which is especially beneficial in environments that require frequent provisioning of storage resources. It also enhances scalability and flexibility, as new applications can be deployed to create storage resources without manual intervention.

7.9 Regional Persistent Disks in GKE

Problem

Ensuring the high availability of stateful applications in Google Kubernetes Engine (GKE) requires the use of persistent storage that can tolerate zone failures. Regional persistent disks provide this capability by replicating data across multiple zones. The challenge lies in efficiently provisioning these disks to meet application demands.

Solution

To provision regional persistent disks in GKE, we can either dynamically provision them using a StorageClass or manually create them in advance. Dynamic provisioning is recommended for its flexibility and ease of management. Here's how to do both:

Dynamic Provisioning of Regional Persistent Disks

1. **Create a StorageClass:** Define a `regionalpd-storageclass.yaml` StorageClass that specifies the replication type and allowed topologies (zones).

```
kind: StorageClass
apiVersion: storage.k8s.io/v1
metadata:
  name: regionalpd-storageclass
provisioner: pd.csi.storage.gke.io
parameters:
  type: pd-balanced
  replication-type: regional-pd
volumeBindingMode: WaitForFirstConsumer
allowedTopologies:
- matchLabelExpressions:
```

```
- key: topology.gke.io/zone
  values:
  - europe-west1-b
  - europe-west1-c
```

Apply the StorageClass:

```
$ kubectl apply -f regionalpd-storageclass.yaml
```

2. **Create a PersistentVolumeClaim (PVC):** Define a PVC that references the StorageClass.

```
apiVersion: v1
kind: PersistentVolumeClaim
metadata:
  name: regional-pvc
spec:
  accessModes:
    - ReadWriteOnce
  resources:
    requests:
      storage: 500Gi
  storageClassName: regionalpd-storageclass
```

Apply the PVC:

```
$ kubectl apply -f regional-pvc.yaml
```

3. **Create a Pod:** Define a `task-pv-pod.yaml` pod that uses the PVC.

```
kind: Pod
apiVersion: v1
metadata:
  name: task-pv-pod
```

```
spec:
  volumes:
    - name: task-pv-storage
      persistentVolumeClaim:
        claimName: regional-pvc
  containers:
    - name: task-pv-container
      image: nginx
      ports:
        - containerPort: 80
          name: "http-server"
      volumeMounts:
        - mountPath: "/usr/share/nginx/html"
          name: task-pv-storage
```

Apply the Pod Definition:

```
$ kubectl apply -f task-pv-pod.yaml
```

Manual Provisioning of Regional Persistent Disks

If dynamic provisioning does not meet our needs, we can manually create and configure regional persistent disks:

1. **Create a Regional Persistent Disk:** Use the Google Cloud Console or gcloud CLI to create a regional persistent disk. Ensure the disk is available in the desired zones.

```
$ gcloud compute disks create regional-disk \
    --type=pd-balanced \
    --size=500GB \
    --region=europe-west1 \
    --replica-zones=europe-west1-b,europe-west1-c
```

2. **Create PersistentVolume (PV):** Define a `regional-pv.yaml` PV that references the manually created disk.

```
apiVersion: v1
kind: PersistentVolume
metadata:
  name: regional-pv
spec:
  capacity:
    storage: 500Gi
  accessModes:
    - ReadWriteOnce
  gcePersistentDisk:
    pdName: regional-disk
    fsType: ext4
  persistentVolumeReclaimPolicy: Retain
```

Apply the PV Definition:

```
$ kubectl apply -f regional-pv.yaml
```

3. **Create PVC and Pod:** Define a PVC that binds to the manually created PV, and then create a pod to use the PVC as demonstrated in the dynamic provisioning steps.

Discussion

Using regional persistent disks in GKE ensures that our data is replicated across multiple zones, providing high availability and resilience against zone failures. Dynamic provisioning is generally preferred because it simplifies management and scales with application demands. The CSI driver over the in-tree provisioner is recommended due to better support and ongoing updates. The lifecycle of a PersistentVolume in Kubernetes is managed by the platform itself. This includes dynamic provisioning and deletion of storage resources, eliminating the need for manual intervention. PersistentVolumes can be backed by various storage solutions, including Google Cloud's persistent disks, NFS solutions like Filestore, and managed services like Cloud Volumes Service.

- **Filestore**: A managed NFS solution on Google Cloud. For setup instructions, refer to the Filestore documentation.
- **Cloud Volumes Service**: A fully managed cloud-based data storage service offering advanced data management capabilities and highly scalable performance.

Summary

Kubernetes storage management uses efficient storage solutions to ensure the stability and scalability of containerized applications. With its robust mechanisms, such as persistent volumes (PVs), Persistent Volume Claims (PVCs), and storage classes, Kubernetes offers a comprehensive suite of tools to manage persistent and ephemeral storage needs effectively. One of the significant advancements discussed is the Container Storage Interface (CSI), which decouples storage plugins from Kubernetes core and allows storage vendors to develop independently and innovate faster. This separation enhances the modularity and flexibility of Kubernetes, enabling users to adopt the latest storage technologies without waiting for Kubernetes' release cycles. The dynamic provisioning capabilities provided by CSI and other Kubernetes features streamline storage management by automating the creation and management of storage volumes based on user-defined specifications. This automation is crucial for modern applications that demand agile and scalable storage solutions. The ability to define custom StorageClasses tailored to specific application needs is another powerful feature that enables applications to leverage storage optimized for performance, redundancy, or other particular requirements. The dynamic nature of Kubernetes storage provisioning, which automatically allocates resources as needed, significantly reduces the operational overhead on administrators and allows for more efficient resource utilization. Practical examples and use cases demonstrate the real-world application of these concepts, from setting up NFS-backed persistent storage to leveraging local persistent volumes for high-performance needs. These examples underscore the flexibility and power of Kubernetes in managing diverse storage requirements seamlessly. Effective storage management is integral to the success of containerized applications in Kubernetes. The features and tools provided by Kubernetes simplify the storage provisioning process and ensure that storage solutions are scalable, reliable, and aligned with the dynamic nature of modern applications. As Kubernetes continues to evolve, its storage capabilities provide robust support for the next generation of cloud-native applications.

CHAPTER 8

Networking in Kubernetes

One of the most critical components of any Kubernetes deployment is networking. Efficient and secure networking is the backbone that connects all services, enabling seamless communication, load balancing, and traffic management within and beyond the cluster.

This chapter aims to provide a comprehensive understanding of networking in Kubernetes, covering essential concepts, configurations, and best practices. By delving into the intricacies of Kubernetes networking, we will equip you with the knowledge and skills necessary to navigate and optimize your cluster's network infrastructure.

We will start with the foundational principles of Kubernetes networking, explaining how pods, services, and nodes interact within the cluster. From there, we will explore the various types of services and how to configure them, including ClusterIP, NodePort, and LoadBalancer, to ensure your applications are accessible and resilient.

Next, we will guide you through the setup and management of load balancers, ensuring high availability and scalability for your applications. Network policies will also be a focal point, demonstrating how to enforce security rules and control traffic flow within your cluster.

Furthermore, we will delve into network Access Control Lists (ACLs), providing insights into securing your network and preventing unauthorized access. We will also cover advanced topics, including traffic routing with

G. Stencel and L. Berton, *Kubernetes Recipes*,
https://doi.org/10.1007/979-8-8688-1325-2_8

Istio, a robust service mesh that offers fine-grained control over traffic behavior, and CertManager, simplifying certificate management for securing communications.

Finally, we will explore external DNS integration, enabling dynamic DNS updates for Kubernetes services and other advanced networking tools and techniques that can enhance your cluster's performance and security.

By the end of this chapter, you will have a thorough understanding of Kubernetes networking and be equipped with practical knowledge to implement, manage, and optimize your network infrastructure. Whether you are a developer, system administrator, or DevOps engineer, this chapter will provide the essential insights needed to master networking in Kubernetes and harness its full potential for your applications.

Debugging Kubernetes Networking

When we are debugging our application connectivity, many Kubernetes and network resources are involved when we try to access our application.

In a Kubernetes cluster with MetalLB as the load balancer, the traffic flow when accessing a pod can be visualized as a multi-step process. I'll create a simplified ASCII diagram to show the flow from an external client to a pod, including the role of MetalLB.

Assumptions:

- **External Client**: The source sending traffic into the cluster
- **MetalLB**: Provides LoadBalancer IP to services, typically using BGP or Layer 2 mode
- **Service**: A Kubernetes service (type: LoadBalancer) to route traffic

Pod: The application running inside a pod that receives the traffic

Node: A physical/virtual machine in the Kubernetes cluster that runs the pod

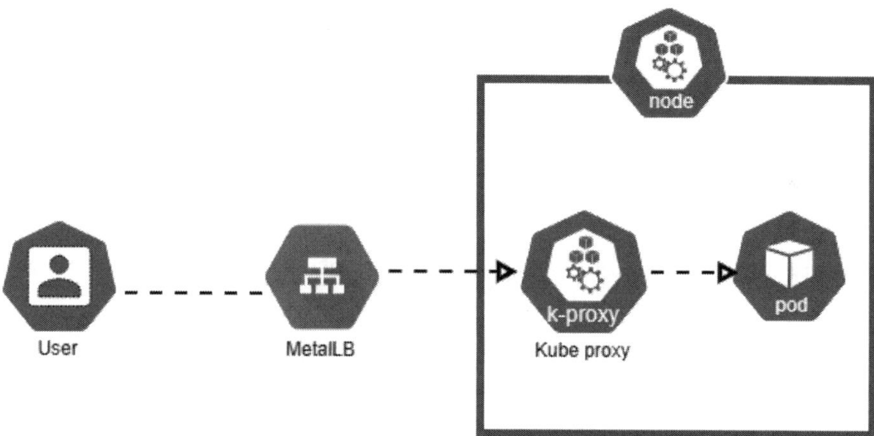

***Figure 8-1.** Breakdown of traffic flow with MetalLB illustration*

Breakdown of Traffic Flow:

External Client → MetalLB LoadBalancer IP:

An external client (e.g., a browser or API client) sends a request to the external IP provided by MetalLB.

This external IP is assigned to a service of type LoadBalancer in the Kubernetes cluster.

MetalLB → Kubernetes Node:

MetalLB directs the traffic to one of the Kubernetes nodes in the cluster. This routing depends on how MetalLB is configured (e.g., in Layer 2 mode or BGP mode).

In Layer 2 mode, MetalLB responds to ARP requests for the assigned external IP, ensuring traffic is routed to the appropriate node.

In BGP mode, MetalLB advertises routes to the external IP to upstream routers, directing traffic to the nodes.

Kubernetes Node → kube-proxy:

When the traffic arrives at the node, the kube-proxy component running on the node handles the traffic.

Based on the service definition, kube-proxy routes the traffic to one of the backend pods associated with the service.

Kubernetes Node → Pod:

kube-proxy selects one of the pods that match the service's label selector.

Traffic is sent to the selected pod over the internal network.

Pod (Application):

Finally, the pod receives the traffic, and the application running inside the pod handles the request (e.g., serving a web page or processing an API request).

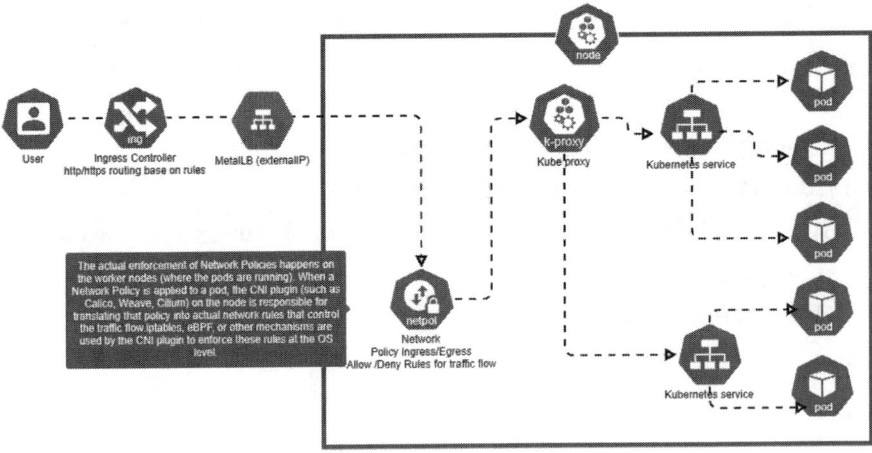

Figure 8-2. *Traffic flow in a Kubernetes cluster*

Debugging networking issues in Kubernetes can involve several steps and tools. It's essential to approach it systematically and deploy tools or debugging pods correctly. Here's a guide to help you with debugging networking issues in Kubernetes.

Netshoot

```
                    dP                dP                           dP
                    88                88                           88
88d888b. .d8888b. d8888P .d8888b. 88d888b. .d8888b. .d8888b. d8888P
88'  `88 88ooood8   88   Y8ooooo. 88'  `88 88'  `88 88'  `88   88
88    88 88.  ...   88         88 88    88 88.  .88 88.  .88   88
dP    dP `88888P'   dP   `88888P' dP    dP `88888P' `88888P'   dP
```

Figure 8-3. *Netshoot logo*

Purpose: Docker and Kubernetes network troubleshooting can become complex. With a proper understanding of how Docker and Kubernetes networking works and the right set of tools, you can troubleshoot and resolve these networking issues. The netshoot container has a set of powerful networking troubleshooting tools that can be used to troubleshoot Docker networking issues. Along with these tools come a set of use cases that show how this container can be used in real-world scenarios.

Network Namespaces: Before using this tool, it's important to go over one key topic: network namespaces. Network namespaces provide isolation of the system resources associated with networking. Docker uses network and other types of namespaces (pid, mount, user, etc.) to create an isolated environment for each container. Everything from interfaces, routes, and IPs is completely isolated within the network namespace of the container.

Kubernetes also uses network namespaces. Kubelet creates a network namespace per pod where all containers in that pod share that same network namespace (eths, IP, TCP sockets, etc.). This is a crucial difference between Docker containers and Kubernetes pods.

The cool thing about namespaces is that you can switch between them. You can enter a different container's network namespace and perform some troubleshooting on its network's stack with tools that aren't even installed on that container. Additionally, netshoot can be used to troubleshoot the host itself by using the host's network namespace. This allows you to perform any troubleshooting without installing any new packages directly on the host or your application's package.

Determine Where to Debug From

Before deploying any debugging tools, it's important to identify where the issue might be occurring. Potential areas include

Pods: Check if the pod has networking issues (e.g., cannot reach another pod or service).

Services: Ensure that the service is routing traffic correctly to the pods.

Network Policies: Ensure no network policies are blocking traffic.

Ingress/Load Balancer: Debug traffic between your external clients and the Kubernetes cluster (e.g., ingress controller).

Nodes/Cluster Network: Check node-level networking (e.g., routing issues, Container Network Interface (CNI) plugin issues).

Deploy a Debugging Pod

A common practice in Kubernetes is to deploy a debugging pod with networking tools like curl, wget, dig, ping, etc., to test network connectivity.

You can deploy a simple pod with networking tools using the following YAML manifest:

```
apiVersion: v1
kind: Pod
metadata:
  name: network-debug
  labels:
    purpose: debug
spec:
  containers:
  - name: network-debug
    image: nicolaka/netshoot:latest
    command:
      - sleep
      - "3600"
    resources:
      requests:
        memory: "64Mi"
        cpu: "250m"
    securityContext:
      capabilities:
        add: ["NET_ADMIN", "NET_RAW"]
```

nicolaka/netshoot: This image contains various networking tools, making it useful for debugging.

The pod runs a sleep command to keep it alive, giving you time to execute various network tests.

To create the debugging pod, save the above YAML and apply it:

```
kubectl apply -f network-debug.yaml
```

Exec into the Debug Pod

Once the debugging pod is up and running, you can use kubectl exec to enter the pod and run tests like curl, ping, dig, etc.

Here's an example:

```
kubectl exec -it network-debug -- /bin/bash
```

Inside the pod, you can perform network tests such as the following:

Ping a Service: ping <service-name>

Curl a Pod or Service: curl http://<service-ip>:<port>

Test DNS Resolution: dig <service-name>

Check Pod Logs and Events

Logs and events can provide additional clues:

Pod Logs: If a pod is failing due to a network issue, check its logs:

```
kubectl logs <pod-name>
```

Describe Resources: The output of kubectl describe provides information about events and errors:

```
kubectl describe pod <pod-name>
kubectl describe svc <service-name>
```

Verify Network Policies

If network policies are used in your cluster, ensure they do not block traffic between the pods. You can check the current network policies:

```
kubectl get networkpolicy
```

Use the kubectl describe to view the details of the network policies applied to a specific namespace or pod.

Check Service and Endpoint Configurations

Services and their associated endpoints can also be a source of issues. Verify that services have the correct endpoints:

```
kubectl get svc <service-name> -o wide
kubectl get endpoints <service-name>
```

If the endpoints are missing or incorrect, check the health of the pods targeted by the service.

Debug Cluster Networking Issues

If you suspect issues at the cluster level (e.g., CNI plugin), some additional checks can be performed:

> **Check Node Routes and IP Tables**: Networking issues between nodes could arise from incorrect routing or firewall rules.
>
> **Check CNI Plugin Logs**: If you are using a CNI plugin like Calico, Flannel, or Weave, check its logs for issues.

Capture Network Traffic

You may need to capture network traffic between components for more advanced debugging. Use tools like tcpdump or Wireshark within the pod to capture packets:

```
kubectl exec -it network-debug -- tcpdump -i eth0
```

Additional Tips

Multi-cluster or Multinode Debugging: Ensure you test networking from different nodes and different clusters if applicable.

Network Connectivity Between Pods: Use kubectl exec into different pods to test connectivity between them.

8.1 Set Up a Load Balancer

Problem

In a Kubernetes cluster, ensuring that your applications are highly available and can efficiently handle varying traffic loads is crucial. When deploying services that need to be accessible from outside the cluster, a single point of access or failure is insufficient. You need a mechanism to distribute incoming traffic across multiple pods to maintain high availability and reliability. The challenge is setting up a load balancer that evenly distributes network traffic to different pods, scales with your application, and provides fault tolerance.

Specific issues a load balancer solves for us are things like

High Availability: Ensuring that your service remains available even if one or more pods fail

Scalability: Automatically distributing traffic to newly created pods as your application scales

Ease of Access: Providing a single, stable IP address or DNS name for clients to connect to your service

Traffic Management: Efficiently managing incoming traffic to prevent any single pod from becoming a bottleneck

Solution

Configuring a Load Balancer in Kubernetes

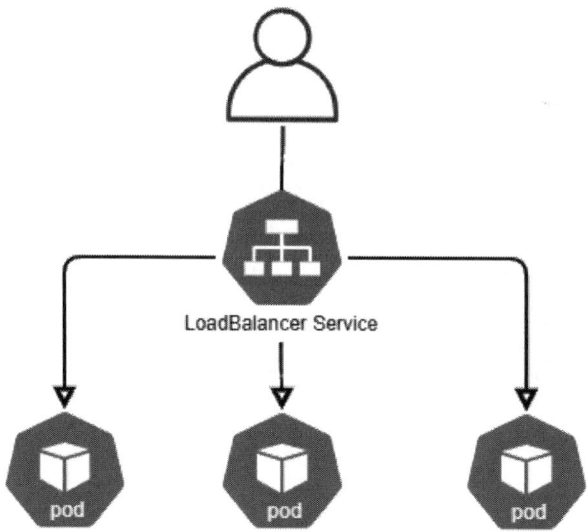

Figure 8-4. *Kubernetes load balancer explanation*

1. **Creating a Deployment**

   First, create a deployment for your application to ensure multiple replicas are running. This example uses a Nginx deployment.

```
apiVersion: apps/v1
kind: Deployment
metadata:
  name: nginx-deployment
spec:
  replicas: 3
  selector:
    matchLabels:
      app: nginx
  template:
    metadata:
      labels:
        app: nginx
    spec:
      containers:
      - name: nginx
        image: nginx:1.14.2
        ports:
        - containerPort: 80
```

   Apply the deployment:

```
kubectl apply -f deployment.yaml
```

```
root@gregPowerPC:/mnt/g/My Drive/KubernetesRecipes/book/networking/8.1# kubectl apply -f deployment.yaml
deployment.apps/nginx-deployment created
root@gregPowerPC:/mnt/g/My Drive/KubernetesRecipes/book/networking/8.1# kubectl get pods
NAME                               READY   STATUS              RESTARTS   AGE
nginx-deployment-d556bf558-j4bk9   0/1     ContainerCreating   0          4s
nginx-deployment-d556bf558-qvrn9   0/1     ContainerCreating   0          4s
nginx-deployment-d556bf558-vmxp4   0/1     ContainerCreating   0          4s
root@gregPowerPC:/mnt/g/My Drive/KubernetesRecipes/book/networking/8.1# kubectl get pods
NAME                               READY   STATUS    RESTARTS   AGE
nginx-deployment-d556bf558-j4bk9   1/1     Running   0          86s
nginx-deployment-d556bf558-qvrn9   1/1     Running   0          86s
nginx-deployment-d556bf558-vmxp4   1/1     Running   0          86s
root@gregPowerPC:/mnt/g/My Drive/KubernetesRecipes/book/networking/8.1#
```

Figure 8-5. *Applying deployment.yaml*

2. **Exposing the Deployment as a Service**

   Next, create a service of type LoadBalancer to expose the deployment. This will automatically provision a load balancer in your cloud provider (e.g., AWS, GCP, Azure).

```
apiVersion: v1
kind: Service
metadata:
  name: nginx-service
spec:
  type: LoadBalancer
  selector:
    app: nginx
  ports:
  - protocol: TCP
    port: 80
    targetPort: 80
```

   Apply the service configuration:

```
kubectl apply -f service.yaml
```

3. **Verifying the Load Balancer**

   After creating the service, Kubernetes will provision an external load balancer. You can verify this by describing the service:

   ```
   kubectl get services
   ```

   You should see an external IP address assigned to your service. This IP can be used to access your application.

```
root@gregPowerPC:/mnt/g/My Drive/KubernetesRecipes/book/networking/8.1# kubectl apply -f service.yaml
service/nginx-service created
root@gregPowerPC:/mnt/g/My Drive/KubernetesRecipes/book/networking/8.1# kubectl get services
NAME            TYPE           CLUSTER-IP     EXTERNAL-IP   PORT(S)        AGE
kubernetes      ClusterIP      10.96.0.1      <none>        443/TCP        32m
nginx-service   LoadBalancer   10.96.213.89   <pending>     80:31390/TCP   17s
root@gregPowerPC:/mnt/g/My Drive/KubernetesRecipes/book/networking/8.1#
```

Figure 8-6. *Listing services' details to get their IPs*

4. **Testing High Availability and Scalability**

   To test high availability, you can scale your deployment up or down and observe how the load balancer distributes traffic to the available pods.

   Scale the deployment:

   ```
   kubectl scale deployment/nginx-deployment --replicas=5
   ```

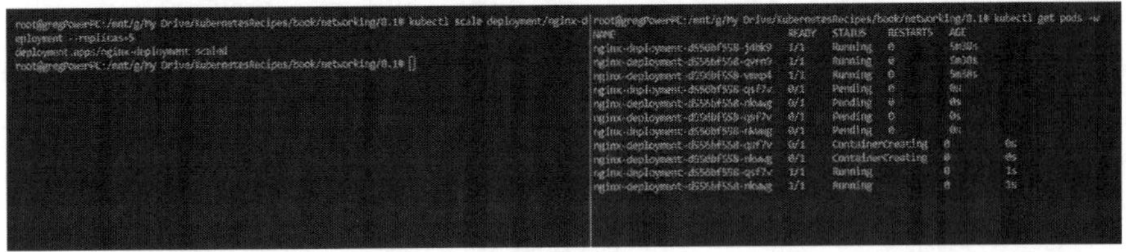

Figure 8-7. *Manually scaling deployment while watching its status live on the right*

Check the status of the pods:

```
kubectl get pods -l app=nginx
```

```
root@gregPowerPC:/mnt/g/My Drive/KubernetesRecipes/book/networking/8.1# kubectl get pods -l app=nginx
NAME                               READY   STATUS    RESTARTS   AGE
nginx-deployment-d556bf558-j4bk9   1/1     Running   0          6m16s
nginx-deployment-d556bf558-nkwwg   1/1     Running   0          28s
nginx-deployment-d556bf558-qsf7v   1/1     Running   0          28s
nginx-deployment-d556bf558-qvrn9   1/1     Running   0          6m16s
nginx-deployment-d556bf558-vmxp4   1/1     Running   0          6m16s
root@gregPowerPC:/mnt/g/My Drive/KubernetesRecipes/book/networking/8.1#
```

Figure 8-8. *Getting pods by label app=nginx*

Let's replace our deployment by applying the one in Figure 8-9.

```
root@gregPowerPC:/mnt/g/My Drive/KubernetesRecipes/book/networking/8.1# kubectl apply -f deployment-showips.yam
deployment.apps/nginx-deployment configured
root@gregPowerPC:/mnt/g/My Drive/KubernetesRecipes/book/networking/8.1# kubectl get pods
NAME                                READY   STATUS    RESTARTS   AGE
nginx-deployment-85d747f754-gmwzc   1/1     Running   0          40s
nginx-deployment-85d747f754-jwttl   1/1     Running   0          41s
nginx-deployment-85d747f754-m94ml   1/1     Running   0          42s
root@gregPowerPC:/mnt/g/My Drive/KubernetesRecipes/book/networking/8.1#
```

Figure 8-9. *Configuring deployment and listing pods*

To see the traffic on our computer, we need to forward port:

```
kubectl port-forward service/nginx-service 80:80
```

Now, we can either

```
curl http://127.0.0.1
```

or just visit the browser to see circulating pods—this is how the service takes action to which the pod user is directed.

You should receive responses from pods indicating that the load balancer distributes traffic among them.

Conclusion

Setting up a load balancer in Kubernetes involves creating a deployment for your application and exposing it using a service of type LoadBalancer. This approach ensures high availability, scalability, and a single point of access for your services. Following the steps outlined above, you can configure a load balancer to manage traffic to your Kubernetes applications efficiently.

8.2 Problem Statement: Applying Network Policies in Kubernetes

In a Kubernetes cluster, ensuring secure communication between pods is crucial for maintaining the overall security of the applications running within the cluster. By default, all pods in a Kubernetes cluster can communicate with each other, which may not be desirable from a security standpoint. The challenge is restricting and controlling network traffic between pods to enforce security boundaries, prevent unauthorized access, and mitigate potential attack vectors. NetworkPolicies provide a means to achieve fine-grained control over the traffic flow within the cluster, but configuring them correctly can be complex.

With network policies, we can achieve unrestricted communication because, by default, there are no restrictions on which pods can communicate with each other, potentially leading to security vulnerabilities. Also, we can get granular traffic control if we need precise control over which pods or namespaces can communicate to enforce security policies. This approach guarantees "isolation," ensuring specific applications or microservices are isolated from others for security or compliance reasons. Defining and applying network policies requires understanding Kubernetes networking and policy syntax.

Solution: Configuring Network Policies in Kubernetes

Understanding Network ACLs

Network ACLs in Kubernetes can be implemented using NetworkPolicies. These policies allow you to define rules that specify the allowed ingress (incoming) and egress (outgoing) traffic for pods.

Creating a Basic Ingress NetworkPolicy

First, create a simple NetworkPolicy that allows ingress traffic to specific pods based on labels and denies all other traffic.

To test the given Kubernetes NetworkPolicy, which allows ingress traffic from pods labeled with the role: frontend to pods labeled with app: my-app on TCP port 80, you can follow these steps:

Apply the NetworkPolicy: Save the YAML content into a file (e.g., network-policy.yaml) and apply it using kubectl:

```
kubectl apply -f network-policy.yaml
```

Ensure that the NetworkPolicy has been applied successfully by running

```
kubectl get networkpolicy -n default
```

You'll need two sets of pods to test the policy:

my-app Pod: The pod that receives the traffic

frontend Pod: The pod that sends the traffic

Deploy the frontend pod:

```
apiVersion: v1
kind: Pod
metadata:
```

```
  name: frontend
  labels:
    role: frontend
spec:
  containers:
  - name: busybox
    image: busybox
    command: ["sleep", "3600"]
```

Apply this pod definition:

```
kubectl apply -f frontend-pod.yaml
```

Test Connectivity from the frontend Pod to the my-app Pod:

Use kubectl exec to access the frontend pod and try connecting to the my-app pod on port 80. First, get the IP address of the my-app pod:

```
kubectl get pod my-app -o wide
```

Now, exec into the frontend pod and use wget or curl to test the connection:

```
kubectl exec -it frontend -- wget --spider http://<my-app-
pod-ip>:80
```

If the policy works correctly, this connection should succeed because the frontend pod has the correct label (role: frontend).

Test Connectivity from a Pod Without the frontend Label:

Create another test pod without the role: frontend label, such as

```
kubectl run backend --image=busybox --command -- sleep 3600
```

Then, try to connect to the my-app pod from the backend pod:

```
kubectl exec -it backend -- wget --spider http://<my-app-
pod-ip>:80
```

This connection should be blocked because the backend pod doesn't have the necessary label.

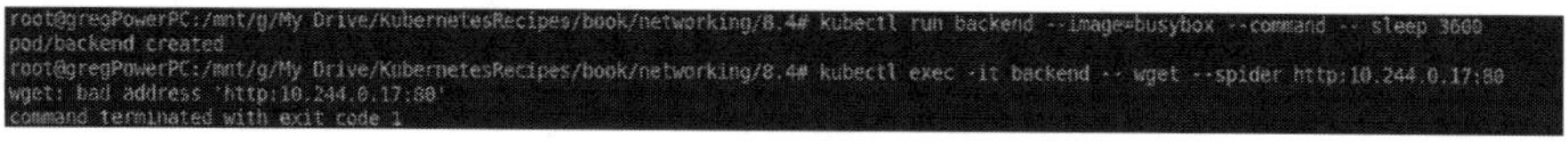

```
root@gregPowerPC:/mnt/g/My Drive/KubernetesRecipes/book/networking/8.4# kubectl run backend --image=busybox --command -- sleep 3600
pod/backend created
root@gregPowerPC:/mnt/g/My Drive/KubernetesRecipes/book/networking/8.4# kubectl exec -it backend -- wget --spider http:10.244.0.17:80
wget: bad address 'http:10.244.0.17:80'
command terminated with exit code 1
```

Figure 8-10. *Checking network policies*

Clean Up:

After testing, you can clean up the resources by deleting the pods and the NetworkPolicy:

```
kubectl delete pod my-app frontend backend
kubectl delete -f network-policy.yaml
```

These steps should help you confirm whether the NetworkPolicy is working as expected!

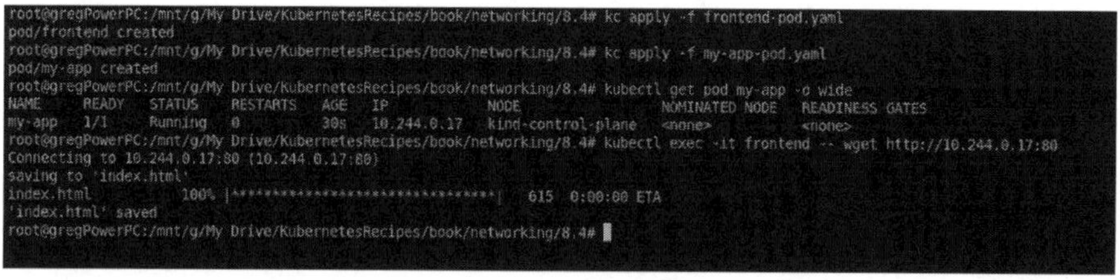

```
root@gregPowerPC:/mnt/g/My Drive/KubernetesRecipes/book/networking/8.4# kc apply -f frontend-pod.yaml
pod/frontend created
root@gregPowerPC:/mnt/g/My Drive/KubernetesRecipes/book/networking/8.4# kc apply -f my-app-pod.yaml
pod/my-app created
root@gregPowerPC:/mnt/g/My Drive/KubernetesRecipes/book/networking/8.4# kubectl get pod my-app -o wide
NAME     READY   STATUS    RESTARTS   AGE   IP            NODE                 NOMINATED NODE   READINESS GATES
my-app   1/1     Running   0          30s   10.244.0.17   kind-control-plane   <none>           <none>
root@gregPowerPC:/mnt/g/My Drive/KubernetesRecipes/book/networking/8.4# kubectl exec -it frontend -- wget http://10.244.0.17:80
Connecting to 10.244.0.17:80 (10.244.0.17:80)
saving to 'index.html'
index.html           100% |********************************|   615  0:00:00 ETA
'index.html' saved
root@gregPowerPC:/mnt/g/My Drive/KubernetesRecipes/book/networking/8.4#
```

Figure 8-11. *Applying frontend-pod.yaml and checking its status*

Creating a Basic Egress NetworkPolicy

An egress NetworkPolicy in Kubernetes is used to control the outbound traffic from pods to external IPs or services. Here's an example of an egress NetworkPolicy that restricts egress traffic, allowing traffic only to a specific IP range on a particular port.

Example Egress NetworkPolicy

The following NetworkPolicy allows pods with the label app: my-app to send egress traffic only to IPs in the CIDR range 192.168.1.0/24 on TCP port 443 (usually used for HTTPS):

```
apiVersion: networking.k8s.io/v1
kind: NetworkPolicy
metadata:
  name: allow-specific-egress
  namespace: default
spec:
  podSelector:
    matchLabels:
      app: my-app
  policyTypes:
  - Egress
  egress:
  - to:
    - ipBlock:
        cidr: 172.19.239.0/24
    ports:
    - protocol: TCP
      port: 80
```

(Note: If our localhost network is different than 172.19.239.0, please change it to match yours.)

Explanation:

> **podSelector**: Targets pods labeled with app: my-app
>
> **policyTypes: - Egress**: Specifies this policy is for egress traffic (outgoing traffic)

egress.to.ipBlock: Allows egress to the CIDR block 192.168.1.0/24

egress.ports: Specifies that only TCP traffic on port 443 is allowed

Testing the Egress NetworkPolicy

1. **Deploy a Pod Matching the Policy**:

   You can create a pod labeled app: my-app to test the policy, for example:

   ```
   apiVersion: v1
   kind: Pod
   metadata:
     name: my-app
     labels:
       app: my-app
   spec:
     containers:
     - name: busybox
       image: busybox
       command: ["sleep", "3600"]
   ```

   Apply the pod:

   ```
   kubectl apply -f pod-egress.yaml
   ```

2. **Test Egress Connectivity**:

   Exec into the my-app pod and try to connect to an IP within the 192.168.1.0/24 range on port 443.

To test something within your network on your host, run some simple python3 web server with a one-liner like

```
python3 -m http.server 80
```

```
root@gregPowerPC:/mnt/g/My Drive/KubernetesRecipes/book/networking/8.2# python3 -m http.server 80
Serving HTTP on 0.0.0.0 port 80 (http://0.0.0.0:80/) ...
127.0.0.1 - - [09/Sep/2024 22:35:26] "GET / HTTP/1.1" 200 -
```

***Figure 8-12.** Running ad hoc python web server*

```
kubectl exec -it my-app -- wget --spider https://172.19.239.62
```

```
root@gregPowerPC:/mnt/g/My Drive/KubernetesRecipes/book/networking/8.2# kubectl exec -it my-app -- wget --spider http://172.19.239.62
Connecting to 172.19.239.62 (172.19.239.62:80)
remote file exists
```

***Figure 8-13.** Checking the egress policy by accessing the web server*

This connection should succeed as it matches the egress policy.

Next, try connecting to an IP outside the allowed CIDR range:

```
kubectl exec -it my-app -- wget --spider
https://google.com
```

This connection should fail because the NetworkPolicy only allows egress traffic to the 192.168.1.0/24 range.

3. **Check Logs**:

   You can verify the behavior by checking the logs in the cluster or using tools like tcpdump to inspect traffic going in and out of the pods.

   Warning if you are on a fresh cluster ...

If your NetworkPolicy is not blocking egress traffic and you can still access external services, the issue may stem from a few common causes. Let's go over them and how to fix the issue:

Ensure Your CNI Plugin Supports NetworkPolicies:

NetworkPolicies are implemented by the underlying Container Network Interface (CNI) plugin in Kubernetes. Not all CNI plugins support NetworkPolicies, and even if they do, some may only support ingress but not egress policies.

Check the CNI Plugin:

Ensure you're using a CNI plugin that supports egress NetworkPolicies, such as

Calico

Cilium

Weave

Kube-Router

You can check which CNI plugin you're using by looking at the Kubernetes cluster configuration or inspecting the networking pods running in the kube-system namespace:

```
kubectl get pods -n kube-system
```

If you're using a CNI plugin like Flannel, note that Flannel does not support NetworkPolicies by itself.

Fix: If you're using a CNI plugin that doesn't support egress policies, you will need to install or switch to one that does, such as Calico.

You can install Calico using the following command (for a standard setup):

```
kubectl apply -f https://docs.projectcalico.org/manifests/
calico.yaml
```

Now with CNI installed, let's try applying the network policy again.

It is best practice to delete netpol and apply it again, as it will fail when reapplied:

```
kubectl apply -f egress-netpol.yaml
```

And retry if egress is blocking:

```
kubectl exec -it my-app -- wget --spider https://google.com
```

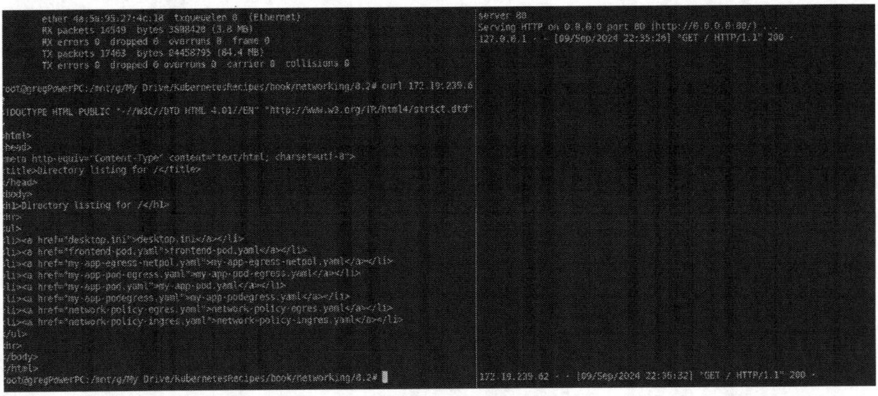

Figure 8-14. *Checking netpol accessibility*

Verifying Network ACLs

You can test connectivity between pods to verify that the network ACLs (NetworkPolicies) are working as expected.

Create a pod with the label role: frontend:

```
apiVersion: v1
kind: Pod
metadata:
```

```
  name: frontend-pod
  labels:
    role: frontend
spec:
  containers:
  - name: busybox
    image: busybox
    command: ["sleep", "3600"]
```

Apply the pod configuration:

```
kubectl apply -f frontend-pod.yaml
```

Attempt to connect to the my-app pod from the frontend-pod:

```
kubectl exec frontend-pod -- curl http://my-app-pod-ip:80
```

You should see a successful response, indicating that the NetworkPolicy allows traffic from the frontend pod.

Next, create a pod without the role: frontend label:

```
apiVersion: v1
kind: Pod
metadata:
  name: backend-pod
  labels:
    role: backend
spec:
  containers:
  - name: busybox
    image: busybox
    command: ["sleep", "3600"]
```

Apply the pod configuration:

```
kubectl apply -f backend-pod.yaml
```

Attempt to connect to the my-app pod from the backend-pod:

```
kubectl exec backend-pod -- curl http://my-app-pod-ip:80
```

The connection should be denied this time, demonstrating that the NetworkPolicy is enforcing the specified ingress rules.

Advanced NetworkPolicies

You can combine ingress and egress rules in a single NetworkPolicy for more advanced scenarios and use namespace selectors.

Here's an example of a more complex NetworkPolicy:

```
apiVersion: networking.k8s.io/v1
kind: NetworkPolicy
metadata:
  name: web-allow-frontend-egress
  namespace: default
spec:
  podSelector:
    matchLabels:
      app: web
  policyTypes:
  - Ingress
  - Egress
  ingress:
  - from:
    - namespaceSelector:
        matchLabels:
          project: frontend
  egress:
  - to:
    - ipBlock:
        cidr: 10.0.0.0/8
```

```
    ports:
    - protocol: TCP
      port: 443
```

This policy allows ingress traffic to pods with the label app: web from any pod in namespaces labeled project: frontend and allows egress traffic to the 10.0.0.0/8 IP range on port 443.

Apply the NetworkPolicy:

```
kubectl apply -f web-allow-frontend-egress.yaml
```

Conclusion

Applying network ACLs in Kubernetes using NetworkPolicies is essential for securing your cluster by controlling inbound and outbound traffic. By defining precise rules for ingress and egress traffic, you can enforce security boundaries, prevent unauthorized access, and ensure that only legitimate traffic is allowed. Following the steps outlined above, you can configure and verify NetworkPolicies to meet your specific security requirements in Kubernetes, thereby enhancing the overall security posture of your applications.

8.3 Problem Statement: Creating Service Types in Kubernetes

In a Kubernetes cluster, services play a crucial role in enabling communication between different components of an application and exposing applications to external clients. However, not all services have the same requirements. Some must be accessible within the cluster, while others must be exposed to external traffic. Kubernetes offers different types of services to address these varying needs, but choosing and configuring the appropriate service type can be challenging. The problem is understanding the various service types and their use cases to effectively manage traffic and access in a Kubernetes environment. In a cluster, there is a need for internal communication to ensure that services are only accessible within the cluster. Exposing services to external clients must be done securely and efficiently. Load balancing is essential to distribute incoming traffic evenly across multiple pods while managing port mappings to ensure the correct traffic routing. Additionally, service discovery is important to enable other components within the cluster to find and communicate with services seamlessly.

Solution: Configuring Service Types in Kubernetes

We will use standard Nginx deployment for all the services running on port 80 (target port in service):

```
apiVersion: apps/v1
kind: Deployment
metadata:
  name: nginx-deployment
spec:
  replicas: 3
  selector:
    matchLabels:
      app: nginx
  template:
    metadata:
      labels:
        app: nginx
    spec:
      containers:
```

```
- name: nginx
  image: nginx:latest
  ports:
  - containerPort: 80
```

ClusterIP Service

The ClusterIP service is the default service type, providing internal access to services within the cluster. It is used for communication between pods. Choosing this value makes the service only reachable from within the cluster.

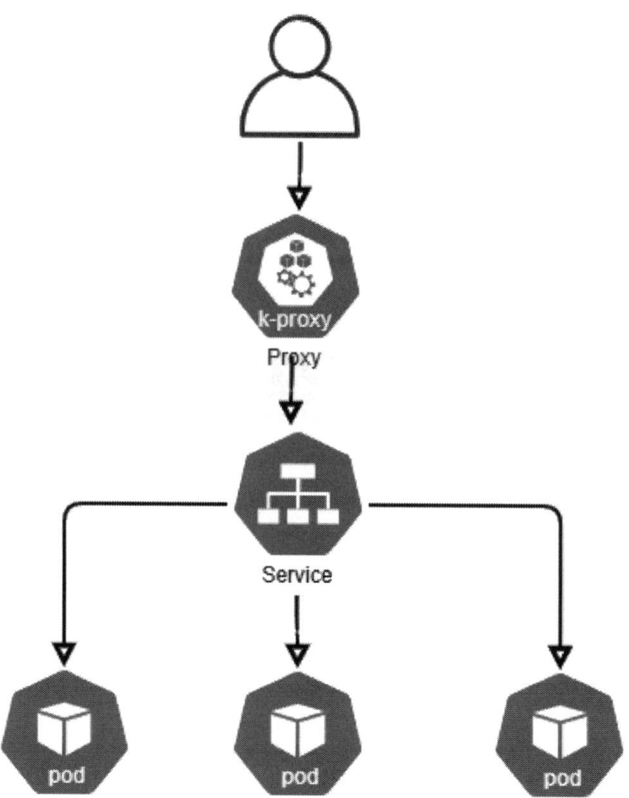

Figure 8-15. *Network flow with kproxy and a load balancer in k8s*

```
apiVersion: v1
kind: Service
metadata:
  name: nginx-service
spec:
  selector:
    app: nginx
  ports:
    - protocol: TCP
      port: 80
      targetPort: 80
  type: ClusterIP
```

We will check now if apps are available by service name:

```
curl http://nginx-service:80
```

If we see a message that cannot resolve the host, we have probably done it from within our host—we need some resources within the cluster to be able to use Kubernetes DNS.

```
root@gregPowerPC:/mnt/g/My Drive/KubernetesRecipes/book/networking/8.3# curl http://nginx-service:
curl: (6) Could not resolve host: nginx-service
```

***Figure 8-16.** Checking Nginx availability by our service (load balancer) name*

To do that, we will use a busybox helper container within the same cluster:

```
kubectl run -i --tty --rm debug --image=busybox
--restart=Never -- sh
 nslookup nginx-service
```

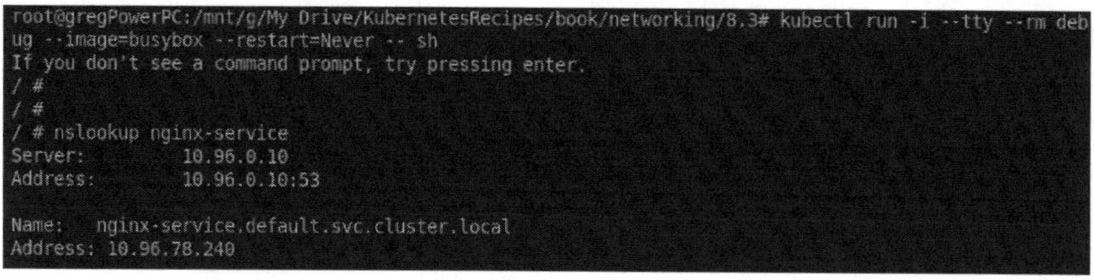

```
root@gregPowerPC:/mnt/g/My Drive/KubernetesRecipes/book/networking/8.3# kubectl run -i --tty --rm deb
ug --image=busybox --restart=Never -- sh
If you don't see a command prompt, try pressing enter.
/ #
/ #
/ # nslookup nginx-service
Server:         10.96.0.10
Address:        10.96.0.10:53

Name:   nginx-service.default.svc.cluster.local
Address: 10.96.78.240
```

Figure 8-17. *Checking Nginx availability with an additional debug pod to access it via the same Kubernetes "network"*

And voila! We can see the service is visible to it and available under a longer name where the namespace is visible: nginx-service.default.svc.cluster.local.

We can also use wget to see the full HTML Nginx response.

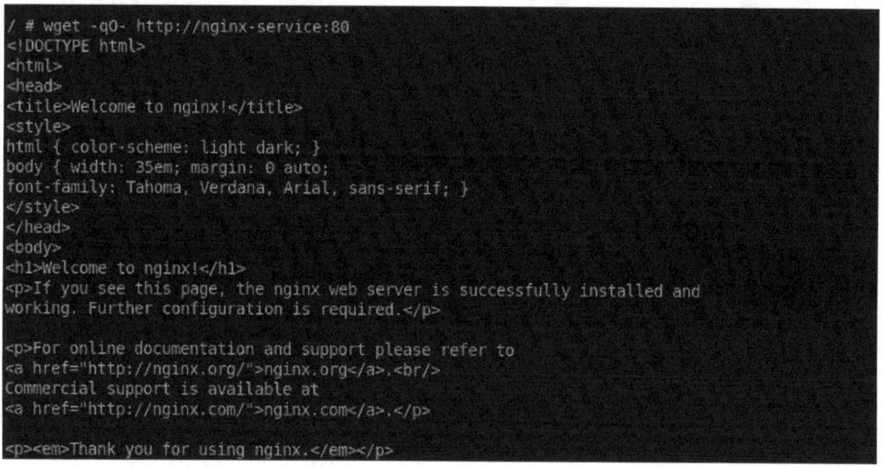

```
/ # wget -qO- http://nginx-service:80
<!DOCTYPE html>
<html>
<head>
<title>Welcome to nginx!</title>
<style>
html { color-scheme: light dark; }
body { width: 35em; margin: 0 auto;
font-family: Tahoma, Verdana, Arial, sans-serif; }
</style>
</head>
<body>
<h1>Welcome to nginx!</h1>
<p>If you see this page, the nginx web server is successfully installed and
working. Further configuration is required.</p>

<p>For online documentation and support please refer to
<a href="http://nginx.org/">nginx.org</a>.<br/>
Commercial support is available at
<a href="http://nginx.com/">nginx.com</a>.</p>

<p><em>Thank you for using nginx.</em></p>
```

Figure 8-18. *Executing wget on our helper busybox pod*

We need to clean the ClusterIP service before going to the next step:

```
kubectl delete -f clusteripservice.yaml
```

Additionally, we can expose the service to the public Internet using an ingress or a gateway.

NodePort Service

The NodePort service exposes the service on each node's IP at a static port. This type allows external traffic to access the service via <NodeIP>:<NodePort>.

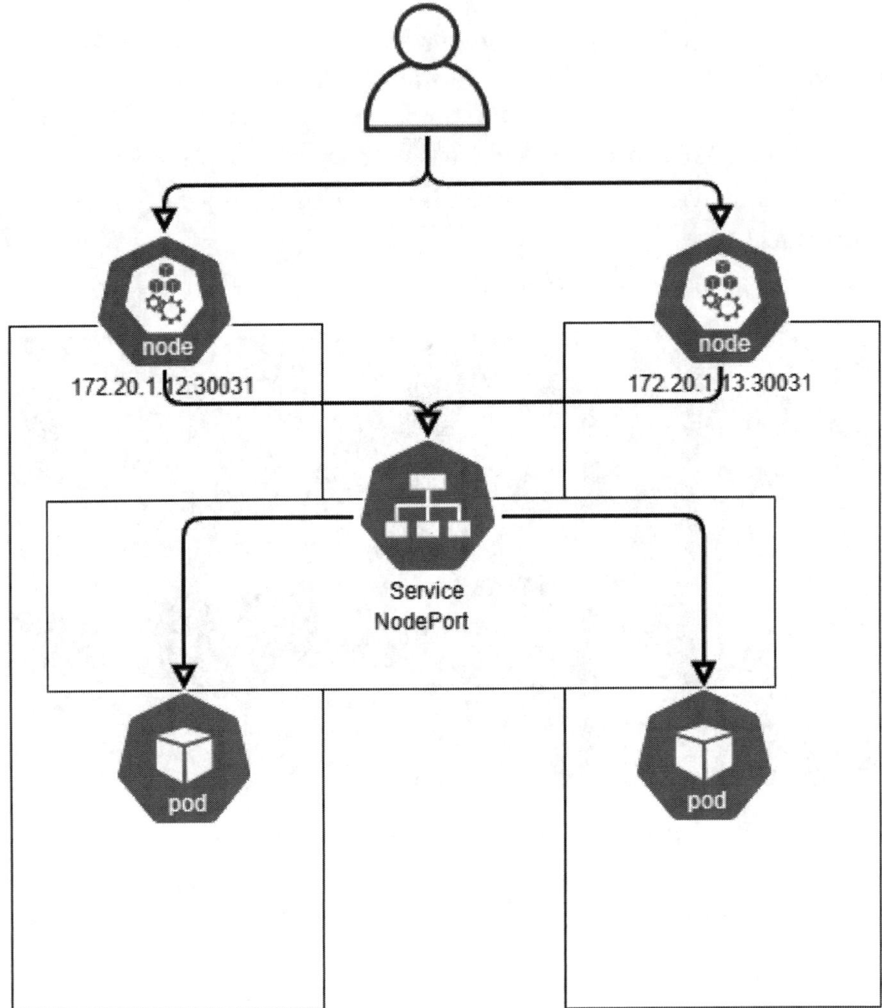

Figure 8-19. *Flow of the NodePort service type*

```
apiVersion: v1
kind: Service
metadata:
  name: nginx-nodeport-service
spec:
  selector:
    app: nginx
  ports:
    - protocol: TCP
      port: 80
      targetPort: 80
      nodePort: 30007
  type: NodePort
```

This YAML file defines a service named nginx-nodeport-service, which exposes port 80 on the Nginx pods. The service type is NodePort, which will map the internal service port to a port on each node's IP address. In this example, the service will be accessible on port 30007 on each node.

Apply the service configuration:

```
kubectl apply -f nodeportservice.yaml
```

Verify the NodePort service:

```
kubectl get svc nginx-nodeport-service
```

Access the Nginx service:

With the node IP and NodePort, you can access the Nginx service from outside the cluster using a web browser or curl:

```
curl http://<NodeIP>:30007
```

Here's how to get the node IP:

```
kubectl get nodes -o wide
```

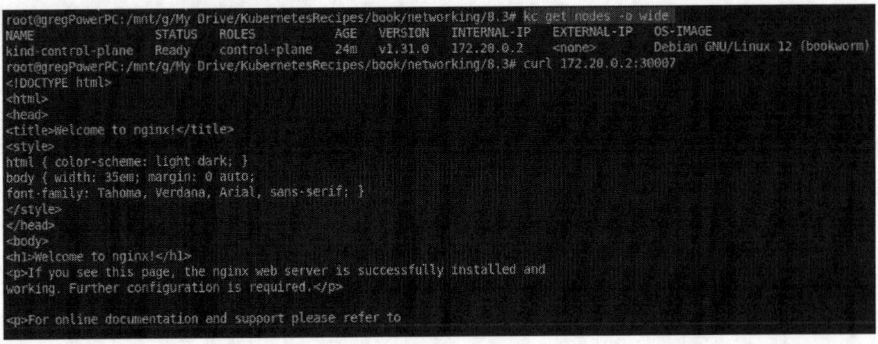

```
root@gregPowerPC:/mnt/g/My Drive/KubernetesRecipes/book/networking/8.3# kc get nodes -o wide
NAME                 STATUS   ROLES           AGE   VERSION   INTERNAL-IP   EXTERNAL-IP   OS-IMAGE
kind-control-plane   Ready    control-plane   24m   v1.31.0   172.20.0.2    <none>        Debian GNU/Linux 12 (bookworm)
root@gregPowerPC:/mnt/g/My Drive/KubernetesRecipes/book/networking/8.3# curl 172.20.0.2:30007
<!DOCTYPE html>
<html>
<head>
<title>Welcome to nginx!</title>
<style>
html { color-scheme: light dark; }
body { width: 35em; margin: 0 auto;
font-family: Tahoma, Verdana, Arial, sans-serif; }
</style>
</head>
<body>
<h1>Welcome to nginx!</h1>
<p>If you see this page, the nginx web server is successfully installed and
working. Further configuration is required.</p>

<p>For online documentation and support please refer to
```

Figure 8-20. *Getting node IPs*

LoadBalancer Service

Section “Set Up a Load Balancer” comprehensively covers the load balancer service. We encourage you to refer to that section to gain a deeper understanding.

ExternalName Service

The ExternalName service maps a service to a DNS name, allowing access to external services within the cluster.

```
apiVersion: v1
kind: Service
metadata:
  name: my-database
spec:
  type: ExternalName
  externalName: google.com
```

Apply the service configuration:

```
kubectl apply -f my-externalname-service.yaml
```

DNS Resolution: When a pod inside your cluster tries to resolve my-database, Kubernetes will return the DNS name db.example.com.

Connection: The pod can connect to the external database as if connecting to a service inside the cluster.

Let's use a curl image to access the externalName service from within the cluster:

```
kubectl run -i --tty --rm debug --image=curlimages/curl
--restart=Never -- sh
```

And now let's run

```
curl http://my-database:80
```

Here, we can see the response from Google, which we have set as externalName for testing.

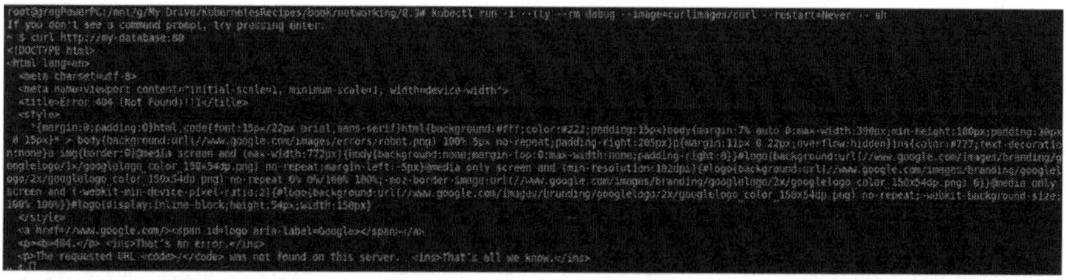

***Figure 8-21.** Execing into the curl pod and executing curl within it*

Accessing this service within the cluster will resolve to the specified external DNS name.

Conclusion

Understanding and configuring the different service types in Kubernetes is essential for managing traffic, ensuring proper access, and maintaining applications' availability and scalability. By following the step-by-step guide outlined above, you can effectively set up and use ClusterIP,

NodePort, LoadBalancer, and ExternalName services to meet your application's specific needs. Each service type serves a unique purpose, enabling you to optimize communication within your cluster and with external clients.

8.4 Problem Statement: Traffic Routing with Istio, CertManager, ExternalDNS, and External Secrets in Kubernetes

In a Kubernetes cluster, managing traffic routing, securing communications, automating DNS updates, and securely handling external secrets are critical for maintaining a robust and scalable application environment. Each of these tasks presents unique challenges:

Traffic Management: Ensuring efficient and reliable traffic routing within the cluster and implementing advanced traffic control features such as canary releases, A/B testing, and fault injection

Secure Communication: Automating issuing and renewing SSL/TLS certificates to secure communications within the cluster

DNS Management: Automating creating and updating DNS records for Kubernetes services

Secret Management: Securely managing and injecting sensitive information such as API keys, passwords, and tokens into the cluster

Solution: Implementing Traffic Routing with Istio, CertManager, ExternalDNS, and External Secrets

Traffic Routing with Istio

Installing Istio

First, install Istio on your Kubernetes cluster. Follow the official Istio documentation to download and install the Istio CLI and install the necessary components.

As of today, the latest version is 1.23.1 (please change accordingly):

```
curl -L https://istio.io/downloadIstio | sh -
cd istio-1.23.1
 export PATH=$PWD/bin:$PATH
```

Now we can install Istio using the demo profile:

```
 istioctl install -f samples/bookinfo/demo-profile-no-
gateways.yaml -y
```

Figure 8-22. *Installing Istio*

There are excellent instructions for up-to-date versions of Istio and sample folders with example applications. Please follow the instructions to get it working.

For reference, Figure 8-23 shows how the response from the app should look like.

***Figure 8-23.** Bookstore application output*

When we have the app deployed, we will open it to outside traffic:

```
kubectl apply -f samples/bookinfo/gateway-api/bookinfo-
gateway.yaml
```

***Figure 8-24.** Applying a gateway for the bookstore application*

By following examples from "Getting Started," you should be able to have the app running in the browser with port-forward:

```
kubectl port-forward svc/bookinfo-gateway-istio 8080:80
```

root@gregPowerPC:/mnt/g/My Drive/KubernetesRecipes/book/networking/8.4/istio-1.23.1# kubectl get gateway
NAME CLASS ADDRESS PROGRAMMED AGE
bookinfo-gateway istio bookinfo-gateway-istio.default.svc.cluster.local True 105s
root@gregPowerPC:/mnt/g/My Drive/KubernetesRecipes/book/networking/8.4/istio-1.23.1# kubectl port-forward svc/bookinfo-gateway-istio 8080:80
Forwarding from 127.0.0.1:8080 -> 80
Forwarding from [::1]:8080 -> 80
Handling connection for 8080
Handling connection for 8080

Figure 8-25. *Forwarding ports for the app*

The Comedy of Errors
Wikipedia Summary: The Comedy of Errors is one of William Sha
plays. It is his shortest and one of his most farcical comedies, with
the humour coming from slapstick and mistaken identity, in addit
word play.
Learn more about Istio →
Book Details
ISBN-10 Publisher Pages Type
1234567890 PublisherA 200 paperback
Book Reviews
"An extremely entertaining play by Shakespeare. The slapstick humour is refreshing!"
"Absolutely fun an entertaining. The p thematic depth wh compared to other Shakespeare."

Figure 8-26. *Application web page output*

If we want to see the Kiali dashboard and the traffic route, see Figure 8-27.

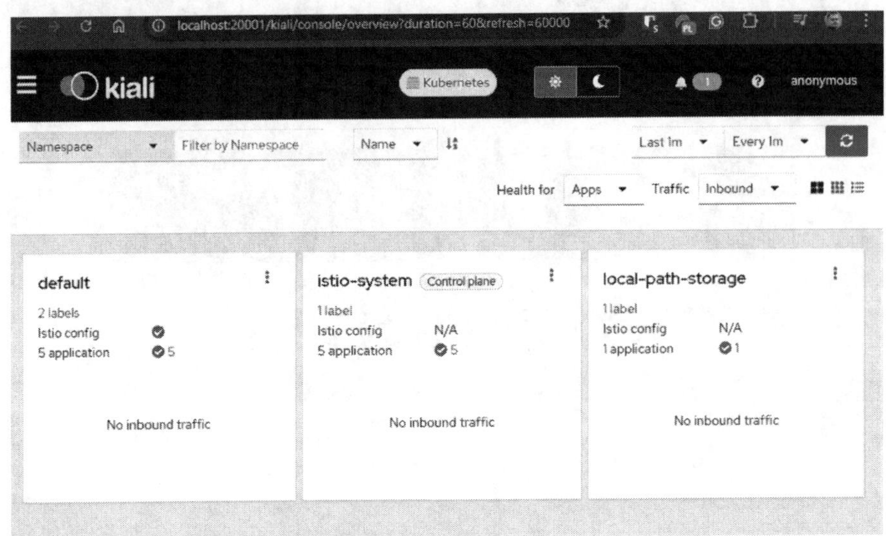

Figure 8-27. *Kiali dashboard*

This is a basic example of deploying an application using Istio and managing traffic, security, and observability. You can extend this setup with advanced features like A/B testing, canary releases, and circuit breaking.

Secure Communication with CertManager

Installing CertManager

Install CertManager to automate SSL/TLS certificate management:

```
kubectl apply -f https://github.com/jetstack/cert-manager/
releases/download/v1.0.4/cert-manager.yaml
```

Issuing Certificates

Create an issuer or ClusterIssuer to define how certificates should be obtained. An issuer is responsible for obtaining certificates. In this example, we'll use a self-signed certificate issuer. You could also create issuers for external providers like Let's Encrypt, but let's keep it simple here:

```
apiVersion: cert-manager.io/v1
kind: ClusterIssuer
metadata:
  name: letsencrypt-prod
spec:
  acme:
    server: https://acme-v02.api.letsencrypt.org/directory
    email: user@example.com
    privateKeySecretRef:
      name: letsencrypt-prod
    solvers:
    - http01:
        ingress:
          class: nginx
```

Apply the issuer configuration:

```
kubectl apply -f clusterissuer.yaml
```

Create a Certificate resource to request a certificate. Define the Certificate resource, automatically requesting a certificate from the specified issuer:

```
apiVersion: cert-manager.io/v1
kind: Certificate
metadata:
  name: example-com
```

```
  namespace: default
spec:
  secretName: example-com-tls
  issuerRef:
    name: letsencrypt-prod
    kind: ClusterIssuer
  commonName: example.com
  dnsNames:
  - example.com
```

Apply the certificate configuration:

```
kubectl apply -f certificate.yaml
```

Explanation:

> **kind: Issuer**: Refers to the cert-manager issuer object, which defines how certificates are issued
>
> **selfSigned: {}**: Specifies that this issuer will generate a self-signed certificate

Certificate:

> **secretName**: Name of the secret where the certificate and private key will be stored
>
> **issuerRef**: Refers to the issuer (or ClusterIssuer) to be used for generating the certificate
>
> **commonName**: The main domain for the certificate
>
> **dnsNames**: A list of additional DNS names covered by the certificate

Here's how to check the certificate:

```
kubectl describe certificate example-com -n default
```

```
root@gregPowerPC:/mnt/g/My Drive/KubernetesRecipes/book/networking/8.5# kubectl describe certificate example-com -n default
Name:         example-com
Namespace:    default
Labels:       <none>
Annotations:  <none>
API Version:  cert-manager.io/v1
Kind:         Certificate
Metadata:
  Creation Timestamp:  2024-09-03T23:04:04Z
  Generation:          1
  Resource Version:    9112
  UID:                 8e55d730-165e-4653-8e5f-6affb70cafcf
Spec:
  Common Name:  example.com
  Dns Names:
    example.com
  Issuer Ref:
    Kind:       ClusterIssuer
    Name:       letsencrypt-prod
  Secret Name:  example-com-tls
Status:
  Conditions:
    Last Transition Time:        2024-09-03T23:04:04Z
    Message:                     Issuing certificate as Secret does not exist
    Observed Generation:         1
    Reason:                      DoesNotExist
    Status:                      False
    Type:                        Ready
    Last Transition Time:        2024-09-03T23:04:04Z
    Message:                     Issuing certificate as Secret does not exist
    Observed Generation:         1
    Reason:                      DoesNotExist
    Status:                      True
    Type:                        Issuing
  Next Private Key Secret Name:  example-com-mgr7l
Events:
  Type    Reason     Age   From                                       Message
  ----    ------     ----  ----                                       -------
  Normal  Issuing    53s   cert-manager-certificates-trigger          Issuing certificate as Secret does not exist
  Normal  Generated  53s   cert-manager-certificates-key-manager      Stored new private key in temporary Secret resource "example-com-mgr7l"
  Normal  Requested  53s   cert-manager-certificates-request-manager  Created new CertificateRequest resource "example-com-1"
root@gregPowerPC:/mnt/g/My Drive/KubernetesRecipes/book/networking/8.5# 
```

Figure 8-28. *Describing the certificate*

Automating DNS with ExternalDNS

We will cover installation, configuration, and how to integrate ExternalDNS with a cloud DNS provider (like AWS Route 53) for automatic DNS updates when services are created in your cluster.

Install ExternalDNS:

First, we need to install ExternalDNS using the provided YAML file. This YAML configures ExternalDNS to watch Kubernetes services and automatically update DNS records in your DNS provider (e.g., AWS Route 53, Google Cloud DNS, etc.).

```
kubectl apply -f https://github.com/kubernetes-sigs/external-
dns/releases/download/v0.7.6/external-dns.yaml
```

Configure ExternalDNS for a DNS Provider:

In this example, we'll assume you're using AWS Route 53 for DNS management. You must provide AWS credentials to allow ExternalDNS to update Route 53 records. The credentials should be provided using IAM roles or by mounting AWS credentials into the ExternalDNS pod.

Create an AWS IAM Role/Policy:

You will need an AWS IAM policy that allows ExternalDNS to manage Route 53 records. See Figure 8-29 for an example IAM policy.

```
{
    "Version": "2012-10-17",
    "Statement": [
        {
            "Effect": "Allow",
            "Action": [
                "route53:ChangeResourceRecordSets",
                "route53:ListHostedZones",
                "route53:ListResourceRecordSets"
            ],
            "Resource": [
                "arn:aws:route53:::hostedzone/YOUR_HOSTED_ZONE_ID"
            ]
        }
    ]
}
```

Figure 8-29. *Example IAM policy*

Attach this policy to the IAM role or user that ExternalDNS will use.

Create a Kubernetes secret for AWS credentials (optional).

You can create a Kubernetes secret with AWS credentials if you're not using IAM roles.

```
kubectl create secret generic aws-credentials \
  --from-literal=aws-access-key-id=YOUR_AWS_ACCESS_KEY \
  --from-literal=aws-secret-access-key=YOUR_AWS_SECRET_KEY
```

You will then mount this secret into the ExternalDNS deployment by modifying the ExternalDNS YAML file.

Modify ExternalDNS Deployment (if Using AWS):

Edit the external-dns.yaml file to configure ExternalDNS for AWS Route 53. In this case, you will add flags that specify the provider (AWS), region, and zone ID and optionally reference the AWS credentials secret created earlier.

```
apiVersion: apps/v1
kind: Deployment
metadata:
  name: external-dns
spec:
  template:
    spec:
      containers:
      - name: external-dns
        args:
        - --source=service
        - --source=ingress
        - --domain-filter=mydomain.com  # Only manage DNS
          records for this domain
        - --provider=aws
        - --aws-zone-type=public
        - --registry=txt
        - --txt-owner-id=my-cluster-id
        env:
```

```
        - name: AWS_ACCESS_KEY_ID
          valueFrom:
            secretKeyRef:
              name: aws-credentials
              key: aws-access-key-id
        - name: AWS_SECRET_ACCESS_KEY
          valueFrom:
            secretKeyRef:
              name: aws-credentials
              key: aws-secret-access-key
```

Create a Service and Annotate It for ExternalDNS:

Now that ExternalDNS is installed and configured, you can develop services in your Kubernetes cluster and annotate them for DNS management. ExternalDNS will create or update the DNS records automatically.

Here's an example of a service definition:

```
apiVersion: v1
kind: Service
metadata:
  name: my-service
  annotations:
    external-dns.alpha.kubernetes.io/hostname: myapp.example.
    com  # DNS record to be created
spec:
  selector:
    app: my-app
  ports:
  - protocol: TCP
    port: 80
    targetPort: 8080
  type: LoadBalancer
```

Apply the Service Configuration:

After defining the service with the necessary DNS annotations, apply the configuration to the cluster:

```
kubectl apply -f my-service.yaml
```

Once applied, ExternalDNS will detect the service and automatically create or update the DNS record (myapp.example.com) in your DNS provider (AWS Route 53 in this example).

Verify the DNS Record:

You can verify that the DNS record was created successfully by using a command-line tool like dig:

```
dig myapp.example.com
```

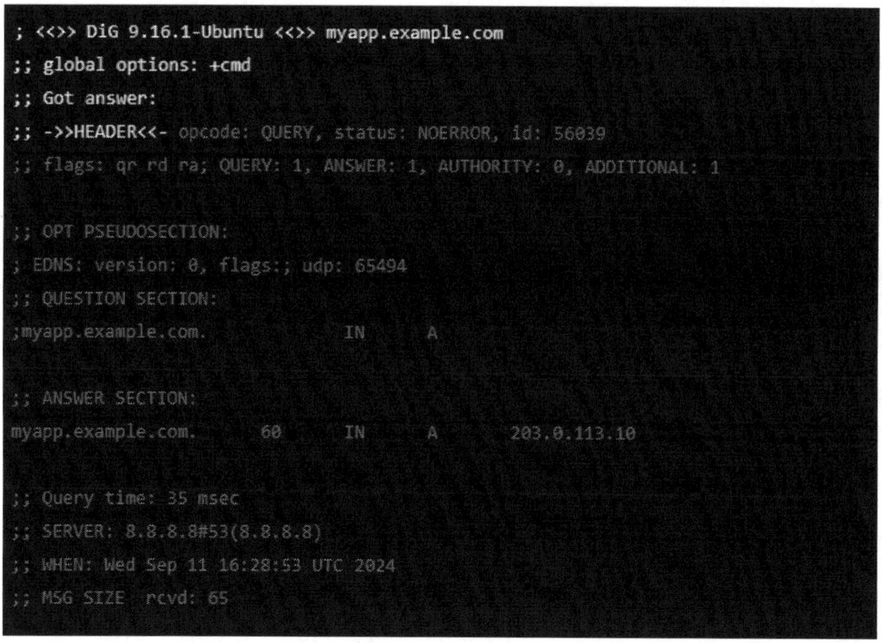

```
; <<>> DiG 9.16.1-Ubuntu <<>> myapp.example.com
;; global options: +cmd
;; Got answer:
;; ->>HEADER<<- opcode: QUERY, status: NOERROR, id: 56039
;; flags: qr rd ra; QUERY: 1, ANSWER: 1, AUTHORITY: 0, ADDITIONAL: 1

;; OPT PSEUDOSECTION:
; EDNS: version: 0, flags:; udp: 65494
;; QUESTION SECTION:
;myapp.example.com.            IN      A

;; ANSWER SECTION:
myapp.example.com.     60      IN      A       203.0.113.10

;; Query time: 35 msec
;; SERVER: 8.8.8.8#53(8.8.8.8)
;; WHEN: Wed Sep 11 16:28:53 UTC 2024
;; MSG SIZE  rcvd: 65
```

Figure 8-30. *Verifying the DNS record with the dig command*

This should return the IP address of your Kubernetes service's external LoadBalancer.

Optional: Debugging and Logs:

You can monitor ExternalDNS logs to troubleshoot issues. Use the following command to view logs from the ExternalDNS pod:

```
kubectl logs deployment/external-dns
```

This will display logs showing the DNS changes made by ExternalDNS, including any errors if something goes wrong.

Conclusion

We have provided instructions on how to install ExternalDNS using a YAML file, configured it for the AWS Route 53 DNS provider, and created a Kubernetes service and annotated it to create DNS records automatically.

This setup allows for automatic DNS management in your Kubernetes cluster, simplifying the process of exposing services to the Internet using custom domain names.

Managing Secrets with External Secrets

Installing External Secrets

Install External Secrets to manage secrets from external secret management systems like AWS Secrets Manager or HashiCorp Vault.

For AWS Secrets Manager:

```
kubectl apply -f https://raw.githubusercontent.com/external-
secrets/kubernetes-external-secrets/master/deploy/crds.yaml
kubectl apply -f https://raw.githubusercontent.com/external-
secrets/kubernetes-external-secrets/master/deploy/operator.yaml
```

Configuring External Secrets

Create an ExternalSecret resource to fetch secrets from AWS Secrets Manager:

```
apiVersion: 'Kubernetes-client.io/v1'
kind: ExternalSecret
metadata:
  name: my-secret
  namespace: default
spec:
  backendType: secretsManager
  data:
  - key: my-app/db-password
    name: db-password
```

Apply the external secret configuration:

```
kubectl apply -f externalsecret.yaml
```

Conclusion

Managing traffic routing, securing communications, automating DNS updates, and securely handling external secrets are critical tasks in a Kubernetes environment. By leveraging Istio for advanced traffic management, CertManager for automated SSL/TLS certificate management, ExternalDNS for dynamic DNS updates, and External Secrets for secure secret management, you can enhance the security, reliability, and scalability of your Kubernetes applications. Following the steps outlined above, you can implement and configure these tools to meet the specific needs of your applications.

8.5 Problem Statement: Traffic Split Configuration, Retry Rule, and Timeout in Kubernetes

In a Kubernetes cluster, managing how traffic is distributed among different service versions, handling retries for failed requests, and setting appropriate timeouts are crucial for ensuring reliability and smooth operation. However, implementing these features requires a good understanding of traffic management and the configuration of proper rules and policies. The challenge is to efficiently split traffic between service versions, implement retry mechanisms to improve resilience, and set timeouts to avoid long-running requests that could impact the application's performance.

Specific issues include splitting traffic between different service versions for canary deployments, A/B testing, or gradual rollouts. Another issue is the retry mechanism, which automatically retries failed requests to improve service reliability and handle transient failures. Lastly, setting appropriate timeouts is crucial to ensure that requests do not run indefinitely, preventing negative impacts on the system's overall performance.

Solution: Configuring Traffic Split, Retry Rules, and Timeouts in Kubernetes

Traffic Split Configuration with Istio

Installing Istio

First, install Istio on your Kubernetes cluster. You will find instructions in the previous section if you still need to do so. Follow the official Istio documentation to download and install the Istio CLI and install the necessary components:

```
istioctl install --set profile=demo
```

Label the namespace where you want to enable Istio sidecar injection:

```
kubectl label namespace default istio-injection=enabled
```

Deploying Multiple Versions of a Service

Deploy two versions of a sample application, such as an HTTPbin service:

```
apiVersion: apps/v1
kind: Deployment
metadata:
  name: httpbin-v1
spec:
  replicas: 1
  selector:
    matchLabels:
      app: httpbin
      version: v1
  template:
    metadata:
      labels:
        app: httpbin
        version: v1
    spec:
      containers:
      - image: docker.io/kennethreitz/httpbin
        name: httpbin
        ports:
        - containerPort: 80
---
apiVersion: apps/v1
```

```
kind: Deployment
metadata:
  name: httpbin-v2
spec:
  replicas: 1
  selector:
    matchLabels:
      app: httpbin
      version: v2
  template:
    metadata:
      labels:
        app: httpbin
        version: v2
    spec:
      containers:
      - image: docker.io/kennethreitz/httpbin
        name: httpbin
        ports:
        - containerPort: 80
```

Apply the deployments:

```
kubectl apply -f httpbin-v1.yaml
```

Create a service for the application:

```
apiVersion: v1
kind: Service
metadata:
  name: httpbin
spec:
  ports:
```

```
  - port: 80
    name: http
  selector:
    app: httpbin
```

Apply the service:

```
kubectl apply -f httpbin-service.yaml
```

Defining VirtualServices and DestinationRules

Define an Istio VirtualService and DestinationRule to split traffic between the two versions:

```
apiVersion: networking.istio.io/v1alpha3
kind: VirtualService
metadata:
  name: httpbin
spec:
  hosts:
  - "*"
  gateways:
  - httpbin-gateway
  http:
  - route:
    - destination:
        host: httpbin
        subset: v1
      weight: 50
    - destination:
        host: httpbin
        subset: v2
      weight: 50
```

```
---
apiVersion: networking.istio.io/v1alpha3
kind: DestinationRule
metadata:
  name: httpbin
spec:
  host: httpbin
  subsets:
  - name: v1
    labels:
      version: v1
  - name: v2
    labels:
      version: v2
```

Apply the configurations:

```
kubectl apply -f httpbin-virtualservice-destinationrule.yaml
```

Configuring Retry Rules

Define a VirtualService with retry rules to handle failed requests:

```
apiVersion: networking.istio.io/v1alpha3
kind: VirtualService
metadata:
  name: httpbin
spec:
  hosts:
  - "*"
  gateways:
  - httpbin-gateway
  http:
```

```
    - route:
      - destination:
          host: httpbin
          subset: v1
        weight: 50
      - destination:
          host: httpbin
          subset: v2
        weight: 50
      retries:
        attempts: 3
        perTryTimeout: 2s
        retryOn: gateway-error,connect-failure,refused-stream
```

Apply the configuration:

```
kubectl apply -f httpbin-retry.yaml
```

Configuring Timeouts

Define a VirtualService with timeout rules to limit the duration of requests:

```
apiVersion: networking.istio.io/v1alpha3
kind: VirtualService
metadata:
  name: httpbin
spec:
  hosts:
  - "*"
  gateways:
  - httpbin-gateway
  http:
  - route:
```

```
  - destination:
      host: httpbin
      subset: v1
    weight: 50
  - destination:
      host: httpbin
      subset: v2
    weight: 50
  timeout: 5s
```

Apply the configuration:

```
kubectl apply -f httpbin-timeout.yaml
```

Verification

Get the service IP:

```
kubectl get svc
```

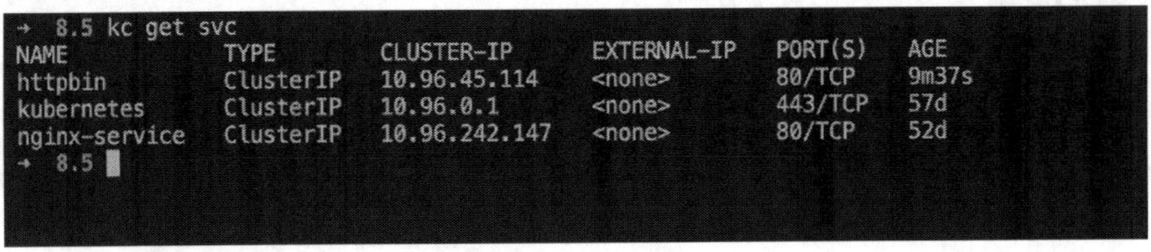

```
→  8.5 kc get svc
NAME            TYPE        CLUSTER-IP      EXTERNAL-IP   PORT(S)   AGE
httpbin         ClusterIP   10.96.45.114    <none>        80/TCP    9m37s
kubernetes      ClusterIP   10.96.0.1       <none>        443/TCP   57d
nginx-service   ClusterIP   10.96.242.147   <none>        80/TCP    52d
→  8.5
```

Figure 8-31. *Getting the service IP*

We need to remember that when trying to curl the service IP during testing, we need to be inside the Kubernetes cluster—doing it from the host machine, which is running kind we are not "inside cluster". We can either deploy the testing pod and exec into it to try out curl, or we can do a simple temporary hack with the kubectl port-forward command:

```
kubectl port-forward svc/httpbin 8888:80
```

Let's see if now anything is running on this port by doing curl `http://127.0.0.1:8888`.

```
→  8.5 kubectl port-forward svc/httpbin 8888:80
Forwarding from 127.0.0.1:8888 -> 80
Forwarding from [::1]:8888 -> 80
Handling connection for 8888
Handling connection for 8888
Handling connection for 8888

    </div>
</div>
</body>

</html>%
→  8.5 curl 127.0.0.1
curl: (7) Failed to connect to 127.0.0.1 port 80 after 0 ms: Couldn't connect to server
→  8.5 curl 127.0.0.1:8888
\<!DOCTYPE html>
<html lang="en">

<head>
    <meta charset="UTF-8">
    <title>httpbin.org</title>
    <link href="https://fonts.googleapis.com/css?family=Open+Sans:400,700|Source+Code+Pro:300,600|Titillium+Web:40
        rel="stylesheet">
    <link rel="stylesheet" type="text/css" href="/flasgger_static/swagger-ui.css">
```

***Figure 8-32.** Forwarding the service port and checking its availability*

As seen in the screenshot above, the web page is being returned, and we can now test it:

1. **Traffic Splitting**: To verify traffic splitting, send multiple requests to the service and observe the distribution between versions:

   ```
   for i in {1..10}; do curl http://<service-ip>; done
   ```

2. **Retry Mechanism**: To verify retries, induce a failure and observe the retry attempts by checking the logs of the Istio sidecar proxy.

3. **Timeouts**: To verify timeouts, create a delay in one of the versions' responses and ensure the request is terminated according to the configured timeout.

Conclusion

Configuring traffic split, retry rules, and timeouts in Kubernetes using Istio allows for advanced traffic management, enhancing your applications' reliability, scalability, and performance. Following the steps outlined above, you can effectively implement these configurations to control traffic distribution, handle transient failures, and enforce timeouts, ensuring a robust and resilient application environment.

8.6 Problem Statement: Iptables and Nftables in Kubernetes

Maintaining network security and managing traffic flow at a granular level are crucial for ensuring the integrity and performance of applications in a Kubernetes cluster. Iptables and Nftables are powerful tools for configuring network packet filtering and network address translation (NAT) rules, providing a way to control network traffic and enforce security policies. However, integrating and managing these tools in a Kubernetes environment can be challenging. The problem lies in effectively configuring Iptables and Nftables rules to secure the cluster, manage traffic, and handle dynamic changes in a Kubernetes environment.

Key Challenges:

- Network security involves securing communication between pods and services while safeguarding the cluster against unauthorized access.
- Traffic management focuses on regulating and managing traffic flow with fine-grained control, including filtering and network address translation (NAT).

- Dynamic environments require adaptation to the constantly changing nature of Kubernetes, where pods and services are frequently created or removed.
- Complexity arises from handling Iptables and Nftables rules, ensuring their correct implementation and ongoing maintenance.

Solution: Iptables and Nftables in Kubernetes

In Kubernetes, Iptables and Nftables are crucial for managing network traffic and communication between different components within the cluster. They are used primarily to control traffic routing, filtering, and translation to and from pods, services, and nodes. Here's how they are used in Kubernetes core components:

1. **Kube-Proxy**:

   Kube-proxy is a critical component that maintains network rules on nodes that route traffic to services. It can work in different modes, such as Iptables mode or Nftables mode, depending on how the cluster is set up:

   Iptables Mode:

   In this mode, kube-proxy uses Iptables to route service traffic. It creates Iptables rules to direct external and internal traffic to the appropriate pods based on the cluster IP or service IP.

   When a client tries to access a Kubernetes service, Iptables rules created by kube-proxy intercept the traffic and route it to one of the pods backing that service. Load balancing is done via round-robin across the available pods.

Iptables manages NAT and forwards packets based on the rules defined by kube-proxy. It handles both ClusterIP and NodePort types of services.

Examples of Iptables chains used include KUBE-SERVICES, KUBE-NODEPORTS, and KUBE-POSTROUTING.

Nftables Mode:

In Nftables mode, kube-proxy uses Nftables instead of Iptables for the same purpose. Nftables is the successor to Iptables, offering better performance and flexibility. The core functionality remains similar: handling traffic routing and load balancing between services and pods.

Nftables provides a more efficient and scalable way of managing complex network rules within Kubernetes, especially in large clusters.

2. **CNI (Container Network Interface) Plugins**:

   The CNI plugin is responsible for setting up the network interfaces for pods and configuring the necessary network rules. It may use Iptables or Nftables to handle traffic routing, NAT, and filtering.

   When a pod is created, the CNI plugin typically sets up routes for it, configures NAT, and may use Iptables/Nftables to ensure that it can communicate with other pods, services, and external resources.

   Some CNI plugins, like Calico, Weave, or Flannel, rely heavily on Iptables to manage networking within the cluster.

3. **Network Policies**:

   Kubernetes network policies allow users to control the communication between pods using Iptables (or sometimes Nftables, depending on the CNI implementation). These policies define which pods can communicate with others, providing network-level security.

   When enforcing network policies, Iptables rules are dynamically generated to ensure traffic follows the policies. For example, if a policy allows only traffic from specific pods or namespaces, Iptables will create rules that filter traffic accordingly.

4. **Service Discovery**:

   Kubernetes uses Iptables to implement service discovery. For example, when a pod tries to connect to a service by its ClusterIP, Iptables rules created by kube-proxy redirect the traffic to one of the pods backing the service.

   In this case, Iptables (or Nftables) performs NAT to change the destination IP address to the pod's IP address and forwards the traffic to the correct pod.

5. **Pod-to-Pod Communication**:

   Kubernetes uses Iptables to ensure that pods within the same node can communicate with each other and with pods on different nodes. Iptables rules route traffic to the correct pod IPs, considering the overlay or underlay network configuration (depending on the CNI plugin used).

This is crucial for internal cluster communication and ensuring that Kubernetes networking operates seamlessly across nodes.

6. **Load Balancing**:

   Kube-proxy in Iptables mode (or Nftables mode) provides load balancing for services in the cluster. When a service has multiple pods backing it, Iptables rules distribute traffic among these pods in a round-robin fashion or based on other algorithms.

For NodePort services, Iptables rules also handle traffic outside the cluster, redirecting it to the appropriate pod.

Differences Between Iptables and Nftables in Kubernetes

Nftables is a more modern replacement for Iptables, offering improved performance, more efficient rule management, and easier scaling for large numbers of rules. However, Iptables is still widely used in many Kubernetes setups due to its maturity and compatibility with existing tools.

Kube-proxy supports both Iptables and Nftables, and the choice between them depends on the system's configuration and the network plugin in use.

In summary, Iptables and its successor, Nftables, play a crucial role in managing network traffic within Kubernetes. They are used by kube-proxy to route traffic between services and pods, by CNI plugins to set up pod networks, and by network policies to enforce security rules within the cluster.

In Kubernetes, Iptables rules are dynamically created by core components like kube-proxy and CNI plugins to manage networking across the cluster. Below are examples of Iptables components related to Kubernetes resources:

1. **Service IP Rules (ClusterIP)**:

   Kubernetes creates Iptables rules for routing traffic to services, which can be accessed via a ClusterIP. Here's an example of how Iptables handles traffic routing for a service:

```
-A KUBE-SERVICES -d 10.96.0.10/32 -p tcp -m comment
--comment "default/nginx-service: cluster IP" -m tcp
--dport 80 -j KUBE-SVC-XXXXXXX
-A KUBE-SVC-XXXXXXX -m statistic --mode random
--probability 0.50000000000 -j KUBE-SEP-XXXXXXXX
-A KUBE-SVC-XXXXXXX -j KUBE-SEP-YYYYYYYY

-A KUBE-SEP-XXXXXXXX -s 192.168.1.20/32 -m comment
--comment "default/nginx-pod-1" -j KUBE-MARK-MASQ
-A KUBE-SEP-XXXXXXXX -p tcp -m tcp -j DNAT --to-
destination 192.168.1.20:80

-A KUBE-SEP-YYYYYYYY -s 192.168.1.21/32 -m comment
--comment "default/nginx-pod-2" -j KUBE-MARK-MASQ
-A KUBE-SEP-YYYYYYYY -p tcp -m tcp -j DNAT --to-
destination 192.168.1.21:80
```

   Explanation:

   The KUBE-SERVICES chain routes traffic destined for the service IP 10.96.0.10 (e.g., nginx-service) on port 80 to the KUBE-SVC-XXXXXXX chain.

   The KUBE-SVC-XXXXXXX chain load-balances traffic between backend pods, distributing it randomly (via statistic --mode random).

Traffic is forwarded to either of the endpoints (KUBE-SEP-XXXXXXXX or KUBE-SEP-YYYYYYYY), which DNATs the traffic to the specific pod IP addresses (192.168.1.20 or 192.168.1.21).

2. **NodePort Service Rules**:

   When you expose a service via a NodePort, Iptables ensures that traffic arriving at the node on a specific port is forwarded to the service's backend pods:

```
-A KUBE-NODEPORTS -p tcp -m comment --comment "default/
nginx-service: NodePort" -m tcp --dport 30001 -j KUBE-
MARK-MASQ
-A KUBE-NODEPORTS -p tcp -m comment --comment "default/
nginx-service: NodePort" -m tcp --dport 30001 -j KUBE-
SVC-XXXXXXX

-A KUBE-SVC-XXXXXXX -j KUBE-SEP-XXXXXXXX
-A KUBE-SEP-XXXXXXXX -s 192.168.1.20/32 -p tcp -m tcp
--dport 80 -j DNAT --to-destination 192.168.1.20:80
```

   Explanation:

   The KUBE-NODEPORTS chain is responsible for handling traffic coming to port 30001 (the NodePort assigned to nginx-service).

   The rule forwards traffic to the KUBE-SVC-XXXXXXX chain, which routes the traffic to the appropriate pod via the KUBE-SEP-XXXXXXXX chain.

   DNAT is applied to forward traffic from the node's external interface to the pod's IP address.

3. **Pod-to-Pod Communication Rules**:

   When pods communicate with each other within the cluster, Iptables ensures that the traffic is properly routed to the destination pod, for example:

   ```
   -A KUBE-FORWARD -s 10.244.0.0/16 -m comment --comment
   "allow pod-to-pod communication" -j ACCEPT
   -A KUBE-FORWARD -d 10.244.0.0/16 -m comment --comment
   "allow pod-to-pod communication" -j ACCEPT
   ```

   Explanation:

   The KUBE-FORWARD chain ensures that traffic from any pod in the 10.244.0.0/16 CIDR (assuming this is the pod network range) is allowed to pass to other pods. This ensures pod-to-pod communication.

4. **Network Policy Rules**:

   If network policies are applied, Iptables rules are created to allow or deny traffic between specific pods or namespaces based on the policy.

   For example, a network policy allows traffic from a specific namespace:

   ```
   -A KUBE-NWPLCY-XXXXXXX -s 10.244.1.0/24 -d
   10.244.0.0/24 -p tcp --dport 80 -j ACCEPT
   ```

   Explanation:

   This rule allows traffic from pods in the 10.244.1.0/24 subnet (representing a specific namespace) to communicate with pods in the 10.244.0.0/24 subnet on port 80.

5. **Masquerading (NAT) Rules**:

   Kubernetes uses masquerading for traffic leaving the cluster to ensure that replies are routed back correctly:

   ```
   -A KUBE-POSTROUTING -s 10.244.0.0/16 ! -d 10.244.0.0/16
   -j MASQUERADE
   ```

   Explanation:

   The KUBE-POSTROUTING chain applies the MASQUERADE rule, which ensures that traffic originating from the pod network (10.244.0.0/16) and destined for external networks is properly NATed. This allows pods to communicate with external services, and return traffic is routed correctly.

6. **Internal DNS Resolution Rules**:

   Kubernetes uses Iptables to route DNS queries from pods to the cluster's DNS service (typically kube-dns or CoreDNS):

   ```
   -A KUBE-SERVICES -d 10.96.0.10/32 -p udp -m comment
   --comment "kube-system/kube-dns: dns cluster IP" -m udp
   --dport 53 -j KUBE-SVC-XXXXXXX
   -A KUBE-SVC-XXXXXXX -j KUBE-SEP-XXXXXXXX
   -A KUBE-SEP-XXXXXXXX -s 192.168.1.100/32 -p udp -m udp
   --dport 53 -j DNAT --to-destination 192.168.1.100:53
   ```

   Explanation:

   The service with ClusterIP 10.96.0.10 represents the DNS service (in this case, CoreDNS or kube-dns).

   Traffic on port 53 (DNS) is routed to the DNS pod (192.168.1.100) via DNAT.

Summary

In Kubernetes, Iptables plays a vital role in managing the network by creating rules for

Routing service traffic (via ClusterIP, NodePort, or LoadBalancer)

Enabling pod-to-pod communication

Enforcing network policies for pod-level security

Applying NAT and masquerading rules for external traffic

These Iptables rules are automatically generated and maintained by components like kube-proxy and CNI plugins, ensuring smooth communication within the cluster and with external services.

8.7 Problem Statement: Implementing Network Security in Kubernetes

In a Kubernetes cluster, securing network communication between various components is crucial to protect against unauthorized access, data breaches, and other security threats. Network security involves multiple aspects, including enforcing network policies, securing communication channels, and monitoring network traffic for suspicious activity. The challenge lies in effectively implementing these security measures while maintaining the performance and functionality of the applications.

Unauthorized Access: Preventing unauthorized entities from accessing services and data within the cluster

Data Encryption: Ensuring that data in transit is encrypted to prevent interception and eavesdropping

Network Policies: Enforcing fine-grained network policies to control traffic flow between pods and services

Monitoring and Logging: Continuously monitoring network traffic and logging activities to detect and respond to security incidents

Solution: Implementing Network Security in Kubernetes

Step-by-Step Guide with Examples

1. Enforcing Network Policies

Network policies in Kubernetes allow you to specify how pods communicate with each other and other network endpoints. They use labels to select pods and define rules about what traffic is allowed to and from those pods.

Creating a Basic NetworkPolicy

Create a simple NetworkPolicy that allows ingress traffic only from specific pods.

Here's an example configuration:

```
apiVersion: networking.k8s.io/v1
kind: NetworkPolicy
metadata:
  name: allow-specific-ingress
```

```
  namespace: default
spec:
  podSelector:
    matchLabels:
      app: my-app
  policyTypes:
  - Ingress
  ingress:
  - from:
    - podSelector:
        matchLabels:
          role: frontend
    ports:
    - protocol: TCP
      port: 80
```

Apply the NetworkPolicy:

```
kubectl apply -f allow-specific-ingress.yaml
```

Verifying the NetworkPolicy

To verify the NetworkPolicy, create test pods and check connectivity.

Create a frontend pod:

```
apiVersion: v1
kind: Pod
metadata:
  name: frontend-pod
  labels:
    role: frontend
spec:
  containers:
```

```
  - name: busybox
    image: busybox
    command: ["sleep", "3600"]
```

Create a backend pod:

```
apiVersion: v1
kind: Pod
metadata:
  name: backend-pod
  labels:
    role: backend
spec:
  containers:
  - name: busybox
    image: busybox
    command: ["sleep", "3600"]
```

Apply the pods:

```
kubectl apply -f frontend-pod.yaml
kubectl apply -f backend-pod.yaml
```

Test connectivity:

```
kubectl exec frontend-pod -- curl http://my-app-pod-ip:80
kubectl exec backend-pod -- curl http://my-app-pod-ip:80
```

Only the request from the frontend pod should succeed.

2. Securing Communication with TLS

Use CertManager to automate the creation and management of TLS certificates for encrypting traffic.

Installing CertManager

Install CertManager using the provided manifest:

```
kubectl apply -f https://github.com/jetstack/cert-manager/
releases/download/v1.0.4/cert-manager.yaml
```

Creating an Issuer

Define an issuer to obtain certificates from Let's Encrypt:

```
apiVersion: cert-manager.io/v1
kind: ClusterIssuer
metadata:
  name: letsencrypt-prod
spec:
  acme:
    server: https://acme-v02.api.letsencrypt.org/directory
    email: user@example.com
    privateKeySecretRef:
      name: letsencrypt-prod
    solvers:
    - http01:
        ingress:
          class: nginx
```

Apply the issuer configuration:

```
kubectl apply -f clusterissuer.yaml
```

Creating a Certificate

Request a certificate for your application:

```
apiVersion: cert-manager.io/v1
kind: Certificate
metadata:
```

```
  name: my-app-cert
  namespace: default
spec:
  secretName: my-app-tls
  issuerRef:
    name: letsencrypt-prod
    kind: ClusterIssuer
  commonName: my-app.example.com
  dnsNames:
  - my-app.example.com
```

Apply the certificate configuration:

```
kubectl apply -f certificate.yaml
```

3. Monitoring and Logging Network Traffic

Use tools like Prometheus and Grafana for monitoring and Fluentd or ELK (Elasticsearch, Logstash, Kibana) Stack for logging.

Installing Prometheus and Grafana

Deploy Prometheus and Grafana using Helm:

```
helm install prometheus prometheus-community/kube-
prometheus-stack
helm install grafana grafana/grafana
```

Setting Up Fluentd

Deploy Fluentd to collect logs:

```
apiVersion: apps/v1
kind: DaemonSet
metadata:
```

```
  name: fluentd
  namespace: logging
spec:
  selector:
    matchLabels:
      app: fluentd
  template:
    metadata:
      labels:
        app: fluentd
    spec:
      containers:
      - name: fluentd
        image: fluentd/fluentd
        env:
        - name: FLUENTD_ARGS
          value: "--no-supervisor -q"
        volumeMounts:
        - name: varlog
          mountPath: /var/log
        - name: fluentdconf
          mountPath: /fluentd/etc
  volumes:
  - name: varlog
    hostPath:
      path: /var/log
  - name: fluentdconf
    configMap:
      name: fluentd-config
```

Apply the DaemonSet:

```
kubectl apply -f fluentd-daemonset.yaml
```

4. Implementing Intrusion Detection

Use tools like Falco to detect and respond to suspicious activity in your Kubernetes cluster.

Installing Falco

Deploy Falco using Helm:

```
helm install falco falcosecurity/falco
```

Conclusion

Implementing network security in Kubernetes involves multiple layers of security measures, including enforcing network policies, securing communication with TLS, monitoring and logging network traffic, and implementing intrusion detection. By following the steps outlined above, you can effectively enhance the security of your Kubernetes cluster, protecting it from unauthorized access and ensuring secure communication between components. This comprehensive approach helps maintain a robust and secure Kubernetes environment.

8.8 Problem Statement: Network Automation and Software-Defined Networking (SDN) in Kubernetes

Manually managing network configurations in a Kubernetes cluster can be time-consuming and error-prone, especially as the cluster scales. Network automation and software-defined networking (SDN) provide a way to dynamically configure, manage, and optimize network resources through software-based solutions. Integrating network automation and SDN into Kubernetes to achieve efficient, scalable, and flexible network management is challenging.

Specific Issues

1. **Manual Configuration**: Manually managing network configurations can lead to errors and inconsistencies, especially in large-scale environments.
2. **Scalability**: Ensuring that the network can scale efficiently by adding new nodes and services.
3. **Flexibility**: Adapting the network to changing requirements and workloads without manual intervention.
4. **Optimized Traffic Management**: Ensuring efficient traffic routing, load balancing, and network resource utilization.

Solution: Implementing Network Automation and SDN in Kubernetes

Step-by-Step Guide with Examples

1. Understanding Network Automation and SDN

Network automation involves using software to manage network configurations and operations automatically. SDN decouples the network control plane from the data plane, enabling centralized network control and management.

2. Setting Up Calico for Network Automation

Calico is a popular Kubernetes networking and network security solution that provides network automation and SDN capabilities.

Installing Calico

Install Calico using the provided manifest:

```
kubectl apply -f https://docs.projectcalico.org/manifests/
calico.yaml
```

Verifying Calico Installation

Check that the Calico components are running:

```
kubectl get pods -n calico-system
```

3. Configuring Calico Network Policies

Calico allows you to define network policies to control traffic flow within your Kubernetes cluster.

Creating a Calico Network Policy

Create a network policy to allow traffic from specific pods:

```
apiVersion: projectcalico.org/v3
kind: NetworkPolicy
metadata:
  name: allow-frontend
  namespace: default
spec:
  selector: app == 'my-app'
  ingress:
    - action: Allow
      source:
        selector: role == 'frontend'
      destination:
        ports:
          - 80
```

Apply the network policy:

```
kubectl apply -f calico-networkpolicy.yaml
```

4. Setting Up Flannel for SDN

Flannel is another SDN solution for Kubernetes, providing a simple overlay network to manage pod communication.

Installing Flannel

Install Flannel using the provided manifest:

```
kubectl apply -f https://raw.githubusercontent.com/coreos/
flannel/master/Documentation/kube-flannel.yml
```

Verifying Flannel Installation

Check that the Flannel components are running:

```
kubectl get pods -n kube-system -l app=flannel
```

5. Automating Network Configuration with Ansible

Ansible is an automation tool that can be used to automate network configurations in Kubernetes.

Installing Ansible

Install Ansible on your control machine:

```
sudo apt-get install ansible
```

Creating an Ansible Playbook

Create a playbook to automate network configurations:

```
- name: Configure Kubernetes Network
  hosts: kube-nodes
  tasks:
    - name: Apply Calico Network Policy
      kubernetes. core.k8s:
        state: present
        definition: "{{ lookup('file', 'calico-networkpolicy.
        yaml') }}"
```

Running the Ansible Playbook

Execute the playbook to apply the network configurations:

```
ansible-playbook -i inventory.ini configure-network.yaml
```

6. Using Open vSwitch (OVS) for Advanced SDN

Open vSwitch is a multilayer virtual switch used to automate network configurations and provide SDN capabilities.

Installing Open vSwitch

Install Open vSwitch on your nodes:

```
sudo apt-get install openvswitch-switch
```

Configuring Open vSwitch

Create a script to configure OVS bridges and ports:

```
#!/bin/bash
ovs-vsctl add-br br0
ovs-vsctl add-port br0 eth1
```

Run the script on your nodes:

```
./configure-ovs.sh
```

7. Implementing Network Monitoring and Analytics

Use tools like Prometheus and Grafana for monitoring network performance and analytics.

Installing Prometheus and Grafana

Deploy Prometheus and Grafana using Helm:

```
helm install prometheus prometheus-community/kube-
prometheus-stack
helm install grafana grafana/grafana
```

Configuring Network Metrics Collection

Configure Prometheus to collect network metrics from Calico and Flannel.

Conclusion

Implementing network automation and SDN in Kubernetes can significantly enhance the efficiency, scalability, and flexibility of your network management. By leveraging tools like Calico, Flannel, Ansible, and Open vSwitch, you can automate network configurations, optimize traffic management, and adapt to changing requirements seamlessly. This approach ensures a robust and scalable network infrastructure that supports the dynamic nature of Kubernetes environments.

8.9 Problem Statement: Implementing Cloud-Native Network Functions (CNFs) and Virtual Network Functions (VNFs) in Kubernetes

In modern network architectures, leveraging Cloud-Native Network Functions (CNFs) and Virtual Network Functions (VNFs) is essential for providing scalable, efficient, and flexible network services. CNFs and VNFs offer functionalities such as firewalls, load balancers, and routing, which are critical for managing network traffic and ensuring security. The challenge is to integrate and manage these functions within a Kubernetes environment, ensuring seamless deployment, scalability, and performance.

Specific Issues

1. **Integration**: Integrating CNFs and VNFs into Kubernetes while maintaining compatibility and performance
2. **Scalability**: Ensuring that CNFs and VNFs can scale efficiently with the Kubernetes cluster
3. **Performance**: Maintaining high performance and low latency for network functions
4. **Management**: Simplifying the management and orchestration of network functions

Solution: Implementing Cloud-Native Network Functions and Virtual Network Functions in Kubernetes

Step-by-Step Guide with Examples

1. Understanding CNFs and VNFs

CNFs are network functions designed to run in cloud-native environments, utilizing microservices and container orchestration platforms like Kubernetes. VNFs are virtualized network functions traditionally deployed on virtual machines, but they can also be containerized for use in Kubernetes.

2. Deploying CNFs with Kubernetes

Example: Deploying a Cloud-Native Firewall Using Calico

Calico can be used to implement network policies acting as a firewall in a Kubernetes cluster.

Installing Calico

Install Calico using the provided manifest:

```
kubectl apply -f https://docs.projectcalico.org/manifests/
calico.yaml
```

Creating a NetworkPolicy for Firewall Rules

Define a NetworkPolicy to act as a firewall:

```
apiVersion: projectcalico.org/v3
kind: NetworkPolicy
metadata:
  name: allow-web
```

```
  namespace: default
spec:
  selector: app == 'my-app'
  ingress:
    - action: Allow
      source:
        selector: role == 'web'
      destination:
        ports:
          - 80
  egress:
    - action: Allow
      destination:
        ports:
          - 443
```

Apply the NetworkPolicy:

```
kubectl apply -f calico-firewall-policy.yaml
```

3. Deploying VNFs with Kubernetes

Example: Deploying a Virtual Router Using FRR (Free Range Routing)

FRR is an open source routing software suite that can be containerized and deployed as a VNF in Kubernetes.

Creating a Deployment for FRR

Create a Kubernetes deployment for the FRR container:

```
apiVersion: apps/v1
kind: Deployment
metadata:
```

```
  name: frr-deployment
spec:
  replicas: 1
  selector:
    matchLabels:
      app: frr
  template:
    metadata:
      labels:
        app: frr
    spec:
      containers:
      - name: frr
        image: frrouting/frr
        ports:
        - containerPort: 179
          name: bgp
        - containerPort: 2601
          name: frr-zebra
        - containerPort: 2605
          name: frr-bgp
```

Apply the deployment:

```
kubectl apply -f frr-deployment.yaml
```

Creating a Service for FRR

Create a service to expose the FRR container:

```
apiVersion: v1
kind: Service
metadata:
```

```
  name: frr-service
spec:
  selector:
    app: frr
  ports:
  - protocol: TCP
    port: 179
    targetPort: 179
  - protocol: TCP
    port: 2601
    targetPort: 2601
  - protocol: TCP
    port: 2605
    targetPort: 2605
```

Apply the service:

```
kubectl apply -f frr-service.yaml
```

4. Automating CNF and VNF Management with Helm

Helm can be used to simplify the deployment and management of CNFs and VNFs.

Creating a Helm Chart

Create a Helm chart for your CNF or VNF. Here's an example structure for an FRR Helm chart:

```
helm create frr-chart
```

Modify the values, YAML, and templates in the Helm chart to match your deployment and service configurations.

Deploying with Helm

Deploy the Helm chart:

```
helm install frr frr-chart
```

5. Monitoring and Scaling CNFs and VNFs

Using Prometheus and Grafana for Monitoring

Deploy Prometheus and Grafana to monitor the performance and health of CNFs and VNFs:

```
helm install prometheus prometheus-community/kube-
prometheus-stack
helm install grafana grafana/grafana
```

Autoscaling CNFs and VNFs

Use Kubernetes Horizontal Pod Autoscaler (HPA) to scale CNFs and VNFs based on resource usage.

Example: Configuring HPA for FRR

Create an HPA configuration:

```
apiVersion: autoscaling/v2beta2
kind: HorizontalPodAutoscaler
metadata:
  name: frr-hpa
spec:
  scaleTargetRef:
    apiVersion: apps/v1
    kind: Deployment
    name: frr-deployment
```

```
  minReplicas: 1
  maxReplicas: 10
  metrics:
  - type: Resource
    resource:
      name: cpu
      target:
        type: Utilization
        averageUtilization: 50
```

Apply the HPA configuration:

```
kubectl apply -f frr-hpa.yaml
```

Conclusion

Implementing Cloud-Native Network Functions (CNFs) and Virtual Network Functions (VNFs) in Kubernetes allows for scalable, flexible, and efficient network service management. By following the steps outlined above, you can deploy, manage, and scale CNFs and VNFs within your Kubernetes environment, ensuring robust and high-performance network functionalities. Leveraging tools like Calico, FRR, Helm, Prometheus, and HPA enhances the overall network management capabilities, aligning with modern cloud-native and software-defined networking practices.

8.10 Troubleshooting Common Networking Issues in Kubernetes

Networking is a critical component of Kubernetes, enabling communication between pods, services, and external clients. However, network-related issues can arise, disrupting the functionality of your applications. This section provides strategies and best practices for diagnosing and resolving common networking problems in Kubernetes, including service connectivity issues, misconfigured network policies, and load balancer setup errors.

8.10.1 Debugging Service Connectivity Problems

Service connectivity issues can prevent pods from communicating with each other or with external clients. Here's how to troubleshoot these issues.

Verify Service Definitions

Check Service YAML: Ensure that the service is correctly defined with the appropriate selector, ports, and type.

```
kubectl describe service <service-name>
```

Confirm Labels: Verify that the pods have the labels matching the service's selector.

```
kubectl get pods --show-labels
```

Check Pod Status and Readiness

Pod Status: Ensure that all pods targeted by the service are in a Running state.

```
kubectl get pods
```

Readiness Probes: Confirm that readiness probes are passing, indicating the pod is ready to receive traffic.

```
kubectl describe pod <pod-name>
```

Inspect DNS Resolution

DNS Configuration: Kubernetes uses CoreDNS or kube-dns for service discovery. Check if DNS is functioning correctly.

```
kubectl get pods -n kube-system -l k8s-app=kube-dns
```

Test DNS Inside the Cluster: Execute a DNS query from within a pod.

```
kubectl exec -ti <pod-name> -- nslookup <service-name>
```

Test Network Connectivity Inside the Cluster

Ping Between Pods: Use ping to test connectivity (if ICMP is allowed).

```
kubectl exec -ti <source-pod> -- ping
<destination-pod-ip>
```

Port Connectivity: Use curl or telnet to test specific ports.

```
kubectl exec -ti <pod> -- curl http://<service-
name>:<port>
```

Examine Service Endpoints

List Endpoints: Ensure that the service has associated endpoints.

```
kubectl get endpoints <service-name>
```

No Endpoints Found: If no endpoints are listed, verify that the service selectors correctly match the pod labels.

Review kube-proxy Configuration

kube-proxy Status: Ensure that kube-proxy is running and correctly configured.

```
kubectl get pods -n kube-system -l k8s-app=kube-proxy
```

Logs: Check kube-proxy logs for errors.

```
kubectl logs <kube-proxy-pod> -n kube-system
```

8.10.2 Troubleshooting Misconfigured Network Policies

Understand the Intended Network Policies

Policy Objectives: Clearly define what traffic should be allowed or denied.

Scope: Determine which pods and namespaces the policies apply to.

Verify Network Policy Definitions

YAML Validation: Ensure that the network policy YAML files are syntactically correct.

```
kubectl apply --dry-run=client -f <network-policy.yaml>
```

Policy Rules: Check ingress and egress rules for correctness.

```
kubectl describe networkpolicy <policy-name>
```

Use Network Policy Auditing Tools

Tools: Utilize tools like Calico Network Policy Analyzer to visualize and audit network policies.

Policy Reports: Generate reports to identify conflicting or overlapping policies.

Test Connectivity Between Pods

Isolated Testing: Deploy test pods in the relevant namespaces and attempt to communicate according to the policy rules.

```
kubectl exec -ti <test-pod> -- curl http://<target-service>:<port>
```

Observe Denials: If communication fails, it might indicate a policy is blocking the traffic.

Review Network Plugin Logs

Plugin Specifics: Depending on the CNI plugin (e.g., Calico, Weave, Cilium), check the corresponding logs for policy enforcement issues.

```
kubectl logs <cni-plugin-pod> -n kube-system
```

Common Misconfigurations and Fixes

Missing Egress Rules: Ensure that egress traffic is permitted if needed.

Overly Restrictive Selectors: Verify that label selectors accurately target the intended pods.

Default Deny Policies: Remember that Kubernetes network policies are additive; multiple policies can restrict traffic more than intended.

8.10.3 Resolving Load Balancer Setup Errors

Load balancers distribute incoming traffic to services in Kubernetes. Misconfigurations can lead to inaccessible services or uneven traffic distribution.

Verify Load Balancer Configuration

Service Type: Ensure the service is of type LoadBalancer.

```
kubectl get service <service-name>
```

Annotations: Check for necessary annotations required by the cloud provider or load balancer.

```
kubectl describe service <service-name>
```

Check Cloud Provider Settings

Provisioning Status: Confirm that the cloud provider has successfully provisioned the load balancer.

Resource Limits: Ensure that you haven't exceeded the quota for load balancers in your cloud environment.

Inspect Service Annotations

Provider-Specific Settings: Annotations may control aspects like load balancer type, health checks, and SSL termination.

Documentation Reference: Consult your cloud provider's documentation for required and optional annotations.

Monitor Load Balancer Health

Health Checks: Verify that health checks are correctly configured and passing.

Backend Status: Ensure that backend pods are healthy and responsive.

Logs: Check load balancer logs for any errors or warnings.

Review Firewall and Security Group Settings

Ingress Rules: Ensure that firewall rules allow traffic to the load balancer's IP and ports.

Egress Rules: Confirm that necessary egress traffic is permitted from the load balancer to the backend pods.

Examine Kubernetes Event Logs

Event Inspection: Look for events related to the service and load balancer.

```
kubectl describe service <service-name>
```

Common Issues: Events may indicate provisioning failures, misconfigurations, or connectivity problems.

Chapter Summary

This chapter equips developers, admins, and DevOps engineers with practical insights to manage Kubernetes networking, ensuring high availability, security, and optimal performance. From debugging tools to advanced SDN integrations, this is a comprehensive guide to mastering Kubernetes networking.

CHAPTER 9

Performance Observability in Kubernetes

This chapter focuses on achieving performance observability within Kubernetes environments. We explore the essential tools that help you maintain visibility in a Kubernetes environment. Whether monitoring with Prometheus, managing logs with Fluentd, or tracing microservices with Jaeger, each tool plays a crucial role in ensuring your applications run smoothly and efficiently. We'll walk you through the problems these tools solve, how to integrate them into your setup, and their benefits to your day-to-day operations. If you're working with Kubernetes, understanding these tools is key to staying on top of your infrastructure, ensuring that you can catch issues before they become problems, and keeping everything running at peak performance.

9.1 Metrics Server

Problem

To effectively scale applications in Kubernetes, it's essential to have access to real-time resource metrics like CPU and memory usage. Without these metrics, autoscaling and capacity planning become challenging.

G. Stencel and L. Berton, *Kubernetes Recipes*,
https://doi.org/10.1007/979-8-8688-1325-2_9

Solution

The metrics server is a Kubernetes component that collects resource metrics from nodes and pods and exposes them via the Kubernetes API. Components like Horizontal Pod Autoscaler (HPA) use these metrics to make scaling decisions based on real-time resource utilization.

Here's an example configuration:

```
apiVersion: v1
kind: Deployment
metadata:
  name: metrics-server
  namespace: kube-system
spec:
  selector:
    matchLabels:
      k8s-app: metrics-server
  template:
    metadata:
      labels:
        k8s-app: metrics-server
    spec:
      containers:
        - name: metrics-server
          image: k8s.gcr.io/metrics-server/metrics-
          server:v0.4.1
          args:
            - --kubelet-insecure-tls
          ports:
            - containerPort: 443
              name: https
```

Discussion

The metrics server is crucial for enabling Kubernetes autoscaling features and providing insights into the resource utilization of workloads. It's lightweight and easy to deploy, making it a standard component in most Kubernetes clusters. By exposing real-time metrics, the metrics server allows for more efficient scaling and resource management, ensuring that applications have the resources they need to perform optimally.

Using the `--kubelet-insecure-tls` flag with the metrics server disables TLS certificate verification, posing significant security risks, such as exposure to MITM attacks; hence, it should only be used in non-production environments. For production setups, secure the metrics server by configuring proper TLS certificates signed by a trusted Certificate Authority (CA) and replacing the insecure flag with `--kubelet-certificate-authority` to verify kubelet communications:

```
args:
- --kubelet-certificate-authority=/path/to/ca.crt
 - --kubelet-preferred-address-types=InternalIP,Hostname,
ExternalIP
```

Additionally, implement RBAC to restrict permissions, apply network policies to control access, and configure `--kubelet-preferred-address-types` for optimal communication. These measures ensure secure and reliable metrics server operation, enabling accurate autoscaling and resource monitoring while maintaining robust security.

Ensure the metrics server has minimal permissions:

```
apiVersion: rbac.authorization.k8s.io/v1
kind: Role
metadata:
  namespace: kube-system
  name: metrics-server-role
```

```
rules:
  - apiGroups: [""]
    resources: ["pods", "nodes", "nodes/stats"]
    verbs: ["get", "list", "watch"]
---
apiVersion: rbac.authorization.k8s.io/v1
kind: RoleBinding
metadata:
  name: metrics-server-role-binding
  namespace: kube-system
roleRef:
  apiGroup: rbac.authorization.k8s.io
  kind: Role
  name: metrics-server-role
subjects:
  - kind: ServiceAccount
    name: metrics-server
    namespace: kube-system
```

Restrict access to the metrics server for enhanced security:

```
apiVersion: networking.k8s.io/v1
kind: NetworkPolicy
metadata:
  name: metrics-server-policy
  namespace: kube-system
spec:
  podSelector:
    matchLabels:
      k8s-app: metrics-server
  ingress:
    - from:
```

```
    - podSelector:
        matchLabels:
          component: kube-apiserver
  ports:
    - protocol: TCP
      port: 443
```

See Also

- Horizontal Pod Autoscaler in Chapter 6

9.2 Prometheus

Problem

Kubernetes environments need a reliable way to monitor the performance and health of various services and infrastructure. Traditional monitoring tools often struggle with the dynamic nature of containerized environments, leading to gaps in visibility and delayed response times to issues.

Solution

Prometheus is a powerful monitoring and alerting toolkit designed specifically for dynamic cloud-native environments. It scrapes metrics from endpoints, stores them in a time-series database, and provides a flexible querying language to analyze these metrics. Integrating Prometheus with Kubernetes allows you to monitor various aspects of your applications and infrastructure, enabling proactive alerting and insights into system health.

Here's an example configuration:

```
apiVersion: monitoring.coreos.com/v1
kind: Prometheus
metadata:
  name: k8s
spec:
  serviceAccountName: prometheus-k8s
  serviceMonitorSelector:
    matchLabels:
      team: frontend
  resources:
    requests:
      memory: 400Mi
```

Event-Driven Monitoring

Instead of relying on periodic scraping, configure Prometheus to scrape metrics based on Kubernetes events, ensuring that data from even the shortest-lived containers is captured. Configure Prometheus to trigger a scrape when a pod transitions into the Running state. Use Kubernetes event resources combined with Prometheus `kubernetes_sd_configs` to dynamically discover and monitor short-lived pods:

```
scrape_configs:
  - job_name: 'kubernetes-pods-shortlived'
    kubernetes_sd_configs:
      - role: pod
    relabel_configs:
      - source_labels: [__meta_kubernetes_pod_phase]
        action: keep
        regex: Running
```

Discussion

Prometheus is highly adaptable to Kubernetes environments due to its service discovery capabilities and native integration with the ecosystem. It excels in environments with ephemeral workloads where traditional monitoring might miss crucial metrics. Combining Prometheus with alerting tools like Alertmanager allows you to set up complex alerting rules that respond to system anomalies in real time.

The most convenient way to install Prometheus is via Prometheus Operator, a Kubernetes operator that provides Kubernetes native deployment and management of Prometheus and related monitoring components. It provides the following:

- Kubernetes custom resources to deploy and manage Prometheus, Alertmanager, and related components.
- Simplified deployment configuration is used to configure the fundamentals of Prometheus, such as versions, persistence, retention policies, and replicas from a native Kubernetes resource.
- Prometheus target configuration to automatically generate monitoring target configurations based on familiar Kubernetes label queries; no need to learn a Prometheus-specific configuration language.

Prometheus operates on a pull-based model and relies on periodic scraping dictated by `scrape_interval`. While Kubernetes' `kubernetes_sd_configs` facilitates dynamic target discovery, Prometheus does not inherently react to Kubernetes events like pod state transitions. This can result in gaps in monitoring short-lived pods unless the `scrape_interval` is tuned appropriately.

Here are recommendations for event-driven monitoring:

1. **Adjusting the `scrape_interval` Value**: Choose a shorter `scrape_interval` for specific jobs to reduce gaps in capturing metrics from ephemeral workloads, for instance:

    ```
    scrape_configs:
      - job_name: 'kubernetes-pods-shortlived'
        kubernetes_sd_configs:
          - role: pod
        scrape_interval: 5s
        relabel_configs:
          - source_labels: [__meta_kubernetes_pod_phase]
            action: keep
            regex: Running
    ```

2. **External Triggers with PushGateway**: Use Prometheus PushGateway for transient jobs or pods. This enables ephemeral workloads to push metrics directly before termination.

3. **Custom Exporters or Sidecars**: Deploy lightweight exporters or sidecars with applications that can aggregate and buffer metrics to ensure they are retained even if the main application terminates.

4. **Enhanced Integration Tools**: Combine Prometheus with tools like Alertmanager or custom Kubernetes controllers to create reactive monitoring:

    - Use Kubernetes event resources to trigger external systems that notify or configure Prometheus dynamically.

- Implement event-driven automation using custom Kubernetes operators.

5. Monitoring ephemeral workloads with techniques such as integration with Prometheus Operator or Grafana Loki can enhance visibility into Kubernetes clusters. These tools enable more granular monitoring of logs and metrics context.

6. Employing custom resource definitions (CRDs) and operators can orchestrate metric collection during critical pod lifecycle events, enhancing monitoring coverage.

These strategies ensure metrics for short-lived pods are reliably captured and stored, enabling a robust monitoring and alerting framework suitable for dynamic Kubernetes environments.

See Also

- **Prometheus Operator**: Prometheus Operator GitHub (`https://github.com/prometheus-operator/prometheus-operator`)

9.3 InfluxDB

Problem

High-performance applications, particularly in IoT and DevOps, generate large volumes of time-series data that need to be ingested, stored, and queried efficiently. Traditional databases often need help with the volume and velocity of time-series data, leading to performance bottlenecks.

Solution

InfluxDB is a purpose-built time-series database that excels at high-performance data ingestion and querying. It's optimized for handling time-stamped data, making it ideal for monitoring metrics, logs, and events from distributed systems. In a Kubernetes environment, InfluxDB can be used to store metrics from various sources, such as application performance data, system metrics, and more.

Here's an example configuration:

```
apiVersion: v1
kind: ConfigMap
metadata:
  name: influxdb-config
  namespace: monitoring
data:
  influxdb.conf: |
    [http]
      enabled = true
      bind-address = ":8086"
      auth-enabled = true
```

Discussion

InfluxDB is particularly useful when you need to handle large volumes of time-series data with high write and query performance. It integrates well with other observability tools like Grafana for visualization. However, managing retention policies and resource allocation is necessary to avoid performance degradation as data volume grows.

See Also

- **Telegraf**
- **Kapacitor**

9.4 Fluentd

Problem

In distributed systems, collecting, aggregating, and forwarding logs from various sources can become complex, leading to fragmented log data and difficulty in troubleshooting issues.

Solution

Fluentd is a data collector that provides a unified logging layer, capable of collecting logs from multiple sources, transforming them, and routing them to various destinations like Elasticsearch, S3, or InfluxDB. It's designed to be flexible and can be easily integrated into Kubernetes environments to ensure consistent and centralized logging.

Here's an example configuration:

```
apiVersion: apps/v1
kind: DaemonSet
metadata:
  name: fluentd
  namespace: logging
spec:
  selector:
```

```
    matchLabels:
      name: fluentd
  template:
    metadata:
      labels:
        name: fluentd
    spec:
      containers:
        - name: fluentd
          image: fluent/fluentd:v1.11
          env:
            - name: FLUENT_ELASTICSEARCH_HOST
              value: "elasticsearch.default.svc.cluster.local"
          volumeMounts:
            - name: varlog
              mountPath: /var/log
```

Discussion

Fluentd's flexibility makes it a powerful tool for centralized logging in Kubernetes. It can handle diverse log formats and destinations, which is critical in complex environments. By standardizing log collection and forwarding, Fluentd helps reduce troubleshooting time and improve overall system observability.

See Also

- **Fluent Bit**

9.5 ELK (Elasticsearch, Logstash, Kibana) Stack

Problem

Managing, searching, and visualizing logs from a distributed system is challenging. Without a centralized system, it's difficult to correlate logs and gain actionable insights from the data generated by various applications and services.

Solution

ELK Stack, consisting of Elasticsearch, Logstash, and Kibana, provides a comprehensive solution for log collection, search, analysis, and visualization. In a Kubernetes environment, ELK Stack can centralize logging, enabling you to search and analyze logs efficiently and create dashboards for real-time monitoring.

Here's an example configuration:

```
apiVersion: apps/v1
kind: StatefulSet
metadata:
  name: elasticsearch
  namespace: logging
spec:
  serviceName: elasticsearch
  replicas: 3
  selector:
    matchLabels:
      app: elasticsearch
  template:
```

```
    metadata:
      labels:
        app: elasticsearch
    spec:
      containers:
        - name: elasticsearch
          image: docker.elastic.co/elasticsearch/
                 elasticsearch:7.10.1
          ports:
            - containerPort: 9200
              name: http
            - containerPort: 9300
              name: transport
          env:
            - name: discovery.type
              value: "zen"
            - name: cluster.name
              value: "elasticsearch-cluster"
            - name: network.host
              value: "0.0.0.0"
          volumeMounts:
            - name: elasticsearch-data
              mountPath: /usr/share/elasticsearch/data
  volumeClaimTemplates:
    - metadata:
        name: elasticsearch-data
      spec:
        accessModes: ["ReadWriteOnce"]
        resources:
          requests:
            storage: 10Gi
```

Discussion

ELK Stack is powerful but resource-intensive, requiring careful scaling and management in production environments. Elasticsearch provides storage and search capabilities, Logstash handles data collection and transformation, and Kibana offers a user-friendly interface for querying and visualizing data. Together, they provide a robust solution for managing logs in Kubernetes environments.

Here are key elements of the configuration snippet:

1. **Selector and Labels:**
    - `selector.matchLabels` ensures that the pods created by the StatefulSet are correctly identified.
    - Labels in the template and selector match, maintaining coherence.
2. **VolumeClaimTemplates:**
    - Specifies persistent storage for Elasticsearch data (`elasticsearch-data`).
    - Uses `ReadWriteOnce` access mode and requests 10 Gi of storage.
3. **Pod Template:**
    - Defines the pod's `spec` including container details.
    - Includes environment variables for essential Elasticsearch configuration (`discovery.type`, `cluster.name`, etc.).
4. **Container Ports:**
    - Specifies ports for HTTP (9200) and transport (9300).

5. **Volume Mounts:**

    - Mounts the persistent volume at `/usr/share/elasticsearch/data`.

9.6 Jaeger

Problem

Distributed systems, especially microservices architectures, often suffer from performance bottlenecks and latency issues that are difficult to diagnose without detailed tracing of requests across services.

Solution

Jaeger is an open source distributed tracing system that helps monitor and troubleshoot complex microservices architectures. It enables you to trace the flow of requests through your system, identify performance bottlenecks, and understand service dependencies. Integrating Jaeger with Kubernetes allows you to gain insights into the performance of your services in real time.

Here's an example configuration:

```
apiVersion: jaegertracing.io/v1
kind: Jaeger
metadata:
  name: simplest
spec:
  strategy: allInOne
```

To install the Jaeger Operator and enable the CRD `jaegertracing.io/v1` in your Kubernetes cluster, follow these steps:

1. Install the Jaeger Operator using Helm:

   ```
   helm repo add jaegertracing https://jaegertracing.github.io/helm-charts
   helm repo update
   ```

   ```
   helm install jaeger-operator jaegertracing/jaeger-operator --namespace observability --create-namespace
   ```

   Alternatively, you can deploy the operator using its Kubernetes manifests:

   ```
   kubectl create namespace observability
   kubectl apply -f https://raw.githubusercontent.com/jaegertracing/jaeger-operator/main/deploy/manifests/jaeger-operator.yaml
   ```

2. Verify the installation and ensure the `jaeger-operator` pod is running:

   ```
   kubectl get pods -n observability
   ```

3. Check the CRD `jaegers.jaegertracing.io` is installed:

   ```
   kubectl get crd | grep jaeger
   ```

4. Deploy a Jaeger instance with the following manifest:

   ```
   apiVersion: jaegertracing.io/v1
   kind: Jaeger
   metadata:
     name: simplest
   ```

```
spec:
  strategy: allInOne
```

Apply the manifest:

```
kubectl apply -f jaeger-instance.yaml
```

5. Expose the Jaeger service to access the tracing user interface. Use a NodePort or Ingress:

```
kubectl expose svc simplest-query --type=NodePort -n
observability
```

Discussion

Jaeger provides visibility into the flow of requests across microservices, making it easier to troubleshoot latency issues and optimize performance. It integrates well with Kubernetes and other observability tools, offering a comprehensive view of system behavior. By analyzing trace data, you can improve the resilience and performance of your distributed applications.

Using the Jaeger CRD operator in Kubernetes simplifies and automates the deployment and management of distributed tracing for microservices. By enabling Kubernetes-native configurations, it integrates seamlessly with the ecosystem, allowing developers to manage Jaeger instances using standard Kubernetes tools like `kubectl` declaratively. The operator handles complex tasks such as scaling, resource allocation, upgrades, and backend storage configuration, ensuring consistency across environments. It supports various deployment strategies, from development-friendly all-in-one setups to production-grade distributed architectures. The operator provides real-time insights into service interactions, making troubleshooting latency issues easier, optimizing performance, and improving system resilience. Additionally, Jaeger's integration with observability tools like Prometheus, Grafana, and OpenTelemetry further enhances monitoring capabilities, allowing organizations to maintain efficient and reliable microservices-based systems.

9.7 Zipkin

Problem

When services in a distributed system experience latency, it can be challenging to pinpoint the root cause without detailed tracing of how requests flow through the system.

Solution

Zipkin is a distributed tracing system that collects timing data needed to troubleshoot latency problems in service architectures. It helps track the flow of requests and visualize their path through different services. In a Kubernetes environment, Zipkin can be integrated with microservices to provide insights into the performance and dependencies of your system.

Here's an example configuration:

```
apiVersion: apps/v1
kind: Deployment
metadata:
  name: zipkin
  namespace: tracing
spec:
  replicas: 1
  selector:
    matchLabels:
      app: zipkin
  template:
    metadata:
      labels:
        app: zipkin
    spec:
```

```
containers:
  - name: zipkin
    image: openzipkin/zipkin
    ports:
      - containerPort: 9411
```

Discussion

Zipkin is an effective tool for diagnosing latency and performance issues in distributed systems. It provides a detailed view of how requests are handled across services, allowing you to identify and address bottlenecks. While Zipkin and Jaeger are similar, each has unique features, and the choice between them may depend on specific use cases and existing toolchains.

See Also

- **Brave:** Brave Docs

9.8 Grafana

Problem

Visualizing metrics and data from various sources in a centralized, customizable dashboard is critical for effective monitoring and observability in Kubernetes environments. Without a centralized view, it's challenging to correlate data and gain actionable insights.

Solution

Grafana is an open source platform for monitoring and observability, allowing you to create and share dashboards that visualize data from various sources like Prometheus, InfluxDB, and Elasticsearch. It provides powerful querying capabilities and supports alerting to help teams monitor system health in real time.

Here's an example configuration:

```
apiVersion: v1
kind: ConfigMap
metadata:
  name: grafana-datasources
  namespace: monitoring
data:
  datasource.yaml: |
    apiVersion: 1
    datasources:
      - name: Prometheus
        type: prometheus
        access: proxy
        url: http://prometheus:9090
        isDefault: true
```

Discussion

Grafana's versatility makes it an essential tool in Kubernetes environments. It can integrate with various data sources and supports a wide range of plugins, making it possible to visualize almost any kind of data. Grafana's alerting capabilities also ensure that teams are notified when critical thresholds are breached, allowing for timely interventions.

See Also

- Grafana Plugin Directory

9.9 Kibana

Problem

Logs generated by distributed systems are often difficult to search and analyze without a centralized interface. This can lead to delays in troubleshooting and identifying issues within the system.

Solution

Kibana, part of ELK Stack, is a powerful tool for searching, visualizing, and analyzing log data stored in Elasticsearch. It provides a user-friendly interface for exploring logs and creating visualizations that help teams quickly identify and resolve issues in a Kubernetes environment.

Here's an example configuration:

```
apiVersion: apps/v1
kind: Deployment
metadata:
  name: kibana
  namespace: logging
spec:
  replicas: 1
  selector:
    matchLabels:
      app: kibana
  template:
    metadata:
      labels:
```

```
      app: kibana
  spec:
    containers:
      - name: kibana
        image: docker.elastic.co/kibana/kibana:7.10.1
        ports:
          - containerPort: 5601
```

Discussion

Kibana is essential for teams that rely on Elasticsearch for log storage. Its visualization capabilities enable teams to create dashboards that provide real-time insights into log data, making it easier to monitor system health and diagnose issues. In Kubernetes environments, Kibana is often used alongside Fluentd and Elasticsearch to form a comprehensive logging solution.

9.10 OpenTelemetry

Problem

In modern microservices architectures, observability data is scattered across various sources and formats, making it difficult to achieve a unified view of system performance and health.

Solution

OpenTelemetry provides a set of APIs, libraries, agents, and instrumentation tools to generate, collect, and export telemetry data (traces, metrics, logs) from your applications and infrastructure. It aims to standardize observability practices and can be integrated with a wide range of backends like Jaeger, Prometheus, and others in a Kubernetes environment.

Here's an example configuration:

```
apiVersion: apps/v1
kind: Deployment
metadata:
  name: opentelemetry-collector
  namespace: observability
spec:
  replicas: 1
  selector:
    matchLabels:
      app: opentelemetry-collector
  template:
    metadata:
      labels:
        app: opentelemetry-collector
    spec:
      containers:
        - name: otel-collector
          image: otel/opentelemetry-collector:latest
          ports:
            - containerPort: 55680
              name: otlp-grpc
            - containerPort: 55681
              name: otlp-http
```

Discussion

OpenTelemetry is a critical component for achieving end-to-end observability in modern cloud-native environments. It supports a wide range of languages and frameworks, making it a versatile choice for standardizing the collection of telemetry data across diverse systems. By unifying telemetry data, OpenTelemetry simplifies the process of monitoring and troubleshooting complex systems.

9.11 Locust

Problem

Testing the performance and scalability of web applications under load is crucial to ensure they can handle high traffic. However, traditional load-testing tools may not provide the flexibility needed to simulate complex user behaviors.

Solution

Locust is an open source load-testing tool that allows you to simulate user behavior using Python code. This flexibility allows you to create detailed load test scenarios that mimic real-world usage patterns. In a Kubernetes environment, Locust can be used to stress test services, identify bottlenecks, and validate the scalability of your applications.

SequentialTaskSet

Tasks are executed sequentially in the order they are defined within the class:

```
from locust import HttpUser, SequentialTaskSet, task

class UserBehavior(SequentialTaskSet):
    @task
    def index(self):
        self.client.get("/")
        print("Visited the index page.")
```

```
    @task
    def profile(self):
        self.client.get("/profile")
        print("Visited the profile page.")

class WebsiteUser(HttpUser):
    tasks = [UserBehavior]
    min_wait = 5000
    max_wait = 9000
```

LoadTestShape

If you need to define custom load patterns, use LoadTestShape, for instance:

```
from locust import LoadTestShape

class CustomShape(LoadTestShape):
    def tick(self):
        """
        Define user count and runtime pattern.
        """
        run_time = self.get_run_time()
        if run_time < 60:
            return (10, 1)  # 10 users, 1 spawn rate
        elif run_time < 120:
            return (20, 2)  # 20 users, 2 spawn rate
        else:
            return None  # End the test
```

Discussion

Locust provides a flexible and scriptable environment for load testing, making it an excellent tool for testing Kubernetes-based applications. Using Python to define user behavior, you can create complex load tests that closely resemble real-world scenarios, helping you identify and address performance issues before they impact users. Locust can run in a Kubernetes cluster to test services. Consider deploying Locust using

1. **Locust Helm chart** or a custom Kubernetes deployment
2. **ConfigMaps** for test scripts and configurations
3. `kubectl` to scale Locust workers dynamically for stress tests

In Locust 2.x, the `TaskSet` class implementation has been deprecated and replaced with `SequentialTaskSet` and `LoadTestShape.` The `SequentialTaskSet` ensures tasks are executed sequentially in the order they are defined within the class. This is particularly useful when the order of task execution is critical for the test scenario. Additionally, in `SequentialTaskSet`, the `@task` decorator no longer requires a weight parameter, as tasks are executed in sequence rather than being distributed based on weight. The `SequentialTaskSet` is then assigned to the `tasks` attribute of the `HttpUser` class to define the user behavior in a structured and orderly manner.

9.12 Vegeta

Problem

Simulating high traffic to test the resilience and performance of web services is essential, especially for services expected to handle large volumes of requests. However, it's challenging to generate this traffic in a controlled and efficient manner.

Solution

Vegeta is an HTTP load-testing tool that can generate high traffic to test the resilience and performance of your web services. It's simple to use and can be integrated into CI/CD pipelines to automate performance testing in a Kubernetes environment.

Here's an example usage:

```
echo "GET http://your-service-endpoint" | vegeta attack
-duration=30s -rate=1000 | tee results.bin | vegeta report
```

Discussion

Vegeta is a powerful and lightweight tool for generating HTTP load. Its simplicity and speed make it a good choice for quick performance tests or integration into automated testing pipelines. In Kubernetes, Vegeta can be used to test service endpoints directly, ensuring that they can handle the expected load without degradation in performance.

See Also

- **Gatling**

9.13 KubeVirt

Problem

Running Virtual Machine Instances (VMIs) alongside containerized applications in Kubernetes can be challenging, especially when trying to manage both types of workloads using a unified platform.

Solution

KubeVirt is a virtualization API for Kubernetes that enables the management of VMIs alongside containerized workloads. It extends Kubernetes to support VMs as first-class citizens, allowing you to run VMs and containers in the same environment using the same tools and workflows.

Here's an example configuration:

```
apiVersion: kubevirt.io/v1
kind: VirtualMachine
metadata:
  name: myvm
  namespace: default
spec:
  running: true
  template:
    spec:
      domain:
        devices:
          disks:
            - disk:
                bus: virtio
              name: containerdisk
      volumes:
        - name: containerdisk
          containerDisk:
            image: kubevirt/cirros-container-disk-demo
```

Discussion

KubeVirt is a virtualization API for Kubernetes that enables the management of Virtual Machine Instances (VMIs) alongside containerized workloads. It bridges the gap between traditional VM workloads and modern containerized applications, allowing you to manage both within a single Kubernetes cluster. This is particularly useful for organizations transitioning from VM-based infrastructure to containerized microservices, as it provides a path to gradually move workloads without maintaining separate platforms.

Before deploying KubeVirt components, it is essential to install the KubeVirt Operator. The operator handles the deployment, scaling, and lifecycle management of these components. It simplifies the operational complexity of managing KubeVirt by automating various administrative tasks. Here are installation steps for the KubeVirt Operator:

- **Step 1: Add the Operator's CRDs**

  Start by applying the custom resource definitions (CRDs) required by KubeVirt. These define the new API resources managed by KubeVirt.

  ```
  kubectl create -f https://github.com/kubevirt/kubevirt/
  releases/download/v<version>/kubevirt-crds.yaml
  ```

  Replace `<version>` with the desired KubeVirt release version (e.g., `v1.4.0`).

- **Step 2: Deploy the Operator**

  Deploy the KubeVirt Operator from the official repository.

  ```
  kubectl create -f https://github.com/kubevirt/kubevirt/
  releases/download/v<version>/kubevirt-operator.yaml
  ```

- **Step 3: Monitor the Installation**

  Check the status of the operator and its components to ensure they are running as expected.

  1. Verify that the operator pods are running:

     ```
     kubectl get pods -n kubevirt
     ```

  2. Check the status of the CRDs:

     ```
     kubectl get crds
     ```

  You should see resources related to KubeVirt listed, such as `virtualmachines.kubevirt.io`.

- **Step 4: Configure the Operator**

  Use the KubeVirt custom resource to configure and deploy the KubeVirt components in your cluster.

  1. Apply the KubeVirt resource to start the deployment of the KubeVirt runtime:

     ```
     kubectl create -f https://github.com/kubevirt/
     kubevirt/releases/download/v<version>/kubevirt.yaml
     ```

  2. Verify the status of the KubeVirt installation:

     ```
     kubectl get kubevirt -n kubevirt
     ```

     Look for the `Phase` field to confirm that the installation is complete (it should display `Deployed`).

  3. Customize the KubeVirt deployment by editing the `kubevirt` custom resource:

     ```
     kubectl edit kubevirt kubevirt -n kubevirt
     ```

Example Configuration File for CRDs

You can use a specific configuration file like the following:

kubevirt-crds.yaml

```
apiVersion: apiextensions.k8s.io/v1
kind: CustomResourceDefinition
metadata:
  name: virtualmachines.kubevirt.io
spec:
  group: kubevirt.io
  names:
    kind: VirtualMachine
    listKind: VirtualMachineList
    plural: virtualmachines
    singular: virtualmachine
  scope: Namespaced
  versions:
    - name: v1
      served: true
      storage: true
      schema:
        openAPIV3Schema:
          type: object
          properties:
            spec:
              type: object
              properties:
                running:
                  type: boolean
```

Save this to a file and apply it:

```
kubectl apply -f kubevirt-crds.yaml
```

9.14 Harvester

Problem

Managing VMs and containerized workloads separately can be cumbersome and inefficient, particularly in hybrid cloud environments that require both types of infrastructure.

Solution

Harvester is an open source hyper-converged infrastructure (HCI) solution by SUSE that integrates KVM, KubeVirt, and Longhorn to manage VMs and containerized workloads within Kubernetes. It provides a unified platform for deploying and managing both types of workloads, simplifying infrastructure management.

Here's an example configuration:

```
apiVersion: harvesterhci.io/v1beta1
kind: VirtualMachine
metadata:
  name: harvester-vm
spec:
  template:
    spec:
      domain:
        cpu:
          cores: 2
        devices:
          disks:
            - disk:
                bus: virtio
              name: rootdisk
```

```
    volumes:
      - name: rootdisk
        containerDisk:
          image: harvester/cirros:latest
```

Discussion

Harvester provides a comprehensive solution for organizations that need to manage both VMs and containers in a unified environment. It's particularly valuable in environments where a mix of legacy VM-based applications and modern containerized workloads must coexist. Harvester simplifies this by providing tools to manage everything within Kubernetes, reducing operational complexity and improving efficiency.

See Also

- **Longhorn:** Longhorn GitHub

9.15 Amazon CloudWatch

Problem

How can we effectively monitor Kubernetes clusters deployed on Amazon Web Services (AWS) using Amazon CloudWatch?

Solution

Utilize the native monitoring tools provided by AWS, Azure, and GCP to monitor Kubernetes clusters. These tools offer comprehensive insights into the performance, health, and resource utilization of your Kubernetes deployments.

Here are step-by-step instructions:

1. **Set Up Amazon EKS:**

   - Ensure your Kubernetes cluster is running on Amazon EKS.

2. **Install a CloudWatch Agent:**

   - Deploy the CloudWatch agent on your EKS cluster to collect metrics and logs.

   ```
   kubectl apply -f https://amazon-cloudwatch-agent-
   k8s.s3.amazonaws.com/kubernetes/cloudwatch-
   agent.yaml
   ```

3. **Configure the CloudWatch Agent:**

   - Create a ConfigMap for the CloudWatch agent configuration.

   ```
   apiVersion: v1
   kind: ConfigMap
   metadata:
     name: cloudwatch-agent-config
     namespace: amazon-cloudwatch
   data:
     cloudwatch-config.json: |
       {
         "agent": {
           "metrics_collection_interval": 60,
           "logfile": "/opt/aws/amazon-cloudwatch-
           agent/logs/amazon-cloudwatch-agent.log"
         },
   ```

```
        "metrics": {
          "metrics_collected": {
            "kubernetes": {
              "cluster_name": "YOUR_CLUSTER_NAME",
              "metrics_collection_interval": 60
            }
          }
        }
      }
```

4. **Deploy the ConfigMap:**

```
kubectl apply -f cloudwatch-agent-config.yaml
```

5. **Monitor Metrics in CloudWatch:**

   - Go to the Amazon CloudWatch console to view the metrics collected from your EKS cluster.

Discussion

Amazon CloudWatch provides detailed monitoring and logging for Amazon EKS clusters. By deploying the CloudWatch agent, you can collect metrics and logs from your Kubernetes nodes and pods. CloudWatch integrates seamlessly with AWS services, offering a unified view of your infrastructure and applications.

9.16 Azure Monitor for Containers

Problem

How can we effectively monitor Kubernetes clusters deployed on Microsoft Azure using Azure Monitor for Containers monitoring tools?

Solution

1. **Set Up Azure Kubernetes Service (AKS):**
   - Ensure your Kubernetes cluster is running on AKS.
2. **Enable Azure Monitor for Containers:**
   - Use the Azure CLI to enable monitoring.

   ```
   az aks enable-addons --resource-group MY_RESOURCE_
   GROUP --name MY_AKS_CLUSTER --addons monitoring
   --workspace-resource-id MY_WORKSPACE_ID
   ```
3. **View Metrics in the Azure Portal:**
   - Navigate to the Azure portal, go to your AKS cluster, and open the "Insights" section to view metrics, logs, and health information.

Discussion

Azure Monitor for Containers provides a comprehensive monitoring solution for AKS clusters. It collects metrics, logs, and traces, allowing you to visualize the performance and health of your containers. Azure Monitor integrates with other Azure services, providing end-to-end visibility into your applications.

9.17 Google Cloud Operations

Problem

How can we effectively monitor Kubernetes clusters deployed on the Google Cloud Platform (GCP)?

Solution

1. **Set Up Google Kubernetes Engine (GKE):**
    - Ensure your Kubernetes cluster is running on GKE.
2. **Install Google Cloud's Operations Suite (Formerly Stackdriver):**
    - Enable Google Cloud's operations suite in your GCP project.

    ```
    gcloud services enable monitoring.googleapis.com
    logging.googleapis.com
    ```
3. **Deploy a Monitoring Agent:**
    - Install the Google Cloud operations suite monitoring and logging agents on your GKE cluster.

    ```
    kubectl apply -f https://github.com/
    GoogleCloudPlatform/k8s-stackdriver/blob/master/
    prometheus-to-sd/deployments/prometheus-to-sd.yaml
    ```
4. **View Metrics in the Google Cloud Console:**
    - Go to the Google Cloud Console, navigate to Operations ➤ Monitoring, and view the metrics and logs collected from your GKE cluster.

Discussion

Google Cloud Operations (formerly Stackdriver) offers robust monitoring and logging capabilities for GKE clusters. It provides detailed insights into the performance, availability, and health of your Kubernetes applications. Google Cloud Operations integrates with other GCP services, enabling efficient monitoring and troubleshooting.

Summary

Observability in Kubernetes goes beyond basic monitoring. It involves using tools like Prometheus and Jaeger to gain deep insights and quickly address issues, optimize performance, and maintain efficient operations. Combining these tools creates a strong observability stack that adapts to your needs and ensures the health of Kubernetes clusters. With the right tools, you can confidently manage Kubernetes environments, delivering the expected performance and reliability.

CHAPTER 10

Control Plane Administration and Package Management

A lack of understanding of Kubernetes control plane components leads to misconfigurations. This chapter aims to comprehensively understand control plane administration tasks in Kubernetes and efficient package management using Helm. The goal is to equip readers with the knowledge and skills to manage the control plane and seamlessly deploy packages within Kubernetes clusters.

What is the Kubernetes control plane?

G. Stencel and L. Berton, *Kubernetes Recipes*,
https://doi.org/10.1007/979-8-8688-1325-2_10

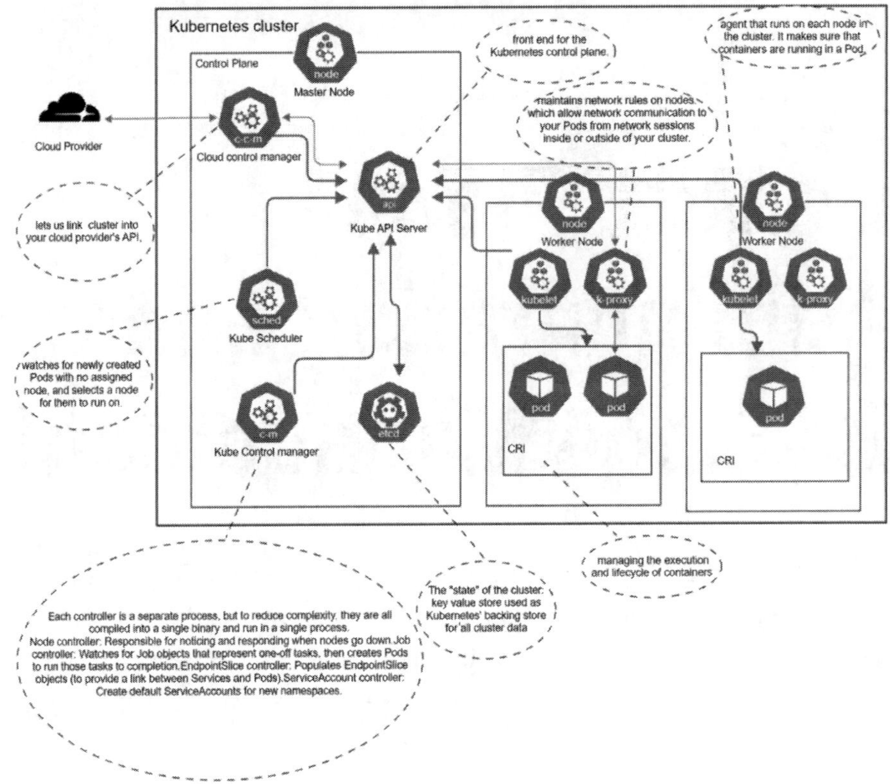

Figure 10-1. *Kubernetes control plane components explanation*

Kube-API Server

The kube-API server is the core component that provides an HTTP API. It serves as the front end of the Kubernetes control plane, and all interactions with the Kubernetes cluster occur via this API.

Its key responsibilities are as follows:

> **API Gateway**: Handles all external and internal requests (e.g., from kubectl or other components).

Authentication and Authorization: Validates requests from users or components and ensures they have permission to perform specific actions.

Data Validation: Validates the configuration and data sent to the API, ensuring it meets the expected schema and standards.

State Management: Works closely with etcd to persist the desired and current state of the cluster.

Communication Hub: Facilitates communication between the control plane components and the worker nodes.

Importance: Without the API server, you can't interact with the cluster, making it a crucial single entry point.

Etcd

Etcd is a distributed, consistent, and highly available key-value store Kubernetes uses to store all cluster data.

Its key responsibilities are as follows:

Persistent Data Store: Stores all Kubernetes cluster states, such as node and pod information, service details, and secrets.

Consistency and Availability: Ensures data is replicated across multiple nodes for redundancy and consistency. This guarantees that the cluster data remains intact even if one node fails.

Source of Truth: Etcd is the primary data store for the cluster's state. It maintains the cluster's desired state so that components like the kube-controller-manager can make necessary adjustments to match the actual state.

Importance: Etcd is essential for the cluster to function. If etcd becomes unavailable, the cluster can't store or retrieve information, leading to functionality loss.

Version Compatibility and Management: It is crucial to ensure that etcd versions are compatible with your Kubernetes versions, as mismatched versions can lead to unexpected behavior and cluster instability. Upgrading etcd should be approached with caution; a structured upgrade path is recommended, typically involving upgrading Kubernetes first followed by etcd to maintain compatibility. Implementing a version control strategy for etcd is essential, which includes tracking the specific versions in use across your cluster to aid in planning upgrades and ensuring consistency. Before applying any upgrades to your production environment, thoroughly testing them in a staging environment is necessary to identify potential issues without impacting your live cluster. Additionally, utilizing automated monitoring tools to keep track of etcd versions and receive alerts for any deprecated or outdated versions helps ensure timely upgrades and reduces the risk of incompatibility. Always perform a full backup of etcd before initiating an upgrade, as having a reliable backup allows you to quickly restore the previous state and minimize downtime in case any issues arise during the upgrade process.

Secure Storage of Sensitive Data: Etcd handles sensitive information, such as Kubernetes secrets, by storing them in an encrypted format. Kubernetes employs built-in encryption mechanisms to encrypt secrets before they are written to etcd, ensuring that sensitive data remains protected at rest. Additionally, communication between Kubernetes components and etcd is secured using Transport Layer Security (TLS), which encrypts data in transit. This dual-layer encryption approach ensures that secrets are safeguarded both while stored and during transmission, mitigating the risk of unauthorized access or data breaches.

Kube-Scheduler

The kube-scheduler assigns unbound (unscheduled) pods to nodes based on specific criteria, such as available resources and scheduling policies.

Its key responsibilities are as follows:

Pod Placement: Monitors the cluster for new pods that haven't been assigned to a node and determines the best node for them.

Resource Optimization: Considers various factors, such as resource requests (CPU, memory), node conditions, pod affinity/anti-affinity rules, taints and tolerations, and custom policies.

Efficient Distribution: Ensures workloads are distributed efficiently across nodes, balancing resource utilization and performance needs.

Importance: Without the scheduler, pods would remain pending and cannot run on any nodes.

Kube-Controller-Manager

The kube-controller-manager runs the various controllers that regulate the cluster's state, ensuring that the system's current state matches the desired state defined in the cluster's configuration.

Its key responsibilities are as follows:

Node Controller: This monitors node availability and takes action if nodes go down (e.g., moving workloads off failed nodes).

Replication Controller: Ensures that a specified number of replicas for a pod are running at all times.

Endpoint Controller: Joins services with pods, updating endpoint objects to facilitate communication between them.

Service Account Controller: Manages default service accounts and tokens for new namespaces.

Other Controllers: Manages additional controllers such as job controllers, namespace controllers, and more.

Importance: It keeps the cluster functioning as expected by automatically reconciling the actual state with the desired state defined by users.

Cloud Controller Manager (Optional)

The cloud controller manager is an optional component that integrates Kubernetes with the underlying cloud infrastructure, allowing Kubernetes to interact with cloud provider APIs.

Its key responsibilities are as follows:

Cloud Integration: This role handles tasks that depend on cloud provider functionality, such as provisioning load balancers, managing storage volumes, and routing traffic.

Node Lifecycle Management: Integrates cloud-specific logic to manage nodes, such as removing nodes that are no longer available from the cloud provider's perspective.

Cloud Services: Manages cloud provider resources like VMs, block storage, and networking.

Cloud Controllers: This splits functionality into different controllers, such as the Node Controller, Route Controller, and Service Controller, based on what cloud provider services the cluster needs to interact with.

Importance: In cloud environments (e.g., AWS, GCP, Azure), the cloud controller manager ensures that Kubernetes can fully utilize the cloud's resources. This component is often optional in on-premise clusters.

Together, these components form the backbone of the Kubernetes control plane, enabling it to effectively manage and orchestrate containers across multiple nodes.

Node Components

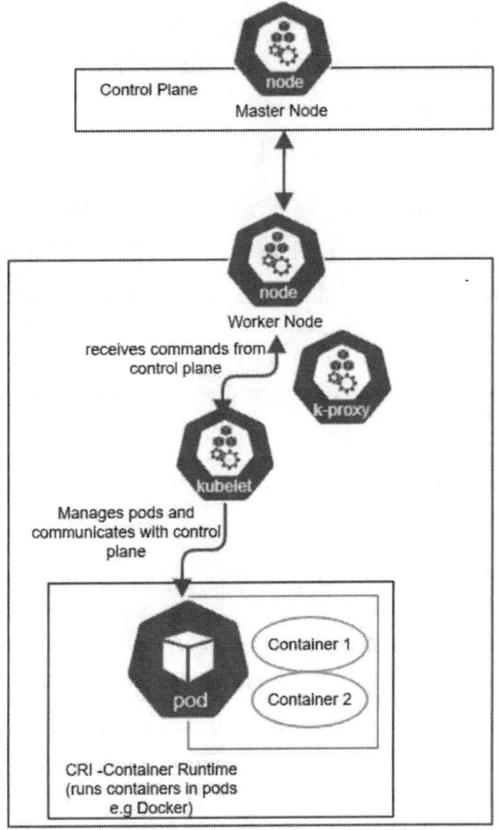

Figure 10-2. *Kubernetes node components*

Kubelet

A key agent running on each node that ensures the containers inside pods are running as expected.

Responsibilities:

Communicate with the control plane (kube-API server) to get the desired pod specifications.

Manage the lifecycle of containers, ensuring they are running healthy and restarting them if needed.

Report the node's status and resource usage back to the control plane.

Kube-Proxy (Optional)

A network component that runs on each node that manages network rules and enables communication between pods and services.

Responsibilities:

Set up networking rules using the underlying OS (Iptables or IPVS) to route traffic to the appropriate pods.

Ensure that network connections from inside and outside the cluster are correctly directed to services.

Container Runtime

The software is responsible for pulling images and running containers on the node.

Responsibilities:

Launch and manage containerized applications in pods.

Interact with the kubelet to create and run containers as defined by pod specifications.

Examples: Docker, containerd, CRI-O

These components work together on each node to maintain the pods' lifecycle, manage network routing, and run containers.

10.1 Assigning Labels, Annotations, and Taints to Nodes

Problem

Managing nodes efficiently within a cluster requires categorizing and controlling their behavior. This is achieved by assigning labels, annotations, and taints to nodes. Labels facilitate grouping and selecting nodes for workloads, annotations store metadata, and taints control which workloads can run on particular nodes.

However, administrators often face challenges such as

Inconsistent Node Management: A proper system for labeling, annotating, or applying taints can help ensure consistency in node selection for workloads.

Complexity in Taint and Toleration Mechanisms: Misconfigured taints and tolerations can prevent workloads from being scheduled appropriately, resulting in resource inefficiencies or failures.

Manual Overhead: Manually managing these node properties can be error-prone, especially in large clusters, and can lead to workload misallocations or improper scheduling.

Given these challenges, the goal is to develop an efficient strategy for assigning labels, annotations, and taints that simplifies node management, enhances workload distribution, and avoids misconfiguration.

Solution

First of all, let's clear our cluster from previous exercises. If we have used KinD, we can easily do it with

```
kind delete cluster
```

```
greg@gregPowerPC:~$ sudo kind delete cluster
Deleting cluster "kind" ...
Deleted nodes: ["kind-control-plane"]
greg@gregPowerPC:~$
```

Figure 10-3. *Cleaning the KinD cluster*

Now, we need to create a multinode cluster in KinD.

Let's use below YAML:

```
kind: Cluster
apiVersion: kind.x-k8s.io/v1alpha4
nodes:
- role: control-plane
- role: worker
- role: worker
```

Let's apply the above YAML with

```
sudo kind create cluster --name k8s-multinode --config
cluster.yaml
```

```
greg@gregPowerPC:~$ sudo kind create cluster --name k8s-multinode --config cluster.yaml
Creating cluster "k8s-multinode" ...
 ✓ Ensuring node image (kindest/node:v1.31.0)
 ✓ Preparing nodes
 ✓ Writing configuration
 ✓ Starting control-plane
 ✓ Installing CNI
 ✓ Installing StorageClass
 ✓ Joining worker nodes
Set kubectl context to "kind-k8s-multinode"
You can now use your cluster with:

kubectl cluster-info --context kind-k8s-multinode

Not sure what to do next? Check out https://kind.sigs.k8s.io/docs/user/quick-start/
```

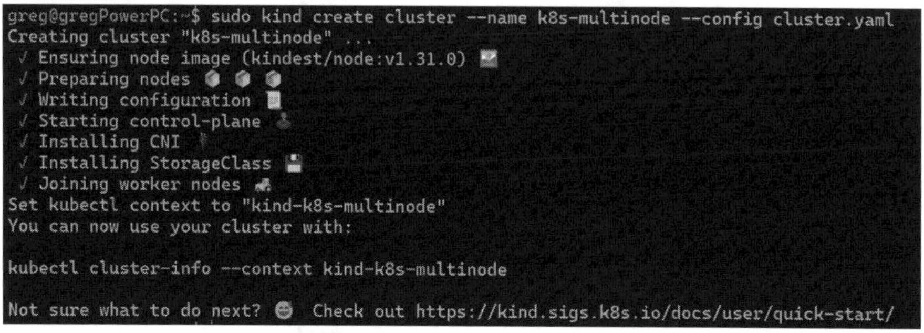

Figure 10-4. *Creating a new KinD cluster*

Let's check if we have more nodes then.

With sudo kubectl, get nodes.

```
greg@gregPowerPC:~$ sudo kubectl get nodes
NAME                          STATUS   ROLES           AGE   VERSION
k8s-multinode-control-plane   Ready    control-plane   50s   v1.31.0
k8s-multinode-worker          Ready    <none>          41s   v1.31.0
k8s-multinode-worker2         Ready    <none>          41s   v1.31.0
```

Figure 10-5. *Getting cluster nodes*

We can see we have our control plane node and two worker nodes.

The solution involves systematically assigning labels, annotations, and taints to nodes using Kubernetes tools and commands. Here's a breakdown of the approach:

Assigning Labels to Nodes: Labels are key–value pairs that help in identifying nodes for scheduling specific workloads. For example, a label can indicate whether a node is for production or testing environments. Administrators can assign labels to nodes using the kubectl command:

```
kubectl label nodes <node-name> <label-key>=<label-value>
```

```
greg@gregPowerPC:~$ sudo kubectl label nodes k8s-multinode-worker usage=gpu
node/k8s-multinode-worker labeled
```

Figure 10-6. *Labeling nodes*

This allows workloads to be assigned to specific nodes by specifying node selectors in their YAML files.

Adding Annotations for Metadata: Annotations are used to attach metadata to nodes without affecting the scheduling of pods. For example, annotations can store operational information like maintenance windows or custom node metadata:

```
kubectl annotate nodes <node-name> <annotation-
key>=<annotation-value>
```

Applying Taints to Nodes: Taints ensure that only workloads with the appropriate tolerations are scheduled on specific nodes. For example, a node designated for critical workloads can be tainted to prevent other workloads from being scheduled there unless they explicitly tolerate the taint:

Step 1: Apply a Taint to a Node

Let's say you have a node named k8s-multinode-worker that you want to reserve for critical workloads. You can taint it using the following command:

```
kubectl taint nodes k8s-multinode-worker
critical=high:NoSchedule
```

```
greg@gregPowerPC:~$ sudo kubectl taint nodes k8s-multinode-worker critical=high:NoSchedule
[sudo] password for greg:
node/k8s-multinode-worker tainted
```

Figure 10-7. *Tainting nodes*

This taint means no pod will be scheduled on "node 1" unless it has a matching tolerance—the effect NoSchedule ensures that pods without the matching tolerance will not be scheduled on the node.

Step 2: Add a Toleration to a Pod

To allow a pod to be scheduled on k8s-multinode-worker, the pod needs a toleration that matches the taint. Here's an example of a pod configuration with the correct toleration:

```
#critical-pod.yaml
apiVersion: v1
kind: Pod
metadata:
  name: critical-pod
spec:
  containers:
    - name: nginx
      image: nginx
```

```
  tolerations:
    - key: "critical"
      operator: "Equal"
      value: "high"
      effect: "NoSchedule"
#regular-pod.yam
apiVersion: v1
kind: Pod
metadata:
  name: regular-pod
spec:
  containers:
    - name: nginx
      image: nginx
```

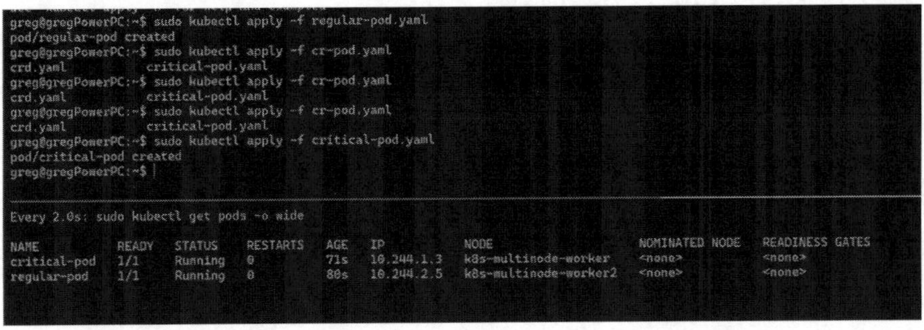

```
greg@gregPowerPC:~$ sudo kubectl apply -f regular-pod.yaml
pod/regular-pod created
greg@gregPowerPC:~$ sudo kubectl apply -f cr-pod.yaml
crd.yaml          critical-pod.yaml
greg@gregPowerPC:~$ sudo kubectl apply -f cr-pod.yaml
crd.yaml          critical-pod.yaml
greg@gregPowerPC:~$ sudo kubectl apply -f cr-pod.yaml
crd.yaml          critical-pod.yaml
greg@gregPowerPC:~$ sudo kubectl apply -f critical-pod.yaml
pod/critical-pod created
greg@gregPowerPC:~$ |

Every 2.0s: sudo kubectl get pods -o wide

NAME           READY   STATUS    RESTARTS   AGE   IP            NODE                     NOMINATED NODE   READINESS GATES
critical-pod   1/1     Running   0          71s   10.244.1.3    k8s-multinode-worker     <none>           <none>
regular-pod    1/1     Running   0          80s   10.244.2.5    k8s-multinode-worker2    <none>           <none>
```

***Figure 10-8.** Applying pod toleration and checking pods*

The toleration's key matches the taint's key (critical).

The value is high, which matches the value in the taint.

The effect is NoSchedule, which aligns with the impact of the taint.

This ensures that the critical pod can be scheduled on k8s-multinode-worker.

Since a regular pod does not have the required toleration, it will not be scheduled on a critical tainted node. Instead, Kubernetes will attempt to place it on a different tainted node.

Automation with Helm and Ansible: For large clusters, manually managing labels, annotations, and taints can be inefficient. Helm charts and Ansible playbooks can automate the process:

Helm: Helm can be used to template node-specific configurations where labels, annotations, and taints can be specified for groups of nodes, improving consistency across environments.

Ansible: Ansible playbooks can be written to apply labels, annotations, and taints across multiple nodes, streamlining cluster-wide updates.

Assigning Labels to Nodes

Imagine you have two types of nodes in your Kubernetes cluster: production and testing nodes. To assign a label indicating this, you can use the following command:

```
# Assign label "environment=production" to a node
kubectl label nodes k8s-multinode-worker2
environment=production
```

```
greg@gregPowerPC:~$ sudo kubectl label nodes k8s-multinode-worker2 environment=production
node/k8s-multinode-worker2 labeled
greg@gregPowerPC:~$ |
```

Figure 10-9. *Labeling a node with a production environment label*

```
# Assign label "environment=testing" to a node
kubectl label nodes k8s-multinode-worker environment=testing
```

You can now create a pod that specifically runs on nodes with the environment=production label.

Here's a pod definition example (pod.yaml):

```
apiVersion: v1
kind: Pod
metadata:
  name: production-app
```

```
spec:
  containers:
  - name: nginx
    image: nginx
  nodeSelector:
    environment: production
```

When this pod is deployed, it will only be scheduled on nodes that have the environment=production label.

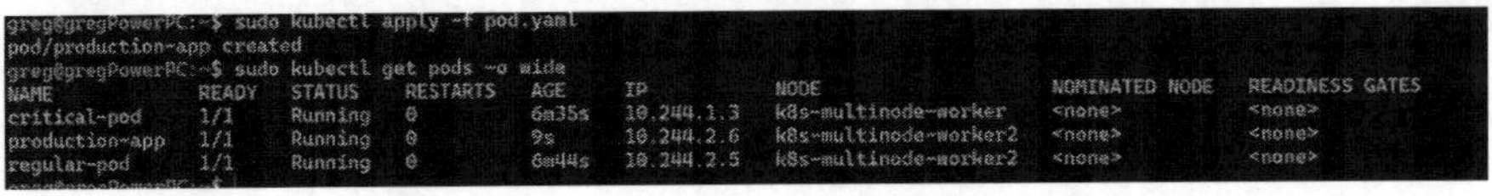

```
greg@gregPowerPC:~$ sudo kubectl apply -f pod.yaml
pod/production-app created
greg@gregPowerPC:~$ sudo kubectl get pods -o wide
NAME             READY   STATUS    RESTARTS   AGE     IP            NODE                     NOMINATED NODE   READINESS GATES
critical-pod     1/1     Running   0          6m35s   10.244.1.3    k8s-multinode-worker     <none>           <none>
production-app   1/1     Running   0          9s      10.244.2.6    k8s-multinode-worker2    <none>           <none>
regular-pod      1/1     Running   0          6m44s   10.244.2.5    k8s-multinode-worker2    <none>           <none>
```

Figure 10-10. *Applying a pod to a production environment*

Adding Annotations to Nodes

Annotations attach metadata to nodes, such as the node's last maintenance date or owner information. These don't affect scheduling but can store valuable data for operators.

```
# Annotate a node with the last maintenance date
kubectl annotate nodes k8s-multinode-worker maintenance-
date="2024-09-01"

# Annotate a node with an owner's name
kubectl annotate nodes k8s-multinode-worker owner="admin-team"
```

You can check the annotations on the node with the following command:

```
kubectl describe node k8s-multinode-worker
```

In the output, you will see the annotations.

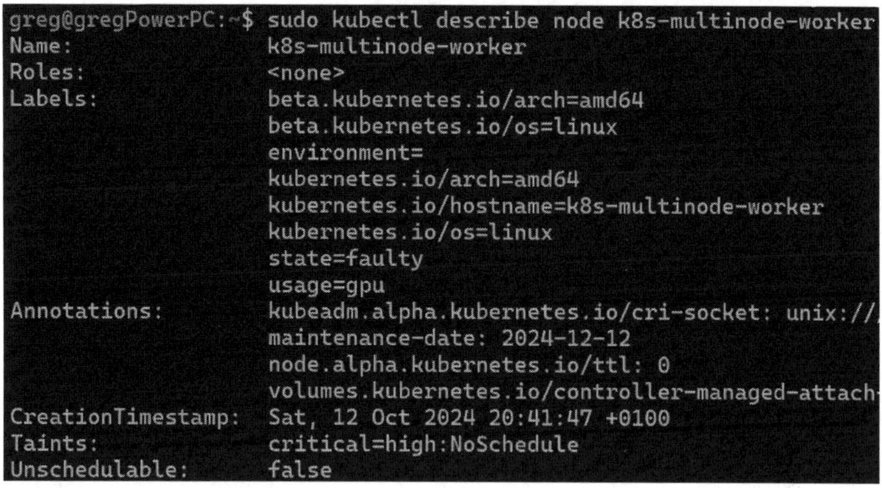

```
greg@gregPowerPC:~$ sudo kubectl describe node k8s-multinode-worker
Name:               k8s-multinode-worker
Roles:              <none>
Labels:             beta.kubernetes.io/arch=amd64
                    beta.kubernetes.io/os=linux
                    environment=
                    kubernetes.io/arch=amd64
                    kubernetes.io/hostname=k8s-multinode-worker
                    kubernetes.io/os=linux
                    state=faulty
                    usage=gpu
Annotations:        kubeadm.alpha.kubernetes.io/cri-socket: unix://
                    maintenance-date: 2024-12-12
                    node.alpha.kubernetes.io/ttl: 0
                    volumes.kubernetes.io/controller-managed-attach
CreationTimestamp:  Sat, 12 Oct 2024 20:41:47 +0100
Taints:             critical=high:NoSchedule
Unschedulable:      false
```

Figure 10-11. *Describing the node*

Automating Labels, Annotations, and Taints with Helm and Ansible

Example: Automating with Helm

You can define a Helm chart that automatically adds labels or taints to nodes as part of the template.

Here's a Helm values file (values.yaml):

```
nodeSelector:
  environment: production
tolerations:
  - key: "critical"
    operator: "Equal"
    value: "true"
    effect: "NoSchedule"
```

This makes it easier to manage node selection and tolerations in Helm-deployed applications.

Example: Automating with Ansible

You can create an Ansible playbook to assign labels and annotations to nodes automatically.

Here's an Ansible playbook (label-annotate-nodes.yaml):

```
- hosts: k8s_nodes
  tasks:
    - name: Label nodes as production
      command: "kubectl label nodes {{ inventory_hostname }}
      environment=production"

    - name: Annotate nodes with maintenance date
      command: "kubectl annotate nodes {{ inventory_hostname }}
      maintenance-date='2024-09-01'"
```

You can run this playbook using

```
ansible-playbook -i inventory/hosts label-annotate-nodes.yaml
```

This playbook will iterate over the nodes defined in the inventory and apply the labels and annotations accordingly.

Outcome

These examples show how to practically assign labels, annotations, and taints to nodes in Kubernetes, improving the organization, scheduling, and management of workloads within the cluster. For large environments, tools like Helm and Ansible can further streamline these processes. By following this structured approach, Kubernetes administrators can efficiently manage node properties, reduce manual overhead, and ensure consistent and accurate scheduling of workloads in the cluster. This enhances operational reliability and resource allocation, facilitating better control plane administration.

10.2 Performing a Drain

Problem

Performing a drain on a node is essential for maintenance, upgrades, or decommissioning purposes. Draining involves safely evicting all running pods from a node ensuring they are rescheduled on other available nodes without causing downtime or disrupting services.

However, administrators often face the following challenges:

Disruption of Critical Services: Draining a node without proper safeguards can lead to service disruptions, especially for pods with no available replicas or improperly configured PodDisruptionBudgets (PDBs).

Failed Pod Rescheduling: Occurs in cases with insufficient resources or node constraints (labels, taints), evicted pods may need to be appropriately rescheduled adequately rescheduled workloads.

Handling DaemonSets and Static Pods: These pods do not get automatically evicted during a drain, requiring manual intervention or additional configuration to handle them appropriately.

Pod Graceful Termination: Pods might be forcefully killed without proper termination handling, leading to data loss or incomplete transactions.

Given these challenges, performing a safe and efficient node drain minimizes disruption while maintaining cluster health during maintenance activities.

Solution

The solution involves a structured approach to draining nodes in Kubernetes, ensuring minimal disruption while handling critical services and pods. The following steps outline how to perform a proper node drain, covering common issues:

Set Up a Pod Disruption Budget (PDB): Before draining a node, you should create a Pod Disruption Budget (PDB) to ensure that certain critical workloads maintain minimum availability during the process. For example, for an application with multiple replicas, a PDB can be created to ensure at least one replica remains running at all times.

First of all, let's remove taint from node 1:

```
kubectl taint nodes k8s-multinode-worker critical=high:NoSchedule-
```

```
greg@gregPowerPC:~/10.2$ sudo kubectl taint nodes k8s-multinode-worker critical=high:NoSchedule-
node/k8s-multinode-worker untainted
greg@gregPowerPC:~/10.2$
```

Figure 10-12. *Removing taint from node 1*

Now, let's create a pod:

```
apiVersion: v1
kind: Pod
metadata:
  name: my-app-pod
  labels:
    app: my-app
spec:
  containers:
    - name: nginx
      image: nginx
kubectl apply -f pod.yaml
```

Here's the Pod Disruption Budget (pdb.yaml):

```
apiVersion: policy/v1
kind: PodDisruptionBudget
metadata:
  name: my-app-pdb
spec:
  minAvailable: 1
  selector:
    matchLabels:
      app: my-app
Apply the PDB:
kubectl apply -f pdb.yaml
```

```
greg@gregPowerPC:~/10.2$ sudo kubectl apply -f pdb.yaml
poddisruptionbudget.policy/my-app-pdb created
```

Figure 10-13. *Creating a Pod Disruption Budget*

Drain the Node: Use the kubectl drain command to evict all running pods from a node safely. This command ensures that pods are gracefully terminated and rescheduled on other nodes and avoids disruptions for those with proper replicas or PDBs.

Here's an example command:

```
kubectl drain k8s-multinode-worker --ignore-daemonsets
--delete-emptydir-data
```

- **--ignore-daemonsets**: Ensures that DaemonSet pods (which are automatically managed by the system) are not evicted
- **--delete-emptydir-data**: Deletes pods using EmptyDir storage since they won't retain data across rescheduling

Handling DaemonSets and Static Pods: DaemonSets and static pods are not automatically evicted during a drain. You need to hold these pods, if necessary, manually:

DaemonSets: You can temporarily disable the DaemonSet on the node by cordoning it and then deleting the DaemonSet pods. When the node is ready, the DaemonSet will automatically create new pods.

Static Pods: You must manually remove their configuration files from the node to remove static pods.

Check Pod Rescheduling: After draining the node, ensure that all evicted pods are rescheduled on other nodes. You can check the pod status using

```
kubectl get pods -o wide
```

```
^Cgreg@gregPowerPC:~$ sudo kubectl get pods -o wide -w
NAME            READY   STATUS    RESTARTS   AGE   IP           NODE                     NOMINATED NODE   READINESS GATES
critical-pod    1/1     Running   0          19m   10.244.1.3   k8s-multinode-worker     <none>           <none>
production-app  1/1     Running   0          13m   10.244.2.6   k8s-multinode-worker2    <none>           <none>
regular-pod     1/1     Running   0          19m   10.244.2.5   k8s-multinode-worker2    <none>           <none>
my-app-pod      0/1     Pending   0          0s    <none>       <none>                   <none>           <none>
my-app-pod      0/1     Pending   0          0s    <none>       k8s-multinode-worker2    <none>           <none>
my-app-pod      0/1     ContainerCreating   0          0s    <none>       k8s-multinode-worker2   <none>           <none>
my-app-pod      1/1     Running             0          3s    10.244.2.8   k8s-multinode-worker2   <none>           <none>
regular-pod     1/1     Running             0          22m   10.244.2.5   k8s-multinode-worker2   <none>           <none>
production-app  1/1     Running             0          15m   10.244.2.6   k8s-multinode-worker2   <none>           <none>
regular-pod     1/1     Terminating         0          22m   10.244.2.5   k8s-multinode-worker2   <none>           <none>
production-app  1/1     Terminating         0          15m   10.244.2.6   k8s-multinode-worker2   <none>           <none>
regular-pod     1/1     Terminating         0          22m   10.244.2.5   k8s-multinode-worker2   <none>           <none>
production-app  1/1     Terminating         0          15m   10.244.2.6   k8s-multinode-worker2   <none>           <none>
regular-pod     0/1     Completed           0          22m   10.244.2.5   k8s-multinode-worker2   <none>           <none>
production-app  0/1     Completed           0          15m   10.244.2.6   k8s-multinode-worker2   <none>           <none>
regular-pod     0/1     Completed           0          22m   10.244.2.5   k8s-multinode-worker2   <none>           <none>
regular-pod     0/1     Completed           0          22m   10.244.2.5   k8s-multinode-worker2   <none>           <none>
production-app  0/1     Completed           0          15m   10.244.2.6   k8s-multinode-worker2   <none>           <none>
production-app  0/1     Completed           0          15m   10.244.2.6   k8s-multinode-worker2   <none>           <none>
```

Figure 10-14. *Getting pods and watching their status live*

And the end status is easier to read. We can see only one app stayed on node 2 because of our pdb.yaml.

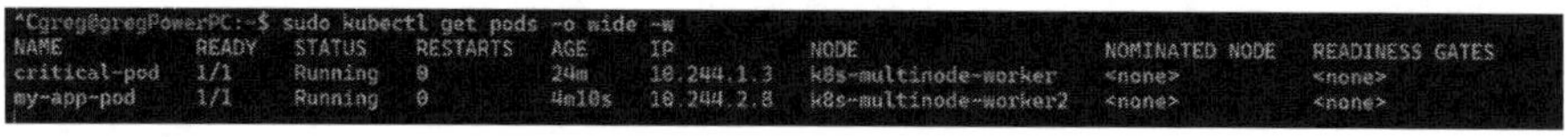

```
^Cgreg@gregPowerPC:~$ sudo kubectl get pods -o wide -w
NAME           READY   STATUS    RESTARTS   AGE     IP           NODE                     NOMINATED NODE   READINESS GATES
critical-pod   1/1     Running   0          24m     10.244.1.3   k8s-multinode-worker     <none>           <none>
my-app-pod     1/1     Running   0          4m10s   10.244.2.8   k8s-multinode-worker2    <none>           <none>
```

***Figure 10-15.** Getting pods from node 2*

If any pods are failing to reschedule due to resource constraints or node taints, consider adjusting node labels, increasing resources, or temporarily removing taints.

As we can see, our disruption budget worked as one pod can't be evicted.

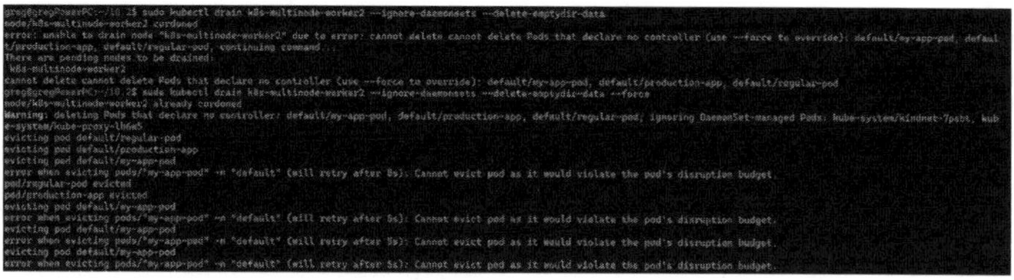

```
greg@gregPowerPC:~/10.2$ sudo kubectl drain k8s-multinode-worker2 --ignore-daemonsets --delete-emptydir-data
node/k8s-multinode-worker2 cordoned
error: unable to drain node "k8s-multinode-worker2" due to error: cannot delete cannot delete Pods that declare no controller (use --force to override): default/my-app-pod, defaul
t/production-app, default/regular-pod, continuing command...
There are pending nodes to be drained:
 k8s-multinode-worker2
cannot delete cannot delete Pods that declare no controller (use --force to override): default/my-app-pod, default/production-app, default/regular-pod
greg@gregPowerPC:~/10.2$ sudo kubectl drain k8s-multinode-worker2 --ignore-daemonsets --delete-emptydir-data --force
node/k8s-multinode-worker2 already cordoned
Warning: deleting Pods that declare no controller: default/my-app-pod, default/production-app, default/regular-pod; ignoring DaemonSet-managed Pods: kube-system/kindnet-7psbt, kub
e-system/kube-proxy-lh6w5
evicting pod default/regular-pod
evicting pod default/production-app
evicting pod default/my-app-pod
error when evicting pods/"my-app-pod" -n "default" (will retry after 5s): Cannot evict pod as it would violate the pod's disruption budget.
pod/regular-pod evicted
pod/production-app evicted
evicting pod default/my-app-pod
error when evicting pods/"my-app-pod" -n "default" (will retry after 5s): Cannot evict pod as it would violate the pod's disruption budget.
evicting pod default/my-app-pod
error when evicting pods/"my-app-pod" -n "default" (will retry after 5s): Cannot evict pod as it would violate the pod's disruption budget.
evicting pod default/my-app-pod
error when evicting pods/"my-app-pod" -n "default" (will retry after 5s): Cannot evict pod as it would violate the pod's disruption budget.
```

***Figure 10-16.** Draining nodes*

Let's quickly remove pdb:

```
kubectl delete -f pdb.yaml
```

```
greg@gregPowerPC:~/10.2$ sudo kubectl delete -f pdb.yaml
poddisruptionbudget.policy "my-app-pdb" deleted
```

***Figure 10-17.** Removing pdb*

```
evicting pod default/my-app-pod
error when evicting pods/"my-app-pod" -n "default" (will retry after 5s): Cannot evict pod as it would violate the pod's disruption budget.
evicting pod default/my-app-pod
pod/my-app-pod evicted
node/k8s-multinode-worker2 drained
```

***Figure 10-18.** Pod evicted and node drained*

We can see that the pod was deleted and our node has been drained.

Uncordon the Node (When Maintenance Is Complete): After performing the necessary maintenance or upgrades on the node, you can uncordon it to allow pods to be scheduled on it again:

```
kubectl uncordon k8s-multinode-worker2
```

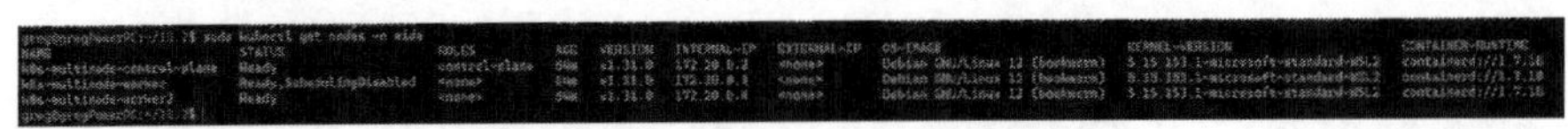

Figure 10-19. *Getting nodes after uncordoning*

Automation with Ansible: To ensure consistent and efficient node management, you can automate node draining using an Ansible playbook for large-scale clusters.

Here's an Ansible playbook example (drain-node.yaml):

```
- hosts: k8s_nodes
  tasks:
    - name: Drain node
      command: "kubectl drain {{ inventory_hostname }}
      --ignore-daemonsets --delete-emptydir-data"
    - name: Uncordon node after maintenance
      command: "kubectl uncordon {{ inventory_hostname }}"
```

Outcome

By following these steps, Kubernetes administrators can safely and efficiently drain nodes for maintenance or decommissioning while ensuring that critical services remain available. Proper use of PodDisruptionBudgets, careful handling of DaemonSets and static pods, and verification of pod rescheduling help avoid service disruptions, enabling smooth operation of the Kubernetes control plane. Automation tools like Ansible can further streamline the process in large environments.

10.3 Cordon and Uncordon to Nodes

Problem

In Kubernetes, cordoning and uncordoning nodes are critical administrative tasks that control whether new pods can be scheduled on specific nodes. When a node is cordoned, no new pods are scheduled while existing workloads continue to run. When a node is uncordoned, it resumes accepting new workloads.

Challenges that administrators often encounter when using cordon and uncordon include

Ensuring Node Availability for Scheduling: In large clusters, it can be difficult to maintain visibility into which nodes are cordoned, leading to potential underutilization of resources.

Manual Process: Cordoning and uncordoning nodes manually in dynamic environments or during rolling updates may introduce delays or inconsistencies, especially in larger-scale clusters.

Draining Coordination: Cordoning is often used alongside draining, and improper management of the two operations can result in incomplete maintenance, missed upgrades, or scheduling issues.

Impact on Cluster Load: Cordoning off nodes without proper planning can lead to an imbalance in resource allocation and overload other nodes that continue accepting new workloads.

Given these challenges, efficient cordon and uncordon practices are essential for managing node availability during maintenance, upgrades, or rolling updates while ensuring balanced cluster performance.

Solution

The solution is to implement structured procedures for cordoning and uncordoning nodes in a Kubernetes cluster, with appropriate automation and visibility tools to manage node status effectively. The following steps outline how to perform these operations efficiently:

Cordon a Node: When you cordon a node, new pods cannot be scheduled on it, but existing pods continue to run. This is useful for preparing the node for maintenance or upgrades without disrupting running workloads.

Let's check the status of our nodes.

Figure 10-20. *Checking status of nodes*

Here's an example command:

```
kubectl cordon k8s-multinode-worker2
```

You can verify the status of the node:

```
kubectl get nodes
```

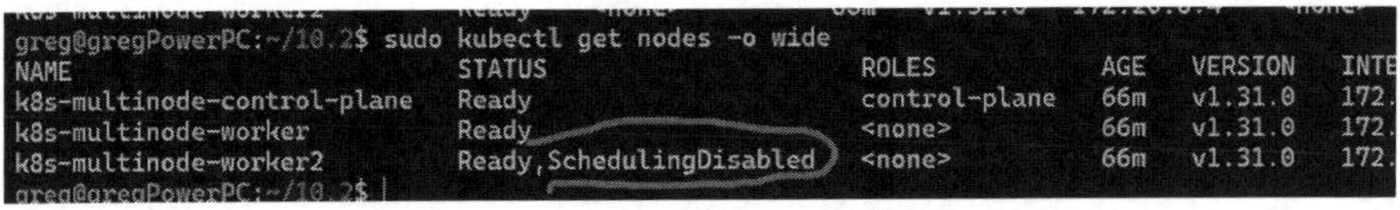

Figure 10-21. *Proving that the worker2 node has disabled scheduling—where no pod can be instantiated on*

The output will show the node as SchedulingDisabled, indicating that no new pods can be scheduled on it.

Uncordon a Node: Once maintenance or upgrades are complete, you can uncordon the node to allow it to accept new workloads again.

Here's an example command:

```
kubectl uncordon k8s-multinode-worker2
```

After uncordoning, the node status will change back to Ready, indicating that it can now accept new pods.

Using Cordon in Rolling Updates and Draining: Cordoning is often the first step in rolling updates or node draining. For example, before performing a node drain, you should cordon the node to prevent new pods from being scheduled on it during the operation.

Here's an example process:

```
kubectl cordon k8s-multinode-worker
kubectl drain k8s-multinode-worker --ignore-daemonsets
--delete-emptydir-data
```

Once the maintenance is complete, uncordon the node:

```
kubectl uncordon k8s-multinode-worker
```

Managing Cordon and Uncordon Across Multiple Nodes: For large clusters, managing the cordon/uncordon state across multiple nodes manually can be time-consuming. To streamline this process, you can use Ansible or kubectl commands with node selectors to cordon/uncordon groups of nodes based on labels or other criteria.

Here's an example of cordoning all nodes with a specific label:

```
kubectl get nodes -l environment=production -o name | xargs -I
{} kubectl cordon {}
```

This command will cordon all nodes labeled as environment=production.

Monitoring Cordon Status with Tools: To avoid accidental over-cordoning and underutilizing resources, administrators can monitor the status of all nodes using Kubernetes Dashboard tools like the Kubernetes Dashboard or Lens. These tools provide visual indicators of node status, helping to identify cordoned nodes quickly.

Outcome

By adopting structured practices for cordon and uncordon operations, Kubernetes administrators can

Efficiently manage node availability during maintenance or updates.

Minimize the risk of overloading other nodes by ensuring proper resource allocation.

Automate repetitive tasks, reducing manual errors and delays.

Maintain clear visibility over which nodes are cordoned and which are available, optimizing cluster resource utilization.

This approach ensures a smoother node management process and minimizes disruption to running workloads while performing maintenance or updates.

10.4 Upgrade Kubernetes

Problem

Upgrading Kubernetes is essential for keeping clusters secure, stable, and equipped with the latest features and bug fixes. However, upgrading Kubernetes clusters, especially in production environments, poses several challenges for administrators:

1. **Downtime and Service Disruptions**: During the upgrade process, control plane components and nodes may experience downtime or service disruption, potentially affecting running workloads and applications.
2. **Compatibility Issues**: New Kubernetes versions might introduce changes that are incompatible with existing configurations, API deprecations, or third-party integrations (e.g., CNI plugins, CSI drivers, Helm charts), causing failures or performance degradation.
3. **Complexity in Multinode and Multi-cluster Environments**: Managing the upgrade process across multiple nodes and clusters while ensuring that workloads are rescheduled correctly and no single point of failure affects the cluster's stability is complex.
4. **Rolling Back**: If an upgrade fails or introduces problems, rolling back to the previous version while maintaining data consistency and cluster health can be difficult.
5. **Coordination with Add-Ons**: Kubernetes upgrades must also be synchronized with critical add-ons like monitoring tools (Prometheus, Grafana), ingress controllers, and security policies, requiring careful planning.

Given these challenges, upgrading Kubernetes must be approached systematically to avoid downtime, ensure compatibility, and minimize operational risks in the control plane and worker nodes.

Solution

A structured and phased approach to upgrading Kubernetes can help mitigate risks and ensure a smooth transition to the new version. The following steps outline best practices for upgrading Kubernetes clusters:

Pre-upgrade Planning:

Back Up the Cluster State: Before starting the upgrade, back up the cluster's etcd data and configurations to ensure data recovery if issues arise during the upgrade.

```
# Backup etcd data from a control plane node
ETCDCTL_API=3 etcdctl snapshot save /tmp/etcd-backup.db \
--endpoints=https://127.0.0.1:2379 \
--cacert=/etc/kubernetes/pki/etcd/ca.crt \
--cert=/etc/kubernetes/pki/etcd/server.crt \
--key=/etc/kubernetes/pki/etcd/server.key
```

Check Kubernetes Version Compatibility: Ensure that your current Kubernetes version is compatible with the new version and that your cluster supports the upgrade path. You can check this on Kubernetes' official upgrade documentation.

Upgrade Third-Party Components: Check that the third-party components (CNI plugins, CSI drivers, Helm charts, etc.) are compatible with the new Kubernetes version. Also, ensure that PodDisruptionBudgets (PDBs) are in place to prevent workloads from being disrupted during the upgrade.

Control Plane Upgrade:

The control plane (API server, scheduler, controller manager) should be upgraded first. For clusters managed by kubeadm, the upgrade can be performed using the following commands:

Upgrade Kubeadm: First, upgrade the kubeadm tool on the control plane node:

```
sudo apt-get update && sudo apt-get install -y
kubeadm=1.24.x-00
```

Upgrade Control Plane Components: After upgrading kubeadm, use it to upgrade the control plane components:

```
sudo kubeadm upgrade plan
sudo kubeadm upgrade apply v1.24.x
```

Upgrade Kubelet and Kubectl: After upgrading the control plane, upgrade kubelet and kubectl on the control plane node:

```
sudo apt-get update && sudo apt-get install -y
kubelet=1.24.x-00 kubectl=1.24.x-00
sudo systemctl restart kubelet
```

Verify Control Plane Upgrade: Verify that the control plane has been successfully upgraded:

```
kubectl get nodes
kubectl get componentstatuses
```

Worker Node Upgrade:

Once the control plane is upgraded, proceed with upgrading the worker nodes in a rolling fashion to avoid service disruptions.

Cordon and Drain the Worker Node: Prevent new workloads from being scheduled on the node and safely evict running pods:

```
kubectl cordon <worker-node>
kubectl drain <worker-node> --ignore-daemonsets --delete-
emptydir-data
```

Upgrade Kubeadm, Kubelet, and Kubectl on Worker Nodes:

```
sudo apt-get update && sudo apt-get install -y
kubeadm=1.24.x-00
```

```
sudo kubeadm upgrade node
sudo apt-get update && sudo apt-get install -y
kubelet=1.24.x-00 kubectl=1.24.x-00
sudo systemctl restart kubelet
```

Uncordon the Worker Node: After successfully upgrading and restarting the node, allow new pods to be scheduled on it:

```
kubectl uncordon <worker-node>
```

Repeat for All Worker Nodes: Perform the same process for all other worker nodes in the cluster.

Post-upgrade Validation:

Check Cluster Health: After upgrading all nodes, check the cluster's overall health to ensure that all components are running correctly:

```
kubectl get nodes
kubectl get pods --all-namespaces
```

Verify API Deprecations: Review the Kubernetes release notes for API deprecations and check for workloads that might use deprecated APIs.

Update Cluster Add-Ons: Ensure that all add-ons (e.g., network plugins, ingress controllers, monitoring tools) are compatible with the new version of Kubernetes and update them as needed.

Rollback Plan:

If the upgrade fails or causes issues, it's important to have a rollback plan:

Restore from the etcd backup if necessary.

Downgrade the kubeadm, kubelet, and kubectl versions to the previous stable version.

Automating the Upgrade Process with Ansible:

Automating the Kubernetes upgrade process for large clusters can be beneficial to ensure consistency. An Ansible playbook can be created to automate the process of cordoning nodes; upgrading kubeadm, kubelet, and kubectl; and uncordoning nodes.

Here's an example Ansible playbook for Kubernetes upgrade:

```
- hosts: k8s_nodes
  tasks:
    - name: Cordon node for upgrade
      command: "kubectl cordon {{ inventory_hostname }}"

    - name: Drain node
      command: "kubectl drain {{ inventory_hostname }}
      --ignore-daemonsets --delete-emptydir-data"

    - name: Upgrade kubeadm
      apt:
        name: kubeadm
        state: latest

    - name: Upgrade kubelet and kubectl
      apt:
        name: "{{ item }}"
        state: latest
      with_items:
        - kubelet
        - kubectl

    - name: Restart kubelet service
      service:
        name: kubelet
        state: restarted

    - name: Uncordon node
      command: "kubectl uncordon {{ inventory_hostname }}"
```

Outcome

By following this structured approach, Kubernetes administrators can successfully upgrade their clusters with minimal downtime and disruption. The process ensures

Controlled Upgrades: Upgrading the control plane and worker nodes incrementally helps maintain cluster availability.

Compatibility Assurance: Pre-upgrade checks, compatibility validation, and post-upgrade validation ensure that workloads and third-party integrations continue to function as expected.

Automation: Automating the upgrade process with tools like Ansible reduces human errors and operational overhead, especially in large-scale environments.

With careful planning and execution, Kubernetes upgrades can be performed efficiently while maintaining cluster stability and workload continuity.

10.5 Helm Package Manager

Problem

Kubernetes is a complex platform with many components and dependencies. Managing applications within a Kubernetes cluster, especially when dealing with microservices, involves handling a large number of resources like pods, services, ConfigMaps, and secrets. Manually creating and managing YAML files for these resources can lead to

Configuration Overload: Manually managing YAML files for multiple services and environments can become unmanageable as the number of resources grows, leading to duplication, human errors, and inconsistencies.

Lack of Reusability: Applications often require similar configurations across different environments (development, staging, production), but manually replicating configurations without a templating system increases maintenance complexity.

Difficult Rollbacks and Upgrades: Updating applications or rolling back changes can be challenging, as Kubernetes doesn't provide version control for application resource configuration changes.

Dependency Management: Manually managing application dependencies (e.g., services, databases, ingress controllers) can cause versioning and compatibility issues, leading to downtime or application failures.

Lack of Standardized Packaging: In large teams or organizations, packaging and sharing applications across teams without a standardized tool creates inconsistency in deployments.

Given these challenges, a better system is required to manage Kubernetes applications in a scalable, reusable, and standardized way.

Solution

Helm—the Kubernetes package manager—provides a solution to these challenges by offering a templating and package management system for deploying and managing Kubernetes applications. Helm allows Kubernetes administrators and developers to define, install, and upgrade applications as reusable charts. Below are the key features and the steps to effectively use Helm to manage Kubernetes applications:

Helm Charts for Application Packaging: Helm uses charts as the standard packaging format for Kubernetes applications. A chart is a collection of files that describe a related set of Kubernetes resources, such as pods, services, ConfigMaps, and more. Helm charts allow for reusability and easy configuration.

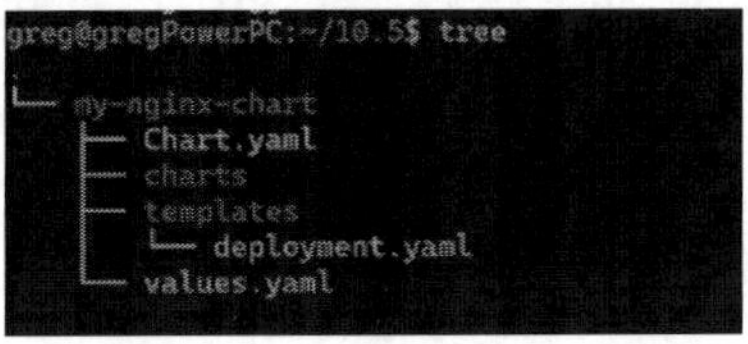

```
greg@gregPowerPC:~/10.5$ tree
.
└── my-nginx-chart
    ├── Chart.yaml
    ├── charts
    ├── templates
    │   └── deployment.yaml
    └── values.yaml
```

Figure 10-22. Directory structure of Helm charts

Add the below content to the Chart.yaml (metadata) file:

```
apiVersion: v2
name: my-nginx-chart
description: A Helm chart for Nginx
version: 1.0.0
appVersion: "1.16.0"
values.yaml (default values):
```

```
Define default configuration values in values.yaml:
replicaCount: 2
image:
```

```
  repository: nginx
  tag: "1.16.0"
templates/deployment.yaml (Kubernetes deployment template):
```

```
Define the Kubernetes deployment template in templates/
deployment.yaml:
apiVersion: apps/v1
kind: Deployment
metadata:
  name: {{ .Release.Name }}-nginx
spec:
  replicas: {{ .Values.replicaCount }}
  selector:
    matchLabels:
      app: nginx
  template:
    metadata:
      labels:
        app: nginx
    spec:
      containers:
      - name: nginx
        image: "{{ .Values.image.repository }}:{{ .Values.
        image.tag }}"
```

Install the Helm Chart:

Initialize Helm (if you haven't already).

If you haven't installed Helm, follow the Helm installation steps for your system.

Run the following command to install the Helm chart you just created:

```
helm install my-nginx ./my-nginx-chart
```

```
greg@gregPowerPC:~/10.5$ helm install my-nginx ./my-nginx-chart
Error: INSTALLATION FAILED: Kubernetes cluster unreachable: Get "http://localhost:8080/version": dial tcp 127.0.0.1:8080: connect: connection refused
greg@gregPowerPC:~/10.5$ sudo helm install my-nginx ./my-nginx-chart
NAME: my-nginx
LAST DEPLOYED: Sat Oct 12 22:08:32 2024
NAMESPACE: default
STATUS: deployed
REVISION: 1
TEST SUITE: None
```

Figure 10-23. *Installing Nginx via Helm*

This will install the chart and deploy Nginx with the default values from values.yaml.

```
greg@gregPowerPC:~/10.5$ sudo kubectl get pods
NAME                              READY   STATUS    RESTARTS   AGE
critical-pod                      1/1     Running   0          55m
my-nginx-nginx-69495fcbf7-dqh5c   1/1     Running   0          4m19s
my-nginx-nginx-69495fcbf7-mbhx9   1/1     Running   0          4m19s
```

Figure 10-24. *Checking if pods were initiated after Helm installation*

Upgrade the Helm Release:

To update the deployment with a new configuration (e.g., changing the replica count), use the helm upgrade command:

```
helm upgrade my-nginx ./my-nginx-chart --set replicaCount=5
```

```
greg@gregPowerPC:~/10.5$ sudo helm upgrade my-nginx ./my-nginx-chart --set replicaCount=5
Release "my-nginx" has been upgraded. Happy Helming!
NAME: my-nginx
LAST DEPLOYED: Sat Oct 12 22:13:12 2024
NAMESPACE: default
STATUS: deployed
REVISION: 2
TEST SUITE: None
greg@gregPowerPC:~/10.5$ sudo kubectl get pods
NAME                              READY   STATUS    RESTARTS   AGE
critical-pod                      1/1     Running   0          56m
my-nginx-nginx-69495fcbf7-7wz2b   1/1     Running   0          5s
my-nginx-nginx-69495fcbf7-dqh5c   1/1     Running   0          4m45s
my-nginx-nginx-69495fcbf7-mbhx9   1/1     Running   0          4m45s
my-nginx-nginx-69495fcbf7-qxrgk   1/1     Running   0          5s
my-nginx-nginx-69495fcbf7-zdzq4   1/1     Running   0          5s
```

Figure 10-25. *Scaling up Nginx pods with Helm to five replicas*

This command updates the running Nginx deployment to use five replicas, overriding the default value in values.yaml.

Uninstall the Helm Release:

Uninstall the release and delete all associated Kubernetes resources:

```
helm uninstall my-nginx
```

```
greg@gregPowerPC:~/10.5$ sudo helm uninstall my-nginx
release "my-nginx" uninstalled
greg@gregPowerPC:~/10.5$ sudo kubectl get pods
NAME           READY   STATUS    RESTARTS   AGE
critical-pod   1/1     Running   0          56m
```

Figure 10-26. *Uninstalling Nginx app with Helm*

This command will remove all the resources deployed by your Helm chart.

Outcome

Using Helm as a Kubernetes package manager offers several advantages:

Simplified Application Management: Helm abstracts the complexity of managing Kubernetes resource definitions, reducing the number of YAML files and manual processes.

Consistency Across Environments: Helm's templating engine ensures that you can reuse the same chart across multiple environments with environment-specific overrides, making it easy to deploy consistent applications.

Easy Rollbacks and Versioning: Helm's versioning and rollback features allow administrators to update applications safely and quickly recover from errors.

Dependency Management: Helm helps manage dependencies between services, ensuring that related applications are installed and configured correctly.

Scalability and Automation: By integrating Helm with CI/CD pipelines and version control systems, Kubernetes administrators can automate application deployments and upgrades, improving operational efficiency.

With Helm, Kubernetes administrators can efficiently manage complex applications, reduce configuration overhead, and maintain control over the versioning and deployment of Kubernetes workloads across different environments.

10.6 Additional Software in the Kubernetes Cluster

Problem

In Kubernetes clusters, additional software is required to enhance functionality, security, and observability beyond the core components (API server, scheduler, etc.). This includes components like networking plugins (CNI), storage solutions (CSI drivers), logging and monitoring tools (Prometheus, Fluentd), ingress controllers (Nginx, Traefik), and security tools (RBAC, network policies).

However, administrators face several challenges when deploying and managing additional software in Kubernetes clusters:

Integration Complexity: Many third-party tools have complex installation and configuration procedures that must be carefully integrated into the existing Kubernetes cluster without causing conflicts or misconfigurations.

Version Compatibility: Ensuring that the additional software is compatible with the specific Kubernetes version and the underlying infrastructure can be difficult, especially when dealing with different CNI plugins, CSI drivers, or third-party security tools.

Resource Management: Additional software consumes cluster resources like CPU, memory, and storage. Without careful resource planning, these components can impact the cluster's performance and the workloads running on it.

Upgrading and Maintenance: Third-party software must be upgraded in a coordinated manner to avoid disruptions or incompatibilities. Without a streamlined process, upgrading these components can introduce service downtime or failures.

Security and Compliance: Additional software, especially security components, needs to be configured and updated regularly to address vulnerabilities and maintain compliance with organizational security policies.

Given these challenges, a systematic approach is necessary to integrate, manage, and maintain additional software in Kubernetes clusters efficiently and securely.

Solution

Administrators should follow a structured approach that includes careful planning, automation, and continuous monitoring to deploy and manage additional software in a Kubernetes cluster successfully. Below are the steps and best practices for adding and managing third-party software in Kubernetes.

Choose the Right Networking Plugin (CNI)

Kubernetes requires a Container Network Interface (CNI) plugin to manage pod networking and communication. Popular CNI plugins include Calico, Flannel, Weave, and Cilium. Each offers unique features such as network policies, security, and scalability.

Install a CNI Plugin (e.g., Calico):

```
kubectl apply -f https://docs.projectcalico.org/v3.20/
manifests/calico.yaml
```

Configure Network Policies: After installing a CNI plugin like Calico that supports network policies, you can define network policies to restrict traffic between pods; note that some CNIs, such as Flannel, do not support network policies natively.

```
apiVersion: networking.k8s.io/v1
kind: NetworkPolicy
metadata:
  name: allow-ingress
spec:
  podSelector:
    matchLabels:
      role: frontend
  policyTypes:
  - Ingress
  ingress:
  - from:
    - podSelector:
        matchLabels:
          role: backend
```

Install Storage Plugins (CSI Drivers)

For dynamic storage provisioning, you need to install CSI (Container Storage Interface) drivers that integrate with your storage provider (e.g., Amazon EBS, Google Cloud Persistent Disk, NFS). These drivers allow Kubernetes to manage persistent volumes for stateful workloads.

Install the CSI Driver (e.g., AWS EBS CSI)

```
kubectl apply -k "github.com/kubernetes-sigs/aws-ebs-csi-
driver/deploy/kubernetes/overlays/stable/ecr/?ref=release-1.9"
Create Storage Class:
apiVersion: storage.k8s.io/v1
kind: StorageClass
metadata:
  name: ebs-sc
provisioner: ebs.csi.aws.com
parameters:
  type: gp2
Use Persistent Volume Claims (PVCs) with the Storage Class:

apiVersion: v1
kind: PersistentVolumeClaim
metadata:
  name: ebs-pvc
spec:
  storageClassName: ebs-sc
  accessModes:
    - ReadWriteOnce
  resources:
    requests:
      storage: 5Gi
```

Install Monitoring and Logging Tools

Observability is critical for managing the health and performance of the cluster. Tools like Prometheus for monitoring, Grafana for visualization, and Fluentd or ELK Stack for logging provide visibility into cluster operations.

Prometheus Installation (Using Helm)

```
helm repo add prometheus-community https://prometheus-
community.github.io/helm-charts
helm repo update
helm install prometheus prometheus-community/kube-
prometheus-stack
```

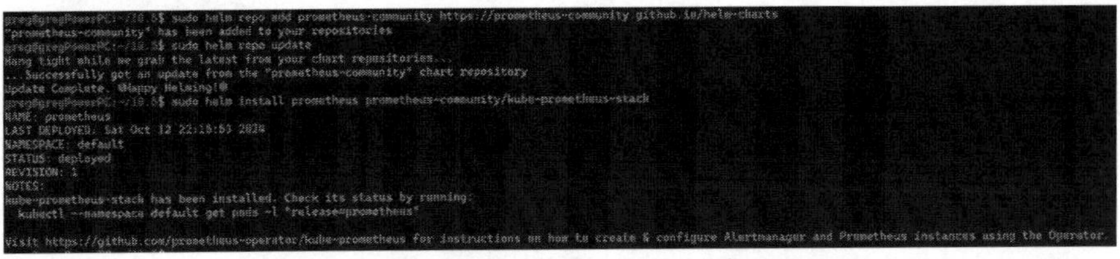

Figure 10-27. *Installing Prometheus with Helm*

Now, install the kube-prometheus-stack Helm chart from the prometheus-community repository. This chart includes Prometheus, Alertmanager, Grafana, and other tools for monitoring your Kubernetes cluster.

Access the Grafana Dashboard:

```
sudo kubectl port-forward service/prometheus-grafana 3000:80
```

Open your browser and visit http://localhost:3000.

Log into Grafana.

The default username is admin.

You can retrieve the default password using the following command:

```
kubectl get secret prometheus-grafana -o jsonpath="{.data.
admin-password}" | base64 --decode
```

Figure 10-28. *Getting the default Prometheus password*

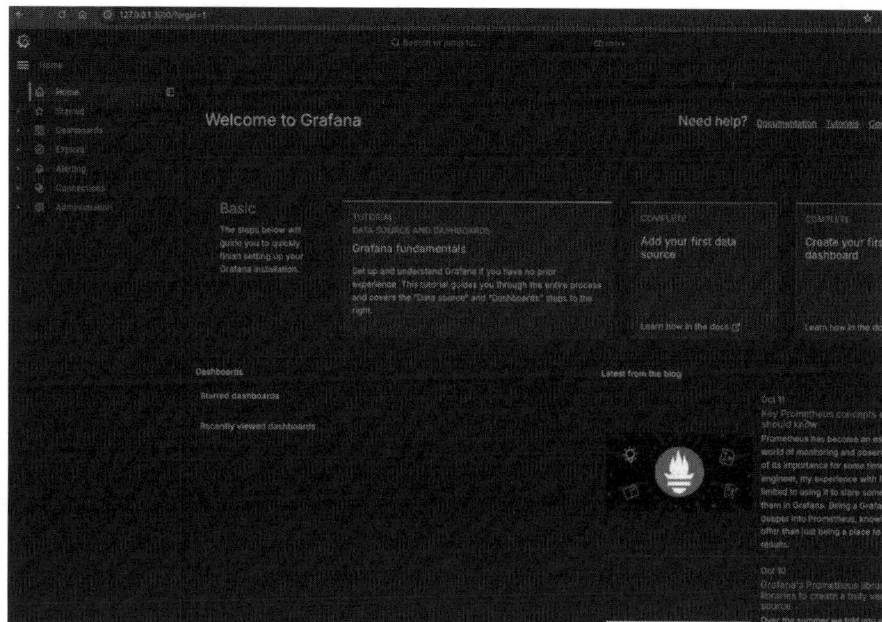

Figure 10-29. *Default Grafana Dashboard*

Grafana Installation

Grafana is often paired with Prometheus to monitor visualization. It can be installed via Helm:

```
helm install grafana stable/grafana
```

Fluentd Installation (for Log Aggregation)

Fluentd collects logs from pods and forwards them to a storage backend (e.g., Elasticsearch):

```
kubectl apply -f https://raw.githubusercontent.com/fluent/
fluentd-kubernetes-daemonset/master/fluentd-daemonset-
elasticsearch-rbac.yaml
```

Set Up Ingress Controllers

Ingress controllers like Nginx or Traefik manage external access to Kubernetes services, handling HTTP/HTTPS routing, load balancing, and SSL termination.

Install the Nginx Ingress Controller:

```
helm repo add ingress-nginx https://kubernetes.github.io/
ingress-nginx
helm install nginx-ingress ingress-nginx/ingress-nginx
```

Define Ingress Resources: After installing the ingress controller, you can define ingress resources to route external traffic to internal services:

```
apiVersion: networking.k8s.io/v1
kind: Ingress
metadata:
  name: example-ingress
spec:
  rules:
  - host: my-app.example.com
    http:
      paths:
      - path: /
        pathType: Prefix
```

```
      backend:
        service:
          name: my-app-service
          port:
            number: 80
```

Security Tools and Policies

Security is a top priority in any Kubernetes cluster. Integrating security software like Open Policy Agent (OPA) for policy management, Istio for service mesh, and RBAC (role-based access control) for access control ensures the cluster is compliant and secure.

Install Open Policy Agent (OPA): OPA helps enforce policies across the cluster:

```
kubectl apply -f https://raw.githubusercontent.com/open-policy-agent/gatekeeper/master/deploy/gatekeeper.yaml
```

Set Up Role-Based Access Control (RBAC): Define roles and role bindings to restrict access to resources:

```
apiVersion: rbac.authorization.k8s.io/v1
kind: Role
metadata:
  namespace: default
  name: pod-reader
rules:
- apiGroups: [""]
  resources: ["pods"]
  verbs: ["get", "list"]
```

Resource Management

Ensure that the additional software you install in the cluster has sufficient resources allocated and does not starve the workloads running in the cluster. Use resource requests and limits to control the resources used by these components.

Here's an example resource limit for Prometheus:

```
apiVersion: apps/v1
kind: Deployment
metadata:
  name: prometheus
spec:
  containers:
  - name: prometheus
    image: prom/prometheus
    resources:
      requests:
        memory: "500Mi"
        cpu: "250m"
      limits:
        memory: "1Gi"
        cpu: "500m"
```

Upgrading Additional Software

As new versions of third-party software are released, upgrading them in your cluster should be done carefully to avoid disruption. Helm charts and custom scripts can be used to manage these upgrades.

Upgrade Helm-Managed Components:

```
helm upgrade prometheus prometheus-community/kube-
prometheus-stack
```

Monitor Upgrades: Use monitoring tools like Prometheus and alerts to track the software's performance and health before and after upgrades.

Outcome

By following a structured approach to deploying and managing additional software in Kubernetes clusters, administrators can achieve the following:

Simplified Integration: Helm charts and automated installation methods reduce the complexity of integrating third-party software into the cluster.

Improved Resource Management: Properly configured resource requests and limits ensure that additional software doesn't overwhelm cluster resources.

Streamlined Monitoring and Security: Integrating observability tools like Prometheus and security tools like Open Policy Agent enables better control over cluster operations, ensuring security and compliance.

Efficient Upgrades: Helm's version management features, combined with careful resource allocation, make upgrading third-party software safer and more efficient.

This approach ensures a scalable and secure Kubernetes environment, enhancing the cluster's capabilities without introducing unnecessary complexity or risks.

10.7 Configure Repository and Plugins

Problem

Kubernetes relies on third-party tools, plugins, and packages to extend its functionality and manage complex workloads. Efficiently configuring repositories for package management and managing plugins is essential for the smooth operation of Kubernetes clusters. These repositories and plugins include

> **Helm Chart Repositories**: To deploy applications, administrators must configure Helm repositories to access and manage Helm charts for different applications.
>
> **Kubernetes Plugins**: Plugins such as CNI (Container Network Interface) plugins, CSI (Container Storage Interface) drivers, and other Kubernetes-related tooling are crucial for enhancing networking, storage, and monitoring capabilities within the cluster.

However, administrators often face several challenges related to configuring repositories and managing plugins:

> **Repository Configuration Complexity**: Setting up and managing multiple Helm chart repositories can be cumbersome, especially when dealing with private or custom repositories. Failure to configure repositories correctly can prevent access to important packages or updates.

Plugin Compatibility: It is critical to ensure that the plugins (network, storage, monitoring) are compatible with the Kubernetes version and other components in the cluster. Misconfigured plugins can lead to network disruptions, storage failures, or performance issues.

Managing Plugin Updates: Plugins require regular updates for security, bug fixes, and new features, but upgrading plugins without proper testing and planning can cause instability in the cluster.

Security Risks in Public Repositories: Using public Helm repositories or plugins without proper vetting can expose the cluster to security vulnerabilities or malicious packages.

Repository Authentication: Configuring authentication for private or internal repositories adds additional complexity, especially when integrating with CI/CD pipelines.

Given these challenges, configuring repositories and managing plugins efficiently and securely is critical for maintaining a stable and scalable Kubernetes environment.

Solution

The solution involves a structured approach to configuring Helm chart repositories and managing Kubernetes plugins effectively. This includes setting up public and private repositories, ensuring plugin compatibility, and automating repository management and plugin updates.

1. **Configure Helm Chart Repositories**:

   Helm is widely used to manage applications in Kubernetes through Helm charts. To deploy applications seamlessly across different environments, you need to configure both public and private Helm chart repositories.

   Add a Public Helm Repository: Adding a Helm chart repository allows you to access pre-built charts for popular applications, for example, to add the official Helm stable repository:

   ```
   helm repo add stable https://charts.helm.sh/stable
   ```

   Add a Private Helm Repository: If you're using a private repository for internal applications, you need to authenticate to access it. This can be done using Helm's repository authentication mechanisms:

   ```
   helm repo add my-private-repo https://my-repo-url
   --username my-user --password my-password
   ```

   Search and Install Charts from Repositories: Once the repository is configured, you can search for available charts and install them in your cluster:

   ```
   helm search repo stable
   helm install my-app stable/nginx
   ```

   Update the Repository and Cache: To ensure that you have the latest charts from all configured repositories, run

   ```
   helm repo update
   ```

2. **Configure Plugins for Kubernetes**:

   Plugins such as networking (CNI), storage (CSI), and monitoring tools are essential for Kubernetes clusters. Managing these plugins ensures that the cluster has the necessary capabilities for advanced use cases.

   Install a CNI Plugin (e.g., Calico for Networking): CNI plugins are responsible for pod networking and communication. Install a CNI plugin using a manifest file or Helm chart:

   ```
   kubectl apply -f https://docs.projectcalico.org/v3.20/
   manifests/calico.yaml
   ```

   Install a CSI Plugin (e.g., AWS EBS CSI Driver for Storage): Storage plugins (CSI) allow for dynamic provisioning of persistent volumes. Install the required CSI driver using a manifest:

   ```
   kubectl apply -k "github.com/kubernetes-sigs/aws-
   ebs-csi-driver/deploy/kubernetes/overlays/stable/
   ecr/?ref=release-1.9"
   ```

   Install Monitoring Plugins (e.g., Prometheus Operator): For observability, install monitoring tools like Prometheus or Grafana using Helm:

   ```
   helm install prometheus prometheus-community/kube-
   prometheus-stack
   ```

3. **Manage Plugin Compatibility**:

   Compatibility is key when adding plugins to Kubernetes. Ensure that the plugin versions are compatible with your Kubernetes version to avoid errors and instability.

   Check the Kubernetes Version: Before installing or updating plugins, check your current Kubernetes version:

   ```
   kubectl version --short
   ```

   Check Plugin Compatibility: Always refer to the plugin documentation to ensure that the plugin's version is compatible with your Kubernetes version. For example, Calico and CSI plugins often release specific versions tied to Kubernetes releases.

   Install Version-Specific Plugins: To ensure compatibility, specify the version of the plugin you want to install:

   ```
   helm install my-plugin --version 1.0.2 stable/my-plugin
   ```

4. **Automate Plugin Updates and Repository Management**:

   To streamline the process of updating repositories and plugins, consider integrating Helm and Kubernetes plugin management into CI/CD pipelines.

   Automate Repository Updates: Use CI/CD pipelines (e.g., Jenkins, GitLab CI) to update Helm repositories and install charts automatically, for example:

   ```
   helm repo update
   helm upgrade my-app stable/nginx --set replicaCount=3
   ```

Monitor Plugin Updates: Tools like kured (Kubernetes Reboot Daemon) can help manage plugin updates and ensure node health after installing or upgrading plugins:

```
kubectl apply -f https://github.com/weaveworks/kured/
releases/download/1.7.0/kured-1.7.0.yaml
```

5. **Secure Access to Repositories and Plugins**:

   For private repositories and critical plugins, use proper authentication and secure access mechanisms to ensure security.

   Use Helm Repository Authentication: For private repositories, authenticate with a username and password or an API token:

```
helm repo add my-private-repo https://my-repo-url
--username user --password pass
```

   Enable TLS for Plugin Communication: Secure plugin communication by enabling TLS and configuring certificates, for example, when configuring the CSI driver:

```
apiVersion: storage.k8s.io/v1
kind: StorageClass
metadata:
  name: secure-csi
parameters:
  csi.storage.k8s.io/provisioner-secret-name: my-secret
  csi.storage.k8s.io/provisioner-secret-namespace:
  default
```

6. **Track and Manage Installed Plugins**:

   Use Helm and Kubernetes commands to track installed plugins, monitor their status, and check for updates.

   List Installed Plugins:

   ```
   helm list
   ```

   View Plugin Status:

   ```
   kubectl get pods --namespace kube-system
   ```

   Check for Updates: Regularly check for available updates for installed plugins:

   ```
   helm search repo stable/nginx --versions
   ```

Outcome

By following these practices for configuring repositories and managing plugins, Kubernetes administrators can achieve the following:

Streamlined Deployment of Applications: With properly configured Helm repositories, both public and private, administrators can easily deploy, upgrade, and manage applications across environments.

Stable and Compatible Plugins: Ensuring plugin compatibility with the Kubernetes version helps prevent disruptions and ensures the smooth operation of networking, storage, and monitoring components.

Automated Management: Automating the update process for repositories and plugins through CI/CD pipelines reduces manual intervention and helps maintain consistency across environments.

Security and Compliance: Using secure authentication mechanisms and TLS ensures that repositories and plugins are protected from unauthorized access, reducing the risk of vulnerabilities.

Efficient Monitoring and Maintenance: Regularly monitoring plugin status and automating updates ensures that the cluster remains healthy and updated with the latest features and security patches.

This approach helps Kubernetes administrators manage repositories and plugins more efficiently, improving the scalability and stability of their Kubernetes environments.

10.8 Install a Package

Problem

Installing packages in Kubernetes is essential for deploying applications, system tools, and additional software that enhance cluster functionality. Typically managed via Helm or other package managers, packages streamline the deployment of complex applications by bundling Kubernetes manifests, dependencies, and configuration files into a single deployable unit.

However, several challenges arise when installing packages in Kubernetes:

Complex Application Deployments: Manually installing applications using raw Kubernetes YAML manifests is prone to human error, duplication, and inconsistencies, especially when dealing with multi-service applications.

Configuration Management: Installing packages manually makes it difficult to manage different configurations for various environments (e.g., development, staging, production). Updating or scaling applications becomes more convenient with a centralized tool for managing configurations.

Dependency Management: Many applications have dependencies (e.g., databases, messaging services) that must be installed and configured together. Failing to manage these dependencies can lead to broken services or incomplete installations.

Rollbacks and Updates: Manually updating or rolling back an installed package can be risky and error-prone, especially when changes affect multiple Kubernetes resources.

Resource Allocation: Ensuring that a package has the appropriate resource limits and requests (e.g., CPU, memory) during installation is critical to avoid overloading the cluster or under-provisioning the application.

To address these issues, Kubernetes administrators need a reliable way to install, configure, and manage packages efficiently.

Solution

Using a package manager like Helm offers a more streamlined approach to installing packages in Kubernetes. It ensures that applications and dependencies are installed, configured, and updated consistently. The following steps outline how to install a package using Helm and how to manage configurations, dependencies, and updates effectively.

Install a Package Using Helm

Helm simplifies package installation by bundling all the necessary Kubernetes manifests into a Helm chart, which can be installed using a single command.

Search for a Package: Helm provides repositories that host pre-configured charts for common applications (e.g., Nginx, MySQL, Prometheus). You can search for a package within a repository:

```
helm search repo nginx
```

Install the Package: Once you have selected the chart you want to install (e.g., Nginx), you can deploy it in the cluster:

```
helm install my-nginx stable/nginx
```

This command installs the Nginx chart under the release name my-nginx, creating all required Kubernetes resources such as deployments, services, and ConfigMaps.

Configure Package Installation

Helm allows you to customize package installations by using a values file or setting individual parameters directly through the command line.

Use a Values File: The values.yaml file contains default configuration values for the Helm chart. To modify these values for your environment (e.g., increasing the number of replicas), you can provide a custom values file during installation:

```
helm install my-nginx stable/nginx -f custom-
values.yaml
Example custom-values.yaml:
replicaCount: 3
image:
  repository: nginx
  tag: "1.19.0"
service:
  type: LoadBalancer
```

Set Values Directly: Alternatively, you can override default values using the --set flag during the Helm installation:

```
helm install my-nginx stable/nginx --set
replicaCount=3,image.tag="1.19.0"
```

Manage Dependencies

Some applications depend on other services (e.g., a web application that depends on a database). Helm charts can declare dependencies, ensuring that all necessary services are installed together.

Define Dependencies in Chart.yaml: Helm supports defining dependencies directly in the Chart.yaml file. For example, a web application might require MySQL as a dependency:

```
dependencies:
- name: mysql
  version: "8.1.0"
  repository: "https://charts.helm.sh/stable"
```

Install a Package with Dependencies: When you install the package, Helm will automatically resolve and install dependencies:

```
helm install my-app ./my-app-chart
```

This command installs both the web application and the MySQL database as part of the deployment.

Handling Package Updates and Rollbacks

Helm simplifies package upgrades and rollbacks, ensuring that changes can be made safely without disrupting services.

Upgrade a Package: To update an installed package with new configuration values or a new version of the chart, use the helm upgrade command:

```
helm upgrade my-nginx stable/nginx --set replicaCount=5
```

This command modifies the existing Nginx deployment and updates it with the new replica count.

Roll Back a Package: If the upgrade introduces issues, Helm allows you to roll back to a previous version of the release:

```
helm rollback my-nginx 1
```

This command restores the Nginx deployment to its previous configuration (version 1).

Resource Allocation for Packages

Ensuring that the application is properly resourced is critical to avoid over- or under-provisioning. Helm charts can be configured to specify resource requests and limits.

Set Resource Requests and Limits: You can set resource limits for the package during installation by specifying them in the values.yaml file or by using the --set flag:

```
resources:
  requests:
    memory: "256Mi"
    cpu: "100m"
  limits:
    memory: "512Mi"
    cpu: "200m"
During installation:
helm install my-nginx stable/nginx --set resources.
requests.memory="256Mi"
```

Automate Package Installation in CI/CD

Helm integrates with continuous integration/continuous deployment (CI/CD) pipelines, allowing you to automate package installation and updates. In a typical CI/CD pipeline (e.g., using Jenkins or GitLab CI), you can trigger Helm commands as part of your deployment process.

Here's an example CI pipeline step:

```
helm repo update
helm install my-app ./my-app-chart --namespace
production
```

This ensures that packages are deployed automatically when new versions of the code or charts are pushed to the repository.

Monitor and Verify Package Installation

After installing a package, monitoring its status and ensuring that all components are running correctly is crucial.

Check Installed Releases: You can list all installed packages and their statuses using

```
helm list
```

Check Pod Status: Verify that the pods related to the installed package are running without issues:

```
kubectl get pods --namespace default
```

Monitor Resource Usage: Use tools like Prometheus and Grafana to monitor the installed package's resource usage to ensure it is running efficiently.

Outcome

By following these best practices for installing packages using Helm in Kubernetes, administrators can achieve the following:

> **Simplified Application Deployment**: Helm streamlines the process of installing complex applications and their dependencies in Kubernetes using pre-configured charts.
>
> **Configuration Flexibility**: Helm's templating system and values.yaml files allow for easy customization of packages for different environments, reducing configuration errors.
>
> **Efficient Dependency Management**: Helm handles dependencies between services, ensuring that related applications are installed and configured correctly together.
>
> **Seamless Updates and Rollbacks**: Helm's version management features simplify updating and rolling back applications, minimizing downtime and risk.
>
> **Resource Optimization**: By configuring resource requests and limits, administrators can ensure that packages run efficiently without overloading the cluster.
>
> **Automation and CI/CD Integration**: Helm can be integrated into CI/CD pipelines to automate the installation, upgrade, and rollback processes, improving operational efficiency and consistency.

This structured approach ensures that Kubernetes packages are installed and managed efficiently, reducing complexity and enhancing cluster stability.

10.9 Helm Bitnami Chart

Problem

Administrators often rely on pre-built Helm charts to streamline the installation process when deploying applications in Kubernetes. Bitnami Helm charts are a popular choice due to their wide range of packaged applications and the stability they offer. Bitnami charts provide pre-configured Helm charts for databases, web applications, monitoring tools, and more. However, several challenges arise when using Bitnami Helm charts in production environments:

Customization of Pre-packaged Solutions: While Bitnami charts come pre-configured, most production environments require extensive customization to match specific infrastructure, security policies, and scaling needs. Adjusting configurations while maintaining stability can be difficult.

Version Management and Updates: It is crucial to track chart versions and ensure compatibility with the Kubernetes cluster and other dependencies. Improperly updating a Bitnami chart may cause application failures or service disruptions.

Dependency Management: Many applications depend on additional services (e.g., databases, caching layers). Managing these dependencies and ensuring they are properly configured with the Bitnami chart can be challenging, especially when upgrading or scaling the application.

Security and Compliance: Ensuring that the Bitnami Helm chart meets security requirements, such as enabling TLS, handling sensitive information like passwords securely, and integrating with external security systems, is essential for production environments.

Resource Optimization: Bitnami charts may come with default resource allocations that could be more optimal for the specific use case, leading to over-provisioning or resource shortages.

Given these challenges, using Bitnami Helm charts effectively in Kubernetes environments requires careful configuration, monitoring, and version control.

Solution

A structured approach to deploying, customizing, and managing Bitnami Helm charts ensures efficient application management in Kubernetes. Below are steps for configuring, installing, and maintaining Bitnami Helm charts.

Configure the Bitnami Helm Repository

Before using Bitnami Helm charts, you need to add the Bitnami repository to your Helm setup.

Add the Bitnami Helm Repository:

```
helm repo add bitnami https://charts.bitnami.com/bitnami
helm repo update
```

```
greg@gregPowerPC:~/10.5$ helm repo add bitnami https://charts.bitnami.com/bitnami
"bitnami" has been added to your repositories
greg@gregPowerPC:~/10.5$ sudo helm repo update
Hang tight while we grab the latest from your chart repositories...
...Successfully got an update from the "prometheus-community" chart repository
Update Complete. ⎈Happy Helming!⎈
```

Figure 10-30. *Adding the repository to Helm*

This adds the Bitnami chart repository to Helm, allowing you to search for and install charts.

Search for Charts: After adding the repository, search for the chart you need:

```
helm search repo bitnami
```

Install a Bitnami Helm Chart

Bitnami provides Helm charts for a wide range of applications, including MariaDB, PostgreSQL, WordPress, Redis, and many others.

Install a Bitnami chart (e.g., for MariaDB):

```
helm install my-mariadb bitnami/mariadb
```

This command installs the MariaDB database using the default settings in the Bitnami chart.

Customizing Bitnami Helm Charts

While Bitnami Helm charts have default configurations, most production environments require customization. You can customize the installation by modifying the values.yaml file or using the --set flag to override specific parameters.

> **Customizing Resource Requests and Limits**: Customize the resource allocations for your environment to prevent over-provisioning or resource exhaustion:

```
resources:
  limits:
    cpu: 500m
    memory: 512Mi
  requests:
    cpu: 250m
    memory: 256Mi
During installation:
helm install my-mariadb bitnami/mariadb --set
resources.limits.cpu=500m
```

Customize Persistence: Enable persistent storage for stateful applications such as databases:

```
persistence:
  enabled: true
  size: 8Gi
  storageClass: "standard"
```

Apply these customizations by providing a values.yaml file during installation:

```
helm install my-mariadb bitnami/mariadb -f custom-values.yaml
```

Managing Dependencies

Some applications depend on additional services, like databases or caching systems. Bitnami charts often allow you to manage these dependencies directly within the Helm chart configuration.

Installing Dependent Services: For example, if you're deploying WordPress using a Bitnami chart, you may also need to deploy MySQL as a dependency:

```
helm install my-wordpress bitnami/wordpress
```

The Bitnami WordPress chart has an option to deploy MySQL as a sub-chart. You can customize the MySQL configuration directly within the WordPress Helm chart using the values file.

Using External Dependencies: Configure the external service in the "values file" if you prefer to use an external database instead of the built-in MySQL.yaml:

```
externalDatabase:
  host: my-external-db
  port: 3306
  user: wordpress
  password: password
  database: wordpress_db
```

Version Management and Updates

Upgrading a Bitnami chart version or the application itself needs careful planning to avoid disruption.

Check for Chart Updates: Regularly check for available updates to the chart or its dependencies:

```
helm search repo bitnami/mariadb --versions
```

Upgrading an Installed Chart: Use the helm upgrade command to update the application while maintaining existing data and configurations:

```
helm upgrade my-mariadb bitnami/mariadb --set
replicaCount=3
```

Rolling Back a Failed Update: If the update causes problems, you can easily roll back to a previous version:

```
helm rollback my-mariadb 1
```

Security Best Practices for Bitnami Helm Charts

Security should always be a priority, especially for production environments. Bitnami Helm charts come with options to enhance security, including enabling TLS, handling sensitive data, and integrating with external security systems.

Enable TLS: For applications like MariaDB or PostgreSQL, Bitnami charts allow you to enable TLS for secure communication:

```
tls:
  enabled: true
```

Apply this during installation:

```
helm install my-mariadb bitnami/mariadb --set tls.
enabled=true
```

Secure Secrets: Bitnami charts allow for handling sensitive information (passwords, keys) securely through Kubernetes secrets:

```
existingSecret: my-secret
```

RBAC and SecurityContext: Enforce role-based access control (RBAC) and configure security contexts for the containers:

```
podSecurityContext:
  runAsUser: 1001
  fsGroup: 1001
securityContext:
  capabilities:
    drop:
      - ALL
```

Resource Management for Bitnami Charts

Adjust the resource allocations to ensure efficient use of cluster resources without over- or under-provisioning. This can be done by specifying resource requests and limits in the values.yaml file.

Here's an example resource configuration:

```
resources:
  limits:
    cpu: 1
    memory: 1Gi
  requests:
    cpu: 500m
    memory: 512Mi
During installation:
helm install my-mariadb bitnami/mariadb --set resources.limits.
cpu=1 --set resources.limits.memory=1Gi
```

Monitor and Verify Installation

After installing a Bitnami Helm chart, monitor the application's health and performance.

Check Release Status: List installed Helm releases and their statuses:

```
helm list
```

Monitor Application Pods: Check the status of pods to ensure they are running as expected:

```
kubectl get pods --namespace default
```

Monitor Resource Usage: Use monitoring tools like Prometheus or Grafana to track the installed application's resource consumption.

Outcome

By following these steps for using Bitnami Helm charts, Kubernetes administrators can achieve the following:

Efficient Application Deployment: Bitnami charts simplify the installation of complex applications and dependencies, streamlining deployment in Kubernetes environments.

Customization and Flexibility: Bitnami charts provide a flexible system for customizing configurations, allowing administrators to tailor deployments for various environments (development, staging, production).

Simplified Dependency Management: Bitnami charts support built-in dependency management, ensuring that applications and their supporting services (e.g., databases, caches) are installed and configured properly.

Version Control and Rollback: Helm's built-in versioning allows for easy updates and rollbacks, ensuring that changes to the environment can be made safely without risking application downtime.

Enhanced Security: Bitnami charts come with security features such as TLS, secret management, and RBAC, ensuring that applications are deployed securely in production environments.

Resource Optimization: Administrators can fine-tune resource requests and limits to ensure efficient use of cluster resources, avoiding both over-provisioning and resource shortages.

Using Bitnami Helm charts simplifies deploying and managing complex applications in Kubernetes, providing a reliable and scalable solution for both development and production environments.

CHAPTER 11

Security in Kubernetes

This chapter provides a comprehensive guide to enhancing the security posture of Kubernetes environments. It covers a wide array of security practices designed to protect workloads, sensitive data, and network communications within the Kubernetes cluster. The goal is to equip readers with practical knowledge to secure Kubernetes across various levels, from managing secrets and container-level security to implementing advanced access control mechanisms and securing service meshes. This chapter also delves into service mesh architectures, with a particular focus on Istio, a popular service mesh solution. By the end of the chapter, readers will gain a holistic understanding of how to manage and improve security in a Kubernetes-based system, including best practices for deploying and managing service meshes.

In modern cloud-native environments, security is paramount. Kubernetes, as the leading orchestration platform, brings flexibility and scalability but also introduces security challenges. This chapter focuses on mitigating risks and securing Kubernetes environments, ensuring both workloads and sensitive data are protected from potential threats.

We begin by addressing external secret management and the creation of native sidecar containers, which allow secure and modular extensions of containerized applications. Pod security, one of the foundational aspects of Kubernetes, is explored through topics such as configuring Pod Security

G. Stencel and L. Berton, *Kubernetes Recipes*,
https://doi.org/10.1007/979-8-8688-1325-2_11

Admission (PSA), AppArmor, and Seccomp (Secure Computing Mode)—tools that ensure container processes and system interactions are tightly controlled.

Next, the chapter covers authorization mechanisms, ranging from API access control, role-based access control (RBAC), and attribute-based access control (ABAC) to more advanced federated systems using OpenID and X.509 credentials.

In the latter part, we dive into the world of service meshes, starting with an overview of why they are needed for securing microservices architectures. Istio is introduced as a leading service mesh solution, and we explore how to configure it for secure traffic routing, service discovery with Istiod, and certificate management via Istio's Certificate Authority (CA). The chapter concludes with insights into telemetry gathering and best practices for managing and maintaining service mesh environments.

11.1 Interact with External Secrets

Problem

Kubernetes applications frequently require access to sensitive information such as API keys, passwords, and certificates to interact with external systems. Storing and managing these secrets securely is a significant challenge. Exposing this sensitive data in an unprotected form within the cluster poses risks such as unauthorized access, leakage, and exploitation. Additionally, handling secrets improperly can lead to compliance violations and security breaches, compromising both the application and its external systems. The challenge is to securely store, access, and transmit these secrets while ensuring they remain protected throughout their lifecycle within the Kubernetes environment.

Solution

To address these security challenges, Kubernetes offers several mechanisms to manage secrets securely:

Kubernetes Secrets API: Use Kubernetes' built-in Secrets API to store and manage sensitive data in an encoded form. While Kubernetes secrets are base64 encoded, they should be combined with proper access controls to limit who can view and modify them. Ensure that secrets are encrypted at rest by configuring Kubernetes to use encryption providers, such as KMS (Key Management Services).

External Secret Management: Utilize external secret management tools, such as HashiCorp Vault, AWS Secrets Manager, or Azure Key Vault, which integrate seamlessly with Kubernetes. These tools enable the storage and dynamic retrieval of secrets from secure, centralized services, reducing the risk of storing sensitive data within the cluster.

Secret Injection Through Environment Variables or Volumes: Inject secrets into pods securely via environment variables or mounted volumes. This ensures that secrets are available to the application without hardcoding them into the application configuration files or codebase.

Role-Based Access Control (RBAC): Implement strict RBAC policies to limit access to secrets. Only authorized pods and users should be able to read or modify secrets, minimizing the risk of unauthorized access.

Dynamic Secrets: Use dynamic secret generation where possible. Tools like HashiCorp Vault support generating short-lived credentials, ensuring that even if a secret is compromised, its lifespan is limited.

Audit and Monitoring: Enable auditing of secret access to monitor who is using and retrieving secrets. Regularly review and rotate secrets to reduce the risk of long-term compromise.

To interact with external secrets in Kubernetes, you typically need to integrate Kubernetes with an external secret management system such as AWS Secrets Manager, HashiCorp Vault, or Azure Key Vault. The External Secrets Operator is a common solution that allows Kubernetes to retrieve secrets from external secret stores.

Below are some examples to illustrate how you can interact with external secrets in Kubernetes using the External Secrets Operator.

Prerequisites:

Kubernetes cluster running

External Secrets Operator installed in the cluster

You can install it with Helm or use the official manifests:

```
helm repo add external-secrets https://charts.external-secrets.io
helm install external-secrets external-secrets/external-secrets
```

Example 1: Using AWS Secrets Manager

Step 1: Create an IAM Policy and Role

Create an IAM policy that allows access to your secrets in AWS Secrets Manager. Then, attach this policy to an IAM role that can be assumed by your Kubernetes service account.

Step 2: Configure External Secrets

First, define a ClusterSecretStore or SecretStore resource to configure the integration with AWS Secrets Manager.

```
apiVersion: external-secrets.io/v1beta1
kind: ClusterSecretStore
metadata:
  name: aws-secrets-manager
spec:
```

```
  provider:
    aws:
      service: SecretsManager
      region: us-west-2
      auth:
        secretRef:
          accessKeyIDSecretRef:
            name: aws-credentials
            key: access-key-id
          secretAccessKeySecretRef:
            name: aws-credentials
            key: secret-access-key
```

This configuration tells the External Secrets Operator to use AWS Secrets Manager as the secret store.

Step 3: Create the ExternalSecret Resource

Next, define the ExternalSecret resource that references your secret in AWS Secrets Manager.

```
apiVersion: external-secrets.io/v1beta1
kind: ExternalSecret
metadata:
  name: my-app-secret
spec:
  secretStoreRef:
    name: aws-secrets-manager
    kind: ClusterSecretStore
  target:
    name: my-kubernetes-secret
  data:
    - secretKey: api-key
      remoteRef:
        key: my-app/api-key
```

This ExternalSecret resource creates a Kubernetes secret my-kubernetes-secret using the secret stored in AWS Secrets Manager under the key my-app/api-key.

Step 4: Access the Secret in Kubernetes

Now, your Kubernetes workloads can use the my-kubernetes-secret like any other Kubernetes secret.

```
apiVersion: v1
kind: Pod
metadata:
  name: secret-app
spec:
  containers:
    - name: app
      image: nginx
      env:
        - name: API_KEY
          valueFrom:
            secretKeyRef:
              name: my-kubernetes-secret
              key: api-key
```

Example 2: Using HashiCorp Vault

Step 1: Configure the SecretStore for Vault

You can configure Vault as a ClusterSecretStore similar to AWS Secrets Manager.

```
apiVersion: external-secrets.io/v1beta1
kind: ClusterSecretStore
metadata:
  name: vault-secret-store
spec:
  provider:
```

```
  vault:
    server: http://vault-server:8200
    path: secret/data
    version: v2
    auth:
      tokenSecretRef:
        name: vault-token
        key: token
```

Step 2: Define an ExternalSecret for Vault

Next, you create an ExternalSecret that pulls a secret from HashiCorp Vault.

```
apiVersion: external-secrets.io/v1beta1
kind: ExternalSecret
metadata:
  name: vault-app-secret
spec:
  secretStoreRef:
    name: vault-secret-store
    kind: ClusterSecretStore
  target:
    name: my-kubernetes-vault-secret
  data:
    - secretKey: api-key
      remoteRef:
        key: my-app/api-key
```

Step 3: Access the Secret in Kubernetes

Once the ExternalSecret is synced, you can use the secret in your applications, just like in the AWS example.

```
apiVersion: v1
kind: Deployment
metadata:
  name: vault-app
spec:
  template:
    spec:
      containers:
        - name: app
          image: nginx
          env:
            - name: API_KEY
              valueFrom:
                secretKeyRef:
                  name: my-kubernetes-vault-secret
                  key: api-key
```

Example 3: Using Azure Key Vault

Step 1: Configure SecretStore for Azure Key Vault

To use Azure Key Vault, define a ClusterSecretStore pointing to Azure.

```
apiVersion: external-secrets.io/v1beta1
kind: ClusterSecretStore
metadata:
  name: azure-key-vault
spec:
  provider:
    azurekv:
      tenantId: "<your-tenant-id>"
      clientId: "<your-client-id>"
      clientSecretSecretRef:
```

```
        name: azure-credentials
        key: client-secret
      vaultUrl: "https://<your-keyvault-name>.vault.azure.net/"
```

Step 2: Create an ExternalSecret for Azure Key Vault

Next, create an ExternalSecret for your secret in Azure Key Vault.

```
apiVersion: external-secrets.io/v1beta1
kind: ExternalSecret
metadata:
  name: azure-app-secret
spec:
  secretStoreRef:
    name: azure-key-vault
    kind: ClusterSecretStore
  target:
    name: my-kubernetes-azure-secret
  data:
    - secretKey: db-password
      remoteRef:
        key: my-app/db-password
```

Outcome

Combining these strategies, Kubernetes environments can securely manage interactions with external secrets, minimizing the risk of exposure and ensuring compliance with security best practices.

These examples demonstrate how to interact with external secrets using the External Secrets Operator in Kubernetes. By connecting to external secret management systems like AWS Secrets Manager, HashiCorp Vault, or Azure Key Vault, you can securely manage and inject secrets into your Kubernetes workloads without hardcoding sensitive information.

11.2 Create a Native Sidecar Container

Problem

Creating a Native Sidecar Container in Kubernetes for Enhanced Application Functionality

In a Kubernetes environment, applications often require additional services to work efficiently, such as logging, monitoring, or data synchronization. These supporting functionalities are typically handled by other applications or services running in parallel. One of the most common approaches to solve this challenge is using sidecar containers.

However, configuring and integrating these sidecar containers natively within Kubernetes clusters can be complex. Developers often face issues in managing the lifecycle of sidecars, ensuring proper communication between the primary and sidecar containers, and coordinating resource consumption. Moreover, ensuring that sidecar containers are portable and independent can be a challenge, especially when dealing with various Kubernetes environments or updates.

Solution

Implementing a Native Sidecar Container for Logging and Monitoring in Kubernetes

A sidecar container is a useful pattern in Kubernetes to enhance the functionality of the main application container. By running a sidecar alongside the main container within the same pod, you can decouple supporting tasks, like logging or monitoring, from the main application. This design allows developers to extend the functionality of applications without modifying the main application code.

A common example involves running a logging agent (like Fluentd) as a sidecar container that collects and processes logs from the main application container. This approach allows logs to be collected, aggregated, and sent to an external logging service like Elasticsearch.

Here are steps to implement this:

Define the Sidecar in the Pod's YAML: You can define a sidecar container in the Pod's YAML file as part of the PodSpec. This way, the sidecar container and the primary container run together within the same pod.

Share Volumes: For the main container and sidecar to communicate or share data, you can use shared volumes. In the case of logging, the main container writes logs to a shared volume, and the sidecar container reads these logs and forwards them to a centralized logging system.

Ensure Proper Resource Allocation: Allocate CPU and memory resources properly between the main and sidecar containers to avoid resource contention.

Example: Logging Sidecar Using Fluentd

Below is an example of a pod YAML file where Fluentd is used as a sidecar to collect logs from the main application container:

```
apiVersion: v1
kind: Pod
metadata:
  name: app-with-sidecar
spec:
  containers:
```

```
  - name: main-app
    image: my-app-image:v1
    volumeMounts:
    - name: log-volume
      mountPath: /var/log/app
  - name: logging-sidecar
    image: fluentd:latest
    volumeMounts:
    - name: log-volume
      mountPath: /var/log/app
    env:
    - name: FLUENTD_OUTPUT
      value: "elasticsearch"
  volumes:
  - name: log-volume
    emptyDir: {}
```

Explanation:

The main-app container is the primary application container.

The logging-sidecar container runs Fluentd to collect logs from the main container.

Both containers share the log-volume volume, where the logs are written and then read by the Fluentd sidecar container.

Fluentd forwards these logs to an external service like Elasticsearch, making log aggregation simple and centralized.

Benefits:

Decoupling: Sidecar containers allow for separation of concerns by decoupling logging and monitoring services from the main application.

Modularity: Sidecar containers are reusable and portable, meaning the same Fluentd sidecar configuration can be applied to other services that require logging.

Scalability: By using sidecars, you can scale the main container independently of the supporting services, leading to better resource optimization.

This native Kubernetes pattern simplifies application management and deployment, especially in cloud-native environments, improving scalability and maintainability.

11.3 Configure Pod Security Admission per Namespace

Problem

In Kubernetes, security is a top concern, and managing security across different namespaces presents a challenge. Certain workloads may require stricter security policies, while others may need more lenient settings. Without proper mechanisms, there is a risk of deploying insecure pods that can compromise the cluster's security posture.

Kubernetes' Pod Security Admission (PSA) enforces security policies at the pod level, but it's essential to have fine-grained control to apply these security policies based on the specific needs of each namespace. Ensuring that different namespaces can enforce varying levels of security (e.g., restricting privileged containers, limiting volume mounts) helps maintain a secure and flexible cluster.

Solution

Implementing Pod Security Admission per Namespace in Kubernetes

Kubernetes provides Pod Security Admission (PSA) to enforce security profiles on pods at the namespace level. By configuring PSA, cluster administrators can ensure that pods in different namespaces adhere to specific security policies. This is done by applying different Pod Security Standards (PSS), such as Privileged, Baseline, and Restricted, based on the risk level and security needs of each namespace.

Here are steps to configure Pod Security Admission per namespace:

> **Enable Pod Security Admission**: PSA is a built-in admission controller in Kubernetes, but it needs to be enabled in the cluster configuration. This typically requires modifying the API server to ensure that PSA is active.

Enable PSA in the API server configuration.

If you're managing your Kubernetes cluster using static pod manifests (common in kubeadm setups), you can enable PSA by updating the kube-apiserver manifest.

The API server manifest is usually located at /etc/kubernetes/manifests/kube-apiserver.yaml on the master node. Edit the manifest to include PSA. Add PodSecurity to the --enable-admission-plugins flag. Ensure that PSA is listed before any other admission plugins that might affect pod creation.

```
apiVersion: v1
kind: Pod
metadata:
  name: kube-apiserver
  namespace: kube-system
spec:
  containers:
  - name: kube-apiserver
    image: k8s.gcr.io/kube-apiserver:v1.25.0
    command:
    - kube-apiserver
    - --enable-admission-plugins=PodSecurity,NamespaceLifecycle,
      LimitRanger,ServiceAccount,DefaultStorageClass,Default
      TolerationSeconds,NodeRestriction,RuntimeClass, etc.
    # other flags
    volumeMounts:
    - mountPath: /etc/kubernetes/pki
      name: k8s-certs
      readOnly: true
  volumes:
  - name: k8s-certs
    hostPath:
      path: /etc/kubernetes/pki
      type: Directory
```

Kubernetes will automatically restart the API server when the manifest file is updated. Verify that PSA is enabled by checking the API server logs or using the following command:

```
kubectl get --raw /api/v1/namespaces/kube-system/pods | grep
kube-apiserver
```

You should see PodSecurity listed among the enabled admission plugins.

Define Pod Security Levels for Namespaces:

Kubernetes provides three predefined security levels for namespaces:

Privileged: Minimal restrictions, most flexible, suitable for trusted workloads

Baseline: Ensures standard security practices are followed; blocks unsafe practices like running privileged containers

Restricted: The strictest security settings, preventing privilege escalation, restricting capabilities, and limiting volume types

Label Namespaces: To configure different levels of pod security per namespace, you must label each namespace with the appropriate pod security level. For example, you can label a namespace as "Restricted" to apply the strictest security policies.

Test and Validate Policies: After configuring the PSA policies for namespaces, it's important to test and validate that the pods deployed in those namespaces conform to the expected security standards.

Example: Configuring Pod Security Admission for Two Namespaces

In this example, we'll configure two namespaces, one with Baseline security and the other with Restricted security, using Kubernetes labels.

Step 1: Create the Namespaces

```
apiVersion: v1
kind: Namespace
metadata:
  name: baseline-namespace
---
apiVersion: v1
kind: Namespace
metadata:
  name: restricted-namespace
```

Step 2: Apply Pod Security Standards via Namespace Labels

```
# Label baseline-namespace to enforce the 'baseline'
security profile
kubectl label namespace baseline-namespace \
  pod-security.kubernetes.io/enforce=baseline

# Label restricted-namespace to enforce the 'restricted'
security profile
kubectl label namespace restricted-namespace \
  pod-security.kubernetes.io/enforce=restricted
```

These labels ensure that any pod created in the baseline-namespace will have to comply with the Baseline security profile and any pod in the restricted-namespace must adhere to the Restricted security profile.

Step 3: Deploy Pods and Validate

To verify if the policy works, you can attempt to deploy pods with varying security contexts in each namespace.

```
# Pod definition for baseline-namespace (allowed under
Baseline policy)

apiVersion: v1
kind: Pod
metadata:
  name: baseline-pod
  namespace: baseline-namespace
spec:
  containers:
  - name: myapp
    image: nginx
    securityContext:
      runAsNonRoot: true

# Pod definition for restricted-namespace (blocked if not
compliant with Restricted policy)
apiVersion: v1
kind: Pod
metadata:
  name: restricted-pod
  namespace: restricted-namespace
spec:
  containers:
  - name: myapp
    image: nginx
    securityContext:
      privileged: true
```

In the second example, the pod in the restricted-namespace will be denied because it violates the Restricted security profile by attempting to use the privileged security context, which is not allowed in restricted settings.

Explanation:

Namespace Labels: By labeling namespaces with different PSA enforcement levels, you ensure that only pods that comply with the respective security standard can be deployed in that namespace.

Security Profiles: The baseline-namespace allows less strict pods, which follow typical security standards, while the restricted-namespace enforces more stringent restrictions like forbidding privileged containers.

Benefits:

Granular Control: Different namespaces can enforce different security policies, ensuring workloads are appropriately protected based on their sensitivity.

Compliance: Enforcing Pod Security Standards ensures that workloads comply with security best practices.

Flexibility: PSA allows administrators to define policies based on risk levels for different namespaces without affecting other workloads or namespaces.

By configuring Pod Security Admission per namespace, Kubernetes clusters can enforce tailored security policies at a granular level, reducing the risk of deploying insecure workloads and improving overall security.

11.4 Configure AppArmor per Pod

Problem

Configuring AppArmor Profiles for Pods to Enhance Container Security in Kubernetes

Kubernetes allows workloads to run in isolated containers, but securing those workloads requires additional layers of protection. AppArmor is a Linux kernel security module that restricts the actions of programs based on pre-configured profiles. In a Kubernetes cluster, workloads running as pods may require specific security restrictions to protect the underlying system. The challenge lies in effectively applying and managing AppArmor profiles to restrict pods' permissions and mitigate potential vulnerabilities without disrupting application functionality.

If not properly configured, workloads might be able to perform harmful operations, such as accessing sensitive host resources or escalating privileges. To ensure containers do not perform unauthorized actions, configuring AppArmor profiles per pod becomes crucial for enhancing security.

Solution

Applying AppArmor Profiles per Pod in Kubernetes

AppArmor helps enforce fine-grained access control by limiting the system calls that pods can make. By applying an AppArmor profile to a pod, you can define what actions the pod's containers are allowed to perform, limiting their potential attack surface. Kubernetes supports AppArmor, and you can assign an AppArmor profile to each container within a pod by annotating the pod specification.

Here are steps to configure AppArmor per pod:

Prepare AppArmor Profiles: AppArmor profiles are defined and managed at the host level. You need to create and load the AppArmor profile on the nodes running your Kubernetes cluster. Each profile defines the allowed system calls and permissions for the container processes.

Annotate the Pod: Once the AppArmor profile is loaded on the node, you can assign it to individual pods by using annotations. The annotation specifies the AppArmor profile that will be enforced for the containers within the pod.

Enforce and Test the AppArmor Profile: After applying the AppArmor profile, it's essential to verify that the container is constrained as expected and cannot perform unauthorized actions.

Example: Configuring an AppArmor Profile for a Pod

Below is an example of how to apply an AppArmor profile to a pod running a Nginx container. In this case, we assume you have an AppArmor profile called nginx-profile already defined and loaded on the Kubernetes node.

Step 1: Define and Load the AppArmor Profile

On the host machine (outside of Kubernetes), you define the AppArmor profile. Here's a simplified example of what the profile might look like:

```
# /etc/apparmor.d/nginx-profile
profile nginx-profile flags=(attach_disconnected,mediate_
deleted) {
```

```
  # Allow basic file access and network operations
  file,
  network,
  capability net_bind_service,

  # Deny access to sensitive files
  deny /etc/shadow r,
  deny /etc/passwd w,

  # Prevent privilege escalation
  deny ptrace,
  deny mount,
}
```

Once defined, you load the profile into the system:

```
sudo apparmor_parser -r /etc/apparmor.d/nginx-profile
```

Step 2: Annotate the Pod YAML to Apply the AppArmor Profile

In the pod specification, you need to annotate the pod definition to use the nginx-profile AppArmor profile for the container:

```
apiVersion: v1
kind: Pod
metadata:
  name: nginx-apparmor-pod
  annotations:
    container.apparmor.security.beta.kubernetes.io/nginx-
container: localhost/nginx-profile
spec:
  containers:
  - name: nginx-container
    image: nginx
    ports:
    - containerPort: 80
```

Explanation:

The annotation container.apparmor.security.beta.kubernetes.io/nginx-container specifies that the nginx-container in this pod will use the nginx-profile AppArmor profile.

The value localhost/nginx-profile refers to the profile already defined on the host machine where the pod runs.

The nginx-profile will enforce the system call restrictions defined in the AppArmor profile, limiting what the Nginx container can do.

Step 3: Deploy and Test the Pod

You can deploy this pod using kubectl:

```
kubectl apply -f nginx-apparmor-pod.yaml
```

Once the pod is running, test the container's behavior to ensure the AppArmor profile is being enforced. For example, you can check whether the container is blocked from reading or writing to sensitive files as defined in the AppArmor profile.

Benefits of AppArmor in Kubernetes:

Fine-Grained Control: AppArmor provides detailed control over the system calls that each container can make, ensuring only the required actions are permitted.

Mitigate Security Risks: With AppArmor, containers are restricted from performing harmful or unnecessary actions, reducing the likelihood of privilege escalation or unauthorized access.

Namespace-Specific Protection: Different workloads can have different security needs, and AppArmor allows administrators to apply unique security profiles tailored to the specific behavior of each container.

Lightweight and Easy to Use: AppArmor is relatively lightweight compared with other security modules like SELinux, and it's easy to apply per pod through annotations in Kubernetes.

Challenges:

Profile Management: AppArmor profiles need to be managed on each node in the cluster, which can become complex in larger clusters or multi-cloud environments.

Compatibility: Some workloads might need more privileges than others, so you need to carefully tailor the profiles to balance security and functionality.

By configuring AppArmor per pod, Kubernetes administrators can ensure that pods run with the minimum necessary permissions, enhancing the security posture of the entire cluster while minimizing the risk of container-based attacks.

11.5 Configure Seccomp per Pod to Restrict Syscalls

Problem

Configuring Seccomp per Pod to Restrict Syscalls in Kubernetes

In Kubernetes, containers may require access to various system calls (syscalls) to interact with the underlying kernel. However, allowing containers unrestricted access to all syscalls can increase the attack surface, potentially leading to security vulnerabilities. For instance, containers could exploit kernel-level vulnerabilities or make unauthorized changes to the host system.

To mitigate these risks, it is essential to restrict the syscalls that a container can use, ensuring that only the necessary ones are permitted. Seccomp (Secure Computing Mode) is a Linux kernel feature that allows filtering and limiting the syscalls a container can invoke. The challenge lies in configuring Seccomp in Kubernetes per pod to enforce these restrictions while ensuring the application remains functional.

Solution

Implementing Seccomp Profiles per Pod in Kubernetes

Kubernetes allows you to apply Seccomp profiles to pods to restrict the syscalls that their containers can invoke. Seccomp profiles define which syscalls are allowed or denied, thus enhancing security by reducing the container's ability to interact with the kernel in dangerous ways.

Kubernetes supports different Seccomp profiles, such as

Unconfined: No restrictions on syscalls (least secure).

Default: Blocks known dangerous syscalls but allows most others (moderate security).

Custom: A custom profile can be defined to tailor specific syscalls allowed or denied (maximum security control).

Here are steps to configure Seccomp per pod:

Create or Use an Existing Seccomp Profile: You can use Kubernetes's default Seccomp profile or create your own custom profile. A Seccomp profile is defined in JSON format and is loaded into the host system.

Annotate the Pod to Use Seccomp: Kubernetes allows you to apply a Seccomp profile to a pod through annotations. The profile can be applied to all containers in the pod or on a per-container basis.

Test and Validate: After configuring the Seccomp profile, you should test the pod to ensure it can perform necessary operations without violating syscall restrictions.

Example: Applying a Custom Seccomp Profile to a Pod

Step 1: Create a Custom Seccomp Profile

Here's an example of a Seccomp profile in JSON format that allows basic syscalls but denies certain sensitive ones like ptrace and kexec:

```
{
  "defaultAction": "SCMP_ACT_ERRNO",
  "syscalls": [
    {
      "names": ["read", "write", "exit", "sigreturn"],
      "action": "SCMP_ACT_ALLOW"
    },
    {
      "names": ["ptrace", "kexec_load", "open_by_handle_at"],
      "action": "SCMP_ACT_ERRNO"
    }
  ]
}
```

The profile specifies a defaultAction of SCMP_ACT_ERRNO, which means any syscall not explicitly allowed will return an error.

Syscalls like read, write, exit, and sigreturn are allowed.

Syscalls like ptrace, kexec_load, and open_by_handle_at are explicitly blocked, preventing the container from performing these potentially dangerous actions.

Step 2: Apply the Seccomp Profile to a Pod

Once the Seccomp profile is defined and loaded on the node, you can apply it to a pod using Kubernetes annotations:

```
apiVersion: v1
kind: Pod
metadata:
  name: seccomp-pod
  annotations:
    seccomp.security.alpha.kubernetes.io/pod: localhost/my-
    seccomp-profile
spec:
  containers:
  - name: my-container
    image: nginx
```

The annotation seccomp.security.alpha.kubernetes.io/pod applies the custom Seccomp profile my-seccomp-profile to all containers in the pod.

The localhost/ prefix indicates that the profile is stored locally on the node.

Step 3: Deploy the Pod and Test

Apply the pod configuration with the following command:

```
kubectl apply -f seccomp-pod.yaml
```

You can then verify that the Seccomp profile is enforced by trying to execute syscalls that are restricted. For example, if the container tries to invoke the ptrace syscall, it should be blocked and result in an error.

Using the Default Seccomp Profile

Kubernetes also provides a default Seccomp profile, which blocks known dangerous syscalls. To apply the default profile, simply annotate the pod as follows:

```
apiVersion: v1
kind: Pod
metadata:
  name: default-seccomp-pod
  annotations:
    seccomp.security.alpha.kubernetes.io/pod: runtime/default
spec:
  containers:
  - name: my-container
    image: nginx
```

In this case, the runtime/default profile will apply the default syscall restrictions to the pod.

Explanation:

Syscall Filtering: Seccomp works by filtering syscalls that the container is allowed to make. Any syscall not permitted by the profile is denied, thus reducing the risk of malicious or accidental kernel-level access.

Custom Profiles: A custom Seccomp profile offers fine-grained control over which syscalls are allowed. This allows you to tailor security policies based on the specific needs of the application.

Annotations: Kubernetes uses annotations to apply Seccomp profiles, making it straightforward to configure security policies per pod or container.

Benefits of Using Seccomp:

Reduced Attack Surface: By limiting the syscalls a container can invoke, Seccomp drastically reduces the kernel's exposure to malicious or unintended actions.

Compatibility with Workloads: You can create custom profiles that match the exact needs of your workloads, allowing for a secure yet functional environment.

Flexible Application: Seccomp profiles can be applied to individual pods or containers, providing flexibility in managing different security needs across a cluster.

Ease of Use: Kubernetes' support for Seccomp through annotations simplifies the integration of syscall restrictions into the deployment process.

Challenges:

Profile Management: Managing Seccomp profiles, especially custom ones, can be complex, particularly in larger clusters where various workloads have different security needs.

Application Breakage: If the Seccomp profile is too restrictive, it might block syscalls that the application needs, leading to failure. Careful testing is required.

By configuring Seccomp per pod, Kubernetes administrators can ensure that containers are restricted to the minimum necessary syscalls, improving the overall security posture of the cluster while protecting the kernel from unnecessary exposure.

11.6 Authorization (API Access Control, X.509 Credentials, JSON Web Tokens, Attribute-Based Access Control, Role-Based Access Control, and Federating with OpenID Identity Providers)

Problem

Implementing Comprehensive Authorization Mechanisms in Kubernetes

Kubernetes provides various ways to manage authorization—the process that ensures that only authenticated users or service accounts can perform specific actions on resources within the cluster. Given the diverse needs of modern cloud-native applications, it is essential to implement fine-grained access control mechanisms to protect sensitive resources and ensure that only authorized entities have the correct permissions.

This challenge encompasses different aspects of authorization in Kubernetes, such as API access control, managing X.509 certificates, JSON Web Tokens (JWTs), attribute-based access control (ABAC), role-based access control (RBAC), and integrating external identity providers like OpenID. Each of these mechanisms serves a specific use case, and understanding how to use them in combination or separately is crucial to building a secure Kubernetes cluster.

Solution

Implementing Comprehensive API Access Control in Kubernetes

Kubernetes supports multiple authorization methods, and understanding when and how to use each is essential for securing API access. Below are the key authorization mechanisms:

API access control

X.509 credentials

JSON Web Tokens (JWTs)

Attribute-based access control (ABAC)

Role-based access control (RBAC)

Federating with OpenID identity providers

1. **API Access Control**

   API access control governs who can access the Kubernetes API and perform operations like creating pods, modifying configurations, or accessing cluster resources. The API server uses an authentication layer to identify the requesting user, followed by an authorization layer to determine if the user is allowed to perform the requested action.

   Kubernetes supports multiple authentication methods, including client certificates, bearer tokens, and OpenID Connect (OIDC) tokens. Once authenticated, authorization decisions are made using either RBAC, ABAC, or Webhook authorization methods.

2. **X.509 Credentials**

   Kubernetes uses X.509 client certificates to authenticate API requests. These certificates can be generated and managed by Kubernetes' built-in Certificate Authority (CA) or an external CA.

   Example: X.509 Client Certificate Authentication

   To authenticate a user using an X.509 certificate, the following steps are involved:

   Step 1: Generate X.509 Certificates

   Use openssl to generate a client certificate signed by the Kubernetes CA:

   ```
   openssl genrsa -out user-key.pem 2048
   openssl req -new -key user-key.pem -out user.csr -subj
   "/CN=username/O=group"
   openssl x509 -req -in user.csr -CA ca.crt -CAkey ca.key
   -CAcreateserial -out user-cert.pem -days 365
   ```

   Step 2: Configure Kubernetes API Access

   Once generated, the user certificate and key can be added to the kubeconfig file:

   ```
   users:
   - name: username
     user:
       client-certificate: /path/to/user-cert.pem
       client-key: /path/to/user-key.pem
   ```

   Kubernetes will then authenticate the user based on the certificate's validity.

3. **JSON Web Tokens (JWTs)**

   JWTs are often used in Kubernetes for service-to-service authentication, particularly in scenarios involving external identity providers. Kubernetes' service accounts issue JWTs to pods, allowing pods to authenticate with the API server securely.

   Example: Using a JWT for API Access

   A JWT can be included as a bearer token in an API request's Authorization header:

   ```
   curl -H "Authorization: Bearer $TOKEN" https://<api-server-url>/api/v1/namespaces/default/pods
   ```

   Here, $TOKEN is the JWT that was issued by the service account.

4. **Attribute-Based Access Control (ABAC)**

   ABAC allows access control policies to be defined based on attributes of the request, such as user identity, resource type, and action. These policies are typically stored in a JSON file on the API server.

   Example: ABAC Policy JSON File

   ```
   {
     "apiVersion": "abac.authorization.kubernetes.io/
     v1beta1",
     "kind": "Policy",
     "spec": {
       "user": "alice",
       "namespace": "default",
       "resource": "pods",
   ```

```
    "readonly": true
  }
}
```

In this policy, user "alice" has read-only access to pods in the "default" namespace.

5. **Role-Based Access Control (RBAC)**

   RBAC is the most commonly used authorization method in Kubernetes. It allows administrators to define roles that group specific permissions and bind these roles to users, groups, or service accounts.

   Example: Role and RoleBinding for RBAC

   Step 1: Create a Role

```
apiVersion: rbac.authorization.k8s.io/v1
kind: Role
metadata:
  namespace: default
  name: pod-reader
rules:
- apiGroups: [""]
  resources: ["pods"]
  verbs: ["get", "watch", "list"]
```

   Step 2: Create a RoleBinding

```
apiVersion: rbac.authorization.k8s.io/v1
kind: RoleBinding
metadata:
  name: read-pods
  namespace: default
```

```yaml
subjects:
- kind: User
  name: alice
  apiGroup: rbac.authorization.k8s.io
roleRef:
  kind: Role
  name: pod-reader
  apiGroup: rbac.authorization.k8s.io
```

Here, the user "alice" is given permission to read pods in the "default" namespace.

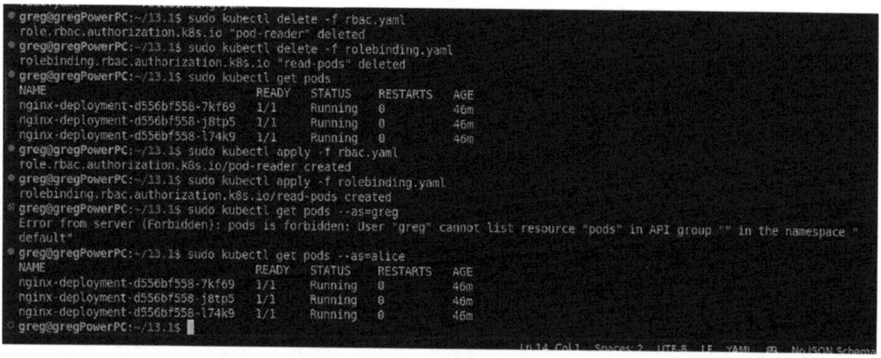

```
greg@gregPowerPC:~/13.1$ sudo kubectl delete -f rbac.yaml
role.rbac.authorization.k8s.io "pod-reader" deleted
greg@gregPowerPC:~/13.1$ sudo kubectl delete -f rolebinding.yaml
rolebinding.rbac.authorization.k8s.io "read-pods" deleted
greg@gregPowerPC:~/13.1$ sudo kubectl get pods
NAME                              READY   STATUS    RESTARTS   AGE
nginx-deployment-d556bf558-7kf69   1/1     Running   0          46m
nginx-deployment-d556bf558-j8tp5   1/1     Running   0          46m
nginx-deployment-d556bf558-l74k9   1/1     Running   0          46m
greg@gregPowerPC:~/13.1$ sudo kubectl apply -f rbac.yaml
role.rbac.authorization.k8s.io/pod-reader created
greg@gregPowerPC:~/13.1$ sudo kubectl apply -f rolebinding.yaml
rolebinding.rbac.authorization.k8s.io/read-pods created
greg@gregPowerPC:~/13.1$ sudo kubectl get pods --as=greg
Error from server (Forbidden): pods is forbidden: User "greg" cannot list resource "pods" in API group "" in the namespace "
default"
greg@gregPowerPC:~/13.1$ sudo kubectl get pods --as=alice
NAME                              READY   STATUS    RESTARTS   AGE
nginx-deployment-d556bf558-7kf69   1/1     Running   0          46m
nginx-deployment-d556bf558-j8tp5   1/1     Running   0          46m
nginx-deployment-d556bf558-l74k9   1/1     Running   0          46m
greg@gregPowerPC:~/13.1$
```

Figure 11-1. *Applying RoleBinding and checking pods as a user alice*

6. **Federating with OpenID Identity Providers**

   Kubernetes can integrate with OpenID Connect (OIDC) identity providers like Google, Keycloak, or Dex for external user authentication. This allows Kubernetes to leverage an existing identity provider for managing user identities and issuing tokens.

Example: Configuring OpenID Connect in Kubernetes

Step 1: Configure the API Server for OIDC

In the Kubernetes API server configuration, enable OIDC by adding the following flags:

```
--oidc-issuer-url=https://accounts.google.com
--oidc-client-id=kubernetes
--oidc-username-claim=email
```

Step 2: Issue a Token

Users can authenticate with the external identity provider, and the identity provider issues a token that can be used to access Kubernetes APIs:

```
curl -H "Authorization: Bearer $OIDC_TOKEN"
https://<api-server-url>/api/v1/namespaces/default/pods
```

The API server validates the token with the OIDC provider before granting access.

Benefits of a Comprehensive Authorization Strategy:

Granular Access Control: RBAC and ABAC allow fine-grained access control, limiting the actions users or service accounts can perform based on specific conditions.

Flexible Identity Integration: Federating with OIDC identity providers allows Kubernetes to integrate with external authentication mechanisms, ensuring secure and centralized identity management.

Security and Compliance: Using methods like X.509 credentials, JWTs, and Seccomp ensures that only authorized entities access the API, improving security and meeting compliance requirements.

Scalability: Kubernetes supports scalable and flexible authorization policies, making it suitable for large clusters with multiple teams and workloads.

By implementing a combination of these authorization mechanisms, Kubernetes administrators can enforce robust access control policies, enhance security, and ensure that only authorized users and services have access to cluster resources.

11.7 Service Mesh

Problem

Implementing a Service Mesh for Observability, Security, and Traffic Management in Kubernetes

As applications grow and become composed of many microservices, managing the complexity of service-to-service communication becomes a significant challenge. Issues such as observability (knowing what happens between services), security (protecting inter-service communication), and traffic control (managing service failures or traffic spikes) must be addressed.

A service mesh solves this by providing a dedicated infrastructure layer to manage service-to-service communication in a microservices architecture. Without a service mesh, developers must manually implement features like load balancing, traffic routing, service discovery, and security, leading to increased development complexity and potential security risks.

Solution

Implementing a Service Mesh in Kubernetes

A service mesh introduces a new layer in your Kubernetes architecture, often by deploying sidecar proxies alongside application containers. These sidecars handle service communication, observability, and security, abstracting these concerns away from application code. Popular service mesh tools include Istio, Linkerd, and Consul.

Here are key features of a service mesh:

Traffic Management: Provides fine-grained control over traffic routing between services, enabling features like blue/green deployments, canary releases, and traffic splitting

Security: Enables automatic mutual TLS (mTLS) between services, ensuring encrypted communication without requiring changes to application code

Observability: Collects metrics, logs, and traces from service interactions, making it easier to monitor and debug applications

Resiliency: Supports advanced traffic policies like retries, timeouts, and circuit breaking to improve the reliability of service communication

Here are steps to implement a service mesh in Kubernetes (example using Istio):

Install Istio: Begin by installing Istio in your Kubernetes cluster. This involves installing the Istio control plane components and enabling automatic sidecar injection for application pods.

Configure Traffic Management: Define routing policies, load balancing, and failure recovery mechanisms using Istio's custom resources.

Enable mTLS: Configure Istio to enforce mutual TLS for service-to-service communication, securing interactions between services.

Set Up Observability Tools: Integrate tools like Prometheus, Grafana, and Jaeger for metrics, dashboards, and tracing.

Step-by-Step Example: Deploying a Service Mesh with Istio

Step 1: Install Istio in Kubernetes

First, install Istio using the Istio CLI or Helm.

Download and install the Istio CLI:

```
curl -L https://istio.io/downloadIstio | sh -
cd istio-1.x.x
export PATH=$PWD/bin:$PATH
```

Install Istio using the istioctl command:

```
istioctl install --set profile=demo -y
```

Enable automatic sidecar injection for the default namespace:

```
kubectl label namespace default istio-injection=enabled
```

This will automatically inject the Istio sidecar proxy (Envoy) into any pod deployed in the default namespace.

Step 2: Deploy a Sample Application

Deploy a simple microservices application, like the "bookinfo" application, to demonstrate traffic routing and observability:

```
kubectl apply -f https://raw.githubusercontent.com/istio/istio/
master/samples/bookinfo/platform/kube/bookinfo.yaml
```

Step 3: Configure Traffic Management

To route traffic to different versions of a microservice, you can define Istio's VirtualService and DestinationRule resources.

For example, route 90% of traffic to version 1 of the reviews service and 10% to version 2:

```
apiVersion: networking.istio.io/v1alpha3
kind: VirtualService
metadata:
  name: reviews
spec:
  hosts:
  - reviews
  http:
  - route:
    - destination:
        host: reviews
        subset: v1
      weight: 90
    - destination:
        host: reviews
        subset: v2
      weight: 10
---
apiVersion: networking.istio.io/v1alpha3
kind: DestinationRule
```

```
metadata:
  name: reviews
spec:
  host: reviews
  subsets:
  - name: v1
    labels:
      version: v1
  - name: v2
    labels:
      version: v2
```

This setup directs most traffic to version 1 of the reviews service while sending a small portion to version 2 for testing.

Step 4: Enable mTLS for Security

To enforce mutual TLS between services, define a PeerAuthentication resource to ensure all communication within the namespace uses mTLS:

```
apiVersion: security.istio.io/v1beta1
kind: PeerAuthentication
metadata:
  name: default
  namespace: default
spec:
  mtls:
    mode: STRICT
```

This configuration ensures that all services within the default namespace communicate using mutual TLS, enhancing security.

Step 5: Set Up Observability Tools

Istio provides built-in integrations with observability tools like Prometheus for metrics, Grafana for dashboards, and Jaeger for distributed tracing.

Install Prometheus and Grafana:

```
kubectl apply -f https://raw.githubusercontent.com/istio/istio/
master/samples/addons/prometheus.yaml
kubectl apply -f https://raw.githubusercontent.com/istio/istio/
master/samples/addons/grafana.yaml
```

Install Jaeger for tracing:

```
kubectl apply -f https://raw.githubusercontent.com/istio/istio/
master/samples/addons/jaeger.yaml
```

Once installed, you can access the Grafana dashboards and Jaeger tracing UI to observe metrics and traces between services.

Benefits of Using a Service Mesh:

Traffic Control and Resiliency: A service mesh provides traffic routing, load balancing, and failure handling (e.g., retries, circuit breaking) without modifying the application code.

Enhanced Security: Mutual TLS (mTLS) secures service-to-service communication, ensuring data in transit is encrypted and authenticated.

Improved Observability: A service mesh automatically collects metrics, logs, and traces for inter-service communication, providing deep visibility into the system.

Policy Enforcement: With tools like Istio, you can enforce fine-grained policies for traffic control, rate limiting, and security across all services.

Decoupling Communication Logic from the Application: Developers can focus on business logic, while the service mesh handles network concerns such as load balancing, failover, and security.

Challenges:

> **Complexity**: Introducing a service mesh adds a new layer of complexity to the infrastructure, which can increase the operational burden on teams managing the cluster.
>
> **Performance Overhead**: Sidecar proxies introduce some performance overhead, especially in highly loaded environments, though this is generally outweighed by the benefits.

A service mesh provides a scalable, secure, and reliable way to manage microservices in Kubernetes, enabling better traffic management, security policies, and observability without modifying application code.

11.8 Why a Service Mesh with Istio

Problem

Why Use a Service Mesh with Istio in Kubernetes?

As applications evolve into microservices architectures, managing communication between numerous services becomes increasingly complex. A service mesh like Istio provides a dedicated infrastructure layer that handles service-to-service communication, offering enhanced security, traffic management, observability, and more without requiring changes to application code. Here's why integrating Istio as a service mesh in Kubernetes is highly beneficial.

Solution

1. **Enhanced Security**

   Mutual TLS (mTLS): Istio automates mTLS encryption between services, ensuring that all inter-service communication is both authenticated and encrypted. This protects against man-in-the-middle attacks and eavesdropping.

   Example: By enabling mTLS in Istio, you can ensure that services like frontend and backend communicate securely without manually configuring SSL certificates for each service.

   Fine-Grained Access Control: Istio allows you to define and enforce security policies that control which services can communicate and under what conditions.

   Example: Implementing an Istio AuthorizationPolicy that only allows the payment-service to access the order-service.

2. **Advanced Traffic Management**

   Traffic Routing: Istio provides sophisticated routing rules, enabling features like A/B testing, canary deployments, and blue/green deployments without changing application code.

   Example: Deploy a new version of a microservice (v2) and route 10% of traffic to it while 90% continues to go to the stable version (v1), using Istio's VirtualService and DestinationRule configurations.

Fault Injection: Simulate failures to test the resiliency of your services.

Example: Introduce a delay or abort requests to a service to see how dependent services handle the situation.

3. **Improved Observability**

   Distributed Tracing: Istio integrates with tracing systems like Jaeger and Zipkin, allowing you to trace requests across service boundaries and identify bottlenecks.

   Example: Trace a user request from the web-service through auth-service to database-service to diagnose latency issues.

   Metrics Collection: Istio automatically collects metrics such as request count, latency, and error rates, exporting them to monitoring systems like Prometheus.

   Example: Use Grafana dashboards to visualize real-time metrics and monitor the health of your services.

   Access Logs: Detailed logs of service traffic help in debugging and auditing.

4. **Policy Enforcement**

   Rate Limiting: Control the number of requests a service can handle, preventing abuse and ensuring fair resource usage.

   Example: Limit the api-service to handle a maximum of 100 requests per second per client.

Quota Management: Allocate resource quotas to different services or teams.

Custom Policies: Define and enforce organizational policies across services.

5. **Resilience and Fault Tolerance**

   Automatic Retries and Timeouts: Istio can automatically retry failed requests and enforce timeouts, improving the user experience without changing application code.

   Example: Configure Istio to retry a failed request to inventory-service up to three times before returning an error.

   Circuit Breaking: Prevent cascading failures by isolating unhealthy services.

   Example: If payment-service is experiencing failures, Istio can stop sending requests to it temporarily.

6. **Simplified Service Discovery**

   Dynamic Service Discovery: Istio keeps track of services and their endpoints, automatically updating routing rules as services scale up or down.

   Example: When new instances of search-service are added, Istio automatically includes them in load balancing.

7. **Platform Agnostic and Language Independent**

   Polyglot Support: Istio works with services written in any language, as it operates at the network layer.

Example: Whether you have services in Java, Go, Python, or Node.js, Istio uniformly manages communication between them.

Multi-environment Support: Istio can span across different environments, including on-premise and cloud-based Kubernetes clusters.

8. **Developer Productivity**

   Offloading Cross-Cutting Concerns: Developers can focus on business logic, as Istio handles networking, security, and observability.

   Example: No need to implement custom retry logic or monitoring code within each service; Istio provides these features out of the box.

9. **Extensibility**

   Custom Plugins and Adapters: Istio supports extensions to integrate with other systems and customize behavior.

   Example: Use Istio adapters to integrate with external policy engines or logging systems.

How Istio Works in Kubernetes

Istio uses a sidecar proxy (Envoy) that is injected alongside each service instance within a Kubernetes pod. This sidecar intercepts all inbound and outbound traffic to the service, allowing Istio to apply policies and collect telemetry data.

Here are its key components:

Envoy Proxy: A high-performance proxy that handles all network traffic between services

Pilot: Manages and distributes routing rules to the Envoy proxies

Citadel: Provides strong service identity and certificate management for mTLS

Galley: Validates and processes configuration changes

Getting Started with Istio

Step 1: Install Istio

Install Istio using the provided installation scripts or Helm charts. Enable automatic sidecar injection in your Kubernetes namespaces.

```
# Download Istio
curl -L https://istio.io/downloadIstio | sh -

# Navigate to the Istio package directory
cd istio-1.x.x

# Install Istio with demo configuration
istioctl install --set profile=demo -y

# Label the namespace for automatic sidecar injection
kubectl label namespace default istio-injection=enabled
```

Step 2: Deploy Your Services

Deploy your microservices as usual. The sidecar proxy will be automatically injected.

```
apiVersion: apps/v1
kind: Deployment
metadata:
  name: my-service
spec:
  replicas: 3
  selector:
    matchLabels:
      app: my-service
  template:
    metadata:
      labels:
        app: my-service
    spec:
      containers:
      - name: my-service-container
        image: my-service-image
```

Step 3: Define Istio Configurations

Create VirtualServices, DestinationRules, and Policies to control traffic, security, and observability.

```
# Example VirtualService for traffic routing
apiVersion: networking.istio.io/v1alpha3
kind: VirtualService
metadata:
  name: my-service
spec:
  hosts:
  - my-service
  http:
  - route:
```

```
  - destination:
      host: my-service
      subset: v1
```

Benefits Summary:

Security: Automatic mTLS, authentication, and authorization policies secure your services without code changes.

Observability: Gain deep insights into your microservices with built-in metrics, logs, and tracing.

Traffic Management: Control traffic flow and API calls with fine-grained routing rules.

Resilience: Improve fault tolerance with retries, timeouts, and circuit breakers.

Operational Efficiency: Simplify operations by centralizing network policies and configurations.

Outcome

Using a service mesh like Istio in Kubernetes environments offers significant advantages by abstracting complex networking and security challenges. Istio enhances microservices architectures by providing

Consistent and Secure Communication: Protects data in transit and ensures only authorized services communicate

Better Visibility: Offers detailed telemetry data for monitoring and debugging

Improved Reliability: Adds robustness to service interactions, enhancing the overall user experience

Developer Focus: Allows developers to concentrate on core application functionality rather than infrastructure concerns

By integrating Istio into your Kubernetes clusters, you can achieve a more secure, resilient, and observable microservices ecosystem, ultimately leading to faster development cycles and improved service quality.

11.9 Configuring Istio for Enhanced Security in Kubernetes

Problem

In the context of security in Kubernetes, using Istio as a service mesh not only simplifies managing service-to-service communication but also enhances security through mutual TLS (mTLS), fine-grained access control, and policy enforcement. Below is a guide on configuring Istio to enhance the security posture of your Kubernetes environment.

Ensuring Secure Communication and Access Control in Kubernetes Microservices with Istio

In a microservices architecture, securing service-to-service communication is critical. Services may need to authenticate each other, encrypt traffic, and limit access based on policies. Traditional Kubernetes networking lacks built-in mechanisms for service authentication, encryption, and fine-grained access control, which leaves service interactions vulnerable to man-in-the-middle attacks, unauthorized access, and data leaks. A solution is needed to secure these interactions without modifying application code or increasing complexity.

Solution

Configuring Istio to Secure Service-to-Service Communication in Kubernetes

Istio enhances the security of Kubernetes microservices by enabling mutual TLS (mTLS), enforcing role-based access control (RBAC), and applying authorization policies. Below is a step-by-step guide to configure Istio for securing your microservices:

Step 1: Install Istio in Kubernetes

Download and Install the Istio CLI: Download Istio and install the CLI tool (istioctl) for managing the Istio service mesh:

```
curl -L https://istio.io/downloadIstio | sh -
cd istio-1.x.x
export PATH=$PWD/bin:$PATH
```

Install Istio in Kubernetes with a Secure Profile: Choose a profile that includes strong security features like mTLS enabled by default. You can use the default or strict profile for enhanced security:

```
istioctl install --set profile=default -y
```

This installs Istio with default security settings, which include enabling mTLS.

Enable Sidecar Injection: Enable automatic sidecar injection for the namespace where your applications run. The sidecar (Envoy proxy) is essential for applying security policies like mTLS:

```
kubectl label namespace default istio-injection=enabled
```

All pods in the default namespace will now automatically include the Istio sidecar proxy when they are created.

Step 2: Enable Mutual TLS (mTLS) for Service Communication

Mutual TLS (mTLS) ensures that both client and server services authenticate each other using certificates, and it encrypts the traffic between them.

Set mTLS Mode to STRICT: Create a PeerAuthentication policy to enforce STRICT mTLS, which requires all services to communicate securely using mTLS:

```
apiVersion: security.istio.io/v1beta1
kind: PeerAuthentication
metadata:
  name: default
  namespace: default
spec:
  mtls:
    mode: STRICT
Apply the policy:
kubectl apply -f strict-mtls.yaml
```

Now, all communication between services within the default namespace will be encrypted, and both services must authenticate each other using TLS certificates.

Step 3: Apply Fine-Grained Authorization Policies

Istio allows you to create AuthorizationPolicies to control which services or users can access specific resources. These policies help enforce zero trust by only allowing authorized traffic between services.

Define an Authorization Policy for Service Access: Here's an example of an AuthorizationPolicy that only allows the frontend service to access the backend service:

```
apiVersion: security.istio.io/v1beta1
kind: AuthorizationPolicy
metadata:
```

```
  name: backend-policy
  namespace: default
spec:
  selector:
    matchLabels:
      app: backend
  rules:
  - from:
    - source:
        principals: ["cluster.local/ns/default/sa/frontend"]
```

This policy selects the backend service (using the label app: backend) and only allows requests from the frontend service (identified by its service account frontend).

Apply the policy:

```
kubectl apply -f backend-authorization-policy.yaml
```

This ensures that only the frontend service can call the backend service, preventing unauthorized service access.

Step 4: Implement Network Policies

In addition to Istio's application-layer policies, it's good practice to use Kubernetes network policies to control traffic at the network level. This provides an additional layer of security by controlling which pods can communicate within the cluster.

Create a Network Policy: For example, you can create a network policy that only allows traffic between the frontend and backend services:

```
apiVersion: networking.k8s.io/v1
kind: NetworkPolicy
metadata:
  name: allow-frontend-to-backend
  namespace: default
```

```
spec:
  podSelector:
    matchLabels:
      app: backend
  ingress:
  - from:
    - podSelector:
        matchLabels:
          app: frontend
```

This policy will only allow ingress traffic to pods with the app: backend label from pods with the app: frontend label, blocking any other communication.

Apply the policy:

```
kubectl apply -f frontend-backend-network-policy.yaml
```

Step 5: Enable Observability for Monitoring Security Events

Istio integrates with observability tools like Prometheus, Grafana, and Jaeger to monitor and audit service communications, especially important for tracking unauthorized access or communication attempts.

Install Istio's Add-Ons for Observability: Install monitoring and tracing tools for tracking security-related metrics and tracing the flow of requests across services:

```
kubectl apply -f https://raw.githubusercontent.com/istio/istio/
master/samples/addons/prometheus.yaml
kubectl apply -f https://raw.githubusercontent.com/istio/istio/
master/samples/addons/grafana.yaml
kubectl apply -f https://raw.githubusercontent.com/istio/istio/
master/samples/addons/jaeger.yaml
```

Monitor mTLS Connections and Authorization Policies: Use Grafana dashboards to track service-to-service connections, identify failed requests, and monitor which services are communicating with each other. Jaeger allows you to trace the requests and see where potential security violations might be happening.

Step 6: Test Security Policies

Once you've applied the security configurations, you should test whether the policies are correctly enforcing secure service-to-service communication.

Test Unauthorized Access: Attempt to call the backend service from a service other than frontend to ensure that unauthorized access is blocked.

Verify mTLS: Use the following command to check that mTLS is enforced between services:

```
istioctl authn tls-check <frontend-pod> <backend-service>
```

This command verifies whether mTLS is working and enforced between the frontend pod and the backend service.

Conclusion

By configuring Istio in Kubernetes, you can significantly enhance the security of your microservices architecture. The steps outlined above provide robust service-to-service communication security through mutual TLS (mTLS), enforce fine-grained access control with authorization policies, and provide detailed observability to monitor the security of your services. This comprehensive security setup helps mitigate risks such as unauthorized access, data breaches, and man-in-the-middle attacks, making Istio a powerful tool for securing microservices in Kubernetes.

Here's a summary of key security features with Istio:

mTLS for Encrypted Communication: Encrypt service-to-service traffic and ensures services authenticate each other.

Authorization Policies: Control which services or users can access specific resources.

Network Policies: Add an additional layer of security by controlling which pods can communicate at the network level.

Observability Tools: Track, monitor, and audit service communication to detect potential security violations.

By integrating Istio's security capabilities, Kubernetes environments can ensure a secure and scalable microservices architecture.

11.10 Service Discovery with Istiod

In a microservices architecture running on Kubernetes, service discovery is a crucial mechanism that enables services to find and communicate with each other without requiring manual configuration. Istiod, the control plane component of Istio plays a significant role in service discovery by managing the configuration and distribution of service information to the sidecar proxies (Envoy) deployed with each service.

Problem

Managing Dynamic Service Discovery in a Microservices Architecture

As microservices scale and change dynamically (services being added, removed, or updated), traditional methods of configuring service discovery (like hardcoded IP addresses) become inefficient and prone to failure. Kubernetes inherently provides some basic service discovery via DNS and kube-proxy, but it lacks advanced traffic control, observability, and security features. A more powerful and flexible service discovery mechanism is needed to manage the increasingly dynamic service topology.

Solution

Using Istiod for Advanced Service Discovery in Kubernetes

Istiod manages the service discovery, configuration, and certificate distribution to the Envoy sidecars in an Istio service mesh. It extends the default Kubernetes service discovery capabilities by offering more advanced routing, security, and observability features.

Here's how service discovery works with Istiod in Kubernetes:

> **Kubernetes Informs Istiod of Service Changes**: Istiod watches for Kubernetes API events related to services and endpoints. When a new service is created, updated, or removed, Istiod immediately receives this information.

Istiod Propagates Service Information: Istiod processes the information and updates the configuration of the Envoy sidecars (deployed alongside every service). These proxies act as intelligent routers that know how to forward traffic based on the latest service information.

Envoy Sidecars Handle Traffic: Each service in the mesh communicates through its own Envoy proxy, which consults its dynamically updated configuration (provided by Istiod) to route traffic to the appropriate service.

Step-by-Step Guide to Service Discovery with Istiod

Step 1: Install Istio with Istiod

Before you can use Istiod for service discovery, you need to install Istio in your Kubernetes cluster. This step installs Istiod as part of the Istio control plane.

Download and Install the Istio CLI:

```
curl -L https://istio.io/downloadIstio | sh -
cd istio-1.x.x
export PATH=$PWD/bin:$PATH
```

Install Istio with the Default Profile:

```
istioctl install --set profile=default -y
```

This command installs the default Istio profile, including Istiod, which is responsible for service discovery, configuration management, and security policy distribution.

Enable Sidecar Injection:

To ensure that every service in the mesh gets an Envoy proxy for service discovery, enable automatic sidecar injection for the namespace(s) where your services will be deployed:

```
kubectl label namespace default istio-injection=enabled
```

Step 2: Deploy Services in the Mesh

Next, you need to deploy services in your cluster, which will be managed by Istiod for service discovery.

Deploy a Sample Application (e.g., a Simple Service like helloworld):

```
apiVersion: apps/v1
kind: Deployment
metadata:
  name: helloworld-v1
spec:
  replicas: 2
  selector:
    matchLabels:
      app: helloworld
      version: v1
  template:
    metadata:
      labels:
        app: helloworld
        version: v1
    spec:
      containers:
      - name: helloworld
        image: istio/examples-helloworld-v1
        ports:
        - containerPort: 5000
```

Expose the Service:

```
apiVersion: v1
kind: Service
metadata:
  name: helloworld
spec:
  ports:
  - port: 5000
    name: http
  selector:
    app: helloworld
```

When this service is deployed, Istiod automatically detects the service and the endpoints (pods) associated with it.

Step 3: Service Discovery in Action

Once your services are deployed and managed by Istiod, service discovery becomes dynamic and automatic. Here's how it works under the hood:

> **Service Information Collection**:
>
> Istiod continuously monitors the Kubernetes API for changes related to services and pods (like scaling events or new service deployments). Whenever a new pod is created, Istiod is informed of its IP address and updates the list of available service endpoints.
>
> **Dynamic Configuration Updates**:
>
> Istiod generates configuration files for the Envoy proxies based on the current state of the service mesh. It sends this configuration to the Envoy sidecars running alongside each service.

The configuration includes details about service discovery, traffic routing, and policies for security (e.g., mTLS settings).

Service-to-Service Communication:

When a service (e.g., frontend) tries to call another service (e.g., helloworld), the Envoy sidecar for frontend handles the request. The sidecar consults its dynamically updated configuration (from Istiod) to find the appropriate backend service and routes the traffic accordingly.

Envoy proxies handle load balancing between multiple instances of the helloworld service without the application needing to manage this.

Step 4: Traffic Management with Service Discovery

Once services are discovered and registered by Istiod, you can define advanced routing rules using VirtualService and DestinationRule to control traffic between services.

Create a VirtualService for Routing:

Here's an example where Istio routes traffic to version v1 of the helloworld service:

```
apiVersion: networking.istio.io/v1alpha3
kind: VirtualService
metadata:
  name: helloworld
spec:
  hosts:
  - helloworld
  http:
  - route:
    - destination:
        host: helloworld
        subset: v1
```

Create a DestinationRule for Load Balancing:

You can also configure how traffic should be load-balanced across service instances:

```
apiVersion: networking.istio.io/v1alpha3
kind: DestinationRule
metadata:
  name: helloworld
spec:
  host: helloworld
  subsets:
  - name: v1
    labels:
      version: v1
  trafficPolicy:
    loadBalancer:
      simple: ROUND_ROBIN
```

Step 5: Monitor and Debug Service Discovery

Check Service Endpoints: Use the Istio CLI (istioctl) to check which endpoints are registered for a service:

```
istioctl proxy-config endpoints <pod-name>
```

This will list all the service endpoints that Istio has discovered for the given pod.

Visualize the Service Mesh: Istio integrates with observability tools like Prometheus, Grafana, and Kiali. Kiali can be particularly useful for visualizing service dependencies and traffic flows within the mesh.

Install Kiali:

```
kubectl apply -f https://raw.githubusercontent.com/istio/istio/
master/samples/addons/kiali.yaml
```

Access Kiali through your browser to see a graphical representation of service discovery and traffic flow.

Outcome

Service discovery with Istiod significantly enhances how microservices in Kubernetes discover and communicate with each other. It automates the registration of services, provides dynamic updates to service endpoints, and enables advanced traffic management features like load balancing, retries, and circuit breaking.

Key features of Istiod service discovery include

Automatic Registration of Services: Istiod dynamically discovers services and updates their configuration in real time.

Seamless Communication: With Istiod managing Envoy proxies, service-to-service communication is efficient, secure, and resilient.

Advanced Traffic Control: You can use Istio's VirtualService and DestinationRule objects to control how traffic is routed between services.

Resiliency and Security: Istio adds reliability features (e.g., retries, load balancing) and security (e.g., mTLS, policy enforcement) to service discovery without application code changes.

By using Istiod for service discovery, Kubernetes environments become more flexible, resilient, and secure while simplifying the management of microservices at scale.

11.11 Certificate Management with Istio's CA

In Kubernetes, managing service-to-service communication securely is essential, especially in microservices architectures where services frequently interact with each other. To ensure secure communication, Istio's built-in Certificate Authority (CA) automates the generation, distribution, and rotation of TLS certificates. This enables mutual TLS (mTLS) between services, securing the communication channel without manual certificate management.

Problem

Securing Service-to-Service Communication with Automated Certificate Management

Traditional certificate management is a complex process involving certificate generation, distribution, and renewal, especially in dynamic environments like Kubernetes. As services are scaled up or down, keeping track of which services have valid certificates and ensuring that communications remain secure becomes challenging. Without automated solutions, there's a risk of expired certificates or improperly configured services, leading to insecure communication channels.

Solution

Leveraging Istio's Built-In CA for Automated Certificate Management

Istio simplifies certificate management through its built-in CA, which automatically generates and rotates certificates for each service in the mesh. This ensures that all service-to-service communications are encrypted using mutual TLS (mTLS), providing confidentiality and integrity without requiring manual intervention.

How Istio's Certificate Management Works

Istio's CA Generates and Distributes Certificates: When a new service joins the mesh, Istio's CA automatically issues a certificate and private key for the service.

Envoy Proxies Handle Certificate-Based Authentication: Each service has an Envoy sidecar proxy that uses the certificates to establish mTLS connections with other services.

Automated Certificate Rotation: Istio's CA regularly rotates certificates, ensuring that services are always using valid and up-to-date certificates without manual intervention.

Revocation and Renewal: In case of security incidents or certificate expiration, Istio can revoke and renew certificates, maintaining secure communications across services.

Step-by-Step Guide to Certificate Management with Istio's CA

Step 1: Install Istio with mTLS Enabled

To use Istio's built-in CA for certificate management, install Istio with mutual TLS (mTLS) enabled by default.

Download Istio and install the CLI:

```
curl -L https://istio.io/downloadIstio | sh -
cd istio-1.x.x
export PATH=$PWD/bin:$PATH
```

Install Istio with the default profile (includes mTLS):

```
istioctl install --set profile=default -y
```

Alternatively, you can explicitly enable mTLS in strict mode, where all service-to-service communication must use mTLS:

```
istioctl install --set values.global.mtls.enabled=true --set
profile=default -y
```

Step 2: Enable mTLS for a Namespace

By default, mTLS might not be enforced for all namespaces. You need to enable it for the namespaces where your services run.

Enable sidecar injection for a namespace:

```
kubectl label namespace default istio-injection=enabled
```

Create a PeerAuthentication Policy to Enforce mTLS:

```
apiVersion: security.istio.io/v1beta1
kind: PeerAuthentication
metadata:
  name: default
  namespace: default
spec:
  mtls:
    mode: STRICT
```

This policy ensures that all services in the default namespace must use mutual TLS to communicate.

Step 3: How Istio Issues and Distributes Certificates

When a new service is deployed, Istio automatically issues a certificate for the service through its CA.

> **Service-to-Service Authentication**: Each service deployed in the Istio mesh gets an X.509 certificate from the Istio CA. The certificates are issued to the service's service account, which is unique per service or deployment.
>
> **Certificate Storage**: The Envoy sidecar proxy for each service stores and uses the service's private key and certificate. The proxy presents this certificate when establishing secure connections with other services.
>
> **mTLS Handshake**: When two services communicate, their Envoy proxies perform a mutual TLS handshake:

Each service presents its certificate.

Both services verify each other's certificates (using the Istio CA as the trusted root authority).

The connection is encrypted, and the services can securely exchange data.

Step 4: Manage Certificate Rotation and Renewal

Istio manages certificate rotation automatically to ensure that services always have valid certificates. You can view certificate details and manage the certificate lifecycle using the Istio CLI and Kubernetes commands.

View Current Certificates: You can use istioctl to check the certificates issued to a specific service:

```
istioctl proxy-config secrets <pod-name> -n <namespace>
```

This command will display the current certificate used by the service running in the specified pod.

Rotate Certificates: Istio's CA automatically rotates certificates before they expire. You can customize the rotation interval by setting the workloadCertTTL option during Istio installation.

For example, set the certificate lifetime to 90 days:

```
istioctl install --set values.global.workloadCertTTL=90d
```

This ensures that certificates are rotated every 90 days, which is particularly useful for long-running services.

Step 5: Revoking Certificates

In certain cases (e.g., if a service is compromised), you may need to revoke certificates. Istio's CA supports certificate revocation, although this typically requires additional configuration. In Istio, revocation is achieved by managing service accounts and restarting the affected pods, ensuring that new certificates are issued.

Step 6: Integrating External CAs (Optional)

By default, Istio uses its internal CA to generate certificates, but you can configure Istio to integrate with external Certificate Authorities (CAs) for certificate issuance and management.

Integrate with an external CA. If your organization already uses an external CA, you can configure Istio to use it for issuing service certificates.

You'll need to configure Istio to use the external CA's certificate and key as the root of trust.

Modify the Istio control plane to point to the external CA for signing and issuing certificates:

```
istioctl install --set values.global.
pilotCertProvider=kubernetes
```

This will direct Istio to use the external CA for managing service certificates.

Step 7: Monitoring and Observing Certificate Usage

Monitoring certificates and ensuring they are valid and correctly used is crucial for maintaining secure communications.

Monitoring mTLS Traffic: Istio provides observability tools like Prometheus and Grafana, where you can monitor mTLS traffic between services. You can track which services are using mTLS and view the certificate details.

Install Prometheus and Grafana for monitoring:

```
kubectl apply -f https://raw.githubusercontent.com/istio/istio/
master/samples/addons/prometheus.yaml
kubectl apply -f https://raw.githubusercontent.com/istio/istio/
master/samples/addons/grafana.yaml
```

Check TLS Handshake with the Istio CLI: You can verify mTLS connections between services using istioctl:

```
istioctl authn tls-check <source-pod> <destination-service>
```

This command checks whether mutual TLS is enabled between two services and whether the TLS handshake was successful.

Benefits of Istio's Certificate Management:

- **Automated Certificate Issuance**: No need for manual certificate generation or renewal; Istio's CA handles the entire lifecycle.
- **mTLS Enforcement**: Mutual TLS ensures secure, encrypted communication between services without requiring changes to the application code.
- **Automatic Certificate Rotation**: Istio's CA automatically rotates certificates before they expire, ensuring service-to-service communication remains secure.

Strong Identity Management: Certificates are tied to service accounts, ensuring that services can only communicate with authorized services.

Scalable and Efficient: As services scale up or down, Istio automatically handles certificate distribution, ensuring every service in the mesh has the correct credentials.

Outcome

Using Istio's CA for certificate management significantly improves the security of service-to-service communication in Kubernetes. By automating certificate issuance, rotation, and management, Istio eliminates the complexity of managing TLS certificates manually. Additionally, enforcing mutual TLS (mTLS) across services ensures that communications are both encrypted and authenticated, protecting against common security threats such as man-in-the-middle attacks.

By leveraging Istio's certificate management features, Kubernetes clusters can maintain secure, scalable, and reliable communication between microservices, with minimal operational overhead.

11.12 Gather Telemetry Data with the Telemetry API

Telemetry in a service mesh like Istio involves collecting data on metrics, logs, and traces from services to provide observability into how services are performing and interacting. This data helps operators monitor service health, diagnose issues, and optimize performance.

In Istio, telemetry data is gathered automatically by the Envoy sidecar proxies that accompany each service. The Telemetry API in Istio offers a way to configure what metrics, logs, and traces are collected, making it a critical tool for monitoring and debugging microservices.

Problem

Obtaining Detailed Insights into Service-to-Service Communication in Kubernetes

Microservices architectures often lack the visibility necessary to understand how services are interacting, performing, and failing. While Kubernetes provides some basic observability features, they do not provide the deep insights needed for optimizing service-to-service communication, detecting anomalies, or understanding how services impact one another. A robust solution is needed for collecting telemetry data such as metrics, logs, and traces to provide a clear picture of how the system is behaving in real time.

Solution

Using Istio's Telemetry API to Gather Metrics, Logs, and Traces for Enhanced Observability

Istio's Telemetry API enables you to gather data on service-to-service communication, response times, success rates, and other critical performance indicators. By leveraging Istio's telemetry system, you can automatically collect, filter, and analyze data without modifying application code. This is achieved through the Envoy sidecars, which act as the data plane in the Istio service mesh.

The following steps outline how to gather and configure telemetry data using Istio's Telemetry API in Kubernetes:

Step 1: Install Istio with Telemetry Enabled

When you install Istio, telemetry features such as metrics collection, logging, and tracing are enabled by default. You can install Istio using the istioctl command, ensuring that telemetry data is collected from your services.

Download and install the Istio CLI:

```
curl -L https://istio.io/downloadIstio | sh -
cd istio-1.x.x
export PATH=$PWD/bin:$PATH
```

Install Istio with the default profile (telemetry enabled):

```
istioctl install --set profile=default -y
```

This installs Istio with default telemetry settings, enabling automatic metrics, log, and tracing collection from all services within the mesh.

Step 2: Deploy Services in the Mesh

Next, deploy your services in the Istio-enabled namespace. Telemetry data will automatically be collected from all services managed by Istio.

Enable Sidecar Injection for the Namespace:

```
kubectl label namespace default istio-injection=enabled
```

This ensures that all pods deployed in the default namespace will have Envoy sidecar proxies, which collect telemetry data.

Deploy a Sample Application:

For example, deploy the bookinfo application, which is commonly used to demonstrate Istio's telemetry capabilities:

```
kubectl apply -f https://raw.githubusercontent.com/istio/istio/
master/samples/bookinfo/platform/kube/bookinfo.yaml
```

Step 3: Enable and Configure the Telemetry API

Istio's Telemetry API allows you to configure what metrics, logs, and traces are collected from services. The Telemetry API can be used to define

Metrics: Data points such as request counts, response times, and error rates

Logs: Access logs that record incoming and outgoing requests

Traces: Distributed tracing to track request flows across services

Create a Telemetry Custom Resource:

You can create a telemetry custom resource (CR) to define the specific telemetry data you want to collect for a service. Below is an example of a telemetry configuration for a service named reviews:

```
apiVersion: telemetry.istio.io/v1alpha1
kind: Telemetry
metadata:
  name: reviews-telemetry
  namespace: default
spec:
  metrics:
    overrides:
    - match:
        service: reviews.default.svc.cluster.local
      disabled: false
  logging:
    accessLog:
      providers:
        - name: file
```

In this configuration

> **Metrics**: Metrics collection for the reviews service is enabled.
>
> **Logging**: Access logs are collected and written to a file using the file log provider.

Apply the Telemetry Resource:

```
kubectl apply -f telemetry-reviews.yaml
```

This command ensures that metrics and access logs are collected for the reviews service.

Step 4: Collect and View Metrics

Metrics are automatically collected by Istio and can be visualized using monitoring tools such as Prometheus and Grafana.

Install Prometheus for Metrics Collection:

```
kubectl apply -f https://raw.githubusercontent.com/istio/istio/
master/samples/addons/prometheus.yaml
```

Prometheus will scrape the telemetry data from Envoy proxies and store it for querying and alerting.

Install Grafana for Visualization:

```
kubectl apply -f https://raw.githubusercontent.com/istio/istio/
master/samples/addons/grafana.yaml
```

Grafana provides pre-configured dashboards that display Istio metrics, such as service response times, request counts, and error rates.

Access the Grafana Dashboard:

You can access Grafana using port forwarding:

```
kubectl port-forward svc/grafana 3000:3000 -n istio-system
```

Then, open a browser and navigate to http://localhost:3000. The pre-built dashboards will show telemetry data collected from your services, including

Success and failure rates for requests

Latency and response times

Request volume per service

Step 5: Collect and View Logs

Envoy sidecars generate access logs, which record incoming and outgoing requests for each service. These logs can be useful for debugging and auditing traffic.

View Access Logs:

You can view access logs directly from the Envoy sidecars using the istioctl command:

```
istioctl proxy-config log <pod-name> --level debug
```

This command shows detailed access logs for a specific pod, providing insights into what traffic is being handled by the service.

Step 6: Enable and View Distributed Tracing

Distributed tracing provides visibility into how requests flow through multiple services in your mesh, helping you identify performance bottlenecks and track down issues.

Install Jaeger for Distributed Tracing:

```
kubectl apply -f https://raw.githubusercontent.com/istio/istio/
master/samples/addons/jaeger.yaml
```

Jaeger collects trace data from the Envoy proxies and provides a UI to view traces.

Access the Jaeger Dashboard:

Use port forwarding to access Jaeger:

```
kubectl port-forward svc/jaeger 16686:16686 -n istio-system
```

Open a browser and navigate to http://localhost:16686. In the Jaeger UI, you can search for traces and view detailed information about how requests are processed across multiple services in your mesh.

Step 7: Customize Telemetry Data Collection

You can further customize the telemetry data being collected by using the Telemetry API to define what metrics, logs, and traces are important for specific services.

Override Metrics Collection:

You can disable or modify metrics for specific services using the Telemetry API. For example, disable metrics collection for the ratings service:

```
apiVersion: telemetry.istio.io/v1alpha1
kind: Telemetry
metadata:
  name: ratings-telemetry
  namespace: default
spec:
  metrics:
    overrides:
    - match:
        service: ratings.default.svc.cluster.local
      disabled: true
Apply the Custom Configuration:
kubectl apply -f telemetry-ratings.yaml
```

This custom configuration disables metrics collection for the ratings service while allowing other services to continue collecting metrics.

Outcome

Istio's Telemetry API provides a flexible and powerful way to gather detailed metrics, logs, and traces from services in your Kubernetes environment. By leveraging Envoy proxies and configuring the Telemetry

API, you can monitor service performance, track request flows, and ensure the overall health of your microservices architecture. Tools like Prometheus, Grafana, and Jaeger integrate seamlessly with Istio to offer a comprehensive observability solution.

Key benefits of using Istio's Telemetry API are

Automatic Metrics Collection: Metrics such as request counts, success rates, and latency are automatically gathered from all services in the mesh.

Logs for Debugging: Access logs provide valuable insights into the traffic handled by each service.

Distributed Tracing: Traces help you track requests across multiple services, making it easier to identify bottlenecks and performance issues.

Customizable Data Collection: The Telemetry API allows you to tailor what data is collected for specific services, optimizing observability for your environment.

By gathering and analyzing telemetry data, Istio makes it easier to monitor and manage service-to-service communication, ultimately improving the performance and reliability of your Kubernetes applications.

11.13 Configure an Istio Ingress Gateway

An Istio Ingress Gateway allows external traffic to enter your service mesh and route it to services running inside the Kubernetes cluster. Istio's Ingress Gateway provides a flexible way to manage incoming traffic, apply security policies, and route traffic based on advanced criteria like headers, URIs, and more.

Problem

Secure and Manage External Traffic to Microservices in a Kubernetes Cluster

By default, Kubernetes exposes services externally using LoadBalancer or NodePort, but these methods lack advanced features like traffic control, rate limiting, authentication, or encryption for incoming traffic. A more robust solution is needed to handle external traffic securely and route it efficiently within the cluster, especially in a microservices architecture.

Solution

Using Istio's Ingress Gateway for Secure and Flexible Traffic Management

The Istio Ingress Gateway acts as a single entry point for all external traffic entering the cluster, allowing you to define rules for routing, encryption, load balancing, and security policies before traffic reaches your internal services.

Here's a step-by-step guide to configuring the Istio Ingress Gateway:

Step 1: Install Istio

If you haven't installed Istio in your Kubernetes cluster yet, you need to do that first. Follow these steps to install Istio with the Ingress Gateway component.

Download and Install the Istio CLI:

```
curl -L https://istio.io/downloadIstio | sh -
cd istio-1.x.x
export PATH=$PWD/bin:$PATH
```

Install Istio with the Ingress Gateway:

When you install Istio using the default profile, it includes the Ingress Gateway by default:

```
istioctl install --set profile=default -y
```

Step 2: Enable Sidecar Injection for the Namespace

To ensure that services within the namespace are included in the service mesh, enable automatic sidecar injection for the namespace where you will deploy your services:

```
kubectl label namespace default istio-injection=enabled
```

Step 3: Expose Services via the Ingress Gateway

Deploy a Sample Application:

For this example, we'll deploy the bookinfo application, which contains multiple microservices. The goal is to expose the productpage service to external traffic via the Ingress Gateway:

```
kubectl apply -f https://raw.githubusercontent.com/istio/istio/
master/samples/bookinfo/platform/kube/bookinfo.yaml
```

Verify the Deployment:

kubectl get pods

Ensure that all pods are running, including the productpage, reviews, ratings, and details services.

Step 4: Define a Gateway Resource

An Istio Gateway resource configures how external traffic enters the mesh. It defines the ports and protocols allowed into the cluster.

Create a Gateway Configuration:

```
apiVersion: networking.istio.io/v1alpha3
kind: Gateway
metadata:
  name: bookinfo-gateway
```

```
  namespace: default
spec:
  selector:
    istio: ingressgateway  # use Istio's default
    ingress gateway
  servers:
  - port:
      number: 80
      name: http
      protocol: HTTP
    hosts:
    - "*"
```

This gateway configuration allows HTTP traffic on port 80 from any external host ("*") to enter the cluster.

Apply the Gateway Configuration:

```
kubectl apply -f bookinfo-gateway.yaml
```

Step 5: Define a VirtualService

A VirtualService defines the routing rules for traffic entering the mesh via the Ingress Gateway. In this case, we'll route traffic from the gateway to the productpage service.

Create a VirtualService Configuration:

```
apiVersion: networking.istio.io/v1alpha3
kind: VirtualService
metadata:
  name: bookinfo
  namespace: default
spec:
  hosts:
  - "*"
```

```
  gateways:
  - bookinfo-gateway
  http:
  - match:
    - uri:
        prefix: "/productpage"
    route:
    - destination:
        host: productpage
        port:
          number: 9080
```

This configuration routes traffic that matches the /productpage path to the productpage service on port 9080.

Apply the VirtualService Configuration:

```
kubectl apply -f virtualservice-bookinfo.yaml
```

Step 6: Access the Application

Now that the Ingress Gateway and routing rules are configured, you can access the application from outside the cluster.

Find the External IP of the Ingress Gateway:

Run the following command to get the external IP of the Istio Ingress Gateway service:

```
kubectl get svc istio-ingressgateway -n istio-system
```

This will display the external IP (or hostname) of the Ingress Gateway. Look for the EXTERNAL-IP field.

Access the Application:

You can now access the productpage service by opening a browser and navigating to the following URL (replace <EXTERNAL-IP> with the actual IP address of the Ingress Gateway):

```
http://<EXTERNAL-IP>/productpage
```

This will bring up the bookinfo application's productpage service, routed through the Istio Ingress Gateway.

Step 7: Secure the Ingress Gateway with TLS (Optional)

To secure external traffic, you can configure TLS termination at the Ingress Gateway. Here's how to add a TLS certificate to your gateway.

Generate a TLS certificate (using openssl or obtain one from a trusted CA):

```
openssl req -x509 -nodes -days 365 -newkey rsa:2048 \
  -keyout tls.key -out tls.crt -subj "/CN=mydomain.com"
```

Create a Kubernetes secret for the TLS certificate:

```
kubectl create -n istio-system secret tls istio-
ingressgateway-certs \
  --key tls.key --cert tls.crt
```

Update the gateway resource to use TLS:

```
apiVersion: networking.istio.io/v1alpha3
kind: Gateway
metadata:
  name: bookinfo-gateway
spec:
  selector:
    istio: ingressgateway
  servers:
  - port:
      number: 443
      name: https
      protocol: HTTPS
    hosts:
    - "mydomain.com"
```

```
    tls:
      mode: SIMPLE
      credentialName: istio-ingressgateway-certs
```

This configuration terminates HTTPS traffic at the Ingress Gateway using the provided TLS certificate.

Apply the updated gateway configuration:

```
kubectl apply -f bookinfo-gateway-tls.yaml
```

Now, you can access the application securely over HTTPS by navigating to

```
https://mydomain.com/productpage
```

Step 8: Monitor Ingress Traffic

To monitor the traffic passing through the Istio Ingress Gateway, you can use Istio's telemetry capabilities.

Install Prometheus and Grafana:

```
kubectl apply -f https://raw.githubusercontent.com/istio/istio/
master/samples/addons/prometheus.yaml
kubectl apply -f https://raw.githubusercontent.com/istio/istio/
master/samples/addons/grafana.yaml
```

Access Grafana Dashboards:

Use port forwarding to access the Grafana UI:

```
kubectl port-forward svc/grafana 3000:3000 -n istio-system
```

Navigate to http://localhost:3000 in your browser and use Istio's pre-configured dashboards to monitor incoming and outgoing traffic through the Ingress Gateway.

Outcome

By configuring Istio's Ingress Gateway, you can securely expose your internal services to external traffic, manage complex routing rules, and apply security policies such as TLS termination. Istio provides advanced traffic control, observability, and security features, allowing you to handle external traffic more flexibly and securely than traditional Kubernetes ingress controllers.

Key benefits of the Istio Ingress Gateway are

> **Advanced Traffic Control**: Route traffic based on criteria such as headers, URIs, or method types.
>
> **Security**: Terminate TLS traffic at the gateway, enabling secure HTTPS communication.
>
> **Observability**: Leverage Istio's telemetry features to monitor and analyze ingress traffic.
>
> **Scalability**: The Ingress Gateway can scale with your application, managing traffic distribution and load balancing.

By integrating the Istio Ingress Gateway into your Kubernetes environment, you create a robust, secure, and highly configurable entry point for all external traffic into your service mesh.

11.14 Best Practices for Managing a Service Mesh

Managing a service mesh like Istio in a Kubernetes cluster requires a combination of sound operational practices and strategic planning to optimize performance, security, and scalability. Service meshes add significant capabilities, including traffic management, observability, and security, but they also introduce complexity. Following best practices can help mitigate operational challenges and maximize the benefits of your service mesh.

Problem

Managing a service mesh like Istio in a Kubernetes cluster presents a significant challenge due to its inherent complexity and the critical role it plays in optimizing performance, security, and scalability. While service meshes provide powerful capabilities such as traffic management, observability, and secure communication, improper configuration and lack of best practices can lead to performance bottlenecks, security vulnerabilities, and operational inefficiencies. The complexity of service mesh deployment and management necessitates a structured approach to ensure successful implementation and adoption.

Solution

1. **Start Small and Incrementally Expand**

   Best Practice: Don't enable the service mesh for all services at once. Start by applying the service mesh to a limited subset of critical services. Gradually expand coverage as you become familiar with managing the mesh's capabilities and understanding its impact on your environment.

   Why: A service mesh adds complexity, especially for traffic routing, security, and telemetry. Starting small helps you build confidence, establish baseline metrics, and address configuration issues without affecting your entire architecture.

Steps:

Choose non-critical, low-traffic services for initial deployment.

Gradually roll out mesh capabilities to other services after validating performance and functionality.

2. **Enable Mutual TLS (mTLS) for Secure Service-to-Service Communication**

   Best Practice: Enforce mutual TLS (mTLS) to secure all service-to-service communication within your mesh. Use a STRICT policy to ensure that all communication between services is encrypted and authenticated.

   Why: mTLS ensures that both the client and server authenticate each other, providing encryption and preventing unauthorized service-to-service communication. It significantly improves security without requiring changes to application code.

   Steps:

   Enable mTLS in STRICT mode for namespaces or services that require secure communication.

   Regularly monitor mTLS handshakes using Istio tools (istioctl authn tls-check).

   Example: Applying a PeerAuthentication policy to enforce mTLS in a namespace:

```
apiVersion: security.istio.io/v1beta1
kind: PeerAuthentication
metadata:
  name: default
```

```
  namespace: default
spec:
  mtls:
    mode: STRICT
```

3. **Use Istio's Traffic Management Features for Controlled Deployments**

   Best Practice: Leverage Istio's traffic management capabilities, such as canary releases, blue/green deployments, and traffic splitting to introduce new versions of services safely.

   Why: Controlled deployments reduce the risk of introducing breaking changes to production by gradually shifting traffic to new service versions. This allows you to monitor the new version under real-world load before full rollout.

   Steps:

   Use VirtualServices and DestinationRules to manage traffic routing between service versions.

   Route a percentage of traffic to the new version while keeping most traffic on the stable version.

   Example: Traffic splitting between two versions of a service:

```
apiVersion: networking.istio.io/v1alpha3
kind: VirtualService
metadata:
  name: reviews
spec:
  hosts:
```

```
- reviews
http:
- route:
  - destination:
      host: reviews
      subset: v1
    weight: 80
  - destination:
      host: reviews
      subset: v2
    weight: 20
```

4. **Monitor Performance and Latency**

   Best Practice: Continuously monitor service latency, error rates, and throughput using Istio's integrated telemetry tools such as Prometheus, Grafana, and Jaeger.

   Why: Service meshes introduce additional latency due to sidecar proxy communication. Monitoring helps you identify and troubleshoot performance bottlenecks. It also helps ensure your services are functioning as expected and any traffic management policies (like retries or circuit breakers) are applied correctly.

   Steps:

   Install Prometheus and Grafana to collect and visualize metrics.

   Use distributed tracing (e.g., Jaeger) to track request flows and identify performance issues.

   Set up alerts for high latency or failure rates.

Example: Access Grafana dashboards for service performance monitoring:

```
kubectl port-forward svc/grafana 3000:3000 -n
istio-system
```

5. **Optimize Resource Allocation for Sidecars**

   Best Practice: Set appropriate CPU and memory resource limits for the Envoy sidecars that handle the service mesh data plane.

   Why: The Envoy sidecars consume resources for every service, and improper resource limits can lead to resource contention between the application and the sidecar. This can affect the performance of both the application and the service mesh.

   Steps:

   Define resource requests and limits for the Envoy proxies in your deployments.

   Regularly monitor resource usage of sidecars to ensure they are not over- or under-provisioned.

   Example: Defining resource limits for an Envoy sidecar:

```
apiVersion: v1
kind: Pod
metadata:
  name: example-pod
spec:
  containers:
  - name: example-container
```

```
    image: example-image
  - name: istio-proxy
    resources:
      requests:
        cpu: "100m"
        memory: "128Mi"
      limits:
        cpu: "500m"
        memory: "512Mi"
```

6. **Use Authorization Policies to Implement Zero-Trust Security**

   Best Practice: Implement role-based access control (RBAC) using Istio's AuthorizationPolicies to enforce zero-trust principles, allowing services to only communicate with those they are explicitly allowed to.

   Why: Zero trust means assuming that no service is trustworthy by default. Enforcing explicit communication policies prevents unauthorized access and limits potential damage from compromised services.

   Steps:

   Use Istio's AuthorizationPolicy to allow or deny service-to-service communication.

   Apply least privilege principles, ensuring each service can only access what it needs.

Example: Allow only the frontend service to access the backend service:

```
apiVersion: security.istio.io/v1beta1
kind: AuthorizationPolicy
metadata:
  name: backend-policy
  namespace: default
spec:
  selector:
    matchLabels:
      app: backend
  rules:
  - from:
    - source:
        principals: ["cluster.local/ns/default/sa/
        frontend"]
```

7. **Automate Certificate Management**

   Best Practice: Rely on Istio's built-in Certificate Authority (CA) for automatic certificate generation, rotation, and expiration. Use short-lived certificates for enhanced security.

   Why: Manually managing certificates for secure communication is error-prone and time-consuming. Istio's CA automates this process, ensuring that certificates are rotated and renewed without manual intervention.

   Steps:

   Use the default Istio CA for certificate management.

Regularly check certificate expiration and renewal processes.

If required, integrate external CAs for advanced use cases.

Example: Checking certificate status using istioctl:

```
istioctl proxy-config secret <pod-name> -n <namespace>
```

8. **Enable Rate Limiting and Circuit Breaking**

   Best Practice: Implement rate limiting and circuit breaking to protect services from traffic spikes, prevent overloads, and manage failed service dependencies.

   Why: Rate limiting prevents services from being overwhelmed by high traffic. Circuit breaking ensures that services stop sending requests to unhealthy dependencies, reducing the impact of downstream service failures.

   Steps:

   Define DestinationRules for services to enforce rate limits and circuit breakers.

   Monitor service performance and adjust rules based on traffic patterns.

   Example: Configuring a circuit breaker for the payment service:

```
apiVersion: networking.istio.io/v1alpha3
kind: DestinationRule
metadata:
  name: payment-destination
```

```
spec:
  host: payment
  trafficPolicy:
    outlierDetection:
      consecutiveErrors: 5
      interval: 10s
      baseEjectionTime: 30s
      maxEjectionPercent: 50
```

9. **Leverage Service Mesh Observability Features**

   Best Practice: Take advantage of Istio's built-in observability features like metrics, logs, and distributed tracing to get a detailed view of your services' behavior and interactions.

   Why: A service mesh introduces complexity, and having strong observability is crucial for understanding how services are performing and interacting. It also helps in detecting issues before they affect users.

   Steps:

   Set up Prometheus for metrics collection, Grafana for visualization, and Jaeger for tracing.

   Use Kiali to visualize the entire service mesh and get an overview of service health, traffic flow, and potential issues.

10. **Regularly Update Istio**

    Best Practice: Stay up to date with Istio releases and apply security patches and feature updates promptly.

Why: Like any other software, Istio releases regular updates that include security patches, performance improvements, and new features. Keeping Istio updated ensures that your service mesh is secure and takes advantage of the latest optimizations.

Steps:

Subscribe to Istio release announcements.

Use canary upgrades to roll out new versions of Istio without downtime.

Outcome

This chapter provides a comprehensive guide to securing Kubernetes environments, focusing on protecting workloads, sensitive data, and inter-service communication. It delves into various security measures, ranging from foundational practices like managing secrets and pod-level security to advanced strategies such as enforcing access controls and securing service meshes with Istio.

This chapter also emphasizes best practices for secure service mesh management, such as starting with limited scope deployments, automating certificate management, and leveraging Istio's observability tools. By the end, readers will understand how to implement a multilayered security strategy, ensuring Kubernetes environments are robust, compliant, and resilient against threats.

CHAPTER 12

Emerging and Advanced Kubernetes Concepts

In this chapter, we explore **emerging and advanced concepts in Kubernetes**, focusing on technologies and approaches that push the boundaries of container orchestration and cloud-native computing. Kubernetes has evolved far beyond its origins as a container scheduler to match the complexity of modern workloads. Organizations need tools to handle specialized workloads: AI/ML, High-Performance Computing (HPC), and WebAssembly (WASM). The following cutting-edge tools ensure networking, security, and observability scale accordingly: **functions as a service (FaaS)** for serverless deployments, **extended Berkeley Packet Filter (eBPF) with Cilium** for advanced networking and security, and **WebAssembly on Kubernetes**, which introduces lightweight, high-performance compute environments. Additionally, we manage **AI/ML workloads** through Kubernetes, touching on MLOps and AIOps practices, along with techniques for extending Kubernetes with **custom resource definitions (CRDs)** and **API extensions**. This chapter also covers **integrations** with popular platforms like Jenkins and VMware Tanzu, as well as strategies for managing Kubernetes in **air-gapped environments**, which present unique challenges for DevOps teams. This

G. Stencel and L. Berton, *Kubernetes Recipes*,
https://doi.org/10.1007/979-8-8688-1325-2_12

chapter equips readers with a deep understanding of these advanced topics, enabling them to leverage Kubernetes for specialized use cases while maintaining operational control and scalability.

12.1 Functions as a Service (FaaS) on Kubernetes

Problem

Deploying serverless applications, also known as functions as a service (FaaS), on Kubernetes has become increasingly important as organizations look to reduce infrastructure overhead and improve scalability. Traditional FaaS platforms such as AWS Lambda lock users into specific ecosystems, and these services can be difficult to scale on demand while maintaining control over execution environments.

How can we implement FaaS within a Kubernetes environment while maintaining flexibility, observability, and operational control?

Solution

Below, we'll explore a simple use case of deploying a Python function using OpenFaaS on Kubernetes.

1. **Step 1: Install OpenFaaS**

   OpenFaaS can be installed on Kubernetes using Helm.

   Add the OpenFaaS Helm repository:

   ```
   helm repo add openfaas https://openfaas.github.io/
   faas-netes/
   ```

Update the Helm repository:

```
helm repo update
```

Create a namespace for OpenFaaS:

```
kubectl create namespace openfaas
```

Install OpenFaaS in the `'openfaas'` namespace:

```
helm install openfaas openfaas/openfaas --namespace
openfaas --set basic_auth=false
```

2. **Step 2: Deploy the Python Function**

   Now that OpenFaaS is installed, we can create a simple Python function.

   - Create a new function template using OpenFaaS CLI:

     ```
     faas-cli new hello-python --lang python
     ```

   - The directory will contain a handler.py file. Update it with the following code:

     ```
     def handle(req):
         return "Hello from Kubernetes and OpenFaaS!"
     ```

   - Build and deploy the function:

     ```
     faas-cli up -f hello-python.yml
     ```

3. **Step 3: Access the Function**

   Once deployed, the function can be accessed through a LoadBalancer service or port forwarding.

Here's port forwarding to access OpenFaaS UI and gateway:

```
kubectl port-forward svc/gateway -n openfaas 8080:8080
```

Call the function via curl:

```
curl http://127.0.0.1:8080/function/hello-python
```

This will return Hello from Kubernetes and OpenFaaS!

4. **Step 4: Autoscale the Function**

   One of the key benefits of FaaS is scaling. OpenFaaS will automatically scale our function based on demand. This can be configured using Horizontal Pod Autoscalers (HPAs) in Kubernetes.

   Create an HPA to scale function pods automatically:

   ```
   kubectl autoscale deployment hello-python --cpu-percent=50 --min=1 --max=5
   ```

Discussion

In order to deploy FaaS in a Kubernetes ecosystem, leveraging **Kubernetes-native FaaS solutions,** we can use OpenFaaS or Knative. These platforms allow developers to build, deploy, and manage serverless functions while utilizing Kubernetes' orchestration features, like autoscaling and traffic splitting, without being locked into a cloud provider. By deploying FaaS on Kubernetes, we are able to

- Dynamically scale applications based on demand.
- Manage function lifecycle using Kubernetes objects (deployments, pods, etc.).
- Implement observability with tools like Prometheus and Grafana for metrics and alerting.

Running FaaS on Kubernetes offers several advantages over using traditional serverless offerings from cloud providers. With Kubernetes-native solutions like OpenFaaS, we maintain full control over our environment, which allows for integrating security measures, custom metrics, and autoscaling policies. This flexibility can be critical for enterprises that need to avoid vendor lock-in or require stringent compliance.

- **Control Over Execution Environments**: Custom container runtimes give more control over dependencies, unlike cloud offerings that limit our runtime environments.
- **Integration with Kubernetes Tools**: Integrating OpenFaaS with Prometheus allows for seamless observability, while Kubernetes-native autoscaling ensures that functions scale dynamically.
- **Consistent Development Practices**: Developers can write functions in any language supported by OpenFaaS templates, and they're able to use familiar CI/CD pipelines with Kubernetes.

See Also

- **Knative**: A Kubernetes-based platform to deploy and manage serverless applications
- **Kubeless**: Another open source FaaS built on Kubernetes
- **KEDA**: Kubernetes-based event-driven autoscaling used for scaling applications based on event-driven patterns

- **Security Considerations in FaaS**: Understanding the unique security risks in serverless functions and how to secure them

12.2 Enhancing Kubernetes Networking with eBPF and Cilium

Problem

Managing and securing networking within a Kubernetes environment can be challenging, especially at scale. Traditional networking tools can struggle with performance overhead and a lack of fine-grained observability. Moreover, ensuring efficient, low-latency networking while enforcing security policies like network policies in dynamic environments can introduce complexity and bottlenecks.

How can we improve network performance, observability, and security in Kubernetes clusters?

Solution

These steps deploy Cilium on a Kubernetes cluster and enable eBPF for network observability and policy enforcement:

1. **Step 1: Install Cilium in the Cluster**

   Cilium can be deployed as a Kubernetes CNI (Container Network Interface) plugin to replace or enhance existing networking solutions.

   Add the Cilium Helm repository:

   ```
   helm repo add cilium https://helm.cilium.io/
   ```

Install Cilium using Helm with eBPF enabled:

```
helm install cilium cilium/cilium --version 1.10.4 \
  --namespace kube-system \
  --set global.enabled=true \
  --set global.hubble.enabled=true \
  --set global.hubble.relay.enabled=true \
  --set global.hubble.ui.enabled=true \
  --set global.tunnel=disabled \
  --set global.egressMasqueradeInterfaces=eth0 \
  --set global.hostFirewall=true \
  --set global.bpf.monitorAggregation=medium
```

This installs Cilium with eBPF enabled for packet filtering and traffic control. The configuration above also enables Hubble, which is Cilium's observability layer, providing deep visibility into networking, traffic flows, and security policies.

2. **Step 2: Enable Network Policies with Cilium**
Cilium allows us to define powerful network policies based on L3/L4/L7 filtering, DNS, and HTTP. Below is an example policy that restricts traffic to a specific namespace (frontend) and only allows HTTP traffic to the backend service:

```
apiVersion: "cilium.io/v2"
kind: CiliumNetworkPolicy
metadata:
  name: allow-frontend-to-backend
  namespace: frontend
spec:
  endpointSelector:
    matchLabels:
```

```
      app: frontend
  ingress:
  - fromEndpoints:
    - matchLabels:
        app: backend
    toPorts:
    - ports:
      - port: "80"
        protocol: TCP
      rules:
        http:
          paths:
          - method: GET
            path: "/"
```

- This policy permits HTTP GET requests from the frontend pod to the backend pod only over port 80.
- Cilium enforces policies using eBPF at the kernel level, ensuring low-latency processing.

3. **Step 3: Monitor Network Traffic Using Hubble**

   With Hubble enabled, we can monitor the real-time flow of packets within our cluster. Use Hubble CLI or UI for live traffic monitoring.

   Port-forward the Hubble UI to access it from our browser:

```
kubectl port-forward -n kube-system svc/hubble-ui 8081:80
```

   Monitor live network flows:

```
hubble observe --namespace frontend
```

The hubble observe command provides detailed logs of traffic flows, including the source, destination, and policy actions, allowing us to detect and troubleshoot connectivity issues or policy violations.

4. **Step 4: Performance Optimization with eBPF**

   Cilium uses eBPF to optimize packet processing, reducing latency and overhead. Unlike traditional Iptables-based firewalls, which can become bottlenecks, eBPF operates within the Linux kernel, eliminating context switching between kernel and user space for network packet processing.

   Enable eBPF-based NodePort routing for optimized service handling:

   ```
   helm upgrade cilium cilium/cilium --namespace kube-
   system --set global.nodePort.mode=snat --set global.
   loadBalancer.algorithm=maglev
   ```

This enables eBPF for NodePort handling, improving service load-balancing performance by reducing the overhead caused by traditional Iptables-based NAT operations.

Discussion

Cilium, powered by **eBPF (extended Berkeley Packet Filter)**, provides an advanced solution to Kubernetes networking challenges. eBPF is a Linux kernel technology that allows safe and efficient execution of programs directly within the kernel, enabling real-time, low-overhead network analysis and packet filtering. Cilium utilizes eBPF to provide rich networking, security, and observability features within Kubernetes.

Cilium improves Kubernetes networking by offering

- **High-performance packet filtering** with low latency
- **Deep observability** into network flows and connections
- **Enhanced security** by enforcing fine-grained network policies (Layer 7 policies, DNS-aware security)
- **Transparent service mesh** that improves performance by avoiding sidecar proxies

Cilium with eBPF is a powerful tool for modern Kubernetes environments, especially for organizations that demand high performance and advanced security controls. The combination of eBPF and Kubernetes results in

- **Fine-Grained Security Policies**: Cilium enables developers to define network policies that operate not only at Layer 3 and Layer 4 but also at Layer 7. For instance, policies can be made HTTP method–aware, allowing or denying traffic based on request types.
- **Improved Observability**: Hubble, Cilium's observability layer, gives real-time insights into network flows and performance, making it easier to debug connectivity issues or ensure that policies are being enforced as intended.
- **eBPF Efficiency**: Traditional Kubernetes networking relies heavily on Iptables, which can degrade performance as the number of rules scales. Cilium, leveraging eBPF, operates directly in the kernel, significantly reducing this performance bottleneck.

See Also

- **Kubernetes Network Policies**: Learn more about Kubernetes' built-in support for L3/L4 network policies.
- **eBPF for Observability**: Explore how eBPF can be used for tracing, profiling, and security across a broader system, not just networking.
- **Calico**: An alternative CNI solution that provides networking and security for Kubernetes clusters.
- **Hubble**: The observability layer for Cilium, offering deep insights into Kubernetes networking.

12.3 High-Performance Computing (HPC) on Kubernetes for Specialized Workloads

Problem

High-Performance Computing (HPC) workloads traditionally run on specialized hardware and infrastructure that prioritize performance, low-latency networking, and large-scale parallelism. However, these systems are often inflexible, costly, and difficult to manage, especially as demand scales. Organizations want to leverage cloud-native technologies like Kubernetes to run HPC workloads while maintaining performance, scalability, and hardware specialization.

How can we run HPC workloads on Kubernetes while meeting the unique performance demands of HPC environments?

Solution

These steps configure Kubernetes to run an HPC workload using GPUs for a deep learning job and a custom scheduler:

1. **Step 1: Set Up Kubernetes with GPU Support**

   To run GPU-accelerated workloads, Kubernetes must be configured to recognize GPUs. NVIDIA provides device plugins to enable this.

   - Install NVIDIA drivers on all GPU nodes.
   - Deploy the NVIDIA Kubernetes device plugin:

   Create the NVIDIA device plugin DaemonSet:

   ```
   kubectl create -f https://raw.githubusercontent.
   com/NVIDIA/k8s-device-plugin/v0.9.0/nvidia-device-
   plugin.yml
   ```

   This DaemonSet will make GPU resources available to Kubernetes, allowing it to schedule workloads that require GPUs.

2. **Step 2: Define an HPC Job Using GPUs**

   Let's configure an HPC workload that uses GPUs for deep learning model training. Below is an example Kubernetes job YAML file that runs a TensorFlow-based workload on a GPU-enabled node:

   ```
   apiVersion: batch/v1
   kind: Job
   metadata:
     name: gpu-hpc-job
   spec:
     template:
   ```

```
    spec:
      containers:
      - name: tensorflow-gpu
        image: tensorflow/tensorflow:latest-gpu
        command: ["python", "-c", "import tensorflow as
        tf; print(tf.reduce_sum(tf.random.normal([1000,
        1000])))"]
        resources:
          limits:
            nvidia.com/gpu: 1
      restartPolicy: Never
  backoffLimit: 4
```

- This job requests a GPU (nvidia.com/gpu: 1) for running a TensorFlow training script that performs a simple matrix operation.
- Kubernetes will schedule this job on a node that has a GPU available.

3. **Step 3: Optimize Job Scheduling for HPC**

   HPC jobs often require fine-grained control over resource scheduling. Kubernetes allows custom schedulers to handle specialized tasks. For example, we can use **kube-batch** to manage batch scheduling for HPC workloads.

   - Install kube-batch for enhanced batch scheduling:

```
helm repo add kube-batch https://volcano-sh.github.
io/charts/
helm install kube-batch kube-batch/kube-batch
--namespace kube-system
```

- Modify our HPC job to work with kube-batch:

```
apiVersion: batch.volcano.sh/v1alpha1
kind: Job
metadata:
  name: gpu-hpc-job
spec:
  schedulerName: volcano  # Use Kube-batch for
  scheduling
  minAvailable: 1
  tasks:
    - replicas: 1
      name: training
      template:
        spec:
          containers:
          - name: tensorflow-gpu
            image: tensorflow/tensorflow:latest-gpu
            command: ["python", "-c", "import
            tensorflow as tf; print(tf.reduce_
            sum(tf.random.normal([1000, 1000])))"]
            resources:
              limits:
                nvidia.com/gpu: 1
          restartPolicy: Never
```

In this example, kube-batch is used as the scheduler, which optimizes the resource allocation for batch processing, ensuring that HPC workloads are handled efficiently.

4. **Step 4: Monitor and Scale the HPC Workload**
   Kubernetes' autoscaling features can be applied to HPC jobs based on CPU, GPU, or memory usage.

   - Use Horizontal Pod Autoscaler (HPA) to automatically scale the job based on resource usage:

     ```
     kubectl autoscale job gpu-hpc-job --min=1
     --max=10 --cpu-percent=80
     ```

This command automatically scales the number of job replicas based on the CPU usage of the job, optimizing resource usage dynamically.

Discussion

Kubernetes, with its flexibility and scalability, can be used to orchestrate High-Performance Computing (HPC) workloads by incorporating specialized compute resources (e.g., GPUs, FPGAs), custom schedulers, and optimized networking. By leveraging Kubernetes' dynamic resource allocation, autoscaling, and containerization capabilities, organizations can run HPC tasks with high efficiency on commodity or cloud-based clusters.

Here are key strategies for HPC on Kubernetes:

- **Specialized Hardware Support**: Use devices like GPUs or FPGAs for workloads requiring high parallelism or machine learning capabilities.
- **Custom Resource Scheduling**: Tailor Kubernetes' scheduler or use plugins for better control of job priorities and resource allocation.
- **Efficient Networking**: Leverage RDMA (Remote Direct Memory Access) or InfiniBand for low-latency, high-throughput networking.

Running HPC workloads on Kubernetes allows organizations to take advantage of cloud-native features while still meeting the stringent performance and resource demands of HPC applications. Here's how Kubernetes excels in the HPC space:

- **Specialized Hardware**: Kubernetes supports GPUs and FPGAs through device plugins, enabling it to run compute-heavy tasks such as machine learning model training or molecular simulations.
- **Custom Scheduling**: With plugins like kube-batch (or Volcano), Kubernetes can optimize resource allocation for large-scale parallel jobs, improving overall cluster utilization.
- **Elastic Scaling**: Kubernetes allows HPC jobs to scale dynamically based on demand, providing flexibility for workloads that need to scale up or down based on performance requirements.
- **Cost Efficiency**: Kubernetes allows HPC jobs to run in cloud environments, where resources can be dynamically provisioned and decommissioned, providing significant cost savings for organizations compared with dedicated HPC infrastructure.

By adopting Kubernetes for HPC workloads, organizations can leverage the power of distributed computing while maintaining the flexibility to run on-premises or in the cloud.

See Also

- **Volcano**: An open source batch scheduling system for Kubernetes designed for HPC and AI workloads.
- **Kube-batch**: A batch scheduling framework for running large-scale parallel jobs on Kubernetes.
- **NVIDIA Device Plugin**: Enables GPU support for Kubernetes, allowing the scheduling and execution of GPU-accelerated tasks.
- **Kubernetes Autoscaling**: Learn about Kubernetes autoscaling for workloads based on CPU, memory, or custom metrics.

12.4 Running WebAssembly (WASM) on Kubernetes

Problem

WebAssembly (WASM) has emerged as a powerful technology for running lightweight, secure, and fast applications. Originally designed for the Web, WASM is now gaining traction in cloud-native environments due to its low resource usage, fast startup times, and ability to run code in a sandboxed environment. However, integrating WASM into Kubernetes for running microservices or high-performance workloads brings challenges like orchestration, scalability, and observability.

How can we deploy and manage WebAssembly (WASM) workloads in a Kubernetes environment effectively?

Solution

These steps are a practical example of deploying a WebAssembly application using Krustlet (Kubernetes Rust Kubelet) on Kubernetes:

1. **Step 1: Install Krustlet in the Kubernetes Cluster**

   Krustlet (Kubernetes Rust Kubelet) allows Kubernetes to schedule WebAssembly workloads. Before deploying WASM workloads, we need to install Krustlet in our cluster.

   - Install Krustlet using Helm:

     Create a namespace for Krustlet:

     ```
     kubectl create namespace krustlet
     ```

     Install Krustlet using Helm:

     ```
     helm repo add krustlet https://deislabs.github.io/
     krustlet/charts/
     helm install krustlet krustlet/krustlet --namespace
     krustlet
     ```

2. **Step 2: Set Up a WebAssembly (WASM) Application**

   Next, let's prepare a simple WebAssembly application that will run on Kubernetes. We can write the WASM application in Rust or any other language that compiles to WASM.

   Here is an example of a simple Rust-based WebAssembly function:

```
#[no_mangle]
pub extern "C" fn hello_wasm() -> *const u8 {
    b"Hello from WebAssembly on Kubernetes!\0".as_ptr()
}
```

Compile the Rust application to WASM:

```
rustup target add wasm32-unknown-unknown
cargo build --target wasm32-unknown-unknown --release
```

3. **Step 3: Deploy the WebAssembly Application**

   After compiling the WASM application, package it as a Kubernetes pod using the wasm32-wasi target.

   - Below is an example of a Kubernetes YAML manifest that runs the WASM application on Krustlet:

     ```
     apiVersion: v1
     kind: Pod
     metadata:
       name: hello-wasm
     spec:
       runtimeClassName: krustlet-wasi
       containers:
       - name: hello-wasm
         image: webassembly.azurecr.io/hello-wasm:v1
         command: ["/bin/wasm32-wasi"]
         args: ["hello_wasm"]
     ```

   - Apply the manifest to deploy the WASM workload:

     ```
     kubectl apply -f hello-wasm.yml
     ```

4. **Step 4: Access the WebAssembly Application**

   Once deployed, we can access the application via the Kubernetes service. Since WebAssembly workloads typically run as lightweight tasks, we can monitor logs to verify the application output.

   - Check the logs to confirm the WASM workload is running:

     ```
     kubectl logs hello-wasm
     ```

   The output should show Hello from WebAssembly on Kubernetes!

5. **Step 5: Integrate WebAssembly into Kubernetes Workflows**

   Since WASM workloads are lightweight, they are ideal for edge computing or resource-constrained environments. We can further integrate WASM with Kubernetes features like **Horizontal Pod Autoscaler (HPA)** for scaling or **custom resource definitions (CRDs)** for specific workflows. Kubernetes can orchestrate WASM-based microservices alongside traditional containerized applications, ensuring seamless integration.

Discussion

WebAssembly (WASM) can be deployed on Kubernetes using solutions like **Krustlet**, a WebAssembly kubelet implementation, or **Wasmtime**, a lightweight WASM runtime. These tools allow Kubernetes to schedule and run WASM-based workloads alongside traditional containerized applications. WASM's lightweight nature offers significant performance advantages, especially in edge computing, IoT, and microservices architectures.

By running WASM on Kubernetes, we benefit from

- **Security**: WASM runs in a highly sandboxed environment, ensuring strong isolation between workloads.
- **Performance**: WASM workloads have fast startup times and low memory footprints.
- **Portability**: WASM bytecode is platform agnostic, allowing code to run consistently across different architectures.

WebAssembly (WASM) offers several advantages for cloud-native environments, especially in Kubernetes clusters. By leveraging Krustlet or other WASM runtimes, Kubernetes can handle both traditional containerized applications and WebAssembly workloads, offering a new level of flexibility and performance.

- **Security**: WASM workloads run in a sandboxed environment, reducing attack surfaces. This makes them ideal for multi-tenant environments or edge devices where security is critical.
- **Fast Startup Times**: WASM workloads start almost instantly, making them perfect for short-lived tasks or event-driven microservices. Unlike containers, which have higher startup latency, WASM workloads execute with minimal overhead.
- **Portability**: WASM is platform agnostic, meaning the same WASM binary can run on different architectures without modification, enhancing consistency across environments.
- **Edge Computing**: WASM's low resource consumption makes it ideal for IoT and edge use cases, where resources such as CPU and memory are limited.

The ability to orchestrate WASM workloads with Kubernetes allows organizations to benefit from Kubernetes' rich ecosystem (scalability, service discovery, networking) while utilizing WASM for performance-critical workloads.

See Also

- **Krustlet**: Kubernetes kubelet for running WebAssembly workloads in a cloud-native environment
- **Wasmtime**: A fast, secure, and lightweight WebAssembly runtime for running WebAssembly outside the browser
- **WASI (WebAssembly System Interface)**: A standard API for WebAssembly to interact with system resources like file systems and networks
- **Faasm**: An open source serverless platform built for running WebAssembly in Kubernetes

12.5 Deploying AI/ML Workloads on Kubernetes: MLOps, AIOps, and Prompt Engineering

Problem

Artificial intelligence (AI) and machine learning (ML) workloads are resource-intensive and require specialized infrastructure like GPUs or TPUs for efficient training and inference. Managing these workloads at scale involves orchestrating complex pipelines, handling large datasets, and ensuring reproducibility and continuous deployment. The challenge is to build a scalable, flexible, and resilient platform that can handle AI/ML tasks efficiently while allowing collaboration between data scientists and DevOps teams.

How can we leverage Kubernetes to handle AI/ML workloads, streamline machine learning operations (MLOps), and enable prompt engineering for scalable AI/ML development?

Solution

We can deploy and manage AI/ML workloads on Kubernetes using Kubeflow for model training and inference with GPUs.

Practical Example: Deploying AI/ML Pipelines with Kubeflow on Kubernetes

1. **Step 1: Install Kubeflow on Kubernetes**

   Kubeflow is a Kubernetes-native platform for deploying and managing machine learning models. It integrates well with Kubernetes' resource management, allowing for seamless scaling and orchestration of ML workloads.

   - Install Kubeflow using kfctl:

     Download the Kubeflow config file:

     ```
     wget https://raw.githubusercontent.com/kubeflow/
     manifests/v1.3-branch/kfdef/kfctl_k8s_istio.
     v1.3.0.yaml
     ```

Set up an environment variable for our configuration:

```
export CONFIG_URI=$(pwd)/kfctl_k8s_istio.
v1.3.0.yaml
```

Install Kubeflow:

```
kfctl apply -V -f ${CONFIG_URI}
```

This installs Kubeflow and its components in our Kubernetes cluster, setting up pipelines, Jupyter notebooks, and various AI/ML tools.

2. **Step 2: Train a Machine Learning Model with GPUs**

   Kubeflow pipelines allow us to define reusable and scalable machine learning workflows. Let's configure a pipeline to train a model using GPUs.

   Below is an example YAML file for training a model using TensorFlow and Kubernetes' GPU support:

```
apiVersion: kubeflow.org/v1beta1
kind: TFJob
metadata:
  name: mnist-training
spec:
  tfReplicaSpecs:
    Worker:
      replicas: 2
      restartPolicy: OnFailure
      template:
        spec:
          containers:
```

```
- name: tensorflow
  image: tensorflow/tensorflow:latest-gpu
  command:
  - "python"
  - "/mnist.py"
  resources:
    limits:
      nvidia.com/gpu: 1
```

Apply the YAML file to run the training job:

```
kubectl apply -f mnist-training.yaml
```

This job requests GPU resources to run TensorFlow training for the MNIST dataset. Kubernetes will allocate the necessary GPU resources and orchestrate the model training.

3. **Step 3: Build an AI/ML Pipeline with Kubeflow**

   With Kubeflow, we can define an entire AI/ML pipeline that includes data preprocessing, model training, validation, and deployment for inference. Below is an example pipeline using Kubeflow Pipelines DSL (Domain-Specific Language).

   Create a Python script to define the pipeline:

```
import kfp.dsl as dsl

@dsl.pipeline(
    name="Simple ML Pipeline",
    description="A simple ML pipeline to train and
    serve a model"
)
def mnist_pipeline():
```

```
        train_op = dsl.ContainerOp(
            name="train-model",
            image="tensorflow/tensorflow:latest-gpu",
            command=["python", "/mnist.py"],
            arguments=[]
        )
        serve_op = dsl.ContainerOp(
            name="serve-model",
            image="tensorflow/serving:latest",
            command=["tensorflow_model_server", "--model_
            name=mnist_model"]
        )
    if __name__ == "__main__":
        import kfp.compiler as compiler
        compiler.Compiler().compile(mnist_pipeline, "mnist_
        pipeline.yaml")
```

Upload the pipeline to the Kubeflow Pipelines UI and run it to orchestrate the entire workflow from model training to serving.

4. **Step 4: Automate Prompt Engineering**

   AI models, particularly in the domain of Natural Language Processing (NLP), require effective **prompt engineering** to produce optimal results. Kubernetes can automate prompt engineering by deploying inference models in a scalable manner, where prompts are dynamically generated and optimized for AI models like GPT.

Below is an example of a Kubernetes deployment YAML for serving a prompt engineering model:

```
apiVersion: apps/v1
kind: Deployment
metadata:
  name: gpt-prompt-engineering
spec:
  replicas: 3
  selector:
    matchLabels:
      app: gpt-prompt
  template:
    metadata:
      labels:
        app: gpt-prompt
    spec:
      containers:
      - name: gpt-inference
        image: openai/gpt-3
        command: ["python", "/run_inference.py"]
        args: ["--prompt", "How does Kubernetes help AI
        workloads?"]
      resources:
        limits:
          nvidia.com/gpu: 1
```

In this example, Kubernetes deploys an AI inference model to handle prompt-based queries. Kubernetes scales this service dynamically based on traffic.

Discussion

Kubernetes is an ideal platform for managing AI/ML workloads due to its ability to scale resources dynamically, integrate with specialized hardware (like GPUs), and orchestrate complex machine learning pipelines. **MLOps** (Machine Learning Operations) and **AIOps** (Artificial Intelligence for IT Operations) workloads can be deployed, scaled, and managed using Kubernetes, ensuring reproducibility, collaboration, and automation throughout the machine learning lifecycle.

Key features Kubernetes brings to AI/ML workloads include

- **Resource Orchestration**: Automate resource allocation, especially for GPU and TPU workloads.
- **Pipeline Orchestration**: Integrate tools like Kubeflow or Argo to manage complex AI/ML pipelines.
- **Prompt Engineering**: In AI-driven systems, prompt engineering (crafting prompts to guide AI models) can be automated and managed via Kubernetes to provide large-scale inference capabilities for NLP models.

Kubernetes provides a powerful platform for managing AI/ML workloads by integrating with tools like Kubeflow, NVIDIA GPUs, and TensorFlow. Here's how Kubernetes enhances AI/ML workloads:

- **MLOps**: Kubernetes streamlines the deployment of machine learning models by automating tasks like resource allocation, pipeline orchestration, and model serving. This brings continuous integration and delivery (CI/CD) practices to the machine learning lifecycle.

- **AIOps**: Kubernetes allows for the automated monitoring, management, and optimization of AI/ML workflows, enabling self-healing and scaling of infrastructure based on AI-driven insights.
- **Prompt Engineering**: In NLP systems, Kubernetes can efficiently manage the large-scale serving of models that rely on prompt engineering for generating optimal outputs. By automating the inference pipelines, it ensures prompt-based tasks are handled efficiently.

By deploying AI/ML workloads on Kubernetes, organizations can leverage its scalability, resource management, and automation features to manage complex machine learning pipelines. This leads to more efficient collaboration between data scientists and DevOps teams and ensures reproducibility and faster time to market for AI solutions.

See Also

- **Kubeflow**: A Kubernetes-native platform for managing machine learning workflows
- **Argo Workflows**: A workflow engine for Kubernetes that helps manage complex ML and AI pipelines
- **TensorFlow Operator**: A Kubernetes operator for running distributed TensorFlow jobs
- **Kubeflow Pipelines**: A platform for building, deploying, and managing end-to-end machine learning workflows

12.6 Extending Kubernetes: Custom Resource Definitions (CRDs), API Extensions, and FeatureGates

Problem

Kubernetes provides a powerful framework for managing containerized applications, but as the demands of modern applications grow, users may require capabilities beyond Kubernetes' built-in resources. Custom solutions are often needed to meet specific organizational needs or handle advanced use cases like external integrations, complex state management, or introducing new Kubernetes objects.

How can we extend Kubernetes to add new features, manage external APIs, or integrate with specialized workloads while maintaining its scalability and reliability?

Solution

We can create a custom resource definition (CRD) to manage a custom resource in Kubernetes and use API extensions to interact with external APIs:

1. **Step 1: Define a Custom Resource Definition (CRD)**

   Custom resource definitions allow us to create new resource types that act like native Kubernetes resources. Let's create a CRD for managing a custom resource called MyApp, which represents a custom application configuration.

- Below is an example YAML definition for the MyApp CRD:

```
apiVersion: apiextensions.k8s.io/v1
kind: CustomResourceDefinition
metadata:
  name: myapps.example.com
spec:
  group: example.com
  versions:
    - name: v1
      served: true
      storage: true
      schema:
        openAPIV3Schema:
          type: object
          properties:
            spec:
              type: object
              properties:
                replicas:
                  type: integer
                version:
                  type: string
  scope: Namespaced
  names:
    plural: myapps
    singular: myapp
    kind: MyApp
    shortNames:
      - ma
```

- Apply the CRD to our Kubernetes cluster:

  ```
  kubectl apply -f myapp-crd.yaml
  ```

  This creates a new resource type called MyApp that we can manage within the Kubernetes cluster, just like pods or services.

2. **Step 2: Create a Custom Resource (CR)**

   After defining the CRD, we can create a custom resource that conforms to the new MyApp type.

   Here's an example YAML for a MyApp custom resource:

   ```
   apiVersion: example.com/v1
   kind: MyApp
   metadata:
     name: my-app-instance
   spec:
     replicas: 3

     version: "v1.0"
   ```

   Apply the custom resource:

   ```
   kubectl apply -f myapp-instance.yaml
   ```

   This creates an instance of MyApp, which we can manage using the standard kubectl commands. Kubernetes controllers can now watch for changes to the MyApp resources and perform actions accordingly.

3. **Step 3: Extend the Kubernetes API with an External Controller**

   We can extend the Kubernetes API by writing custom controllers that act on our CRDs. These controllers allow us to define custom logic for how Kubernetes should react when our custom resources are created, updated, or deleted.

   Below is an example of how a controller written in Go can watch the MyApp resources and take action (e.g., scaling an application based on replicas):

```
package main
import (
    "context"
    "fmt"

    appsv1 "k8s.io/api/apps/v1"
    metav1 "k8s.io/apimachinery/pkg/apis/meta/v1"
    "k8s.io/client-go/kubernetes"
    "k8s.io/client-go/tools/clientcmd"
)
func main() {
    config, err := clientcmd.BuildConfigFromFlags("",
    "kubeconfig")
    if err != nil {
        panic(err)
    }

    clientset, err := kubernetes.NewForConfig(config)
    if err != nil {
        panic(err)
    }
```

```
    // Watch for changes in MyApp custom resources and
       scale a Deployment
    watch, err := clientset.AppsV1().
    Deployments("default").Watch(context.TODO(),
    metav1.ListOptions{})
    if err != nil {
        panic(err)
    }

    for event := range watch.ResultChan() {
        fmt.Printf("Event: %v\n", event.Type)
        // Custom logic to handle MyApp changes
    }

}
```

This controller watches for changes in the MyApp resources and can scale deployments or perform other actions based on the values in the MyApp spec.

4. **Step 4: Use FeatureGates to Enable Experimental Kubernetes Features**

   FeatureGates allow us to enable or disable specific experimental features in Kubernetes. These are particularly useful for testing new functionality in a non-production environment. Here's an example command to enable a feature gate:

```
kube-apiserver --feature-gates=TTLAfterFinished=true
```

In this example, the **TTLAfterFinished** FeatureGate enables automatic garbage collection of finished jobs based on TTL (time to live). We can experiment with features like this to optimize and extend our Kubernetes setup.

Discussion

Extending Kubernetes involves the use of **custom resource definitions (CRDs)**, **API extensions**, and **FeatureGates** to add new functionalities or enhance existing Kubernetes capabilities. CRDs allow us to define new types of Kubernetes resources that behave like native Kubernetes objects, while API extensions let us extend the Kubernetes API with additional controllers and features. FeatureGates enable or disable experimental features, allowing us to safely test and integrate cutting-edge features.

By extending Kubernetes, we can

- **Create Custom Kubernetes Resources**: Define resources tailored to our application needs, such as new controllers for complex workloads.
- **Integrate with External Services**: Extend the Kubernetes API to interact with external APIs or services, enabling seamless integration with external systems.
- **Enable Experimental Features**: Use FeatureGates to enable or test new Kubernetes features without impacting the stability of our cluster.

Extending Kubernetes through CRDs, API extensions, and FeatureGates provides a robust way to build custom workflows, integrate external systems, and add new functionality to our cluster. Some of the key benefits include

- **Custom Resource Definitions (CRDs)**: CRDs allow us to create new, domain-specific objects that behave just like native Kubernetes resources. This enables users to define custom workflows and logic that fit their exact use cases.

- **API Extensions**: With API extensions, we can integrate external APIs or systems into Kubernetes, enabling Kubernetes to orchestrate more than just containers—like databases, external cloud services, or custom hardware.
- **FeatureGates**: Enabling or disabling experimental features via FeatureGates ensures that our Kubernetes cluster can adopt the latest features at our own pace, helping us innovate while keeping the cluster stable.

These extensions enable organizations to adapt Kubernetes to meet their evolving needs, whether it's managing new types of resources or integrating with external services.

See Also

- **KubeBuilder**: A framework for building Kubernetes APIs using custom resources.
- **Operator SDK**: A toolkit for building Kubernetes operators that extend the functionality of Kubernetes using custom controllers and CRDs.
- **CRDs vs. ConfigMaps**: Understand when to use CRDs vs. Kubernetes native resources like ConfigMaps.
- **FeatureGates in Kubernetes**: Learn more about FeatureGates and how to safely enable or disable them in production environments.

12.7 Integrating Jenkins and VMware Tanzu with Kubernetes for CI/CD and Application Scaling

Problem

As organizations adopt Kubernetes for deploying and managing applications, integrating continuous integration/continuous deployment (CI/CD) pipelines becomes crucial. Jenkins, a widely used CI/CD tool, needs to be scalable, flexible, and able to leverage Kubernetes' capabilities to handle dynamic workloads. Additionally, platforms like **VMware Tanzu Application Platform (TAP)** are becoming essential for streamlining Kubernetes-based application development and deployment.

How can we integrate Jenkins with Kubernetes to create scalable CI/CD pipelines, and how can VMware Tanzu Application Platform further enhance the deployment and management of modern applications?

Solution

We configure scaling with Jenkins agents and introduce VMware Tanzu Application Platform integrating Jenkins with Kubernetes:

1. **Step 1: Install Jenkins on Kubernetes**

   Jenkins can be deployed on Kubernetes as a StatefulSet to take advantage of Kubernetes' scaling features. We can use Helm to deploy Jenkins in our cluster.

   Install Jenkins using Helm.

   Add the Jenkins Helm repository:

   ```
   helm repo add jenkins https://charts.jenkins.io
   ```

Update the Helm repo:

```
helm repo update
```

Install Jenkins in the jenkins namespace:

```
helm install jenkins jenkins/jenkins --namespace
jenkins --create-namespace
```

Once Jenkins is deployed, access the Jenkins UI by port forwarding:

```
kubectl port-forward svc/jenkins 8080:8080
--namespace jenkins
```

2. **Step 2: Configure the Jenkins Kubernetes Plugin**

   The **Jenkins Kubernetes Plugin** allows Jenkins to dynamically create and destroy Kubernetes pods as Jenkins agents. Each build can run in its own isolated Kubernetes pod, ensuring resource efficiency and scalability.

   - Install the Kubernetes plugin in Jenkins:
     - In the Jenkins UI, go to **Manage Jenkins ➤ Manage Plugins ➤ Available**.
     - Search for the "Kubernetes" plugin and install it.
   - After installation, configure the Kubernetes cloud under **Manage Jenkins ➤ Configure System**.
   - Add our Kubernetes cluster details (such as API server URL, credentials, and namespace) in the Kubernetes cloud configuration section.

3. **Step 3: Dynamic Scaling with Jenkins Agents**

   Once Jenkins is configured with Kubernetes, it can dynamically scale agents (pods) to run build jobs based on demand. Below is an example configuration of the Kubernetes plugin for Jenkins agents:

```
apiVersion: v1
kind: Pod
metadata:
  name: jenkins-agent
spec:
  containers:
  - name: jnlp
    image: jenkins/inbound-agent:alpine
    args: ["${computer.jnlpmac} ${computer.name}"]
  - name: build
    image: maven:3.8.1-adoptopenjdk-11
    command: ["/bin/sh", "-c"]
    args: ["mvn clean install"]
```

   - Jenkins will dynamically create and terminate pods (agents) based on the pipeline needs, reducing resource usage when the builds are idle.

4. **Step 4: Scaling Jenkins on Kubernetes**

   Jenkins running on Kubernetes can scale horizontally to handle multiple concurrent build jobs. Use **Horizontal Pod Autoscalers (HPAs)** to automatically scale Jenkins based on CPU and memory usage.

- To enable autoscaling for Jenkins, apply the following HPA manifest:

```
apiVersion: autoscaling/v1
kind: HorizontalPodAutoscaler
metadata:
  name: jenkins-hpa
  namespace: jenkins
spec:
  scaleTargetRef:
    apiVersion: apps/v1
    kind: StatefulSet
    name: jenkins
  minReplicas: 1
  maxReplicas: 5
  targetCPUUtilizationPercentage: 70
```

This HPA will scale Jenkins between one and five replicas based on CPU utilization, ensuring efficient resource usage during high build demand.

Practical Example: Using VMware Tanzu Application Platform for Kubernetes Workloads

1. **Step 1: Set Up VMware Tanzu Application Platform**

   VMware Tanzu Application Platform (TAP) provides a complete development and deployment platform for Kubernetes applications, streamlining CI/CD and deployment processes.

- To install TAP, first ensure we have access to the Tanzu Network to download the necessary packages.
- Install the Tanzu CLI.

  Download and install the Tanzu CLI:

  ```
  curl -O https://network.tanzu.vmware.com/tanzu/
  tanzu-cli-v0.11.1-linux-amd64.tar.gz
  ```

  ```
  tar xvf tanzu-cli-v0.11.1-linux-amd64.tar.gz
  ```

  ```
  sudo install cli/core/v0.11.1/tanzu-core-linux_
  amd64 /usr/local/bin/tanzu
  ```

Follow VMware's installation guide to install TAP into our Kubernetes cluster using the Tanzu CLI.

2. **Step 2: Create and Deploy an Application with TAP**

   Once TAP is installed, we can use it to create and deploy Kubernetes applications easily. Below is an example using TAP's tanzu apps workload command to deploy an application.

   Create a new workload for an application:

   ```
   tanzu apps workload create my-app --git-repo https://
   github.com/my-org/my-app.git
   ```

   ```
   --git-branch main --type web --yes
   ```

   TAP will automatically build the container, generate manifests, and deploy the application to our Kubernetes cluster.

3. **Step 3: Managing CI/CD with TAP**

   VMware Tanzu integrates with CI/CD pipelines by automating the build and deployment process. It abstracts much of the Kubernetes complexity and provides developers with a smooth workflow for pushing code and deploying applications.

   TAP's **Supply Chain Choreographer** manages the entire pipeline, ensuring security and consistency throughout the build, test, and deployment stages.

Discussion

By integrating **Jenkins** with Kubernetes through the **Jenkins Kubernetes Plugin**, we can dynamically scale Jenkins agents, ensuring that CI/CD tasks are handled efficiently across a Kubernetes cluster. Additionally, leveraging **VMware Tanzu Application Platform (TAP)** allows developers to streamline the entire application lifecycle, from building to deploying and scaling applications on Kubernetes, all while maintaining security and operational best practices.

The key benefits of integrating Jenkins and VMware Tanzu with Kubernetes include the following:

- **Dynamic scaling of Jenkins agents** based on demand, reducing overhead and increasing flexibility.
- **VMware Tanzu Application Platform** provides an integrated development environment, making it easier to build, deploy, and manage applications on Kubernetes.
- Enhanced **observability, security, and performance** through Kubernetes-native tools.

By integrating Jenkins and VMware Tanzu with Kubernetes, organizations can unlock the full potential of cloud-native development and CI/CD workflows. Here's how these integrations improve operational efficiency and developer productivity:

- **Jenkins Kubernetes Plugin**: This plugin enables Jenkins to dynamically scale its build agents, reducing resource consumption and optimizing build times. Kubernetes ensures that Jenkins agents are ephemeral and efficient, leading to faster and more scalable builds.
- **Scaling Jenkins**: Horizontal Pod Autoscalers (HPAs) can be used to dynamically scale Jenkins instances based on demand, ensuring that build capacity grows as needed while reducing overhead during idle times.
- **VMware Tanzu Application Platform (TAP)**: TAP simplifies the Kubernetes application lifecycle, enabling developers to focus on writing code while TAP handles deployment, security, and scaling. By integrating TAP with Kubernetes, development teams can streamline CI/CD workflows and automate the deployment of microservices at scale.

Both Jenkins and Tanzu provide Kubernetes-native solutions for orchestrating CI/CD pipelines and managing complex application lifecycles, leading to faster and more secure releases.

See Also

- **Jenkins Kubernetes Plugin**: Learn more about how to configure Jenkins agents with Kubernetes.
- **Kubernetes Horizontal Pod Autoscaler**: A guide to setting up autoscaling for Kubernetes workloads.

- **VMware Tanzu Application Platform**: Explore VMware's documentation on deploying and managing applications on Kubernetes with TAP.
- **Argo CD**: An alternative Kubernetes-native continuous delivery tool for managing application deployments.

12.8 Empowering DevOps in Air-Gapped Environments: Managing Kubernetes and CI/CD

Problem

An **air-gapped environment** refers to a network that is physically isolated from the public Internet or any other external network. This is common in industries with strict security and regulatory requirements, such as finance, defense, or critical infrastructure. Running Kubernetes clusters and enabling DevOps practices in air-gapped environments poses unique challenges, such as managing container images, pushing updates, and running CI/CD pipelines without direct Internet access.

How can Kubernetes and DevOps pipelines be configured and managed in air-gapped environments, and how do we address the challenges of pushing images, applying updates, and resolving common issues?

Solution

We explore how to set up an air-gapped environment for Kubernetes, including pushing images to an air-gapped registry and managing DevOps pipelines:

1. **Step 1: Set Up an Air-Gapped Container Registry**

   In an air-gapped environment, we need to establish a local container registry that can be accessed from within the Kubernetes cluster.

   - Deploy a container registry (e.g., **Harbor**) in our air-gapped environment. Harbor provides a robust registry with security features like image signing and vulnerability scanning.

     Run Harbor with Docker (in our air-gapped environment):

     ```
     docker run -d --name harbor -p 80:80 -p 443:443 -p
     4443:4443 goharbor/harbor:latest
     ```

   - Access Harbor by port forwarding or exposing it through a local DNS. Ensure the air-gapped environment can resolve the registry's address.

2. **Step 2: Pull and Save Container Images**

   Since the air-gapped environment cannot access external registries, we must first pull necessary container images from a connected environment and transfer them to the air-gapped system. In a connected environment, use Docker or Podman to pull and save the required images to a tar file.

   Pull an image from a public registry:

   ```
   docker pull nginx:latest
   ```

Save the image to a tarball:

```
docker save nginx:latest -o nginx-latest.tar
```

Transfer the tarball to the air-gapped environment (using physical media like USB or other secure methods).

3. **Step 3: Load Images into the Air-Gapped Registry**

   Once transferred, the images need to be loaded into the air-gapped registry so that Kubernetes can access them. Load the image tarball into our local registry:

```
docker load -i nginx-latest.tar
```

   Tag the image to point to our local registry:

```
docker tag nginx:latest airgapped-registry.local/
nginx:latest
```

   Push the image to the local registry:

```
docker push airgapped-registry.local/nginx:latest
```

   Make sure Kubernetes nodes are configured to pull images from this local registry.

   - Update Kubernetes deployment YAML to reference the air-gapped registry:

```
apiVersion: apps/v1
kind: Deployment
metadata:
  name: nginx-deployment
spec:
  replicas: 3
```

```
  selector:
    matchLabels:
      app: nginx
  template:
    metadata:
      labels:
        app: nginx
    spec:
      containers:
      - name: nginx
        image: airgapped-registry.local/
        nginx:latest
        ports:
        - containerPort: 80
```

4. **Step 4: Offline Installation and Updates for Kubernetes**

   In an air-gapped environment, we also need to ensure Kubernetes clusters and its dependencies (e.g., Helm charts, Kubernetes components) are kept up to date without Internet access.

   - **Offline Installation**: Many Kubernetes tools, including Helm and kubeadm, offer offline installation options. For example, we can mirror the necessary Kubernetes images and Helm charts and transfer them into our environment.

     Save Kubernetes component images from an external environment:

     ```
     kubeadm config images pull --kubernetes-
     version v1.21.0
     ```

Transfer these images to the air-gapped environment and load them:

```
docker load -i kube-apiserver.tar
docker load -i kube-controller-manager.tar
```

- **Mirroring Helm Charts**: In environments where Helm charts are used, mirror the charts externally, then package and transfer them to the air-gapped environment. For example:

  Mirror Helm chart from a public chart repository:

  ```
  helm pull bitnami/nginx --version 9.3.1
  ```

Transfer the chart to the air-gapped environment and install it locally:

```
helm install nginx ./nginx-9.3.1.tgz
```

Discussion

Running Kubernetes and empowering DevOps in air-gapped environments requires careful planning and setup, particularly for handling dependencies like container images, updates, and communication between tools. DevOps teams need to manage **air-gapped container registries**, mirror necessary dependencies, and configure **Kubernetes clusters** to operate without direct access to external repositories. Key strategies include

- **Creating and Managing Air-Gapped Container Registries**: Use local registries to store and serve container images within the isolated environment.

- **Handling Kubernetes Updates and Dependencies**: Use offline installation tools and mirroring techniques to ensure clusters remain up to date.
- **Dealing with Common Issues**: Be prepared for challenges such as dependency mismatches, certificate management, and limited observability.

Operating DevOps in an air-gapped environment introduces challenges, but with proper planning and tooling, Kubernetes and CI/CD pipelines can function effectively. Key considerations include

- **Image Management**: Without direct access to public registries, managing container images becomes critical. Setting up a reliable local registry, such as Harbor or Docker Registry, is essential for storing and serving images.
- **Offline Kubernetes Installation**: Keeping the Kubernetes cluster updated without Internet access requires mirroring all necessary components, including the control plane and other key dependencies.
- **Handling Common Issues**: In air-gapped environments, common issues include mismatches between software versions (especially when transferring images or packages), managing certificates for internal registries, and troubleshooting without direct Internet access. Careful synchronization of dependencies is critical to avoid disruptions.

Solutions like **Rancher**, **Tanzu**, or **OpenShift** offer additional tooling for managing Kubernetes clusters in air-gapped environments, providing streamlined ways to keep air-gapped environments secure and functional.

See Also

- **Harbor Registry**: A cloud-native registry that secures images with role-based access control, vulnerability scanning, and content signing.
- **Kubernetes Air-Gapped Installation**: Documentation and best practices for setting up air-gapped Kubernetes environments.
- **Mirroring Helm Charts**: Learn how to mirror Helm charts and manage them in an offline environment.
- **Rancher for Air-Gapped Clusters**: A Kubernetes management platform designed for air-gapped environments, including automated image synchronization.

Summary

Kubernetes offers a growing ecosystem of tools for modern workloads, from **serverless computing** with FaaS solutions to the **fine-grained control** of eBPF-powered networking with Cilium. This chapter illustrates how Kubernetes can be adapted to various specialized use cases. We've also seen how **Kubernetes empowers AI/ML** operations by providing scalable, resource-efficient platforms for complex workflows and how lightweight environments like **WebAssembly** can extend Kubernetes' reach-to-edge and IoT use cases.

Beyond workload-specific innovations, **extending Kubernetes** through CRDs and API extensions, as well as managing operations in air-gapped environments, highlights the flexibility and robustness of the Kubernetes platform in constrained or isolated scenarios.

Integrations with CI/CD tools like **Jenkins** and platforms like **VMware Tanzu** further streamline the development and deployment process, enabling organizations to innovate quickly and efficiently in cloud-native environments.

By embracing these emerging and advanced concepts, teams can future-proof their Kubernetes infrastructure, ensuring it meets the demands of evolving workloads while maintaining control over networking, security, and scalability.

CHAPTER 13

Best Practices in Kubernetes

This chapter is dedicated to providing a comprehensive guide on best practices in Kubernetes. The goal is to equip readers with proven methodologies for optimizing Kubernetes environments, ensuring containerized workloads' security, scalability, efficiency, and maintainability. In the dynamic realm of cloud-native computing, Kubernetes stands as a pivotal tool for orchestrating containerized applications. Understanding and implementing best practices becomes crucial as organizations increasingly adopt Kubernetes to manage their workloads. This chapter is dedicated to guiding you through proven methodologies that enhance the security, scalability, efficiency, and maintainability of your Kubernetes environments.

By embracing these best practices, you ensure your applications are robust, resilient, and optimized for performance and resource utilization. The reasoning behind each practice is rooted in real-world challenges and solutions that have been tested and validated in diverse operational contexts.

G. Stencel and L. Berton, *Kubernetes Recipes*,
https://doi.org/10.1007/979-8-8688-1325-2_13

13.1 Using Declarative Configuration

Adopting a declarative approach to configuration allows for consistent and repeatable deployments. It enables version control and easier auditing of changes, promoting transparency and collaboration within teams.

Problem

As Kubernetes environments scale and evolve, managing resources through imperative commands (e.g., kubectl create, kubectl apply) can lead to inconsistencies, operational complexity, and errors. Teams using imperative commands often face challenges like configuration drift, where different environments (development, staging, production) are not in sync, leading to unpredictable deployments. Additionally, manual configuration management increases the risk of human error and makes it difficult to track changes or revert to previous states when necessary. The lack of a repeatable, automated process also slows down delivery pipelines and makes scaling more difficult.

Solution

Declarative configuration offers a solution by allowing users to define the desired state of Kubernetes resources (e.g., pods, services, deployments) in a configuration file (usually YAML or JSON). Kubernetes continuously reconciles the current state with the desired state, ensuring consistency across environments and reducing the need for manual intervention.

By storing configuration files in a version control system (like Git), teams can easily benefit from versioning, auditing, and rolling back changes. Tools like GitOps, which automate the process of synchronizing the desired state with the cluster, can further enhance reliability and scalability.

Example:

Imperative Approach (Problem):

Imperatively creating a deployment

```
kubectl run nginx --image=nginx --replicas=3
```

In this scenario, if the deployment needs to be replicated in another environment, it must be recreated manually using the same command. Any modification to this deployment requires additional manual intervention, increasing the risk of misconfiguration across environments.

Declarative Approach (Solution):

Here's a declarative configuration file (nginx-deployment.yaml):

```
apiVersion: apps/v1
kind: Deployment
metadata:
  name: nginx-deployment
spec:
  replicas: 3
  selector:
    matchLabels:
      app: nginx
  template:
    metadata:
      labels:
        app: nginx
    spec:
      containers:
      - name: nginx
        image: nginx:1.14.2
        ports:
        - containerPort: 80
```

Apply the configuration:

```
kubectl apply -f nginx-deployment.yaml
```

```
greg@gregPowerPC:~/13.1$ sudo kubectl apply -f nginx-deployment.yaml
deployment.apps/nginx-deployment created
greg@gregPowerPC:~/13.1$ sudo kubectl get pods
NAME                                READY   STATUS    RESTARTS   AGE
nginx-deployment-d556bf558-7kf69    1/1     Running   0          8s
nginx-deployment-d556bf558-j8tp5    1/1     Running   0          8s
nginx-deployment-d556bf558-l74k9    1/1     Running   0          8s
greg@gregPowerPC:~/13.1$
```

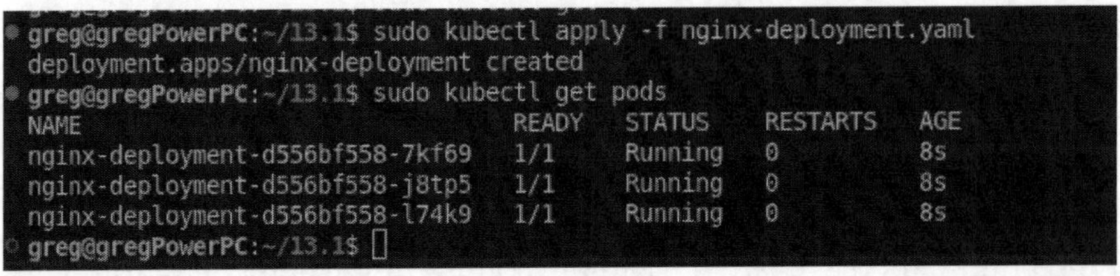

Figure 13-1. *Applying the Nginx deployment and listing pods created from it*

This file defines the desired state of the Nginx deployment. Kubernetes will ensure the system matches the defined state (here, three replicas), scaling and updating resources as necessary.

Benefits:

> **Consistency**: The same file can be used across different environments (development, staging, production), ensuring that the configuration is uniform and reducing the chances of drift.
>
> **Version Control**: The configuration file can be committed to Git, allowing teams to track changes, roll back to previous versions, and maintain an audit trail.
>
> **Automation**: By leveraging tools like GitOps, the process of applying configurations can be automated, improving delivery speed and reducing the need for manual intervention.

For example, with GitOps, a change to the nginx-deployment.yaml file (e.g., updating the number of replicas) can be automatically applied to the Kubernetes cluster by simply committing the updated file to the Git repository:

```
spec:
  replicas: 5  # Updated from 3 to 5
```

By making this change in the configuration file and committing it, GitOps tools like Flux or Argo CD will detect the change and automatically reconcile the cluster to match the desired state (five replicas instead of three).

Outcome

Using declarative configuration in Kubernetes provides a structured, automated, and consistent way to manage resources. By adopting this practice and combining it with version control and GitOps tools, organizations can significantly reduce configuration errors, improve operational efficiency, and ensure a scalable and resilient infrastructure.

13.2 Use Namespaces to Organize Resources

Organizing resources using namespaces enhances manageability and provides logical separation within the cluster. This practice is essential for multi-team environments and supports resource isolation and quota management.

Problem

As Kubernetes clusters grow in size and complexity, managing resources across multiple teams, applications, or environments becomes increasingly challenging. Without proper organization, all resources (pods, services, secrets, etc.) are created in the default namespace, leading to cluttered environments, lack of isolation, and the risk of resource name collisions. Additionally, sharing a common resource pool makes it difficult to enforce resource quotas, access control, and security policies, potentially resulting in conflicts or performance degradation.

The lack of logical separation between different teams, environments (e.g., development, testing, production), or applications can lead to accidental modifications, security vulnerabilities, and difficulties in scaling or maintaining the cluster.

Solution

Implementing Namespaces to Organize Resources

Kubernetes namespaces provide a powerful way to logically separate and organize resources within a cluster. By using namespaces, teams can group related resources together, isolate them from other resources, and apply fine-grained policies for access control, resource limits, and network policies. This ensures that resources from different teams, applications, or environments remain isolated, secure, and manageable.

Namespaces also facilitate scaling and maintaining large clusters by simplifying resource management, enabling better monitoring, and applying role-based access control (RBAC) at the namespace level.

Example:

Problem (Without Namespaces): In a single cluster, imagine resources for multiple applications and environments are deployed together:

Creating a development and production deployment for two different applications

```
kubectl apply -f dev-app1-deployment.yaml
kubectl apply -f prod-app2-deployment.yaml
```

Here, both applications' deployments are created in the default namespace. If two resources have the same name (e.g., a service called frontend), they could overwrite or conflict with each other. Access control becomes complicated, and there's no easy way to limit resources or apply security policies to individual applications or environments.

Solution (Using Namespaces):

Create Separate Namespaces: You can create separate namespaces for each environment (e.g., development, production) or for each team or application.

Create namespaces for different environments

```
kubectl create namespace dev
kubectl create namespace prod
```

```
greg@gregPowerPC:~/13.1$ sudo kubectl create namespace dev
namespace/dev created
greg@gregPowerPC:~/13.1$ sudo kubectl create namespace prod
namespace/prod created
```

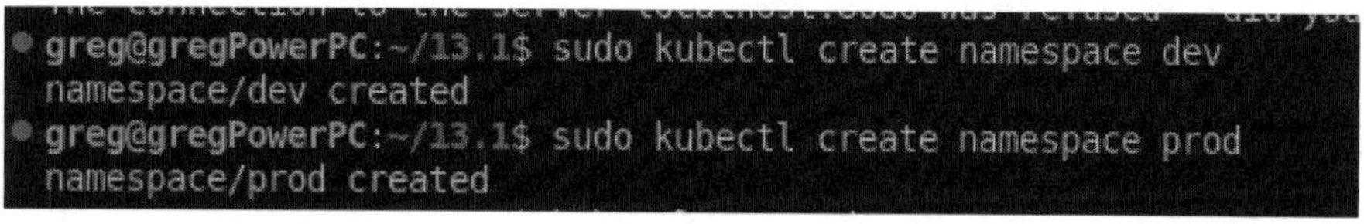

Figure 13-2. *Creating dev and prod namespaces*

Deploy Resources to Specific Namespaces: Specify the namespace in the resource definition or during deployment to keep resources organized.

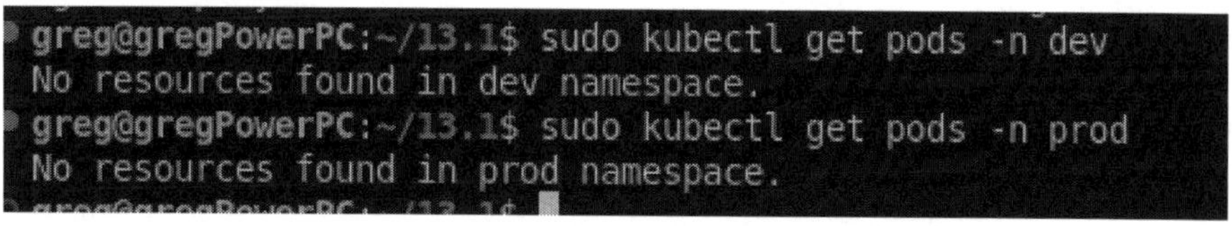

```
greg@gregPowerPC:~/13.1$ sudo kubectl get pods -n dev
No resources found in dev namespace.
greg@gregPowerPC:~/13.1$ sudo kubectl get pods -n prod
No resources found in prod namespace.
```

Figure 13-3. *Getting pods from dev and prod namespaces*

```
# Deploy development resources in the dev namespace
kubectl apply -f dev-app1-deployment.yaml -n dev
```

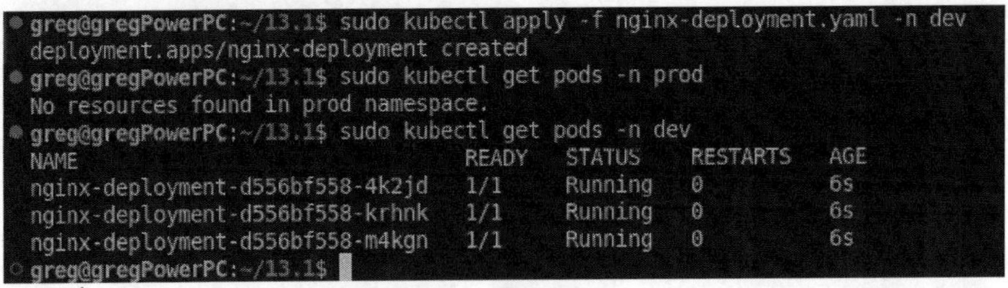

```
greg@gregPowerPC:~/13.1$ sudo kubectl apply -f nginx-deployment.yaml -n dev
deployment.apps/nginx-deployment created
greg@gregPowerPC:~/13.1$ sudo kubectl get pods -n prod
No resources found in prod namespace.
greg@gregPowerPC:~/13.1$ sudo kubectl get pods -n dev
NAME                                READY   STATUS    RESTARTS   AGE
nginx-deployment-d556bf558-4k2jd    1/1     Running   0          6s
nginx-deployment-d556bf558-krhnk    1/1     Running   0          6s
nginx-deployment-d556bf558-m4kgn    1/1     Running   0          6s
greg@gregPowerPC:~/13.1$
```

Figure 13-4. *Applying app1-deployment.yaml to the dev namespace*

```
# Deploy production resources in the prod namespace
kubectl apply -f prod-app2-deployment.yaml -n prod
```

Here's an example of a namespace-specific deployment (dev-app1-deployment.yaml):

```
apiVersion: apps/v1
kind: Deployment
metadata:
  name: app1
  namespace: dev  # Namespace is explicitly defined
spec:
  replicas: 3
  selector:
    matchLabels:
      app: app1
  template:
    metadata:
      labels:
        app: app1
    spec:
      containers:
      - name: app1-container
        image: nginx
```

Resource Quotas and Limits: Namespaces allow you to set resource quotas and limits to control how much CPU, memory, and storage each namespace can use. This ensures that no single team or environment can consume all the cluster's resources.

```
apiVersion: v1
kind: ResourceQuota
metadata:
  name: dev-quota
  namespace: dev
spec:
  hard:
    cpu: "4"
    memory: "16Gi"
```

Access Control with RBAC: Namespaces enable better security by allowing role-based access control (RBAC) policies to be applied at the namespace level. For instance, developers can be given read-only access to the production namespace while having full access to the development namespace.

```
apiVersion: rbac.authorization.k8s.io/v1
kind: Role
metadata:
  namespace: dev
  name: dev-role
rules:
- apiGroups: [""]
  resources: ["pods", "services"]
  verbs: ["get", "list", "create", "delete"]
```

Network Policies for Isolation: Kubernetes namespaces can also be used to apply network policies, ensuring that services and applications in one namespace cannot communicate with those in another unless explicitly allowed.

Outcome

Isolation: Resources in one namespace are isolated from resources in another, preventing conflicts and ensuring better security.

Organization: Resources are neatly organized based on teams, applications, or environments, reducing operational complexity.

Resource Control: By setting resource quotas and limits per namespace, teams can effectively manage resources and avoid performance issues caused by overconsumption.

Improved Security: RBAC and network policies can be applied at the namespace level to enforce strict access control and security boundaries.

Scalability: Namespaces help scale clusters by logically organizing and managing thousands of resources across large teams or multiple applications.

Namespaces are essential for efficiently managing large Kubernetes clusters. By logically separating resources, teams can enforce resource limits, improve security, and maintain better control over the cluster's organization. This best practice enables scalability, enhances manageability, and helps avoid resource conflicts in complex Kubernetes environments.

13.3 Security Enhancements

Enforcing the principle of least privilege minimizes the attack surface. Implementing network policies and properly managing ConfigMaps and secrets safeguard sensitive data and communications within the cluster.

13.3.1 Enforce the Principle of Least Privilege

Problem

Security is critical in a Kubernetes environment, especially when multiple teams, services, or applications share the same cluster. A common problem arises when users or services are granted excessive privileges beyond what they require to perform their tasks. Overly permissive access can lead to unintended actions, accidental misconfigurations, or even the exploitation of vulnerabilities by malicious actors.

Without enforcing the principle of least privilege, where users, services, and applications have only the minimum required permissions, the risk of security breaches increases. For example, a compromised service with excessive access can potentially control sensitive resources or modify critical components of the cluster, impacting the entire system's security and availability.

Solution

Leveraging role-based access control (RBAC) enables Kubernetes to enforce the principle of least privilege. RBAC enables administrators to define granular permissions and assign them to specific roles, ensuring that users and services only have access to the resources they need.

By creating fine-tuned roles and assigning them to specific users or service accounts, teams can limit the scope of actions each entity can perform, minimizing security risks. RBAC helps create clear boundaries within the cluster, making it difficult for unauthorized users or services to access or modify sensitive resources.

1. **Create a Namespace**

   To isolate resources and ensure scoped access:

   ```
   apiVersion: v1
   kind: Namespace
   metadata:
     name: my-namespace
   ```

2. **Define a Role**

   This role allows only read access to pods in a specific namespace:

   ```
   apiVersion: rbac.authorization.k8s.io/v1
   kind: Role
   metadata:
     namespace: my-namespace
     name: pod-reader
   rules:
     - apiGroups: [""]
       resources: ["pods"]
       verbs: ["get", "list", "watch"]
   ```

3. **Create a Service Account**

   A dedicated service account for an application or team:

   ```
   apiVersion: v1
   kind: ServiceAccount
   metadata:
   ```

```
  name: app-service-account
  namespace: my-namespace
```

4. **Bind the Role to the Service Account**

   This binds the pod-reader role to the app-service-account:

```
apiVersion: rbac.authorization.k8s.io/v1
kind: RoleBinding
metadata:
  name: read-pods-binding
  namespace: my-namespace
subjects:
  - kind: ServiceAccount
    name: app-service-account
    namespace: my-namespace
roleRef:
  kind: Role
  name: pod-reader
  apiGroup: rbac.authorization.k8s.io
```

5. **Test with a Pod**

   Deploy a pod using the restricted service account to validate the permissions:

```
apiVersion: v1
kind: Pod
metadata:
  name: test-pod
  namespace: my-namespace
spec:
  serviceAccountName: app-service-account
  containers:
```

```
    - name: nginx
      image: nginx
```

6. **Verify Access**

```
greg@gregPowerPC:~/13.3$ sudo kubectl apply -f 13.3.1/
namespace/my-namespace created
rolebinding.rbac.authorization.k8s.io/read-pods-binding created
role.rbac.authorization.k8s.io/pod-reader created
serviceaccount/app-service-account created
Error from server (Forbidden): error when creating "13.3.1/pod.yaml": pods "test-pod" is forbidden: error looking up servic
e account my-namespace/app-service-account: serviceaccount "app-service-account" not found
greg@gregPowerPC:~/13.3$ sudo kubectl apply -f 13.3.1/
namespace/my-namespace unchanged
pod/test-pod created
rolebinding.rbac.authorization.k8s.io/read-pods-binding unchanged
role.rbac.authorization.k8s.io/pod-reader unchanged
serviceaccount/app-service-account unchanged
```

***Figure 13-5.** Applying the whole folder of the app—showing how sequence matters on the first attempt it fails*

We can see that we need to run the YAMLs in sequence. Role binding to the service account takes time, so there might be a concurrency problem. On the first go, as in the picture above, pod creation failed as binding wasn't finished in time.

After deploying the resources, check again their status.

```
greg@gregPowerPC:~/13.3$ sudo kubectl get pods -n my-namespace
NAME       READY   STATUS    RESTARTS   AGE
test-pod   1/1     Running   0          3m50s
```

***Figure 13-6.** Getting pods from my-namespace*

Use the kubectl exec command to access the test-pod.

Remember we need to assume a service account role. We can do it like below by using an image with the kubectl building:

```
apiVersion: v1
kind: Pod
metadata:
  name: kubectl-pod
  namespace: my-namespace
```

```
spec:
  serviceAccountName: app-service-account
  containers:
    - name: kubectl
      image: bitnami/kubectl:latest
      command:
        - sleep
        - "3600"
```

Create a pod with

```
kubectl apply -f checkerpod.yaml
```

Exec into it:

```
kubectl exec -it kubectl-pod -n my-namespace -- /bin/sh
```

7. **Test Permissions**:

   Now that kubectl is configured, lets test the permissions granted to the app-service-account.
   List pods (allowed):

```
kubectl get pods -n my-namespace
```

Delete pods (denied):

```
kubectl delete pod kubectl-pod -n my-namespace
```

Create pods (denied):

```
kubectl run new-pod --image=nginx -n my-namespace
```

Attempt to perform operations like kubectl get pods, kubectl delete pods, or kubectl create pods using the service account.

Lets have a look at the outcome which is as shown in Figure 13-7.

```
I have no name!@kubectl-pod:/$ kubectl get pods -n my-namespace
NAME          READY   STATUS    RESTARTS   AGE
kubectl-pod   1/1     Running   0          71s
test-pod      1/1     Running   0          31m
I have no name!@kubectl-pod:/$ kubectl delete pod kubectl-pod -n my-namespace
Error from server (Forbidden): pods "kubectl-pod" is forbidden: User "system:serviceaccount:my-namespace:app-service-accoun
t" cannot delete resource "pods" in API group "" in the namespace "my-namespace"
I have no name!@kubectl-pod:/$ kubectl run new-pod --image=nginx -n my-namespace
Error from server (Forbidden): pods is forbidden: User "system:serviceaccount:my-namespace:app-service-account" cannot crea
te resource "pods" in API group "" in the namespace "my-namespace"
I have no name!@kubectl-pod:/$
```

Figure 13-7. *Deleting kubectl-pod from my-namespace*

The test-pod should only be able to list and get pod information in the my-namespace.

Any actions outside the scope of verbs ["get", "list", "watch"] (e.g., creating or deleting pods) should be denied.

By following this example, you can effectively limit permissions and enforce the principle of least privilege within your Kubernetes cluster.

Outcome

By enforcing the principle of least privilege through RBAC in Kubernetes, organizations can significantly bolster their security framework, ensure operational stability, and maintain compliance with regulatory standards. This approach not only mitigates the risk of security breaches and accidental misconfigurations but also promotes a structured and scalable permission management system within the Kubernetes ecosystem. Adopting these practices is essential for maintaining a secure, reliable, and efficient Kubernetes environment, especially in scenarios involving multiple teams, services, or applications sharing the same cluster.

13.3.2 Use Network Policies for Security

Problem

By default, Kubernetes allows unrestricted communication between all pods within a cluster, regardless of application, environment, or namespace. This permissive network model introduces significant security risks, especially in multi-tenant environments or when running sensitive applications. A compromised pod can freely communicate with other pods, potentially accessing sensitive data or spreading an attack.

Administrators can only enforce pod-to-pod communication restrictions with proper controls. Otherwise, network paths are insecure, exposing the cluster to breaches, data leaks, and disruptions.

Solution

Kubernetes network policies restrict and control communication between pods. By implementing network policies, administrators can enforce pod-level isolation and define which pods or services are allowed to communicate based on criteria such as namespaces, labels, and ports. This helps reduce unauthorized access and the risk of lateral movement in case of a breach.

Here are key actions for implementing network policies:

Define Ingress and Egress Rules:

Create policies that specify allowed incoming and outgoing traffic for pods. Control traffic based on labels, namespaces, or IP blocks.

Restrict Communication to Trusted Pods:

Limit communication to specific pods that need access. For example, only frontend pods should be able to communicate with backend pods.

Namespace Isolation:

Enforce network boundaries between namespaces to separate environments like development, staging, and production.

Port and Protocol Filtering:

Control traffic based on specific ports or protocols to ensure only authorized services are reachable.

Here are benefits of using network policies:

Enhanced Security:

Control pod communication to enforce least privilege access, reducing the risk of unauthorized access and lateral movement.

Workload Isolation:

Isolate applications and environments to prevent unintended interactions or security breaches.

Granular Control:

Define specific rules using labels, namespaces, ports, and protocols to allow only necessary traffic.

Reduced Attack Surface:

Block unnecessary communication to minimize exposure and limit potential exploits.

Define Ingress and Egress Rules

To effectively secure your Kubernetes cluster, it's essential to define precise ingress and egress rules that control the flow of traffic to and from your pods. Below is an example of a network policy YAML file that demonstrates how to define these rules:

```
apiVersion: networking.k8s.io/v1
kind: NetworkPolicy
metadata:
  name: allow-specific-traffic
```

```
  namespace: your-namespace
spec:
  podSelector:
    matchLabels:
      app: your-app
  policyTypes:
  - Ingress
  - Egress
  ingress:
  - from:
    - namespaceSelector:
        matchLabels:
          name: trusted-namespace
    - podSelector:
        matchLabels:
          role: frontend
    ports:
    - protocol: TCP
      port: 80
    - protocol: TCP
      port: 443
  egress:
  - to:
    - ipBlock:
        cidr: 10.0.0.0/16
        except:
        - 10.0.0.0/24
    ports:
    - protocol: TCP
      port: 53
    - protocol: UDP
```

```
      port: 53
  - to:
    - namespaceSelector:
        matchLabels:
          name: monitoring
    ports:
    - protocol: TCP
      port: 9090
```

Outcome

Implementing network policies is a critical step for securing Kubernetes clusters. By enforcing rules on pod communication, administrators can achieve greater security, containment, and control over network traffic, significantly improving the cluster's security posture.

13.3.3 Utilize ConfigMaps and Secrets

Problem

Kubernetes applications often require external configuration data, such as database connection strings or API keys, to be managed separately from the application code. While Kubernetes secrets are designed to handle such sensitive information, it's important to note that they are only base64 encoded by default and not truly encrypted. To enhance security, enabling encryption at rest within the Kubernetes configuration is essential. Without a structured approach, sensitive data may be hardcoded into manifests or images, leading to

Security Risks: Sensitive data, such as passwords or tokens, may be exposed in plain text.

Lack of Flexibility: Updating configurations requires rebuilding and redeploying applications.

Complex Environment Management: Managing environment-specific configurations (e.g., development, staging, production) becomes error-prone.

By implementing additional encryption measures, organizations can ensure a more comprehensive protection of their sensitive data within Kubernetes environments.

Solution

Kubernetes provides ConfigMaps and secrets to separate configuration from application code:

ConfigMaps: For non-sensitive data such as environment variables and application settings

Secrets: For sensitive data like credentials, API tokens, or certificates, stored securely

Here are key recommendations for using ConfigMaps and secrets:

Secure Sensitive Data with Secrets:c

Store sensitive information in secrets to ensure it is encrypted and restrict access to authorized components only.

Decouple Configuration from Code:

Use ConfigMaps to manage non-sensitive configuration data separately, making updates easy without modifying application code or manifests.

Dynamic Updates:

Applications can read updated configurations dynamically from ConfigMaps and secrets without requiring image rebuilds or redeployment.

Environment-Specific Management:

Create separate ConfigMaps and secrets for different environments to handle unique settings securely and efficiently.

Access Control:

Apply role-based access control (RBAC) to ensure only authorized users or pods can access specific ConfigMaps or secrets.

Here are benefits of using ConfigMaps and secrets:

Improved Security: Ensures sensitive data is not exposed in plain text or embedded in images

Dynamic and Flexible Configuration: Enables runtime configuration updates without redeployment

Environment-Specific Configurations: Simplifies management of settings across different environments

Enhanced Maintainability: Decouples configuration from code, making applications more portable and maintainable

Reduced Risk: Mitigates potential exposure of sensitive information and hardcoded values

Outcome

Leveraging ConfigMaps and secrets in Kubernetes is essential for secure, scalable, and maintainable configuration management. This approach decouples sensitive and non-sensitive data from application code, facilitates dynamic updates, and supports best practices for managing environment-specific configurations. By adopting these tools, teams can enhance application security and flexibility while reducing operational complexity.

13.4 Resource Optimization

Setting resource quotas and limits prevents resource contention and ensures fair usage among applications. Efficient image management reduces overhead and accelerates deployment times.

13.4.1 Use Resource Quotas and Limits

Problem

In a shared Kubernetes cluster, multiple teams and applications compete for CPU, memory, and storage resources. Without proper management, some applications or users can monopolize these resources, potentially leading to performance degradation for other workloads and even causing the cluster to become unstable. The absence of resource controls can also result in inefficient use of cluster resources, where certain applications may consume excessive resources, leaving less for critical applications. In extreme cases, resource contention can cause outages, slowdowns, or application crashes, which is particularly concerning in production environments.

Resource quotas and limits ensure fair distribution and usage of resources across teams, applications, or namespaces. Organizations risk inefficient resource allocation, poor application performance, and reduced cluster stability without them.

Solution

Enforcing Resource Quotas and Limits in Kubernetes

Kubernetes provides two mechanisms to manage resource consumption:

Resource quotas allow administrators to set maximum limits on the amount of CPU, memory, and other resources that a namespace can consume. This ensures teams or applications stay within their fair share of cluster resources.

Resource limits (at the pod or container level) define the maximum and minimum amounts of CPU and memory that a specific container can use. This ensures that individual applications don't overuse resources or starve others.

Implementing resource quotas at the namespace level and resource limits at the container level allows administrators to control resource allocation, prevent resource contention, and maintain cluster stability.

Example:

Problem (Without Resource Quotas and Limits):

Consider a scenario where multiple teams deploy their applications in the same cluster without defined resource quotas or limits. A single application might consume excessive CPU and memory, starving other applications of necessary resources:

```
apiVersion: apps/v1
kind: Deployment
metadata:
  name: resource-hungry-app
spec:
  replicas: 3
  template:
    spec:
```

```
    containers:
    - name: resource-hungry-app-container
      image: heavy-load-app:1.0
```

In this setup

The resource-hungry app has no resource limits, so it can use as much CPU and memory as it wants.

Other applications in the same namespace or cluster could experience degraded performance due to this single application's excessive resource consumption.

Solution (Using Resource Quotas and Limits):

Set Resource Quotas at the Namespace Level: By defining a resource quota, you can limit the total amount of resources that a namespace can consume, for example, limiting the total CPU and memory available to all applications within the dev namespace:

```
apiVersion: v1
kind: ResourceQuota
metadata:
  name: dev-resource-quota
  namespace: dev
spec:
  hard:
    cpu: "8"  # Maximum total CPU that can be consumed by all
    pods in the namespace
    memory: "32Gi"  # Maximum total memory allowed for the
    namespace
    pods: "20"  # Maximum number of pods allowed in the namespace
```

This resource quota ensures that all applications in the dev namespace cannot collectively use more than 8 CPU cores, 32 GB of memory, or run more than 20 pods, preventing resource overuse in that namespace.

Define Resource Limits for Pods: Resource limits at the container level define how much CPU and memory each container is allowed to use, preventing any single application from hogging resources, for example, defining CPU and memory requests and limits for the resource-hungry-app:

```
apiVersion: apps/v1
kind: Deployment
metadata:
  name: resource-hungry-app
  namespace: dev
spec:
  replicas: 3
  template:
    spec:
      containers:
      - name: resource-hungry-app-container
        image: heavy-load-app:1.0
        resources:
          requests:
            memory: "512Mi"  # Minimum memory the container is
            guaranteed
           cpu: "500m"  # Minimum CPU the container is guaranteed
          limits:
            memory: "2Gi"  # Maximum memory the container
            can consume
            cpu: "1"  # Maximum CPU the container can consume
```

In this configuration

Requests: The minimum amount of CPU and memory the container guarantees. For example, the resource-hungry-app-container is guaranteed 500 m (half a core) of CPU and 512 Mi of memory.

Limits: The maximum amount of CPU and memory the container can consume. It cannot use more than one CPU core and 2 Gi of memory during peak usage.

Monitor Resource Usage with kubectl: To monitor resource usage and ensure that the application is adhering to quotas and limits, Kubernetes administrators can use

```
kubectl describe quota dev-resource-quota --namespace=dev
kubectl top pod --namespace=dev
```

This allows you to check whether the resource-hungry app or any other application is approaching or exceeding the allocated resource limits.

Benefits:

Fair Resource Distribution: Resource quotas ensure that resources are evenly distributed across namespaces or teams, preventing one team from monopolizing cluster resources.

Improved Cluster Stability: Resource limits prevent runaway applications from consuming excessive resources, protecting the cluster from becoming unstable or unresponsive.

Predictable Application Performance: By defining resource requests, applications are guaranteed a baseline level of resources, ensuring that critical applications always have enough CPU and memory to function properly.

Cost Control: In environments where resources are billed (e.g., cloud environments), resource quotas and limits help control costs by preventing resource overconsumption.

Example of a Balanced Configuration

Imagine a shared Kubernetes cluster hosting both development and production workloads. You can use resource quotas to ensure that the production namespace gets more resources than the development namespace, but still enforce limits on individual applications.

Production Namespace Quota:

```
apiVersion: v1
kind: ResourceQuota
metadata:
  name: prod-resource-quota
  namespace: prod
spec:
  hard:
    cpu: "16"
    memory: "64Gi"
    pods: "50"
```

Development Namespace Quota:

```
apiVersion: v1
kind: ResourceQuota
metadata:
  name: dev-resource-quota
  namespace: dev
spec:
  hard:
    cpu: "8"
    memory: "32Gi"
    pods: "20"
```

In this setup

The production environment is allocated more resources (16 CPUs, 64 GB of memory, and up to 50 pods) than the development environment (8 CPUs, 32 GB of memory, and 20 pods).

Both environments have resource limits defined for individual applications, ensuring no single app consumes excessive resources.

Outcome

Resource quotas and limits are essential best practices in Kubernetes to ensure efficient and fair resource allocation across teams and applications. By setting these controls, administrators can maintain cluster stability, prevent resource contention, and ensure that critical applications receive the resources they need to perform reliably. This will also prevent excessive consumption by non-critical workloads.

13.4.2 Efficient Image Management

Problem

Container images are fundamental to Kubernetes deployments, but inefficient management can lead to significant performance, security, and resource usage challenges. Common issues include

- **Image Bloat**: Large or unused images consume storage, slowing deployments and increasing costs.
- **Insecure Images**: The use of unscanned or untrusted images introduces vulnerabilities.
- **Slow Deployments**: Large images or remote registry dependencies delay pod startup.
- **Version Control Issues**: Lack of proper tagging leads to inconsistent deployments across environments.

Solution

Efficient image management in Kubernetes focuses on optimizing image size, securing images, maintaining version control, and using caching to accelerate deployments.

Here are key recommendations for efficient image management:

Minimize Image Size:

- Use lightweight base images (e.g., Alpine, Distroless) to reduce unnecessary packages and dependencies.
- Leverage multi-stage builds to separate build and runtime environments, ensuring the final image contains only what's needed for production.

Implement Semantic Versioning:

Avoid using the latest tag, which can cause inconsistencies.

Use explicit, versioned tags (e.g., v1.0.0) to ensure reliable and predictable deployments.

Scan Images for Vulnerabilities:

Use tools like Trivy, Clair, or registry-integrated scanning to identify and address known vulnerabilities.

Ensure only secure and validated images are deployed into the cluster.

Use Private Registries:

Store and manage images in private registries (e.g., Harbor, Amazon ECR, Google Container Registry) for better security and control.

Enable RBAC to restrict image access.

Leverage Image Caching:

Set imagePullPolicy to IfNotPresent to reduce redundant pulls and improve deployment speed.

Utilize local cluster caching to minimize dependency on external registries.

Optimize Resource Usage:

Specify resource limits for containers to ensure efficient memory and CPU utilization.

Remove unused or outdated images from the registry and nodes to conserve storage.

Here are benefits of efficient image management:

Faster Deployments: Smaller, optimized images reduce pull times and speed up pod startup.

Improved Security: Scanning for vulnerabilities and using trusted registries enhances cluster security.

Lower Resource Consumption: Optimized images reduce storage, memory, and bandwidth requirements.

Environment Consistency: Version control ensures predictable development, staging, and production behavior.

Simplified Maintenance: Easier to manage, update, and track images.

Outcome

Efficient image management is critical to Kubernetes operations, ensuring applications are deployed securely, quickly, and with minimal overhead. By adopting best practices, organizations can enhance deployment reliability, improve security, and reduce resource consumption in their clusters. These practices include optimizing image sizes, scanning for vulnerabilities, versioning, and caching.

13.4.3 Optimize Container Images

Problem

Unoptimized container images can lead to several operational challenges, including

Increased Deployment Times: Larger images take longer to pull from registries, especially in environments with limited network bandwidth.

Excessive Resource Consumption: Bloated images consume more storage and memory, reducing capacity for other workloads.

Security Vulnerabilities: Unnecessary packages and tools increase the attack surface.

Difficult Maintenance: Managing large images complicates updates, troubleshooting, and CI/CD pipelines.

Solution

Optimizing container images involves reducing image size, removing unnecessary dependencies, and ensuring only essential components are included. This approach enhances deployment speed, resource efficiency, security, and maintainability.

Here are key recommendations for optimizing container images:

Use Lightweight Base Images:

To reduce unnecessary libraries and tools, replace large base images (e.g., Ubuntu) with minimal ones like Alpine or Distroless.

Leverage Multi-stage Builds:

Use a build stage for compiling and a separate runtime stage to create a minimal final image.

Keep build tools and dependencies out of the final runtime image.

Remove Unnecessary Files and Layers:

Use a .dockerignore file to exclude files like logs, local configurations, and source control metadata.

Consolidate commands in the Dockerfile to reduce the number of layers and clean up temporary files.

Optimize Dependencies:

Install only production dependencies to exclude unnecessary development tools and libraries.

Use package managers effectively to minimize installed packages.

Order Instructions for Caching:

Place frequently changing instructions (e.g., application code) in the Dockerfile to leverage Docker's layer caching and speed up rebuilds.

Scan for Vulnerabilities:

Image scanning tools like Trivy or Clair can be used to identify and mitigate security vulnerabilities in image layers.

Here are benefits of optimized images:

Faster Deployments: Smaller images pull and deploy faster, improving application startup and scaling times.

Reduced Resource Usage: Optimized images consume less storage and runtime memory, freeing up resources for other workloads.

Enhanced Security: Fewer tools and dependencies reduce the attack surface, making containers less vulnerable.

Easier Maintenance: Simpler, smaller images streamline updates, troubleshooting, and integration into CI/CD pipelines.

Outcome

Optimizing container images is essential for efficient Kubernetes operations. Organizations can enhance performance, reduce resource consumption, and improve security by adopting lightweight base images, multi-stage builds, dependency minimization, and vulnerability scanning. This approach ensures applications are lean, fast, and secure, resulting in a more efficient and manageable Kubernetes ecosystem.

13.5 Operational Excellence

Implementing health checks allows for automatic detection and remediation of failed containers. Regular updates, patches, and audits keep the system secure and compliant with the latest standards.

13.5.1 Implement Health Checks

Problem

In Kubernetes, maintaining the health and availability of applications is critical for reliability.

Solution

Kubernetes provides liveness probes and readiness probes to monitor and manage application health:

> **Liveness Probes**: Detect if an application is running. If the probe fails, Kubernetes restarts the pod to recover from issues like crashes or deadlocks.
>
> **Readiness Probes**: Check if an application is ready to serve traffic. If the probe fails, Kubernetes stops routing traffic to the pod until it becomes ready.

By configuring both probes, Kubernetes can detect failures, redirect traffic, and restart or replace unhealthy pods, ensuring high availability and reliability.

Here are key recommendations for health checks:

Implement Liveness Probes:

Use liveness probes to detect application failures and restart pods automatically.

Common options include HTTP checks, TCP socket checks, or running a command inside the container.

Configure Readiness Probes:

Use readiness probes to ensure only ready pods receive traffic.

Prevent routing traffic to pods that are initializing or recovering from a failure.

Use Delays and Periodicity:

Set appropriate initialDelaySeconds to give applications time to initialize before probes start.

Adjust periodSeconds to balance responsiveness and resource usage.

Match Probes to Application Needs:

Use HTTP probes for web applications to check specific endpoints (e.g., /healthz or /ready).

Use TCP or Exec probes for non-HTTP workloads, such as checking open ports or running diagnostic commands.

Combine Liveness and Readiness Probes:

Liveness probes ensure the application is running correctly, restarting pods when necessary.

Readiness probes ensure that only fully initialized and healthy pods serve traffic.

Here are benefits of health checks:

Improved Availability: Liveness probes enable automatic recovery, reducing downtime caused by crashes or deadlocks.

Prevent Unnecessary Traffic: Readiness probes prevent traffic from being routed to unready pods, avoiding errors during startup or recovery.

Reduced Manual Intervention: Automatic detection and recovery eliminate the need for frequent manual fixes.

Enhanced Cluster Stability: Probes help Kubernetes proactively manage unhealthy pods, ensuring a resilient cluster.

Outcome

Implementing health checks using liveness and readiness probes is a Kubernetes best practice for operational excellence. These probes allow Kubernetes to automatically detect and recover from failures, route traffic only to healthy pods, and restart or replace unhealthy pods, ensuring application stability and high availability in the cluster.

13.5.2 Regularly Update and Patch

Problem

Neglecting regular updates and patching in a Kubernetes environment introduces several risks:

Security Vulnerabilities: Outdated images or components expose the cluster to attacks like privilege escalation, data breaches, and DoS attacks.

Compatibility Issues: Old components may conflict with newer versions, leading to performance degradation or failures.

Missed Improvements: Delayed updates mean missing critical bug fixes, performance enhancements, and new features.

Operational Challenges: Large-scale updates applied infrequently are complex, risk-prone, and disruptive compared with incremental updates.

Organizations risk reduced performance, increased downtime, and compromised security without a strategy for updates and patches.

Solution

A comprehensive update and patching process ensures that Kubernetes clusters remain secure, stable, and efficient. This involves regularly updating container images, Kubernetes versions, and cluster components while automating where possible to reduce manual effort.

Here are key recommendations for updates and patches:

Automate Image Updates:

Use CI/CD pipelines to regularly build, scan, and push updated container images.

Incorporate vulnerability scanning tools (e.g., Trivy, Clair) to detect and fix issues before deployment.

Automatically rebuild images when vulnerabilities are detected to keep applications secure.

Use Rolling Updates for Applications:

Deploy new versions gradually using Kubernetes rolling updates to ensure zero downtime.

Allow Kubernetes to manage the replacement of old pods with updated ones, maintaining availability.

Regularly Upgrade Kubernetes Versions:

Stay current with Kubernetes releases to benefit from security patches, performance enhancements, and new features.

Plan upgrades systematically, testing compatibility with cluster components, network plugins, and storage drivers.

Monitor for Security Patches:

Keep track of Kubernetes Security Announcements, container registry notifications, and cloud provider bulletins.

Automate kernel patch applications and node reboots using tools like kured (Kubernetes Reboot Daemon).

Automate Update Processes:

Use tools like Helm or Argo CD to streamline application updates.

Incorporate vulnerability scanning and remediation into CI/CD pipelines to maintain secure container images and deployments.

Here are benefits of regular updates and patching:

Enhanced Security: Applying updates and patches promptly mitigates known vulnerabilities, reducing attack risks.

Improved Stability and Performance: Frequent updates ensure the cluster operates efficiently with the latest features and bug fixes.

Better Compatibility: Keeping components updated prevents issues caused by outdated versions and maintains feature parity.

Operational Efficiency: Automating updates reduces manual intervention, making the process more efficient and error-free.

Outcome

Regularly updating and patching Kubernetes clusters and container images is critical for maintaining a secure, stable, and efficient environment. By automating updates, leveraging rolling updates for zero downtime, and staying on top of security patches, organizations can protect against vulnerabilities, improve cluster performance, and reduce operational complexity. This best practice ensures Kubernetes environments remain resilient, compliant, and prepared for future demands.

13.5.3 Regularly Review and Audit

Problem

Kubernetes' dynamic nature demands continuous monitoring to maintain security, performance, and compliance. Without regular reviews and audits, organizations face several risks:

Security Vulnerabilities: Misconfigurations, such as overly permissive roles or unscanned container images, can expose clusters to attacks.

Configuration Drift: Unmonitored changes result in deviations from the intended state, causing unpredictable behavior and operational complexity.

Compliance Violations: Lack of audits can lead to non-compliance with regulations, resulting in legal and financial consequences.

Reduced Visibility: With audits, tracking changes, identifying affected resources, and detecting unauthorized access become easier.

Failure to implement regular reviews and audits increases operational risks and undermines the reliability of Kubernetes environments.

Solution

Implement a strategy for regular reviews and audits to maintain security, enforce policies, and detect risks early. This involves tracking access, monitoring resource usage, and auditing security configurations using automated tools and processes.

Here are key recommendations for regular reviews and auditing:

Enable Audit Logging:

Use Kubernetes' built-in audit logging to track API requests and changes.

Forward logs to centralized logging systems like ELK, Fluentd, or Splunk for analysis and long-term storage.

Audit Role-Based Access Control (RBAC):

Review RBAC policies periodically to ensure permissions follow the principle of least privilege.

Use tools like rakkess to visualize and audit RBAC roles and bindings.

Perform Regular Security Audits:

Utilize tools like Kube-bench and Kubesec to audit clusters against benchmarks like CIS Kubernetes.

Scan for misconfigurations, such as overly permissive roles or exposed insecure ports.

Monitor Configuration Changes with GitOps:

Use GitOps tools like Flux or Argo CD to track all changes to Kubernetes manifests in a version-controlled Git repository.

Ensure changes are reviewed and approved before applying them to the cluster.

Audit Container Image Security:

Regularly scan container images for vulnerabilities using tools like Trivy or Clair.

Integrate image scanning into CI/CD pipelines to detect and block unscanned or vulnerable images.

Monitor Resource Usage:

Use tools like Prometheus or Kubecost to monitor resource consumption and detect over- or underutilized resources.

Audit quotas and limits to ensure efficient resource allocation.

Schedule Regular Reports and Alerts:

Automate periodic security and resource usage reports using tools like the Kubernetes Dashboard, Lens, or Datadog.

Set alerts for suspicious activities or configuration changes.

Here are benefits of regular reviews and auditing:

Improved Security: Identifies and mitigates risks, such as misconfigurations or excessive permissions, reducing the attack surface

Compliance and Governance: Ensures adherence to regulatory and organizational policies, critical for industries with strict compliance requirements

Enhanced Visibility: Provides insights into cluster activities, access patterns, and configuration changes, enabling better management

Early Issue Detection: Detects problems like configuration drift or unauthorized changes before they escalate into major issues

Outcome

Regular reviews and auditing are essential for secure and efficient Kubernetes operations. Organizations can maintain a safe, compliant, and transparent Kubernetes environment by enabling audit logging, reviewing RBAC policies, conducting security audits, and using GitOps for configuration tracking. Proactively addressing risks and ensuring configurations align with best practices enhances the reliability and efficiency of Kubernetes clusters.

13.6 Scalability and Reliability

Planning for scalability ensures that applications can gracefully handle increased loads. Understanding the differences between stateful and stateless applications aids in designing appropriate scaling strategies. Handling graceful shutdowns prevents data loss and ensures service continuity.

13.6.1 Scalability Planning

Problem

Without proper scalability planning, Kubernetes environments can face issues such as

- **Over-provisioning or Under-provisioning**: Clusters may need more resources or meet demand, leading to increased costs or degraded performance.
- **Inconsistent Performance During Traffic Spikes**: Applications may experience downtime or poor performance during sudden load increases.

Scaling Inefficiency: Improper or absent configuration of scaling features results in suboptimal resource allocation.

Resource Contention: Failure to plan for CPU, memory, storage, and network requirements can degrade overall cluster performance.

A lack of scalability planning undermines Kubernetes' ability to meet fluctuating demand, leading to inefficiencies, higher costs, and potential service outages.

Solution

Effective scalability planning ensures that Kubernetes clusters can efficiently handle current and future demands. This involves configuring autoscaling mechanisms, monitoring performance, and designing workloads for high availability.

Here are key recommendations for scalability planning:

Horizontal Pod Autoscaling (HPA):

Use HPA to automatically adjust the number of pod replicas based on real-time metrics (e.g., CPU, memory, or custom metrics).

Configure appropriate thresholds to ensure applications scale during traffic spikes and scale down during low-demand periods.

Vertical Pod Autoscaling (VPA):

Implement VPA to dynamically adjust resource requests and limits for pods based on their actual usage.

Prevent resource over- or under-allocation by allowing Kubernetes to optimize CPU and memory allocation automatically.

Cluster Autoscaling:

Enable cluster autoscalers to dynamically add or remove nodes based on workload demands.

Configure minimum and maximum node limits to balance resource availability and cost efficiency.

Define Resource Requests and Limits:

Clearly define CPU and memory requests and limits for each pod to ensure predictable scheduling and prevent resource contention.

Avoid over-allocating resources, which can lead to inefficiencies and higher costs.

Load Testing and Performance Monitoring:

Regularly perform load testing with tools like k6 or Locust to simulate varying traffic conditions.

Monitoring tools like Prometheus and Grafana can track resource utilization, pod availability, and scaling behavior metrics.

Design for High Availability:

Distribute replicas across multiple nodes and availability zones to avoid single points of failure.

Use multi-zone deployments to ensure resilience against node or zone failures.

Here are benefits of scalability planning:

Automatic Resource Management: Autoscaling ensures workloads dynamically receive the resources they need without manual intervention.

Cost Optimization: By scaling down during low demand, clusters minimize unnecessary resource consumption and reduce costs.

Improved Performance: Applications maintain responsiveness during traffic spikes, avoiding downtime or degraded user experiences.

Resilience and Fault Tolerance: Distributing workloads across nodes and zones reduces the risk of service disruptions.

Outcome

Scalability planning is vital to building resilient, efficient, and high-performing Kubernetes environments. By leveraging Kubernetes autoscaling features (HPA, VPA, cluster autoscalers), defining resource requests and limits, and continuously monitoring performance, organizations can ensure their systems are prepared for fluctuating workloads while optimizing costs and maintaining high availability.

13.6.2 Stateful and Stateless Applications

Problem

Kubernetes supports both stateful and stateless applications, but their differing requirements necessitate distinct management strategies. Lack of proper differentiation can lead to:

Mismanagement of Stateful Applications: Improper handling of data persistence, consistency, or failover strategies can lead to data loss and service disruptions.

Overcomplicating Stateless Applications: Unnecessary complexity in managing stateless applications can result in inefficient resource usage and scaling difficulties.

Inefficient Resource Allocation: Treating both application types identically leads to suboptimal performance, especially during scaling or recovery operations.

It is essential to address these differences to maintain performance, reduce operational complexity, and increase resource efficiency.

Solution

Effectively managing stateful and stateless applications requires leveraging Kubernetes-specific tools and configurations tailored to each type.

Here are key recommendations for stateless applications:

Use Deployments:

Stateless applications are managed using Kubernetes deployments, allowing for easy horizontal scaling without the need for persistent storage.

Deployments ensure a specified number of replicas are always running and can be scaled dynamically.

Enable Horizontal Pod Autoscaling (HPA):

Use HPA to automatically adjust the number of pod replicas based on real-time metrics (e.g., CPU or memory usage).

Configure minimum and maximum replica limits to balance resource efficiency and traffic handling.

Leverage External Storage for Data Needs:

Stateless applications that require data storage should rely on external systems like cloud storage or databases. This ensures that the application remains stateless while external services handle persistence.

Here are key recommendations for stateful applications:

Use StatefulSets for Stateful Workloads:

StatefulSets ensure stable network identities and persistent storage for each pod, critical for stateful applications like databases or distributed file systems.

Each pod in a StatefulSet maintains a unique identity and persistent volume across restarts.

Configure Persistent Volumes (PVs) and Persistent Volume Claims (PVCs):

Use PVCs to request storage resources, ensuring data is retained even if pods are rescheduled or deleted.

Define appropriate storage classes to match the application's storage requirements.

Scale Carefully with StatefulSets:

Scaling stateful applications involves provisioning storage for each new replica and ensuring application logic handles distributed state management.

Use Headless Services for Stable Network Identities:

Headless services provide stable DNS names for each pod in a StatefulSet, facilitating communication between stateful components.

Design for Data Persistence and Consistency:

Ensure that stateful applications are configured for redundancy and failover to maintain data integrity during disruptions.

Benefits of managing stateful and stateless applications appropriately include

Efficient Resource Management: Stateless applications benefit from rapid horizontal scaling, while stateful applications maintain consistency and availability during scaling operations.

High Availability: Stateless applications can handle sudden traffic spikes, while stateful applications maintain redundancy and data integrity.

Data Reliability: StatefulSets and PVs ensure data persistence across pod restarts, preserving the application state.

Scalability Optimization: Stateless applications leverage HPA for efficient scaling, while stateful applications use tailored configurations to scale safely.

Outcome

Understanding the differences between stateful and stateless applications is essential for effective Kubernetes management. Stateless applications thrive with deployments and HPA for rapid scaling, while stateful applications rely on StatefulSets, PVs, and headless services for data persistence and stable network identities. Properly managing both types ensures Kubernetes clusters remain efficient, resilient, and capable of handling diverse workloads with high availability and performance.

13.6.3 Graceful Shutdown Handling

Problem

When Kubernetes terminates a pod (e.g., during scaling, updates, or node maintenance), abrupt shutdowns can cause

> **Data Loss**: Incomplete operations may result in lost data, particularly for stateful applications.
>
> **Broken Connections**: Active connections may be interrupted, leading to failed requests and degraded user experience.
>
> **Inconsistent States**: Applications or databases might be left in an unstable state.
>
> **Downtime**: Rapid termination of old pods before new pods are ready can cause temporary service disruptions.

With proper graceful shutdown handling, applications may experience stability, efficiency, and better user satisfaction during termination or updates.

Solution

Graceful shutdown handling ensures applications have time to complete tasks, release resources, and close connections during termination. Kubernetes facilitates this process through termination grace periods, preStop hooks, and readiness probes.

Here are key recommendations for graceful shutdown handling:

Handle SIGTERM in the Application:

Applications should listen for the SIGTERM signal sent by Kubernetes during termination.

Implement logic to complete ongoing tasks and close active connections before shutting down.

Example (Node.js):

```
const server = app.listen(8080, () => console.
log('Server running on port 8080'));

process.on('SIGTERM', () => {
    console.log('SIGTERM received, shutting down
    gracefully');
    server.close(() => {
        console.log('All connections closed, exiting');
        process.exit(0);
    });
});
```

Set a Termination Grace Period:

The pod specification uses terminationGracePeriodSeconds to allow the application enough time to shut down gracefully before being forcibly terminated.

Example:

terminationGracePeriodSeconds: 60

Use preStop Hooks for Custom Cleanup:

Add a preStop hook to perform specific actions (e.g., draining connections or releasing resources) before termination.

Example:

```
lifecycle:
  preStop:
    exec:
      command: ["/bin/sh", "-c", "echo 'Draining
      connections'"]
```

Leverage Readiness Probes:

Configure readiness probes to automatically remove terminating pods from service endpoints, ensuring they no longer receive new traffic.

Example:

```
readinessProbe:
  httpGet:
    path: /ready
    port: 8080
  initialDelaySeconds: 5
  periodSeconds: 10
```

Here are benefits of graceful shutdown:

Prevents Data Loss: Ensures applications complete tasks and save data before shutting down.

Minimizes Downtime: Reduces failed requests by gracefully transitioning traffic away from terminating pods.

Improves User Experience: Handles active connections smoothly, minimizing disruptions.

Efficient Resource Management: Maintains consistent and predictable resource states during termination.

Outcome

Implementing graceful shutdown handling is critical to maintaining stable and efficient Kubernetes environments. Organizations can ensure smooth and reliable shutdowns by designing applications to handle SIGTERM signals, configuring termination grace periods, using preStop hooks for custom cleanup, and leveraging readiness probes to manage traffic. This enhances system stability, protects data integrity, and improves user experience during updates or scaling operations.

13.7 Advanced Management Tools

Leveraging Helm for package management simplifies application deployment and management. Utilizing service meshes enhances observability, security, and traffic management between services. Implementing continuous integration and deployment pipelines streamlines the development lifecycle.

13.7.1 Leverage Helm for Package Management

Problem

Managing applications in Kubernetes can become complex as environments grow, with multiple microservices, custom configurations, and dependencies to handle. Without a standardized and efficient way to manage deployments, several issues may arise:

Complex Configuration Management: As applications scale, maintaining multiple Kubernetes manifests (YAML files) for different environments (e.g., development, staging, production) becomes cumbersome and error-prone.

Inconsistent Deployments: Deploying the same application across different clusters or environments without automation can lead to consistency, version mismatches, and misconfigurations.

Manual Updates: Without a package manager, updating or rolling back applications can require manual intervention, increasing the risk of errors and downtime.

Reusability Challenges: With a templating system, creating reusable and shareable components for Kubernetes deployments, such as databases, monitoring tools, or custom applications, is more effortless.

To address these challenges, Kubernetes administrators and developers need an efficient way to package, deploy, update, and manage applications consistently across environments.

Solution

Leveraging Helm for Package Management in Kubernetes

Helm is a Kubernetes package manager that simplifies application deployment and management. It streamlines application deployment, version control, and configuration management using Helm charts and reusable application templates.

Helm charts package all the necessary Kubernetes resources (deployments, services, config maps, secrets, etc.) into a single chart, making it easy to deploy, update, and manage applications across different environments.

Key features of Helm include

- **Charts**: A Helm chart is a package of pre-configured Kubernetes resources that can be deployed as a unit.
- **Values Files**: Helm allows users to define environment-specific configurations using values.yaml files simplify managing different environments (e.g., development, staging, production).
- **Version Control**: Helm supports versioned charts, making tracking and managing application versions easy.
- **Rollback**: Helm enables quick rollbacks to previous versions of an application, simplifying recovery from failed updates.

Example:

Problem (Without Helm):

In a traditional Kubernetes setup, deploying a microservice might require managing multiple YAML files:

Deployment YAML

Service YAML

ConfigMap YAML

Secret YAML

PersistentVolumeClaim YAML

For example, deploying a web application and database might require the following resources:

```
# Web App Deployment
apiVersion: apps/v1
kind: Deployment
metadata:
  name: web-app
spec:
  replicas: 3
  template:
    spec:
      containers:
      - name: web-app
        image: web-app:latest
        ports:
        - containerPort: 80
# Web App Service
apiVersion: v1
kind: Service
metadata:
  name: web-app-service
spec:
  type: ClusterIP
  selector:
```

```
    app: web-app
  ports:
  - protocol: TCP
    port: 80
    targetPort: 80

# Database Deployment
apiVersion: apps/v1
kind: Deployment
metadata:
  name: database
spec:
  replicas: 1
  template:
    spec:
      containers:
      - name: postgres
        image: postgres:latest
        env:
        - name: POSTGRES_USER
          value: "admin"
        - name: POSTGRES_PASSWORD
          value: "password"
```

Deploying and managing multiple YAML files for every environment increases complexity and the likelihood of configuration drift. Updating these resources requires manual updates across files, increasing the risk of mistakes and inconsistencies.

Solution (Using Helm to Simplify Deployment):

With Helm, you can bundle all these Kubernetes resources into a single Helm chart, simplifying deployment, versioning, and environment management.

Create a Helm Chart: Start by creating a Helm chart for the web application and database:

```
helm create my-app
```

This generates a basic chart structure:

```
my-app/
├── Chart.yaml            # Chart metadata (version, name, etc.)
├── values.yaml           # Default values for configuration
├── templates/            # Template YAML files for Kubernetes
                            resources
└── charts/               # Dependencies (optional)
```

Template the Kubernetes Resources: Instead of manually creating multiple YAML files, you can define templates in the templates/ directory. For example, the web app deployment can be defined as a templated YAML file (templates/deployment.yaml):

```
apiVersion: apps/v1
kind: Deployment
metadata:
  name: {{ .Release.Name }}-web-app
spec:
  replicas: {{ .Values.webApp.replicaCount }}
  selector:
    matchLabels:
      app: {{ .Release.Name }}-web-app
  template:
    metadata:
      labels:
        app: {{ .Release.Name }}-web-app
    spec:
      containers:
```

```
      - name: web-app
        image: "{{ .Values.webApp.image.repository }}:{{
        .Values.webApp.image.tag }}"
        ports:
        - containerPort: 80
```

The values.yaml file provides configurable parameters for the deployment:

```
webApp:
  replicaCount: 3
  image:
    repository: web-app
    tag: latest
```

By using templates and values, the same Helm chart can be reused across different environments with custom configurations.

Deploy the Application with Helm: Use Helm to deploy the application in a Kubernetes cluster:

```
helm install my-app ./my-app
```

This command

Deploys the chart as a release named my-app.

Creates all the necessary Kubernetes resources (deployments, services, config maps) based on the templates and values defined in the chart.

Customize for Different Environments: You can create environment-specific values files (e.g., values-production.yaml) to customize deployments for production environments:

```
webApp:
  replicaCount: 5
  image:
    repository: web-app
    tag: stable
```

Deploy with specific values for production:

```
helm install my-app-production ./my-app -f values-
production.yaml
```

Upgrade and Roll Back: Helm simplifies updates and rollbacks. To upgrade the app:

```
helm upgrade my-app ./my-app -f values.yaml
```

To roll back to the previous version:

```
helm rollback my-app 1
```

Benefits:

Simplified Deployment and Management: Helm packages complex Kubernetes resources into reusable charts, making deployments easier and more consistent.

Version Control and Rollbacks: Helm allows easy management of application versions and quick rollback capabilities in case of failed updates.

Environment-Specific Configurations: Using values files, Helm makes it easy to customize deployments for different environments (e.g., dev, staging, production) without duplicating YAML files.

Reusable Components: Helm charts can be shared and reused across projects and teams, reducing redundancy and simplifying complex deployments.

Automated Updates: Helm makes it easy to upgrade applications with minimal manual intervention, ensuring consistency and reducing the risk of errors.

Example of a Complete Helm Workflow

Create the Helm chart:

```
helm create my-app
```

Define template resources (e.g., deployment.yaml):

```
apiVersion: apps/v1
kind: Deployment
metadata:
  name: {{ .Release.Name }}-web-app
spec:
  replicas: {{ .Values.webApp.replicaCount }}
  template:
    metadata:
      labels:
        app: {{ .Release.Name }}-web-app
    spec:
      containers:
      - name: web-app
        image: "{{ .Values.webApp.image.repository }}:{{
        .Values.webApp.image.tag }}"
        ports:
        - containerPort: 80
```

Deploy the app with Helm:

```
helm install my-app ./my-app
```

Upgrade the application:

```
helm upgrade my-app ./my-app -f values.yaml
```

Roll back the application:

```
helm rollback my-app 1
```

Outcome

Helm significantly simplifies the management of Kubernetes applications by providing an efficient package management solution. By leveraging Helm charts, organizations can quickly deploy, upgrade, roll back, and manage complex applications across different environments. Helm enables consistency, version control, and easy customization, making Kubernetes deployments more scalable, manageable, and maintainable.

13.7.2 Leverage Service Meshes

Problem

As applications grow in complexity, managing service-to-service communication, security, and observability in Kubernetes becomes challenging. Without a service mesh, teams face

Service Communication Complexity: Manually implementing service discovery, load balancing, retries, and circuit breaking leads to inconsistent and error-prone solutions.

Lack of Observability: Limited visibility into service interactions makes troubleshooting and performance monitoring difficult.

Security Challenges: Ensuring secure communication and implementing access control policies across microservices is complex without a unified framework.

Resilience Issues: Manually handling network failures, retries, and timeouts increases the risk of inconsistent behavior and reduces application reliability.

These challenges make it difficult to manage large-scale, microservices-based architectures effectively.

Solution

Service meshes like Istio, Linkerd, and Consul provide a dedicated infrastructure layer for managing communication, security, and observability across microservices. Service meshes simplify operations and enhance reliability by abstracting these concerns from application code.

Key features of service meshes include

Traffic Management: Advanced routing, load balancing, retries, and circuit breaking

Security: Mutual TLS (mTLS) for encrypted communication, access control, and zero-trust security

Observability: Metrics, logs, and distributed tracing for monitoring and debugging

Resilience: Automatic retries, timeouts, and circuit breaking to improve reliability

Here are key recommendations for using service meshes:

Install and Configure a Service Mesh:

Use tools like Istioctl to install the service mesh and configure its control plane and data plane.

Inject sidecar proxies into application pods to intercept and manage traffic.

Simplify Traffic Management:

Use service mesh features for retries, timeouts, and load balancing to eliminate custom logic in application code.

Define policies using VirtualService resources for consistent traffic management.

Enhance Security with mTLS:

Enable mTLS to encrypt service-to-service communication automatically.

Use access control policies to manage which services can communicate.

Improve Observability:

Integrate with tools like Prometheus, Grafana, and Jaeger for metrics, logging, and distributed tracing.

Leverage sidecar proxies to collect telemetry data without modifying application code.

Ensure Resilience:

Implement automatic retries, circuit breaking, and timeouts using service mesh policies.

Centralize resilience logic in the mesh to ensure consistent behavior across services.

Benefits of service meshes include

Simplified Communication: Traffic management features reduce complexity in application code.

Enhanced Security: Centralized security policies and mTLS ensure encrypted, authenticated communication.

Improved Observability: Built-in telemetry provides deep insights into service interactions.

Increased Resilience: Automatic failure recovery mechanisms improve application reliability.

Operational Consistency: Uniform policies simplify managing complex microservices architectures.

Outcome

Leveraging a service mesh in Kubernetes, such as Istio, simplifies the management of microservice communication, security, and observability. By offloading these concerns to the mesh, developers can focus on business logic, ensuring consistent, secure, and reliable service communication. Service meshes are essential for managing complex Kubernetes environments, enabling scalability, resilience, and operational efficiency.

13.8 Cluster Administration

Taints and tolerations help control pod placement on nodes, improving resource utilization. Addressing multi-tenancy and isolation is vital for shared environments. Regular capacity planning ensures that the cluster can meet current and future demands.

13.8.1 Taints and Toleration

Problem

In Kubernetes, clusters often include nodes with specific hardware or operational roles (e.g., GPU nodes or storage-heavy nodes). Without proper control over pod placement, several issues can arise:

> **Inefficient Resource Utilization**: Non-specialized workloads may occupy resource-intensive nodes (e.g., GPU nodes), leading to wasted resources.
>
> **Overloaded Specialized Nodes**: Critical nodes may be overwhelmed by general-purpose workloads, affecting performance or causing failures.
>
> **Inconsistent Node Availability**: High-priority nodes may be unavailable for essential tasks if occupied by less critical workloads.

With mechanisms like taints and tolerations, Kubernetes can efficiently enforce node-level resource allocation, avoiding resource contention and suboptimal performance.

Solution

Taints and tolerations allow pod scheduling to be controlled, ensuring workloads are matched to nodes with the necessary resources or roles.

> **Taints**: These are applied to nodes to mark them as unsuitable for pods unless the pods tolerate the taint.
>
> **Tolerations**: Added to pods to schedule them on nodes with specific taints.

Key taint effects include

NoSchedule: Prevents pods without the toleration from being scheduled on the node

PreferNoSchedule: Prefers to avoid scheduling pods on the node but allows it if necessary

NoExecute: Evicts existing pods from the node if they lack the required toleration

Here are key recommendations for using taints and tolerations:

Apply Taints to Specialized Nodes:

Mark nodes with taints to reserve them for specific workloads.

For example, taint GPU nodes to restrict scheduling to GPU-specific workloads.

Command example:

```
kubectl taint nodes gpu-node-1 dedicated=gpu:NoSchedule
```

Add Tolerations to Pods:

Include tolerations in pod specifications to allow scheduling on tainted nodes.

For example, machine learning pods can tolerate GPU taints to ensure they are scheduled on GPU nodes.

Example (pod with tolerations):

```
tolerations:
  - key: "dedicated"
    operator: "Equal"
    value: "gpu"
    effect: "NoSchedule"
```

Avoid Taints for General Workloads:

Pods without tolerations will be scheduled on untainted nodes, ensuring specialized nodes are reserved for critical workloads.

Use PreferNoSchedule for Flexibility:

Use PreferNoSchedule for workloads that can run on specific nodes but do not strictly require them.

Command example:

```
kubectl taint nodes storage-node dedicated=storage:Pre
ferNoSchedule
```

Benefits of taints and tolerations include

Efficient Resource Utilization: Ensures workloads requiring specialized resources (e.g., GPUs) are matched to appropriate nodes

Workload Isolation: Allows high-priority or sensitive workloads to run on reserved nodes, avoiding interference from general-purpose tasks

Enhanced Performance: Prevents overloading of critical nodes, ensuring they are available for essential tasks

Consistency Across Clusters: Provides predictable scheduling behavior across different environments

Outcome

Taints and tolerations are essential for managing workload placement in Kubernetes. They enable precise control over resource allocation and node usage. By marking specialized nodes with taints and adding tolerations to pods, Kubernetes administrators can ensure that workloads are scheduled efficiently, enhancing cluster performance, resource utilization, and workload isolation. This approach is critical for managing diverse workloads in complex, multi-tenant Kubernetes environments.

13.8.2 Multi-tenancy and Isolation

Problem

In Kubernetes, running workloads from multiple teams, users, or organizations in a shared cluster requires careful management to avoid

> **Security Risks**: Without proper isolation, tenants may access unauthorized resources, services, or secrets, leading to breaches and data leaks.
>
> **Resource Contention**: A single tenant can monopolize cluster resources, starving other workloads.
>
> **Inconsistent Policies**: Structured isolation is the only way to enforce specific policies (e.g., security controls and resource quotas) for different tenants.
>
> **Operational Complexity**: Managing access, networking, and resources for multiple tenants can become cumbersome without adequate tools and strategies.

These challenges can lead to a disorganized, insecure, and inefficient shared environment.

Solution

Kubernetes offers features such as namespaces, RBAC, network policies, resource quotas, and pod security policies (PSPs) to enable multi-tenancy and ensure proper isolation. These tools provide logical, resource, and security boundaries between tenants in a shared cluster.

Here are key recommendations for multi-tenancy and isolation:

Namespaces for Logical Isolation:

Use namespaces to organize resources for each tenant, ensuring logical separation.

Example:

kubectl create namespace development

kubectl create namespace qa

kubectl create namespace production

Benefits:

Each tenant's workloads, services, and secrets are isolated within their namespace.

Tenants operate independently without interfering with others.

RBAC for Access Control:

Use role-based access control (RBAC) to define roles and restrict access to specific namespaces and resources.

Example:

```
apiVersion: rbac.authorization.k8s.io/v1
kind: Role
metadata:
  namespace: development
  name: dev-role
rules:
- apiGroups: [""]
  resources: ["pods", "services", "secrets"]
  verbs: ["get", "list", "create", "update", "delete"]
```

Benefits:

Tenants can only access their own resources.

Unauthorized access is prevented, ensuring data and resource security.

Network Policies for Communication Control:

Restrict pod-to-pod communication between namespaces to prevent unauthorized access.

Example:

```
apiVersion: networking.k8s.io/v1
kind: NetworkPolicy
metadata:
  name: deny-cross-namespace
  namespace: development
spec:
  podSelector: {}
  policyTypes:
  - Ingress
  - Egress
  ingress:
  - from:
    - namespaceSelector:
        matchLabels:
          name: development
```

Benefits:

Tenant workloads are isolated at the network level.

Sensitive services are protected from unauthorized access by other tenants.

Resource Quotas for Fair Allocation:

Limit CPU, memory, and pod usage per namespace to prevent resource monopolization.

Example:

```
apiVersion: v1
kind: ResourceQuota
metadata:
  name: dev-quota
  namespace: development
spec:
  hard:
    cpu: "5"
    memory: "10Gi"
    pods: "50"
```

Benefits:

Resource quotas ensure fair resource distribution.

Prevents one tenant from overconsuming resources at the expense of others.

Pod Security Policies for Secure Workloads:

Enforce security best practices such as non-root users and restricted privileges.

Example:

```
apiVersion: policy/v1beta1
kind: PodSecurityPolicy
metadata:
  name: restricted
spec:
```

```
  privileged: false
  runAsUser:
    rule: MustRunAsNonRoot
```

Benefits:

Ensures tenant workloads adhere to secure deployment practices

Reduces security risks associated with privileged or misconfigured containers

Benefits of multi-tenancy with isolation include

Security: Logical, resource, and network isolation ensures unauthorized access is prevented.

Resource Efficiency: Quotas ensure fair resource usage, preventing monopolization.

Operational Simplicity: Namespaces and RBAC simplify access control and resource organization.

Compliance: Enforcing network, security, and resource policies meets organizational and regulatory requirements.

Scalability: Enables efficient scaling while maintaining clear boundaries between tenants.

Outcome

Leveraging Kubernetes features such as namespaces, RBAC, network policies, resource quotas, and pod security policies can help you achieve secure and efficient multi-tenancy in a shared cluster. These tools ensure tenants are logically wise and resource wise and network wise isolated, minimizing risks, preventing contention, and simplifying management. Proper multi-tenancy and isolation enable Kubernetes to support diverse teams and workloads reliably and securely.

13.8.3 Regular Capacity Planning

Problem

As applications grow in complexity, Kubernetes clusters must efficiently handle varying workloads while maintaining reliable performance. Without regular capacity planning, organizations may face

Resource Shortages: Insufficient resources during peak demand can cause application crashes, degraded performance, or downtime.

Over-provisioning: Excessive resource allocation for peak loads leads to inefficient utilization and increased costs.

Unexpected Scaling Issues: Inadequate preparation for growth or workload changes results in resource contention and instability.

Lack of Predictability: The inability to anticipate when to scale nodes, add storage, or adjust workloads hinders proactive management.

Effective capacity planning is critical for scaling clusters efficiently and ensuring resource optimization while maintaining cost-effective operations.

Solution

Capacity planning ensures that Kubernetes clusters can meet current and future demands while avoiding resource inefficiencies. This involves monitoring resource usage, forecasting growth, and scaling resources dynamically.

Here are key recommendations for capacity planning:

Define Resource Requests and Limits:

Specify CPU and memory requests and limits for each pod to ensure predictable resource allocation.

Prevent resource contention by limiting excessive resource consumption by individual pods.

Example:

```
resources:
  requests:
    memory: "512Mi"
    cpu: "500m"
  limits:
    memory: "1Gi"
    cpu: "1"
```

Benefits:

Ensures pods have sufficient resources to run effectively

Prevents one workload from monopolizing resources, ensuring fair distribution

Enable Horizontal Pod Autoscaling (HPA):

Scale the number of pod replicas automatically based on real-time metrics such as CPU or memory usage.

Example:

```
apiVersion: autoscaling/v2
kind: HorizontalPodAutoscaler
metadata:
  name: web-app-hpa
spec:
  scaleTargetRef:
    apiVersion: apps/v1
    kind: Deployment
    name: web-app
  minReplicas: 3
  maxReplicas: 10
  metrics:
  - type: Resource
    resource:
      name: cpu
      target:
        type: Utilization
        averageUtilization: 70
```

Benefits:

Dynamically adjusts to traffic changes, ensuring efficient resource use

Scales down during low demand to reduce costs

Leverage Cluster Autoscaling:

Enable cluster autoscaling to dynamically adjust the number of nodes in response to resource needs.

Example (GKE):

```
gcloud container clusters update my-cluster \
    --enable-autoscaling --min-nodes 3 --max-nodes 10 \
    --zone us-central1-a
```

Benefits:

Ensures adequate node capacity during high demand

Reduces node count during low usage, optimizing costs

Monitor Resource Usage with Tools Like Prometheus and Grafana:

Use monitoring tools to track CPU, memory, storage, and network usage.

Set up alerts for critical thresholds to anticipate scaling needs.

Example:

Prometheus: Collects real-time metrics

Grafana: Visualizes trends and sends alerts when resources approach limits

Benefits:

Provides actionable insights into resource utilization

Enables proactive scaling and issue resolution

Conduct Regular Audits and Forecasting:

Periodically analyze historical resource usage to identify trends.

Plan future growth based on workload patterns, feature rollouts, and traffic forecasts.

Steps:

Review metrics quarterly or monthly.

Adjust scaling policies based on projected growth.

Plan node and storage capacity expansions.

Benefits:

Prevents surprises during traffic spikes

Ensures clusters can handle future workloads seamlessly

Benefits of regular capacity planning include

Predictable Performance: Applications receive consistent resource allocations, avoiding degradation during peak loads.

Efficient Scaling: Autoscaling dynamically adjusts resources based on demand, minimizing manual intervention.

Cost Optimization: Right-sizing cluster resources prevents over-provisioning, reducing operational expenses.

Improved Reliability: Proactive monitoring and forecasting ensure clusters remain stable and performant.

Proactive Growth Management: Anticipates scaling needs, ensuring readiness for future demands.

Outcome

Regular capacity planning in Kubernetes ensures that clusters can scale efficiently and handle fluctuating workloads without resource shortages or over-provisioning. Organizations can optimize performance, reduce costs, and maintain high availability by defining resource requests and limits, implementing autoscaling, monitoring usage, and conducting regular audits. Proactive capacity planning enables Kubernetes clusters to grow sustainably while reliably and efficiently meeting application demands.

13.9 Use Labels and Annotations

Problem

As Kubernetes environments scale, managing, organizing, and querying resources can become challenging. Without a structured system, issues like the following arise:

Lack of Resource Organization: Difficulty grouping or filtering resources based on criteria like environment, version, or team.

Inconsistent Metadata Management: Deployment details, build history, and notes must be included, reducing visibility.

Challenges in Multi-tenancy: Keeping track of resources across teams, applications, or environments becomes cumbersome.

Inefficient Monitoring and Automation: Automated workflows and monitoring systems need well-defined labels and metadata.

These challenges make managing Kubernetes clusters less efficient and increase the likelihood of errors in resource management and automation.

Solution

Labels and annotations are key-value pairs that provide a structured way to organize and document Kubernetes resources:

Labels: These are used for selecting, grouping, and filtering resources. They are essential for operations like service discovery, scaling, and monitoring.

Annotations: Add non-identifying metadata to resources for documentation, tracking, or tool integration purposes. Annotations are not used to filter or select resources.

Here are key recommendations for using labels and annotations:

Apply Labels for Resource Organization:

Use labels to categorize resources by environment, version, team, or application attributes.

Ensure consistent naming conventions for labels to simplify filtering and querying.

Example:

```
metadata:
  labels:
    app: web-app
    environment: production
    version: v1.0.0
    team: frontend
```

Benefits:

Simplifies grouping and filtering resources

Enables better organization in multi-tenant and multi-environment clusters

Use Labels in Selectors for Automation:

Use label selectors in services, deployments, and monitoring systems to act on specific resources.

Example:

```
apiVersion: v1
kind: Service
metadata:
  name: web-app-service
spec:
  selector:
    app: web-app
    environment: production
```

Benefits:

Targets specific workloads for traffic routing, scaling, or monitoring

Simplifies automation and ensures precise operations

Add Annotations for Metadata and Documentation:

Use annotations to store details like build information, deployment history, or operational notes.

Example:

```
metadata:
  annotations:
    build-info: "Build 1234"
    deployment-date: "2024-01-15"
    operator-notes: "QA-approved deployment"
```

Benefits:

Improves visibility and traceability

Facilitates debugging and auditing

Enable Efficient Monitoring and Alerts:

Labels can be used to filter resources in monitoring tools like Prometheus or Datadog.

Set up environment- or version-specific alerts based on labels.

Example (Prometheus Alert):

```
alert: HighCPUUsage
expr: sum(rate(container_cpu_usage_seconds_
total{environment="production"}[5m])) > 80
```

Benefits:

Focuses monitoring efforts on critical environments

Simplifies setup for environment-specific alerts

Ensure Consistency in Multi-tenant Clusters:

Tenants or teams use labels to identify resources in shared environments.

Example:

```
metadata:
  labels:
    tenant: team-a
    environment: development
```

Benefits:

Isolates resources by tenant or team

Enhances operational clarity in shared clusters

Benefits of labels and annotations include

Efficient Resource Organization: Group and filter resources logically, improving management in large clusters.

Enhanced Metadata Management: Directly store deployment details and build info and operational notes with resources.

Simplified Automation: Use labels to automate workflows like scaling, updates, and monitoring.

Improved Monitoring and Troubleshooting: Enable precise targeting of resources for monitoring and alerts.

Multi-tenancy Support: Isolate and identify resources across teams and environments in shared clusters.

Outcome

Using labels and annotations in Kubernetes is essential for effectively managing, organizing, and documenting resources. Labels enable efficient grouping, filtering, and automation, while annotations provide valuable metadata for tracking and documentation. They improve resource organization, simplify automation and monitoring, and enhance operational visibility. Adopting a systematic approach to labels and annotations is crucial for effectively managing complex Kubernetes environments and multi-tenant setups.

13.10 Immutable Infrastructure

Problem

As applications grow in complexity, managing infrastructure changes dynamically becomes challenging in Kubernetes. Traditional mutable infrastructure—where components are modified in place—introduces issues such as

> **Configuration Drift**: Manual or untracked changes create inconsistencies between environments over time.
>
> **Debugging Challenges**: Changes made directly to infrastructure make troubleshooting harder, with unclear modification history.
>
> **Rollback Complexity**: Reverting changes in mutable systems is error-prone and may require manual intervention.

Unpredictable Behavior: Residual configurations or dependencies from previous states increase the risk of instability.

Security Risks: Uncontrolled changes leave outdated configurations and software, introducing vulnerabilities.

Immutable infrastructure, where components are replaced instead of modified, mitigates these risks. This approach ensures consistency, simplifies management, and enhances reliability.

Solution

Immutable infrastructure treats components as unchangeable after deployment. Updates are handled by creating and deploying new versions, while outdated components are retired. Kubernetes naturally aligns with this model by emphasizing replacement rather than modification.

Key principles of immutable infrastructure are

Immutable Container Images:

Container images should use versioned, immutable tags to ensure consistency and reproducibility.

Avoid mutable tags like latest, as they may point to different versions over time.

Declarative Configuration:

Use Kubernetes YAML manifests to define the desired state of resources, ensuring consistency and ease of replication.

Store configurations in version control for traceability.

Rolling Updates and Rollbacks:

Use Kubernetes' rolling update mechanism to replace old resources with new ones incrementally, ensuring zero downtime.

Leverage rollback capabilities for quick recovery from failed deployments.

Ephemeral Containers and Persistent Volumes:

Use persistent volumes for storing stateful data. Containers themselves should remain stateless for easy replacement.

Infrastructure as Code (IaC):

Use tools like Terraform or Pulumi to define and manage infrastructure components declaratively, ensuring repeatable and consistent deployments.

Example Scenarios and Configurations

Problem: Mutable Infrastructure Setup

A web application is updated manually or through a mutable container tag (latest), leading to inconsistent behavior:

```
apiVersion: apps/v1
kind: Deployment
metadata:
  name: web-app
spec:
  replicas: 3
  template:
    spec:
```

```
      containers:
      - name: web-app-container
        image: web-app:latest
```

Issues:

The latest tag causes inconsistencies between environments.

Updates rely on manual interventions, increasing risks of drift or residual configurations.

Solution: Immutable Infrastructure

Use Versioned Tags for Immutable Containers: Replace mutable tags with versioned, immutable tags:

```
apiVersion: apps/v1
kind: Deployment
metadata:
  name: web-app
spec:
  replicas: 3
  template:
    spec:
      containers:
      - name: web-app-container
        image: web-app:v1.0.0
```

Benefits:

Ensures consistent application versions across environments.

Updates require new images (e.g., web-app:v1.1.0), avoiding direct modifications.

Declarative Configuration for Infrastructure: Use declarative YAML manifests to define infrastructure:

```
apiVersion: apps/v1
kind: Deployment
metadata:
```

```
  name: web-app
spec:
  replicas: 3
  template:
    spec:
      containers:
      - name: web-app-container
        image: web-app:v1.0.0
```

Benefits:

Configurations are tracked in version control (e.g., Git).

Updating infrastructure is as simple as updating the manifest and reapplying it.

Leverage Rolling Updates for Seamless Deployment: Update applications incrementally using rolling updates:

```
apiVersion: apps/v1
kind: Deployment
metadata:
  name: web-app
spec:
  replicas: 3
  strategy:
    type: RollingUpdate
    rollingUpdate:
      maxUnavailable: 1
      maxSurge: 1
  template:
    spec:
      containers:
      - name: web-app-container
        image: web-app:v1.1.0
```

Benefits:

Gradual replacement of pods ensures minimal downtime.

Automatic rollback is available if the update fails.

Use Persistent Volumes for Stateful Applications: Separate data persistence from application containers:

```
apiVersion: apps/v1
kind: StatefulSet
metadata:
  name: stateful-app
spec:
  replicas: 2
  serviceName: "stateful-app"
  template:
    spec:
      containers:
      - name: app-container
        image: stateful-app:v1.0.0
        volumeMounts:
        - name: data-volume
          mountPath: /data
  volumeClaimTemplates:
  - metadata:
      name: data-volume
    spec:
      accessModes: ["ReadWriteOnce"]
      resources:
        requests:
          storage: 10Gi
```

Benefits:

Persistent volumes ensure data is retained even when containers are replaced.

Stateless containers can be easily updated without affecting stored data.

Use Infrastructure as Code (IaC) for Provisioning: Manage cluster infrastructure declaratively using IaC tools like Terraform:

```
resource "google_container_cluster" "primary" {
  name     = "my-cluster"
  location = "us-central1"

  node_config {
    machine_type = "n1-standard-1"
  }

  initial_node_count = 3
}
```

Benefits:

Consistent, repeatable infrastructure provisioning

Easy rollback and tracking of changes

Benefits of Immutable Infrastructure

Consistency Across Environments:

Eliminates configuration drift by replacing resources instead of modifying them.

Ensures reproducible deployments.

Simplified Rollbacks:

Easily revert to a previous version by redeploying an earlier container image.

Improved Debugging and Visibility:

Clear versioning and declarative configurations make tracking changes straightforward.

Enhanced Security:

Reduces untracked changes, ensuring compliance with best practices.

Avoids residual configurations from previous deployments.

Streamlined Automation:

Works seamlessly with CI/CD pipelines to automate building, testing, and deploying immutable artifacts.

Example Workflow for Immutable Infrastructure

Build and Push Immutable Containers:

```
docker build -t web-app:v1.0.0 .
docker push web-app:v1.0.0
```

Deploy Using Declarative YAML:

```
kubectl apply -f web-app-deployment.yaml
```

Rollout Updates with Rolling Updates: Update web-app:v1.0.0 to web-app:v1.1.0 in the YAML and apply:

```
kubectl apply -f web-app-deployment.yaml
```

Handle Persistent Data with Volumes: Ensure all stateful data is stored in PersistentVolumes.

Provision Infrastructure with IaC: Apply infrastructure changes using Terraform or similar tools.

Outcome

Immutable infrastructure simplifies Kubernetes resource management by ensuring components are replaced rather than modified. You can achieve consistent, reliable, and secure deployments by adopting immutable container images, declarative configurations, and Kubernetes' rolling update mechanisms. This approach minimizes operational complexity, improves scalability, and ensures predictable behavior, making it ideal for modern, dynamic Kubernetes environments.

CHAPTER 14

Additional Kubernetes Resources

In a rapidly changing technology landscape, the Cloud Native Computing Foundation (CNCF) is a guiding light for organizations looking to modernize their application development and deployment methods. The CNCF ecosystem includes powerful tools such as Kubernetes, Prometheus, and Helm, which help businesses tackle governance, scalability, and orchestration challenges across various environments.

This chapter examines how CNCF technologies provide a solid foundation for building resilient, scalable, and secure applications. It also discusses strategies for contributing to cloud-native communities, fostering collaboration, and understanding the business value of CNCF technologies. By exploring these insights, readers will be better equipped to leverage CNCF's full potential, whether they are adopters or contributors in this dynamic landscape.

14.1 The Cloud Native Computing Foundation

Problem

Organizations utilizing cloud-native technologies frequently face challenges related to governance, orchestration, and scalability within diverse infrastructure and software stacks. The Cloud Native Computing

G. Stencel and L. Berton, *Kubernetes Recipes*,
https://doi.org/10.1007/979-8-8688-1325-2_14

Foundation (CNCF) plays a crucial role in mitigating these challenges by curating, governing, and promoting open source projects like Kubernetes, Prometheus, and Envoy. Nevertheless, for many organizations, incorporating CNCF principles and tools into existing environments remains a complex undertaking.

Solution

Develop scalable, resilient, and secure applications by utilizing the Cloud Native Computing Foundation's (CNCF) ecosystem, which includes both graduated and incubating projects, certified platforms, and established best practices. Get acquainted with essential CNCF projects such as Kubernetes for container orchestration, Prometheus for monitoring, Helm for application deployment, and Envoy for service proxies. Embrace CNCF principles by adopting microservices architectures, implementing declarative APIs for infrastructure management, and focusing on automation and immutable infrastructure. Achieve dependable deployments by selecting CNCF-certified Kubernetes distributions and enhancing their security with tools like Falco for runtime protection while applying DevSecOps practices. Streamline operations using Prometheus for metrics, Grafana for data visualization, and Argo CD for continuous improvements driven by GitOps.

Discussion

The CNCF ecosystem offers a comprehensive suite of tools to address various challenges in cloud-native development. Kubernetes is a central orchestrator supported by observability tools like Prometheus and service mesh solutions like Envoy. However, the learning curve can be steep. Enterprises must invest in skill development and embrace DevOps cultural shifts to maximize CNCF's benefits. Tools like Helm and GitOps practices simplify deployment but require an upfront commitment to learning their intricacies.

14.2 Contributing to Cloud-Native Communities

Problem

Entering cloud-native communities, such as the Cloud Native Computing Foundation (CNCF), can be daunting for beginners. Many potential contributors are unsure about how to start, locate suitable projects, or navigate the contribution process successfully.

Solution

Engage with cloud-native communities using a structured approach, starting with understanding community dynamics, identifying areas of contribution, and gradually integrating into projects.

Steps to Begin Contributing

1. **Understand the Ecosystem**:
    - Explore CNCF's project landscape to familiarize yourself with different tools and platforms, such as Kubernetes, Prometheus, and Helm.
    - Join community meetings, forums, or mailing lists to understand ongoing discussions.
2. **Pick a Project**:
    - Start with beginner-friendly projects or repositories that label issues as "good first issue" or "help wanted."
    - Projects like Kubernetes and Argo CD often have well-documented contribution guidelines.

3. **Set Up the Environment**:
    - Clone the repository of your chosen project and follow the setup instructions.
    - Install required tools such as Docker, Kubernetes (Minikube or KinD), and programming dependencies.
4. **Start Small**:
    - Contribute by fixing minor bugs, improving documentation, or adding tests.
    - Participate in discussions on issues to understand project maintainers' expectations.
5. **Engage Actively**:
    - To stay updated, join project Slack channels, mailing lists, and working groups.
    - Attend community calls and contribute to roadmaps or design proposals.
6. **Submit Pull Requests (PRs)**:
    - Ensure your PR adheres to the project's contribution guidelines.
    - Be open to feedback and iterate on your submissions as requested by maintainers.
7. **Participate in Events**:
    - To network and learn from peers, engage in community events like KubeCon, meetups, or hackathons.

Discussion

Starting small and building familiarity with a project is critical to success. The cloud-native ecosystem is vast, and finding a niche that aligns with your interests and skills ensures sustained engagement. Documentation, testing, and bug fixes are often overlooked areas with a high demand for contributors. Active communication with maintainers and other contributors fosters a sense of belonging and accelerates learning.

Projects like Kubernetes have comprehensive onboarding materials and contribution handbooks to help new contributors navigate the process. However, patience is crucial, as learning the codebase and tools can take time. Participating in community discussions also builds relationships and exposes contributors to collaboration dynamics.

See Also

- Kubernetes Contributor Guide

14.3 Building and Supporting a Cloud-Native Community

Problem

Creating and nurturing a cloud-native community presents challenges. Both organizations and individuals often struggle to draw in contributors, keep them engaged, and foster a collaborative, inclusive atmosphere. By implementing a strategic plan, the community can achieve a critical mass, which is essential for facilitating project adoption and enhancing innovation.

Solution

To build and sustain a thriving cloud-native community, create a structured plan with clear objectives, open communication, inclusive participation, and consistent support.

Steps to Build and Support a Cloud-Native Community

1. **Define Goals and Values**:
   - Identify the community's purpose (e.g., supporting a specific project, sharing knowledge, or driving innovation).
   - Establish core values like openness, inclusivity, and collaboration to guide community behavior.
2. **Choose the Right Platforms**:
   - Use collaboration tools like Slack, Discord, or mailing lists for communication.
   - Host codebases on open platforms like GitHub or GitLab with clear contribution guidelines.
3. **Foster Onboarding for New Members**:
   - Create comprehensive documentation and beginner-friendly resources.
   - Label issues as "good first issue" to help newcomers contribute easily.

4. **Host Regular Events**:
    - Schedule virtual or in-person meetups, webinars, and community calls to engage members.
    - Organize hackathons or contribution days to encourage participation.
5. **Encourage Contributions Beyond Code**:
    - Recognize and reward non-code contributions like documentation, translations, or community moderation.
    - Highlight contributors in newsletters, blogs, or project documentation.
6. **Implement Feedback Mechanisms**:
    - Actively seek feedback through surveys, discussions, and issue trackers.
    - Use feedback to improve processes and address concerns promptly.
7. **Cultivate Leadership**:
    - Identify and empower contributors to take on leadership roles like maintainers, moderators, or mentors.
    - Provide training or guidance to ensure consistency in community leadership.
8. **Promote Diversity and Inclusion**:
    - Ensure diverse representation in leadership and decision-making roles.
    - Create safe spaces for underrepresented groups and establish codes of conduct.

9. **Measure and Share Success**:
    - Track metrics like contributor growth, active participation, and project adoption.
    - Share milestones and achievements to inspire current and potential members.

Discussion

Building and supporting a cloud-native community requires long-term commitment and adaptability. Early-stage communities often face challenges in achieving active participation. To overcome this, emphasize accessibility by lowering barriers to entry with well-documented onboarding processes. Engaging regularly with members through events and communications strengthens connections and fosters loyalty.

Encouraging contributions beyond coding is critical for sustainability. Contributions like organizing events, maintaining documentation, or managing discussions are invaluable. A transparent leadership structure ensures members feel valued and provides clear pathways for growth.

Communities thrive when members see tangible benefits, such as professional development, networking opportunities, or the satisfaction of contributing to impactful projects.

See Also

- GitHub Open Source Guides

14.4 The Business Value

Problem

Organizations frequently find it challenging to measure the business value of implementing Cloud Native Computing Foundation (CNCF) technologies like Kubernetes, Prometheus, and Envoy. Leadership generally seeks a straightforward rationale for investments emphasizing cost efficiency, scalability, innovation, and security.

Solution

CNCF technologies provide measurable benefits, including operational efficiency, faster innovation cycles, improved system reliability, and enhanced security. These technologies support modern software development practices, enabling businesses to stay competitive in a rapidly evolving market.

Here are steps to realize and demonstrate business value:

1. **Adopt Kubernetes for Container Orchestration**:

   Centralize deployment and management of containerized applications. Achieve higher resource utilization and scalability with Kubernetes' autoscaling capabilities.

2. **Leverage Observability Tools Like Prometheus and Grafana**:

   Monitor application performance and system health in real time. Use metrics to identify inefficiencies and reduce downtime.

3. **Enhance Security Posture with CNCF Tools**:

   Use projects like Falco for runtime security and Open Policy Agent (OPA) for policy enforcement. Implement DevSecOps practices with Kubernetes-native security capabilities.

4. **Accelerate Software Delivery with GitOps and CI/CD**:

   Use tools like Argo CD and Tekton to automate deployments and integrate testing. Shorten development cycles while maintaining high software quality.

5. **Enable Multi-cloud and Hybrid Cloud Strategies**:

   Leverage Kubernetes for consistent application management across multiple cloud environments . Reduce vendor lock-in and increase flexibility to adapt to market demands.

6. **Support Microservices Architectures**:

   Use service mesh solutions like Envoy or Istio to enhance inter-service communication. Achieve fault isolation and better resource management for complex applications.

7. **Leverage Cost Optimization Features**:

   Use Kubernetes autoscaling and resource quotas to minimize over-provisioning. Optimize infrastructure spending while maintaining performance.

Discussion

CNCF technologies enable organizations to modernize their infrastructure and development practices effectively. Kubernetes, known for its scalability, allows businesses to manage traffic spikes automatically, ensuring a better customer experience during peak times. Additionally, observability tools like Prometheus provide actionable insights into performance metrics, which help reduce downtime and improve operational efficiency.

The CNCF ecosystem also includes security-focused tools that mitigate risks associated with containerized environments. By adopting GitOps and CI/CD practices, organizations can streamline software delivery and gain a competitive edge by reducing their time to market.

However, successfully implementing CNCF technologies necessitates initial training, tooling, and infrastructure investments. Organizations must also cultivate a DevOps culture to maximize the advantages of cloud-native approaches.

14.5 KubeCon Events

Problem

Cloud-native professionals and organizations might find it challenging to successfully engage with and gain insights from KubeCon, the leading conference focused on Kubernetes and cloud-native technologies. The vast size of the event, along with numerous tracks and networking chances, can be daunting, particularly for those attending for the first time.

Solution

KubeCon + CloudNativeCon is the leading event for cloud-native enthusiasts, uniting developers, technologists, and industry leaders to delve into the latest developments in Kubernetes, cloud-native architectures, and related technologies. Organized by the Cloud Native Computing Foundation (CNCF), KubeCon acts as a center for learning, networking, and fostering innovation within the vibrant cloud-native ecosystem. Since its launch, KubeCon has evolved into a global series of conferences across North America, Europe, and Asia. Each event features a blend of keynotes, technical sessions, workshops, and community-building events, making it essential for anyone involved in cloud-native technologies. To maximize your experience at KubeCon + CloudNativeCon, develop a strategic approach encompassing preparation, targeted participation, and follow-up after the event. Begin by registering early for discounts and convenient lodging, and establish clear goals, such as mastering new tools or enhancing your network. Utilize the event app to become familiar with the schedule and plan your sessions accordingly. During the conference, attend keynotes and popular sessions to keep abreast of CNCF projects, explore the expo hall for live demonstrations, and participate in hands-on workshops to develop your skills. Make a point to network actively during BoF sessions, social hours, and meetups, and interact with speakers during or after their presentations. After the event, review and share your notes, try out the tools you discovered, and continue to connect through LinkedIn or CNCF channels to maintain the momentum.

Discussion

KubeCon events are essential for keeping current with Kubernetes and cloud-native innovations. They feature technical presentations, opportunities for community engagement, and vendor exhibitions. Careful planning ensures focused involvement and prevents feelings of being overwhelmed.

The most notable benefit of KubeCon is networking. Connecting with the global cloud-native community encourages collaborations, knowledge exchange, and career advancements. Yet, the event's scale may cause you to overlook important sessions or networking chances if not properly organized. Using the event app to schedule your activities and setting achievable daily objectives can assist.

Moreover, joining side events hosted by sponsors and attending after-hours gatherings often leads to casual yet significant conversations, usually yielding deeper insights than the conventional sessions.

See Also

- KubeCon + CloudNativeCon website for schedules and registration `https://www.cncf.io/kubecon-cloudnativecon-events/`
- CNCF's event recordings on YouTube (`https://www.youtube.com/c/cloudnativefdn`) for on-demand session viewing

14.6 TAG Environmental Sustainability

Problem

With the evolution of cloud-native technologies, their environmental footprint grows. Companies need organized direction to reduce energy consumption and carbon emissions while scaling their applications effectively. The absence of standardized tools and processes for evaluating and enhancing the sustainability of cloud-native applications poses a significant barrier to embracing environmentally friendly practices.

Solution

TAG Environmental Sustainability, a Technical Advisory Group (TAG) under the CNCF, strengthens the cloud-native ecosystem by promoting sustainability efforts. It offers organized processes, task groups, and collaborative platforms to help organizations assess, improve, and advocate for environmental sustainability.

Key components of the solution are

Green Reviews Working Group:

Purpose: To incorporate sustainability assessments into cloud-native projects

Actions:

- Conduct assessments of sustainability footprints.
- Utilize existing tools for automation.
- Offer guidance on visualizing outcomes (e.g., dashboards for tracking carbon and energy usage).

Sustainability Advocacy Working Group:

Purpose: To encourage sustainable practices within the CNCF ecosystem through effective communication, marketing, and member engagement

Actions:

- Organize blogs, events, and social media campaigns.
- Oversee outreach programs to raise awareness about sustainability.

Resources provided by TAG Environmental Sustainability are

- Frameworks for conducting sustainability assessments
- Metrics, guidelines, and best practices
- A shared GitHub repository for documentation and tools
- Communication channels like Slack and Zoom for collaboration

Discussion

TAG Environmental Sustainability exemplifies how cloud-native projects can balance scalability with environmental responsibility. By participating in the initiatives led by the group, you can enjoy the following benefits:

- **Organization Benefits:**
  - Gain actionable insights into their environmental impact.
  - Reduce operational costs by optimizing resource usage.
  - Align with global sustainability goals and regulations.
- **CNCF Ecosystem Benefits:**
  - Encourages widespread adoption of eco-friendly practices
  - Strengthens collaboration between developers, maintainers, and stakeholders
  - Positions CNCF as a leader in environmentally conscious innovation

Its challenges include

- Effective measurement in VM environments due to shared infrastructure
- Engaging diverse stakeholders to standardize sustainability efforts across projects

Future enhancements include the following:

- Expand tool support for monitoring across different architectures.
- Promote partnerships to increase tool availability and adoption.
- Advocate for policies to incentivize sustainability.

See Also

- **Resources and Communication:**
  - TAG Environmental Sustainability GitHub Repository
- **Working Group Deliverables:**
  - Green Reviews Charter
  - Sustainability Advocacy Charter

TAG Environmental Sustainability shines brightly as a guiding initiative for environmentally responsible cloud-native innovation, inspiring our community to move together toward a greener future.

14.7 KubeTrain

Problem

Traveling to international conferences like KubeCon + CloudNativeCon often involves carbon-intensive modes of transport, such as air travel, which significantly contributes to environmental degradation. For instance, a single passenger's flight from London to Paris generates 66 kg of CO2, whereas a train ride for the same route emits only 2.4 kg of CO2. However, sustainable travel alternatives like train journeys often face challenges, such as higher costs and longer travel times, deterring widespread adoption.

Solution

Figure 14-1. *kubetrain.io*

KubeTrain is launching a sustainable travel initiative for participants of KubeCon + CloudNativeCon Europe 2024. This program facilitates group train journeys from key European cities to Paris, aiming to minimize the environmental impact of travel while encouraging community interaction and collaboration.

Dedicated train compartments from cities like Amsterdam, London, Berlin, and Zurich dramatically lower CO2 emissions compared with flying. Travel allows attendees to share the ride, engage in onboard activities, and form connections within the Kubernetes community. Sponsors help reduce travel costs, making train journeys more economical and demonstrating their dedication to sustainability. Enjoy amenities such as meals, beverages, and social gatherings upon arrival to enrich your overall experience.

Discussion

KubeTrain not only reduces the carbon footprint from conference travel but also builds a community among cloud-native enthusiasts. By favoring train travel, CO2 emissions are significantly lowered, contributing to a more sustainable conference culture. This initiative demonstrates a practical commitment to the sustainability goals and values of the Cloud Native Computing Foundation (CNCF). Sponsors increase their visibility and credibility by supporting eco-friendly initiatives. Attendees gain benefits from affordable travel options and valuable networking during their journey to the conference. In addition to train journeys taking longer than flights, they require careful planning and flexibility from those traveling. The limited departure cities mean that not all attendees may have direct access to KubeTrain services.

The model has the potential for growth in other global events, fostering a broader culture of sustainable conference travel. Future collaborations with railway companies could further enhance cost efficiency and logistics.

KubeTrain highlights the importance of integrating sustainability into all aspects of technology, including how communities approach knowledge sharing and innovation.

See Also

- **Official Website**: KubeTrain `https://kubetrain.io/`

By choosing KubeTrain, you can contribute to reducing your carbon footprint, engage with like-minded professionals, and help redefine sustainability in the tech ecosystem. Together, let's make every journey count.

14.8 Kubernetes Efficient Power Level Exporter (Kepler)

Problem

Assessing the energy use of applications built on Kubernetes is difficult because of the intricate nature of cloud-native settings. As sustainability becomes more urgent and the necessity to lower CO2 emissions rises, there's a growing need for accurate, real-time energy monitoring solutions that can measure power consumption at the level of Kubernetes pods.

Solution

Kepler (Kubernetes-based Efficient Power Level Exporter) addresses this challenge. It is a Prometheus exporter that utilizes eBPF to probe CPU performance counters and Linux kernel tracepoints. These metrics, combined with data from `sysfs` and machine learning (ML) models, allow for estimating energy consumption by individual pods. Here are steps to implement Kepler in your cluster:

1. **Set Up Kepler:**
    - Deploy Kepler as a DaemonSet in your Kubernetes cluster.
    - Install required dependencies like Prometheus for storing metrics.
2. **Collect Data:**
    - Kepler collects process-level metrics using eBPF.
    - It aggregates these metrics to container and pod levels, correlating process IDs (PIDs) with Kubernetes metadata.
3. **Estimate Power Consumption:**
    - For bare-metal nodes, Kepler directly uses APIs like Intel RAPL or NVIDIA NVML to fetch power metrics.
    - For virtual machines, Kepler employs trained regression models to estimate power consumption using resource utilization metrics.
4. **Visualize Metrics:**
    - Query Kepler-exported metrics through Prometheus or visualize them using Grafana dashboards.
5. **Integrate with ML Models:**
    - Optionally deploy a model server for training and sharing power models based on benchmarked data, ensuring adaptable predictions across diverse architectures.

Discussion

Kepler provides an innovative way to address sustainability in cloud-native environments by enabling granular energy consumption monitoring. However, there are considerations and limitations:

- **Accuracy:**
    - Bare-metal environments provide more accurate real-time metrics than VMs, which rely on estimated models.
    - Idle power estimation in VM scenarios is complex due to shared infrastructure.
- **Extensibility:**
    - The project supports vendor-agnostic architectures and allows integration with external APIs (e.g., IPMI, Redfish).
- **Performance Overhead:**
    - Minimal overhead is introduced by eBPF tracing, but tuning may be necessary for high-performance environments.
- **Future Directions:**
    - Upcoming features include VM-level power pass-through and support for additional power data sources.

Kepler is ideal for organizations aiming to align with green IT practices while gaining insights into the operational energy efficiency of their applications.

See Also

- Kepler GitHub Repository `https://github.com/sustainable-computing-io/kepler`

Summary

The Cloud Native Computing Foundation has revolutionized how organizations approach modern software development. Its curated projects and principles empower businesses to embrace cloud-native strategies, enhancing agility, scalability, and security. By adopting CNCF tools, organizations can streamline application lifecycle management and build stronger, more collaborative communities. Moreover, the insights shared in this chapter on engaging with CNCF communities and realizing the business value of its technologies highlight the multifaceted advantages of being an active participant in this ecosystem. As the cloud-native paradigm evolves, leveraging CNCF's resources and best practices will remain essential for staying competitive and innovative in a digitally driven world.

Index

A

G. Stencel and L. Berton, *Kubernetes Recipes*,
https://doi.org/10.1007/979-8-8688-1325-2

B

D

E

F

I

J

K

L

M

O

P

Q

R

S

V

W, X, Y

Z

Printed in the United States
by Baker & Taylor Publisher Services